ROAD TRIPS
NORTHERN AND CENTRAL ITALY

Sunset over the hills of Chianti

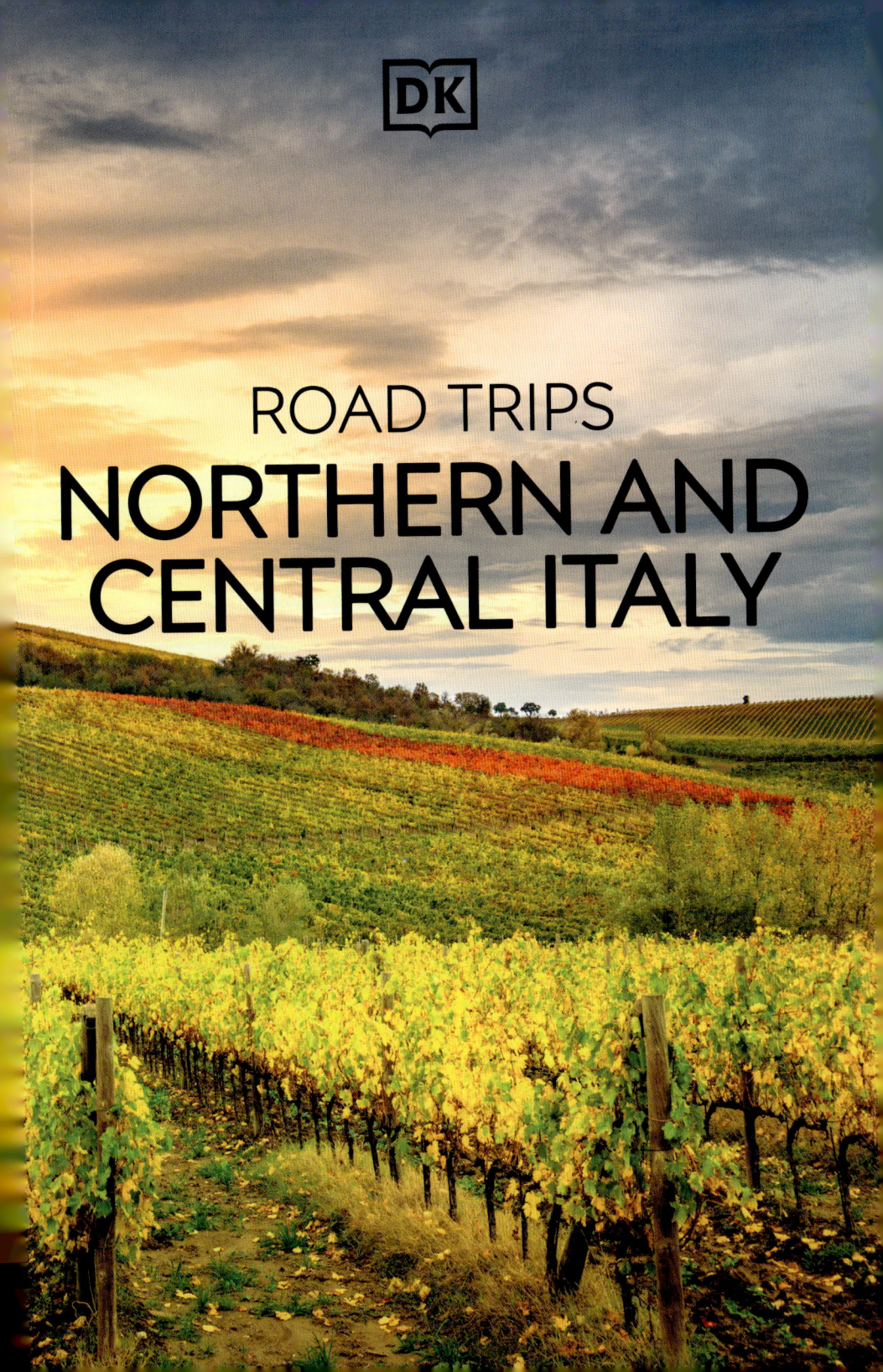

ROAD TRIPS
NORTHERN AND CENTRAL ITALY

DK

Above The church of Santa Maddalena in Val di Funes

CONTENTS

06 ABOUT THIS BOOK

08 INTRODUCING NORTHERN AND CENTRAL ITALY

10 GETTING THERE

12 PRACTICAL INFORMATION

16 DRIVING IN ITALY

22 WHERE TO STAY

24 WHERE TO EAT

26 THE TRIPS

28 **TRIP 1**
IN THE SHADOW OF THE ALPS
Turin to Castello di Rivoli
3–4 DAYS

38 **TRIP 2**
IN THE LAND OF THE TRUFFLE
Barbaresco to Cuneo
3–4 DAYS

48 **TRIP 3**
SACRED MOUNTAINS & ISLAND PALACES
San Carlone to Varese
4–5 DAYS

56 **TRIP 4**
COMO'S VILLAS AND VILLAGES
Como to Brunate
2–3 DAYS

64 **TRIP 5**
LOMBARDY'S GLACIAL VALLEYS
Bergamo to Erbusco
3 DAYS

72 **TRIP 6**
SWITCHBACKS AND LIMONAIE
Arco to Gargnano
1 DAY

78 **TRIP 7**
FROM THE LAKE TO THE PLAINS
Salò to Mantua
3 DAYS

86 **TRIP 8**
THE HIDDEN VALLEYS OF THE ALTO ADIGE
Merano to Brunico
3 DAYS

96 **TRIP 9**
CLASSIC DOLOMITES TOUR
Bolzano to Alpe di Siusi
4–5 DAYS

104 **TRIP 10**
MOUNTAINS AND LAKES
Laghi di Fusine to Trieste
5 DAYS

114 **TRIP 11**
THE VENETO PLAIN
Verona to Venice
4 DAYS

122 **TRIP 12**
DOLOMITES TO VENETO HILLS
Cortina d'Ampezzo to Treviso
4 DAYS

Front cover The scenic route to Greve, Chianti

Above Alfresco dining at a restaurant in Lago d'Orta

Above Piazza Garibaldi at the heart of Narni

130 **TRIP 13**
THE PO DELTA
Ferrara to Ravenna
2–3 DAYS

140 **TRIP 14**
THE AZURE
COAST TO
THE PO VALLEY
Genoa to
Portovenere
4–5 DAYS

148 **TRIP 15**
THE LIGURIAN
COAST AND
APENNINES
Camogli to Riomaggiore
4–5 DAYS

160 **TRIP 16**
SANCTUARIES
AND FORESTS
Fiesole to Anghiari
2–3 DAYS

170 **TRIP 17**
VAL D'ARNO AND
THE CHIANTI HILLS
Ponte Buriano to
Volpaia
2–3 DAYS

178 **TRIP 18**
SACRED PATHS
San Miniato
to San Galgano
4–5 DAYS

188 **TRIP 19**
IN THE SHADOW
OF A VOLCANO
Castiglione d'Orcia to
San Casciano dei Bagni
2–3 DAYS

196 **TRIP 20**
UMBRIAN HILLS,
TUSCAN VALLEYS
Orvieto to Arezzo
3–4 DAYS

206 **TRIP 21**
UMBRIA'S VERDANT
VALLEYS
Perugia to Arrone
3–4 DAYS

216 **TRIP 22**
LANDS OF MYTH
AND LEGEND
Rieti to Lago di
Corbara
3–4 DAYS

226 **TRIP 23**
THE STONE OF
THE APENNINES
Città di Castello
to Jesi
3 DAYS

236 **TRIP 24**
MONTEFELTRO
MOUNTAINS
Rimini to Fano
3–4 DAYS

246 **TRIP 25**
THE HEART OF
LE MARCHE
Loreto to
Grottammare
3–4 DAYS

256 INDEX

260 ACKNOWLEDGMENTS

261 PHRASE BOOK

263 DRIVER'S PHRASE
     BOOK

The rate at which the world is changing is constantly keeping the DK Travel team on our toes. While we've worked hard to ensure that this edition of Road Trips Northern and Central Italy is accurate and up-to-date, we know that opening hours alter, standards shift, prices fluctuate, places close and new ones pop up in their stead. So, if you notice we've got something wrong or left something out, we want to hear about it. Please get in touch at travelguides@dk.com

ABOUT THIS BOOK

The 25 trips in this book capture the diversity of Northern and Central Italy, from the snow-capped mountain ranges on the borders with France and Austria to the hill towns of Tuscany and Umbria; from the dramatic coastline of the Ligurian Cinque Terre to the lakes of Lombardy and the Veneto. A modern, industrialized nation with its finger on the commercial and cultural pulse of Europe, Italy is also a country where traditional values are maintained, and the pace of life outside of its cities is still refreshingly slow.

Our trips embrace the region's world-famous art towns, but rather than being treated as isolated spots on a weekend break, they are included in tours that encourage a wider exploration of the history, culture and landscape that gave rise to them. Other tours go right off the beaten track – to enchanting villages, remote mountain outposts, hidden rocky coves and rarely visited archaeological sites – allowing visitors to explore facets of Northern and Central Italy that many never experience.

Getting Started
The guide begins with all the practical information you need to plan and get the most out of a driving holiday in Northern and Central Italy: how to get there; tips on bringing your own vehicle or hiring one; details of the documentation required; and motoring advice, from the quirks of Italian driving and road signage to where you can buy petrol and what to do if your car breaks down. Health, money and communications are also covered and there is an overview of dining and accommodation options. A language section at the back lists essential words and phrases, including key driving-related vocabulary.

The Trips
The main touring section of the guide is divided into leisurely trips, ranging in duration from one to seven days. Most of the tours are on paved roads, and where they are not, they are on good-quality, unmetalled roads, which should pose no problems for a standard vehicle. The trips encompass every area of Northern and Central Italy. To help visitors choose and plan a trip, each drive begins with a list of highlights and a clearly mapped itinerary. There is advice on the best time of year to do the drive, road conditions, market days and major festival dates. The trip pages contain detailed descriptions of each sight and activity, linked by clear driving instructions. Side panels offer information on places to stay and eat. Tinted boxes feature suggestions for extra activities and background information. These might include details of a local festival or speciality; tips for a wine-tasting tour; or where to go hiking. The flexible nature of the tours means that some can be linked together to create a longer driving holiday, or simply dipped into to plan day trips while based in one particular region. Each trip also features a mapped town or countryside walking tour, designed to take no more than three hours at a leisurely pace with stops on the way.

Using the Sheet Map
A pull-out road map of the entire region is supplied at the back of the guide. This map contains all the information you need to drive around the country and navigate between the different tours. All motorways, major roads, ferry ports and airports – both domestic and international – are clearly identified. There is also a comprehensive index, allowing you to locate sights quickly and easily. The map is further supplemented by a handy distance chart, to enable you to gauge the distances between the major cities. All of these features make the pull-out map an excellent addition to the individual trip-itinerary maps within the book.

Top left Manarola, a Cinque Terre town in Liguria **Top right** Fishing boats moored at Lazise, on the eastern shore of Lake Garda **Centre left** Grey-stone houses in the medieval heart of Abbadia San Salvatore **Centre right** The rolling Tuscan landscape near Montisi **Below left** Fiat 500, Greve in Chianti **Below right** A fresco in the Neo-Classical Villa Melzi, Bellagio

Above Driving in the Upper Tiber region of northern Umbria

INTRODUCING NORTHERN AND CENTRAL ITALY

The culture, cuisine, traditions and landscape of Northern and Central Italy are best appreciated close up, and there is no better way to home in on this endlessly fascinating part of the world than to slow down, leave the busy *autostrada* and explore the countryside by its back roads. Follow one road to a vineyard and meet a prize-winning winemaker; pull over on another to let a shepherd pass with his flock; or take a third to experience the genuine hospitality of a B&B owner proudly introducing you to regional specialities at the breakfast table. In Northern and Central Italy – whether driving through the alpine peaks of the Alto-Adige, over the rolling hillsides of Le Langhe or along the Adriatic coast in Le Marche – the visitor will never be far from beautiful towns rich in culture and history, evocative landscapes and gourmet delights. Travelling the back roads reveals how, beneath the contemporary surface, a world that many thought had ceased to exist half a century ago is alive and well, and as alluring as ever.

When to Go
Each trip includes a recommendation for the ideal time to make the drive. This may be because the scenery is at its best or the rivers are at their highest, or perhaps because the azaleas or apple blossom are in bloom. There might be a local festival taking place, or it could be that a certain food is in season. The weather, of course, is also a factor. The northern half of Italy has a varied climate falling into three distinct geographical zones: in the north, expect cold, alpine winters and warm, wet summers; in the vast central Po valley, summers are hot and humid and winters damp, foggy and freezing; Tuscany, Umbria and Le Marche enjoy a more clement climate, with long, hot summers and relatively mild winters. In general, the best times to visit Northern and Central Italy are spring and autumn, ideally between April and June or September and October, when the climate should be mild without being too hot, and the whole region is generally much less crowded than in high summer.

Times to Avoid
As far as possible, roads and airports should be avoided at the beginning of August and in the days just before and after Ferragosto (15 August), the national summer holiday. The start of school holidays also sees a great surge in traffic levels. Schools break up for summer in mid-June and resume in mid-September. The Easter holidays usually begin on the Thursday before Easter and end on the Monday or Tuesday afterwards. Summer weekends and days around public holidays can also be very busy on the roads.

Festivals
Festivals and fairs take place all over Italy throughout the year. As well as the Easter and Christmas festivities, every town and village has a patron saint, and each one marks its saint's day with special celebrations. Spring and autumn are the best times for *sagre*, festivals devoted to local foods. Mushroom, sausage, olive oil, chestnut and wine *sagre* are common in autumn, while spring *sagre* are often devoted to seasonal fruits like strawberries or cherries. *Carnevale* sees masked and fancy-dress parades in many towns and villages, most spectacularly in Venice and Ivrea. Ferragosto is marked by free outdoor concerts, dancing and often fireworks.

Public Holidays
New Year's Day (1 Jan)
Epiphany (6 Jan)
Easter Sunday and Monday
Liberation Day (25 Apr)
Labour Day (1 May)
Republic Day (2 Jun)
Ferragosto (15 Aug)
All Saint's Day (1 Nov)
Feast of the Immaculate Conception (8 Dec)
Christmas Day (25 Dec)
Santo Stefano (26 Dec)

Left The pretty resort village of Limone sul Garda, on the shores of Lake Garda

Above The springtime ritual of Calendimaggio, celebrated in Assisi

GETTING THERE

The increasing availability of low-cost flights has revolutionized travel to and within Italy. Provincial airports across the country are open to international flights from other European cities, both major and provincial. Arriving at a small airport – where queues for immigration and baggage are short, and where a hire car can easily be collected (often at a discounted rate through the airline company) – generally makes for the best start to a driving holiday in Italy. Travellers from outside Europe may find it cheaper to fly via London or another European hub to take advantage of the many low-cost flights on offer.

Above The Brenner Highway A13 that connects Austria to Italy

Arriving by Air

From the UK and Ireland, airlines such as **British Airways**, **ITA Airways** (formerly Alitalia) and **Aer Lingus** fly to airports throughout Northern and Central Italy, including Milan, Turin, Bologna, Verona, Venice and Pisa. London and Dublin offer the greatest choice but there are also flights from Edinburgh, Manchester, Birmingham and Bristol. Low-cost carriers, including **Jet2**, **Ryanair** and **easyJet**, fly from provincial airports all over the UK and Ireland to small airports across Northern and Central Italy.

Delta and **American Airlines** offer daily flights from New York, Los Angeles, Chicago, Miami and Atlanta to Rome and Milan; one short stopover greatly extends the network. Many European carriers fly to Italy from major US and Canadian cities – **Lufthansa** (via Frankfurt), **KLM** (via Amsterdam) and British Airways (via London).

Air New Zealand offers the best deals from New Zealand to Italy but **Malaysia Airlines**, **Thai Airways**, British Airways, **Qantas** and **Emirates** are all good alternatives; they also fly from Australia. From South Africa, KLM and Lufthansa are often the best options. If you are heading for any of the southerly areas covered by this guide – for instance Umbria or Le Marche – it's worth noting that Rome's Fiumicino is a closer intercontinental option than Milan's twin airports of Linate and Malpensa-Silvio Berlusconi International Airport. If you're heading further north, it may still make sense to fly into Rome if the Italian airline **Aeroitalia** can offer a competitive price for taking you on to your destination.

It's also worth bearing in mind that air companies frequently offer a range of discounted tour packages and "air passes", which allow you to fly to multiple destinations within a designated area, with varying degrees of flexibility.

Italian Airports

Italy's system of naming its airports can be confusing to the uninitiated. Airports are named not only after the nearest major city or the nearest village, but usually after a famous Italian too. For example, Verona airport is known as Verona-Villafranca but also as Valerio Catullo. On road signs, an airport may be referred to by any of its names, or a combination – including by the airport's international code (for example, MXP for Malpensa or VBS for Brescia-Montichiari).

Arriving by Rail

Countless direct services (including many sleepers) link Italy with the major European cities. Connections from Paris (and, via **Eurostar**, from London) run to Turin, Milan, Venice, Bologna, Florence and Pisa.

Rail services operate from German, Swiss and other northern European cities to Milan, Turin, Venice and Verona. There are direct services from Vienna, Spain and the south of France.

Low-cost airlines have forced the train companies to be a little more competitive. Special discount fares are often available online. As the trains can be extremely busy during peak periods (Friday and Sunday evenings, the Christmas and Easter holidays and during July and August), it is advisable to make reservations if you intend to travel at those times.

There are direct motorail train services to Livorno in Tuscany and Alessandria in Piemonte from 's-Hertegenbosch (convenient for the Hook of Holland ferry port) in the Netherlands. Three German railway stations – Hamburg, Dusseldorf and Neu-Isenburg – are boarding points for motorail services to Alessandria and Bolzano. There is no direct motorail connection from either France or Germany, although it is possible to connect through other stations. From France, you can travel to Nice via motorail, then drive across the Italian border. From Germany, you can take the train from one of the motorail stations and connect through Innsbruck.

Arriving by Road

Most roads into Italy from the rest of Europe involve alpine crossings by tunnel or mountain pass. The exceptions are the approach from Slovenia in the northeast (on the A4 motorway) and the route along the French Riviera that enters Italy as the A10 motorway at Ventimiglia.

The most popular route from Geneva and southeast France is via the Mont Blanc tunnel and A5 motorway, entering Italy close to Aosta and Turin. Another busy approach (from Switzerland) uses the St Bernard Pass and Tunnel. The main route from Austria and southern Germany crosses the Brenner Pass and goes down to Verona on the A22 motorway via Trento and the Adige valley. Most motorways are toll roads – you pay as you exit them. Travellers from the UK could take a car to one of the French Channel ports by ferry or on the **Eurotunnel** rail shuttle. Once there, the drive to Genova in the north of Italy takes around 12 hours (a journey of some 1,900 km/1,200 miles). The **AA** and **Michelin** both offer reliable route planners on their websites.

Arriving by Sea

A well-developed network of ferries links Northern and Central Italy with neighbouring Mediterranean countries such as France, Spain, Croatia, Greece and Tunisia. **Minoan Lines** runs large ferries with cabins and vehicle decks from several ports in Greece to Ancona, while **Anek** runs ferries to Venice, the northwest's busiest port, most months of the year. A grand way to travel, the Istrian peninsula and the Dalmatian coast are linked to Venice through the summer by fast catamarans and ferries run by operators such as **Venezia Lines** and **Adriatic Lines**. Venice is also a key port for state-of-the-art cruise ships bound for the Mediterranean. Companies stopping here include **P&O Cruises** and **MSC Crociere**.

In 2021, the Italian government banned cruise ships over 25 tonnes from entering Venice. As such cruise ships now dock at Marghera on the mainland, while smaller ships dock at San Basilio and Santa Maria (in the Giudecca canal).

Genoa's Stazione Marittima is the northwest's main ferry hub, with links to Corsica, Tunis and Barcelona. Ferries from Corsica also arrive at Savona-Vado. Several companies operate these services, including **Tirrenia** and **Grimaldi**.

Far left Malpensa airport, Milan **Left** A ferry carrying passengers and cars to Sicily **Below** High-speed train in Milano Centrale station

DIRECTORY

ARRIVING BY AIR
Aer Lingus
aerlingus.com
Aeroitalia
aeroitalia.com
Air New Zealand
airnz.co.nz
American Airlines
aa.com
British Airways
ba.com
Delta
delta.com
easyJet
easyjet.com
Emirates
emirates.com
ITA Airways
ita-airways.com
Jet2
jet2.com
KLM (Royal Dutch Airlines)
klm.com
Lufthansa
lufthansa.com
Malaysia Airlines
malaysiaairlines.com
Qantas
qantas.com
Ryanair
ryanair.com
Thai Airways
thaiairways.com

ARRIVING BY RAIL
Eurostar
eurostar.com

ARRIVING BY ROAD
LeSuttle
leshuttle.com

ARRIVING BY SEA
Adriatic Lines
adriatic-lines.com
Anek
anek.gr
Grimaldi
grimaldi-lines.com
Minoan Lines
minoan.gr/en
MSC Crociere
msccrociere.it
P&O Cruises
pocruises.com
Tirrenia
tirrenia.it
Venezia Lines
venezialines.com

PRACTICAL INFORMATION

Italy is easy and safe to travel around. The country has an excellent health system and emergency infrastructure, plus the public services have improved significantly in the last decade. Broadband and mobile phone accessibility is almost universal, and, while banks in smaller towns may keep seemingly erratic hours, most have an ATM outside. Despite this, a little know-how goes a long way. Be prepared for all eventualities by considering the following points before you travel.

Above The green neon sign of an Italian pharmacy

Passports and Visas
European Union (EU) nationals can enter Italy and stay indefinitely with a valid passport or identity card. Citizens of the UK, United States, Canada, Australia, New Zealand and some other countries (for example, Brunei and Barbados) can stay for up to three months on production of a passport, but will need to apply for a visa at their local Italian embassy in advance if they wish to stay longer. Citizens of some countries (for example, Bahrain and Bolivia) will need a visa from the outset – for details, visit the website of the **Ministry of Foreign Affairs of Italy**.

Government Advice
Now more than ever, it is important to consult both your and the Italian government's advice before travelling. The **UK Foreign, Commonwealth & Development Office**, the **US State Department**, the **Australian Department of Foreign Affairs and Trade** and the Italian **Ministero della Salute** offer the latest information on security, health and local regulations.

Travel Insurance
All travellers should consider getting travel insurance. A policy will usually cover you for loss or theft of luggage and other property such as passports and money, as well as for personal accident, repatriation in case of severe illness, third-party damage and delayed or cancelled flights. Check that the per-article limit covers your most valuable items. You will need a special cover if you are taking part in sports, or in any activities that are considered hazardous. Most insurance policies also include legal cover up to a specified amount, as do comprehensive motor policies.

Health
Italy has a world-class healthcare system. UK citizens are eligible for free emergency medical care in Italy provided they have a valid European Health Insurance Card (**EHIC**) or UK Global Health Insurance Card (**GHIC**). Australia has a reciprocal health care agreement with Italy and citizens can access essential medical treatment as long as they are registered with **Medicare**. If you have an EHIC or GHIC, be sure to present it as soon as possible. You may have to pay after treatment and reclaim the money later.

For visitors from outside the EU and Australia, payment of medical expenses is the patient's responsibility. As such, it is important to arrange comprehensive medical insurance.

In holiday areas there may be a *guardia medica* – a kind of minor ailments and emergencies clinic – designed to deal with the sort of accidents that befall tourists. All non-residents may be asked to pay a nominal fee, which is set by each region. Otherwise, visiting the *pronto soccorso* (accident and emergency) department of a local hospital is often the quickest way to get reliable treatment – but be aware that you may be charged a small co-pay for a visit plus prescription charges.

If you are taking prescription medicines, it is a good idea to bring the packaging with you in case you run out. Many pharmacists will be happy to sell you a replacement for drugs such as anti-inflammatories, antibiotics and blood pressure medications without needing a prescription. Pharmacies are also a good source of advice on minor ailments. They are signalled by a green cross, and if the one you go to is closed, there will be a notice on display telling you where to find the nearest open pharmacy.

If you are involved in an accident, call 112 or 118 or go to the *pronto soccorso* department of the nearest hospital. If you are in a major town

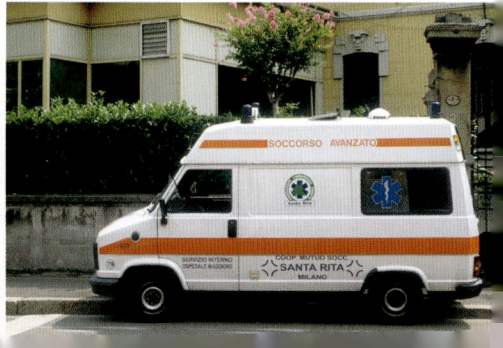

PRACTICAL INFORMATION 13

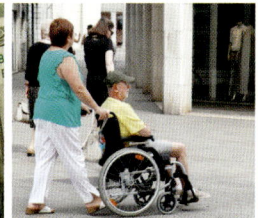

Above left US passports **Above centre** The region is becoming more accessible for travellers with specific requirements **Above right** Military police force

or city, it may be possible to find an English-speaking doctor – or, at least, someone who can translate for you. No inoculations are required for Italy, but mosquito repellent is useful in the summer months.

In recent years, there has been a marked increase in jellyfish numbers in the Mediterranean. None are particularly dangerous, but a sting is painful and can leave weals on the skin for days. To relieve the pain and swelling, wash the wound with sea water (never fresh water, which will react with the sting and worsen the pain) and put a bag of ice on it for five or ten minutes before disinfecting it. In severe cases, seek medical attention.

Personal Security

Italy is a relatively safe place to visit, but you should still take precautions. Bag-snatching scooter drivers are a problem in some Italian cities, so hold bags on the inside of the pavement, especially in crowded tourist areas. Pickpockets are common on public transport and in crowded city centres, so keep your belongings in a safe place or with you at all times.

If you have anything stolen, report the crime within 24 hours to the nearest police station and carry your ID. Unless you speak good Italian, it is better to report a crime in person rather than calling.

To make an insurance claim, you will need a copy of the *denuncia* (crime report). There are two crime-fighting forces in Italy. The *carabinieri*, the military branch, have stations in just about every village; the civil police, *polizia di Stato*, have a station, known as the *questura*, in most sizeable towns. Either can furnish you with a crime report, but English is not always spoken.

Contact your embassy if you have your passport stolen, or in the event of a serious crime or accident.

Italians, especially younger generations, are very accepting of all people, regardless of their race, gender or sexuality. Homosexuality was legalized in 1887 and in 1982, Italy became the third country to recognize the right to legally change your gender. If you do feel unsafe, the **Safe Space Alliance** pinpoints your nearest place of refuge.

Women may receive unwanted and unwelcome attention, especially around tourist areas. If you feel threatened, head straight for the nearest police station.

Below far left Pedestrian crossing signal **Below left** Ambulance **Below middle** Herbal pharmacy **Below** Police officer directing traffic

DIRECTORY

CONSULATES

Australian Consulate General
3rd Floor, Via Borgogna 2, 20122 Milan; italy.embassy.gov.au

British Consulate General
Via San Paolo 7, 20121 Milan; gov.uk/world/organisations/british-consulate-general-milan

Canadian Consulate General
Via Zara 30, Rome; international.gc.ca/country-pays/italy-italie

New Zealand Consulate General
Via Terraggio 17, 20123 Milan; mfat.govt.nz

United States Consulate General
Via Principe Amedeo 2/10, 20121 Milan; it.usembassy.gov/embassy-consulates/milan/

PASSPORTS AND VISAS

Ministry of Foreign Affairs of Italy
esteri.it

GOVERNMENT ADVICE

Australian Department of Foreign Affairs and Trade
smartraveller.gov.au

Ministero della Salute
salute.gov.it

UK Foreign, Commonwealth & Development Office
gov.uk/foreign-travel-advice

US State Department
travel.state.gov

HEALTH

EHIC
ec.europa.eu

GHIC
ghic.org.uk

Medicare Australia
servicesaustralia.gov.au/individuals/medicare

PERSONAL SECURITY

Safe Space Alliance
safespacealliance.com

Mobile Phones and Wi-Fi

In Italy, the city phone code is an integral part of every number and always has to be dialled. So in calling Italy from abroad, the initial zero of the city code must be retained.

European mobiles will work in Italy, but visitors from the US will need a tri-band phone. Coverage is generally good, although it can be patchy near some of the higher mountain ranges. Check with your provider for roaming options and international booster packages, which greatly reduce the cost of phone and data charges while you're abroad. EU visitors can use their devices without being affected by roaming charges – they will be charged the same rates for data, SMS and voice calls as their home.

In the past, you could only use an Italian SIM card if you had a *codice fiscale* (Italian tax code). However, several reliable service providers now offer pre-registered Italian SIM cards for unlocked European-standard GSM phones, giving you an Italian mobile number and reduced-rate calls. Alternatively, international SIM cards work well in Italy – again, as long as you have an unlocked European-standard GSM phone. The main phone operators in Italy are TIM, Vodafone, and Wind Tre.

Wi-Fi is generally available throughout Italy, with cafés and restaurants usually giving you the password for their Wi-Fi on the condition that you make a purchase.

Post

The Italian postal system – **Poste Italiane** – is somewhat erratic. It can be marvellously efficient, but also, appallingly slow at times. If something is urgent, avoid sending it as registered mail, as that tends to be amassed at the collection point before being sent on. Instead, use the postal system's courier service, *Posta Celere*, or, for international deliveries *Pacco Celere Internazionale*; the latter is cheaper and more widely available outside major cities than international operators like DHL, UPS and Fedex. Stamps *(francobolli)* are sold at post offices, tobacconists and at most shops that sell postcards.

Banks and Money

Italy is one of the many European countries using the euro. Most establishments accept major credit, debit and pre-paid currency cards. Contactless payments are becoming increasingly common in Italy, but it's always a good idea to carry some cash for smaller items such as coffee, gelato and pizza-by-the-slice, when visiting markets or more remote areas and for tipping. Waiting staff should be tipped €1–2 and hotel porters and housekeeping will expect €1 per bag or day. Most ticket machines at stations accept credit or debit cards, but some still only accept cash.

The easiest way of drawing cash is to use a debit or credit card at a Bancomat (ATM machine). Most cards have a maximum daily withdrawal limit (typically €250). It is essential to inform your bank that you will be using your card abroad, as many banks have increased security measures such as blocking unusual transactions. Many banks charge high rates of interest (typically 2.5 per cent) for withdrawals and transactions abroad.

Above Popular Italian newspapers

Banking hours in Italy are quite restricted, so it's best to acquire some local currency before you arrive or from a bancomat at the airport or train station. If you want to take cash euros, you might get a better rate of exchange by using online currency operators.

Tourist Information

Most Italian towns have either an APT (*Azienda di Promozione Turistica*) or EPT (*Enti Provinciali per il Turismo*) information office. These can vary enormously in the level of service they offer, but will at least provide maps, travel guides and information on local events. Before you leave for Italy, you can get information from the **Italian State Tourism Board**.

Opening Hours

Most shops open Monday to Saturday 9am–1pm and 4–7pm, but many remain closed for parts of specific days, generally Monday mornings and Saturday afternoons. State-run museums tend to open Tuesday to Saturday 9am–1 or 2pm; the same goes for privately owned museums, but they may also open

Above left Regional bank of the Südtirol **Above centre** Public telephone **Above right** Sign for a post office

for several hours in the afternoon. Sunday opening is generally mornings only. Many large museums now open throughout the day year-round, with late-night openings in summer (till 10pm or later Tuesday to Saturday and till 8pm Sunday). Most archaeological sites open daily, from 9am until dusk.

> Situations can change quickly and unexpectedly. Always check before visiting attractions and hospitality venues for up-to-date opening hours and booking requirements.

Travellers with Specific Requirements

Italy's historic towns and cities are ill-equipped for disabled access. Many buildings do not have wheelchair access or lifts. It is a good idea to always call ahead to ensure that your needs will be met. **AIAS** and **Rome and Italy**, in addition to **Accessible Italy**, provide useful information and general assistance for disabled travellers.

Trenitalia offers assistance to travellers with specific requirements and reduced mobility at over 350 stations, available through their **Sala Blu** website.

Language

Italian is the official language in Italy, though many people also speak regional languages such as Friulian, Piedmontese, Sardinian and Sicilian. The level of English and other foreign languages spoken can be limited, particularly in rural areas, and locals appreciate visitors' efforts to speak Italian, even if only a few words.

Time and Electricity

Italy uses Central European Time (CET), which is one hour ahead of Greenwich Mean Time (GMT). Summer (Daylight Saving) Time comes into effect from 2am on the last Sunday of March, and ceases at 2am on the last Sunday in October. Italian voltage is 220 volts. Plugs have either two (not earthed) or three round pins (which means they may be earthed, but not necessarily so).

Below far left Walking-trail information boards, Pietrarubbia **Below left** "Open" sign **Below middle** The Torrazzo (clock tower) in Crema **Below** Person using an ATM

DIRECTORY

COMMUNICATIONS

Calling Abroad from Italy
00 followed by the country code:
UK +44, Ireland +353, USA +1,
New Zealand +64, Australia +61

Directory Enquiries
1240

International Directory Enquiries
176

Italy Country Code
+39

Operator Services
176 (also for reverse charge and calling card calls)

Poste Italiane
poste.it

ITALIAN AND INTERNATIONAL SIM CARDS

Double Zero Double Four
0044.co.uk

Telestial
telestial.com

TOURIST INFORMATION

Italian State Tourism Board
enit.it

TRAVELLERS WITH SPECIFIC REQUIREMENTS

AIAS
aiasmilano.it

Accessible Italy
accessibleitaly.com

Rome and Italy
romeanditaly.com

Sala Blu
rfi.it/it/stazioni/pagine-stazioni/accessibilita/sale-blu.html

DRIVING IN ITALY

Driving is one of the best ways of exploring Northern and Central Italy – particularly for getting away from the crowds and reaching the more remote areas and sights. For long distances, Italy has a comprehensive motorway system, easily accessed from the rest of Europe. The condition of minor roads may vary in quality, but most are passable with care. Mountainous terrain can make for an exhilarating drive along twisty, hairpin roads, but be sure to take them at a relaxed pace.

Above Sign showing the Italian speed limits for main and secondary roads

Insurance and Breakdown Cover
In Italy it is compulsory for drivers to have third-party motor insurance. Check with your insurance provider that you are fully covered to drive abroad; in some cases, drivers will only be covered for basic Road Traffic Accident insurance – not for theft, or for the legal costs that can ensue in the event of an accident. UK drivers can arrange full breakdown cover while abroad – some companies even offer a package that includes a 24-hour English-language helpline.

What to Take
If you are driving your own foreign-registered car, you should carry your vehicle insurance policy with you – ideally with a statement of cover in Italian, usually provided by your insurer. The insurer should also provide a European Accident Statement form. Additionally, you will need to carry with you the vehicle registration document and a valid driving licence, and for non-EU residents, an international driver's licence issued in your home country. You should also have spare bulbs, a warning triangle and a high-visibility jacket (to be worn if your car breaks down and you have to leave the vehicle). The headlights of right-hand-drive cars will need to be adjusted for left-hand driving, to ensure that the hotspot of the beam lights up the edge of the road and does not dazzle oncoming drivers. All non-EU-registered vehicles must display a country sticker on their car.

Road Systems
Italy was the first country in the world to build a motorway: the Autostrada dei Laghi, which runs from Milan to Varese, and was opened in 1924. Nationwide, there are now more than 8,000 km (4,970 miles) of *autostrade*, built by both state and private companies, with several new roads planned. The privately built motorways are toll roads; non-toll roads are managed by ANAS (Azienda Nazionale Autonoma delle Strade Statali). On a toll road, you pick up a ticket when you join the motorway and pay as you exit. Tolls can be paid in cash, by credit card (such as Visa, MasterCard, American Express or Diners Club), or with a prepaid "ViaCard", available from motorway service stations and toll-booth operators. As you approach a toll station, make sure you get into the correct lane: for payment in cash, follow the white signs; for credit card and ViaCard, look for the blue signs. A white sign with only bank notes and coins indicates a self-service lane; a white sign with a hand holding the bank notes indicates that there will be an operator. Avoid the yellow Telepass lanes; these are for drivers with an onboard device that registers tolls and deducts them from their bank account.

Italian motorways are designated with the letter "A" followed by a numeral – for instance A8, for the Autostrada dei Laghi. Some motorways are also part of the pan-European system, whose roads are designated with an "E" followed by a numeral. Therefore, an Italian motorway can have two numbers: say A11 and E45. On signage, these are indicated in white on a green background.

Secondary roads are known as *strada statale* (SS), *strada provinciale* (SP) or *strada comunale* (SC) – the latter sort is usually very small, and maintained by the local town council. SR (rare) signifies a *strada regionale*. Although the road numbering system is comprehensive, it is not widely used in Italy; you will see the numbers on milestones at the side of the road, but they are not

DRIVING IN ITALY

Above left Roadside mirror near Radda in Chianti **Above right** Automatic lanes at a motorway toll station

always given on signposts. It is useful to know the next place of any size on your route, as it is the town or village name rather than a number that will probably be referred to on the sign. Note that some roads may just be named, and may not use a number.

The privately run motorways have their own website, *autostrade.it*, where you can get live traffic reports by clicking on a map.

Speed Limits and Fines

On motorways, the speed limit for cars and motorcycles over 150 cc is 130 kmph (80 mph); on main roads, it is 110 kmph (70 mph); on secondary roads, 90 kmph (55 mph); and in built-up areas, 50 kmph (30 mph). Speed limits are lower if you are towing *(see p21)*, or if you have held a licence for under three years, in which case you must not exceed 90 kmph (55 mph) on main roads or 100 kmph (62 mph) on motorways. Limits are also lower if there is fog or heavy rain.

The use of speed cameras is becoming more widespread, so avoid disregarding the motorway speed limit. If you incur a fine while you are driving a rental car, the rental company will deduct the money from your credit card when the fine arrives and add a handling fee; speed fines can range from around €150 to in excess of €250, depending on how much over the limit you were driving.

The use of mobile phones (except hands-free) while driving is prohibited. If caught, drivers will be fined. Seat belts, if fitted, are compulsory for both front- and rear-seat passengers. Never drink and drive; the laws are stringent and penalties high. The legal alcohol limit is 0.05 per cent.

Driving with Children

Children under 1.5 m (4 ft 9 in) and 36 kg (79 lbs) must be transported in an appropriate restraint system: up to 18 kg (40 lbs) in a baby seat, and above that in a booster seat. If you are renting a car, baby and booster seats can be hired when you book. Remember to check that there is no airbag fitted if you intend to put a child in the front passenger seat. Service stations are tolerably frequent on motorways, but although toys and sweets are prominently displayed in their bars, children are not well catered for; baby-changing facilities are virtually non-existent, and there is unlikely to be anywhere for older kids to let off steam safely.

DIRECTORY

COMMON ROAD SIGNS

Centro
Town or city centre

Incrocio
Crossroads

Lavori in corso
Roadworks ahead

Parcheggio
Car park

Rallentare
Slow down

Senso unico
One way

Senso vietato
No entry

Sosta vietata
No parking

Strada a doppia corsia
Dual carriageway

Strada panoramica
Scenic route

Tutte le direzioni
All directions

Uscita
Exit

Below far left Hiking-route signs, Val di Planol **Below left** Road climbing through a tunnel to the village of Pieve **Below middle** Moped parking sign **Below right** Drive through the spa town of Pré-Saint-Didier in the Valle d'Aosta **Below** Road signage for Citerna

Above left Motorway in Milan **Above right** The precipitous road out of Elva, in the Valle Maira

Rules of the Road
Remember: always drive on the right. Visitors from countries with left-hand traffic may find roundabouts and crossroads disorientating at first, as well as turning from a one-way street onto a road with two-way traffic – especially if that road is empty.

On motorways, Italian drivers can be aggressive. Some of them believe the inside lane is only for lorries, don't like being overtaken and tend to tailgate. They concentrate on the cars in front of them and those to the side, and if they see a space ahead of them, they will fill it. The best advice is to let them pass.

Unless road signs indicate otherwise, you should give way to vehicles joining your road from the right. Outside built-up areas, use dipped headlights at all times or risk a hefty fine. Surprisingly, in a country where football victories and weddings are celebrated by convoys of cars sounding their klaxons, you should only use the horn in emergencies. The British **Foreign, Commonwealth & Development Office** offers detailed advice on safe Italian road travel in the "Travel Advice by Country" section of its website.

Buying Petrol
Petrol *(benzina)* stations open from early morning until lunchtime, then from 3pm till around 7pm. Outside those hours you will often find an automatic pump that accepts either credit/debit cards or banknotes, although these are less common in rural areas. Petrol stations on motorways tend to be open 24 hours a day. Unleaded *(senza piombo)* petrol, diesel *(gasolio)* and LPG *(PLG)* are universally available.

Electric Vehicles (EV) and Charging Points
Road trips using an EV are possible due to an ever-expanding number of charging points and rental services. While these are increasingly available in urban centres, they can be sporadic in rural areas, particularly in more remote mountainous regions. Plan ahead using online charging point maps like **Chargemap**.

Road Conditions
Italy's motorways often flow freely, although rush hours and summer holidays can see long tailbacks. The busiest times are weekends in July, and the beginning and end of August. Roads are particularly busy on either side of the national summer holiday, Ferragosto (15 August). Saturday and Sunday are good days to travel if you have a long distance to cover, as most lorries and trucks are banned from travelling at weekends.

Road maintenance is a major issue. Italian roads have to contend with freezing winters in the mountains to landslide-inducing rain storms and tarmac-melting summers. "White roads", known as *strade bianche*, have only a gravel or dirt surface, though these are still marked on road maps.

Mountain Roads
Reaching some of Italy's most spectacular viewpoints and mountain passes inevitably involves tackling hairpin bends (the Stelvio Pass in Trentino-Alto Adige has 48 of them in succession) and some steep, narrow roads with sheer drops, such as those on the route through the valleys of the Ortler Mountain range. In spring, road surfaces may have been eroded by heavy winter snow, snow-melt and frost, and it can take some time for repairs to be undertaken, especially off the beaten track.

Unless you are used to driving in snow and ice, it is safer to avoid mountainous areas in winter conditions, especially on unfamiliar roads. In certain areas, snow chains are mandatory from mid-November

Above left Petrol pumps near Lake Garda, Lombardy **Above right** Road signs near Costigliole d'Asti

to mid-April, and you will get fined if you don't have them fitted to your wheels. For advance weather warnings that might affect your journey, always check one of the Italian weather websites, such as *meteo.it* or *ilmeteo.it*.

Taking a Break
Service stations on Italian motorways are less frequent than in the UK and other parts of Europe, and they can be pretty basic, with little more than a toilet and a bar where you can get a coffee and a heated-up pastry or a toasted sandwich. Service stations with fast-food restaurants are on the increase – in particular the Autogrill chain, which offers decent sandwiches and usually has a small supermarket where you can pick up basic supplies and even some local specialities. On the back roads, however, you are more likely to find a pretty village with a bar where you can have a good coffee or snack at a fair price, so if you are getting tired, consider leaving the motorway and taking a break in the nearest town or village. Well-priced set-lunch deals aimed at local workers *(pranzo di lavoro)* are worth looking out for; service will be fast, and you can get a simple, well-cooked three-course meal for under €20.

Breakdown and Accidents
In the event of an accident or breakdown, switch on your hazard warning lights and place a warning triangle 50 m (164 ft) behind your car. If you break down and have pan-European breakdown cover, call the **ACI**, the Italian Automobile Club (803 116 from an Italian phone or 800 116 800 from a foreign mobile connection), or the emergency services. The ACI will tow any foreign-registered vehicle to the nearest affiliated garage free of charge.

If you are in a rental car, call the company and follow their advice; the ACI should still offer a free tow, as long as you can produce your rental contract and flight tickets. If you do have pan-European cover, your provider will contact the nearest garage and make arrangements for you. In case of an accident, depending on its severity, call one of the **emergency services**. If there is any damage to a vehicle or any passengers are hurt, it is obligatory to call the police. You will then need to fill out a European Accident Statement *(see p16)* and take the details of other cars or persons involved. It is a good idea to take photos of the accident from all angles before any of the vehicles are moved.

DIRECTORY
GENERAL DRIVING INFORMATION
Autostrade per l'Italia
autostrade.it
RAC
rac.co.uk
Touring Club Italiano
touringclub.it
RULES OF THE ROAD
Foreign, Commonwealth & Development Office
gov.uk/driving-abroad
BREAKDOWNS AND ACCIDENTS
ACI
aci.it
EMERGENCY SERVICES
Fire Brigade
115
Medical Emergency/Ambulance
118
Police
112 (Carabinieri) / 113 (Polizia Statale)
Roadside Assistance
116
ELECTRIC VEHICLES AND CHARGING POINTS
Chargemap
chargemap.com

Below far left Mountain road in the Dolomites
Below left Symbol of Agip, a petrol company
Below middle Road through the Val d'Orcia, Tuscany **Below** Road signs near Lake Como

Parking

Parking in an Italian town or city can demand a great deal of time and patience. When kerb-space is limited, drivers tend to park anywhere and everywhere: on pavements, at bus stops, even blocking private entrances. It is unwise to follow suit; parking attendants are on the rise, as are *zone di rimozione* (tow-away zones).

In cities and villages alike, double parking is common, triple parking becoming more so. Towns and villages popular with tourists usually have paying car parks just outside the centre, and many places now operate a zoned parking scheme, with the type of zone indicated by the colour of the lines on the side of the road. Blue-zone parking spaces have a maximum stay of between one and two hours, and cost around €1 an hour (though they can be free at lunchtime, after 8pm and on Sundays). White-zone areas are free. Yellow-zone areas are for residents only. For zones where there is a time-limit but no parking fee, Italian cars (including rental cars) come equipped with a *disco orario* (mini clock dial) that you set with your time of arrival and display in the window; if you do not have one, you may be able to get one from the local tourist office or at a tobacconist's shop.

Do not leave any valuables in your car – and certainly nothing visible. In big cities, "illegal parking helpers" may insist on finding you a spot (sometimes an unlawful one) in exchange for a few coins, but it is wiser to follow the rules and pay officially. Secure, indoor, city car parks are expensive, but hotels can offer guest discounts.

Drivers displaying the blue disabled badge can park in designated spaces.

Restricted Traffic and Congestion Charges

The centres of many Italian towns and historic villages are closed to non-resident traffic. These so-called *zona traffico limitato* (restricted traffic zones) are usually indicated by signs displaying the letters "ZTL" in black on a yellow background. Many of these zones are monitored by cameras, and fines are issued to those who enter without authorization. Other towns impose traffic restrictions on certain days, or at certain times of day – Bergamo, for instance, does this in its historic centre, Città Alta. Make sure you read the signs: *lavorativo* or *feriale* means Monday to Saturday, and is marked by two crossed hammers; *festivi* indicates Sundays and public holidays, and is marked by a Christian cross. If your hotel is within a restricted area, you will need a police permit to enter with your car (they will need to know your registration number).

Milan has introduced a congestion-charge scheme (Area C) in an attempt to reduce traffic volumes and pollution. Other towns have implemented Low Emission Zones (LEZ) with Turin giving exemptions to EVs only.

Car Hire

All the major international car rental companies – such as **Avis**, **Budget**, **Hertz** and **Europcar** – operate in Italy. It is worth comparing rates online, as well as investigating any deals offered by your airline; low-cost airlines are particularly competitive in this area. You can also compare the deals you have found yourself with those of a reliable car-rental broker such as **Holiday Autos** or **AutoEurope**.
To rent a car in Italy you need to be

Above Street mirror on a narrow road in Amiata

over 20, and to have held a full licence for at least one year. Be sure that your rental agreement includes collision-damage waiver (CDW) and theft protection, as well as unlimited mileage. Child seats need to be booked in advance. With the rise in inner-city congestion, automatic cars are becoming more widely available.

When you collect the vehicle you will need your driving licence, passport and credit card (from which a security deposit will be deducted). Non-EU nationals must have an international driving permit issued from their home country. Cars are usually supplied with a full tank of petrol, and it is wise to return them refilled or you will be charged at an inflated rate for filling the tank.

Motorbikes and Scooters

Almost 10 per cent of the population has a motorbike or scooter. Two-wheel transport is good for navigating the labyrinth of streets that forms the centre of many cities, and you will usually find somewhere (free) to park, even in the busiest metropolis.

Italy is an exhilarating country to traverse by bike, with roads twisting up and down mountains and along dramatic coastlines, unmade "white"

DRIVING IN ITALY

Above left An Italian campsite in summer **Above right** Terminillo Road, a typical, winding mountain drive

roads to explore and a landscape that changes constantly. Note that if you are on a motorbike or scooter, a helmet is compulsory for both driver and pillion. A driving licence or motorbike driving licence is required for all vehicles over 49cc. Motorcycles must use dipped headlights at all times during the day.

Caravans and Motorhomes/RVs

In recent years, motorhomes have become very popular in Italy. Local councils have established designated camper parks near many popular tourist areas, and larger campsites nearly always accept campers and caravans. Camper van or mobile home rental is becoming increasingly common. Prices are usually around €1,400 for a four-berth vehicle for a week in high season, with unlimited mileage – check out **Comocaravan** for options.

In peak season, you will need to book places in advance at campsites. In quieter areas, free camping is on the increase, but it is illegal. To avoid offending local sensibilities (or ruining other people's views), ask advice from the local traffic police (*vigili*) before parking up for the night. The speed limit for driving with a caravan or trailer is 50 kmph (30 mph) in built-up areas; 70 kmph (45 mph) on secondary and main roads; and 80 kmph (50 mph) on motorways.

Maps and Sat Nav Devices

The best maps for long journeys and overall planning are the *AA Road Atlas Italy* and Touring Club Italiano's *Atlante Stradale d'Italia* (both 1:250,000). Regional maps from Touring Club Italiano (1:200,000) are invaluable for local exploring, but they will not plot every country lane and unsurfaced track. Touring Club Italiano does, however, occasionally produce maps of small areas of particular interest – such as national parks – at 1:50,000 scale. These are rarely sold in shops, but available at park offices.

Satellite navigation applications such as Google Maps or Waze can be used on your mobile phone to get real-time navigation and traffic information. For non-EU drivers, avoid expensive roaming charges by signing up for an international data plan with your provider. Google Maps also has a feature to download maps and save them on your device for use offline. Most car rental firms offer GPS as standard or as an add-on. Be sure to book the option in advance.

DIRECTORY

CAR HIRE

AutoEurope
autoeurope.com

Avis
avis.com

Budget
budget.co.uk

Europcar
europcar.com

Hertz
hertz.com

Holiday Autos
holidayautos.co.uk

CARAVANS AND MOTORHOMES/RVS

Comocaravan
comocaravan.it

Below far left Road signage, Chianti **Below left** Camper van near Lake Como **Below middle** Tourist information map in Valli di Comacchio **Below middle right** Iconic Italian scooter **Below** Getting about in Parco di San Bartolo

WHERE TO STAY

Italy has some of the most memorable places to stay in Europe, ranging from grand hotels oozing *belle époque* glamour to boutique hotels on the cutting edge of contemporary design. Both the *agriturismo* scheme – which allowed the owners of farms, vineyards and country estates to convert historic barns, villas and palaces into rooms and apartments – and the vibrant bed-and-breakfast scene have made it easier for visitors to experience the warm hospitality usually missing in so many chain hotels and *pensioni*.

Above Hotel Splendid, Baveno, on the shores of Lake Maggiore

B&Bs

There are hundreds of B&Bs operating in Italy. The best of these can offer excellent value for money as well as the opportunity to experience exceptional Italian hospitality, whether the setting is a couple of rooms in a simple city apartment or a glamorous suite in a historic palace. The **BB Planet** website is a useful online resource.

The rules state that a B&B should have no more than five rooms and that the owners must live on the premises (although not all B&Bs fully adhere to these rules). In the best-run places, breakfasts can be fantastic affairs, with homemade jams and cakes, fresh croissants and fruit; at the other end of the spectrum, you might be handed a cellophane-packed croissant and a juice box the night before.

If you are looking for a B&B on spec, ask if there are any staff on the premises and, if not, how to contact the owner should the need arise. Also check if breakfast is served on site, or whether they have an arrangement with a local café. Occasionally, B&Bs may allow you free use of the kitchen.

Boutique Hotels

The international trend for boutique hotels has found fertile ground in Italy – not surprisingly, given the plethora of historic buildings as well as the Italian flair for food, hospitality, lifestyle and design. Some boutique hotels are run by hospitality-trade professionals, others by passionate newcomers, often from the worlds of architecture and design. This guide recommends plenty of boutique hotels across Northern and Central Italy. Websites such as **i-escape** and **Mr & Mrs Smith** are also well worth a browse.

Hotels

Italian hotels are given an official rating ranging between 1 and 5 stars (though Milan has the 7-star Town House Galleria – *sevenstars galleria.com*) based on a checklist of facilities and services, such as how many rooms have a telephone or ensuite bathroom, if there is an on-site restaurant, and whether there is 24-hour room service. This means that the star rating is no guide to the subtler, more subjective charms of hotels, such as cleanliness, the decor or the friendliness or helpfulness of staff. If such things are important to you, then the accommodation recommendations made in this guide should help you to find the kind of place you are looking for.

Agriturismi

The *agriturismo* scheme began in the 1980s to enable farmers and landowners to boost falling revenues by renting out converted farm buildings to visitors. They can range from state-of-the-art country hotels to simple self-catering apartments. Some serve food for guests made from homegrown produce, others have on-site restaurants. Many offer activities such as horse riding, and some have developed into little resorts, with swimming pools, tennis courts and mountain bikes to rent.

Booking

It is wise to book well in advance if you are travelling in July and August, or around Easter and the various springtime public holidays. Hotels in coastal and lake resorts often close between October and Easter. Reservations can often be made online, though not all sites belonging to individual hotels are secure, which may be a little unsettling if credit card

Above left Alpine hotel, Courmayeur, in the Valle d'Aosta **Above right** Stylish bedroom in the Hotel Greif, Bolzano

details are requested as a guarantee. You can minimize risk by booking over the phone or by using a hotel-booking site with a secure website.

Facilities and Prices

Double rooms in Italian hotels usually have a double bed *(letto matrimoniale)*, so if you prefer twin beds *(due letti)*, it is wise to request that when you book. Single rooms are rare, and you will often end up having to pay for a single use of a double room.

In hotels, rates are quoted per room; in B&Bs, per person. The more expensive B&Bs will usually cost about as much as a 2- or 3-star hotel, but tend to offer better value in terms of service and surroundings. You will often find rooms at a reduced rate on the web. Weekend rates in city hotels are often great value.

In some cities you will be charged a city tax in addition to the price of the room (usually a few euros per person per night), while in Venice, overnight guests are exempt from paying entry fees for day trippers.

Under Italian law, hotels are required to register guests at police headquarters and issue a receipt of payment *(ricevuta fiscale)*, which you must keep until you leave Italy.

Camping

Camping is becoming increasingly popular in Italy, and there are plenty of sites both on the coast and in the mountains. They are usually open from April to September, though some sites stay open year-round in the south and in Sicily. For the tentless, sites offer bungalows, sleeping up to six, with space for caravans and camper vans.

Self-catering

If you want to focus on a single region, consider renting a villa or rural house. Villas in Northern and Central Italy ranging from simple rustic retreats and seaside apartments to palatial places with pools, maids, chefs and masseurs. The widest choice can be found in Tuscany and Umbria, but Lake Como and the Veneto are also popular villa destinations, with many properties in exquisitely restored country houses. The **Airbnb** website has useful self-catering sections. However, places like Florence have banned Airbnb in its historic centre.

Below far left A relaxing guest lounge **Below left** Spa at the Hotel Victoria, Turin **Below middle** Doorway of a B&B in Castelmuzio **Below** Hotel Ristorante Locanda San Vigilio, on the eastern shore of Lake Garda

DIRECTORY

B&Bs
BB Planet
bbplanet.it

BOUTIQUE HOTELS
Mr & Mrs Smith
mrandmrssmith.com

TabletHotels
tablethotels.com

AGRITURISMI
Official *agriturismo* website
agriturismo.it

CAMPING
Italian campsites
camping.it

SELF-CATERING
Airbnb
airbnb.com

PRICE CATEGORIES
The following price bands are based on a standard double room in high season, including tax and service:

inexpensive – under €150
moderate – €100–€300
expensive – over €300

WHERE TO EAT

One of the great pleasures of travelling in Northern and Central Italy is exploring the rich culinary and winemaking traditions of each region. Every trip in this guide provides the opportunity to sample regional specialities, whether it be the *pesto* and fish dishes of Liguria, the truffles, hams and salamis of Umbria, or the cheeses, dumplings and smoked sausages of the Alto-Adige. Below is a basic guide to the typical kinds of eating places you will find in Italy, from simple pizzerias to sophisticated gourmet haunts.

Above Menu for a pizza restaurant in Riva del Garda, near Lake Garda

Practical Information

Perhaps the most typical Italian breakfast is a croissant (*cornetto*) and coffee at a bar. The coffee comes in a staggering variety of modes, from short and sharp (*un caffè*) to long and milky (*latte macchiato*). An espresso diluted with hot water to make it resemble American filter coffee is an *Americano*; an espresso with a blob of frothy milk is a *caffè macchiato*. Italians wouldn't dream of having a frothy cappuccino at any time of day other than breakfast. In summer, there is usually iced coffee – *caffè freddo*.

The main meal is lunch, normally served in restaurants from noon until 2pm, though in summer resorts you'll find a few restaurants that keep their kitchens open right through to dinner, which is usually served from 7:30–10:30pm. Most restaurants are closed one day a week and display their *giorno di chiusura* (closed day) in the window, although in the summer, many open seven days a week.

Meals begin with an *antipasto*, or starter, followed by the *primo*, or first course – most commonly pasta, risotto or, in winter, a *minestra* (hearty soup). The *secondo* is the meat and fish course, with the *contorno* (vegetables or salad) usually served on a separate dish alongside. Finally, there is the *dolce*, or dessert. House wines can vary in quality, but a quarter (*quarto*), half (*mezzo*) or 1-litre carafe (*caraffa*) will always be at the very least drinkable.

In cities and major towns, credit cards are widely accepted – less so in smaller places and in the country, where it is advisable to carry cash. Tax and service must be included in the bill by law, and a small cover charge (*coperto*) is usually added. Tipping is becoming more common; 10 per cent is usual in smarter or more touristy places.

Italians rarely dress down, so dressing fairly smartly will generally fit the bill. Men – like women – will be expected to wear tops during meals, even at beachside places. Only in the most exclusive restaurants is dress formal, and men required to wear a tie and jacket. Children are welcome in restaurants, even late at night.

Ristoranti, Trattorie, Osterie

These are the three main types of restaurants in Italy, and until some years ago they were quite distinct. A *ristorante* was a "proper" restaurant, with linen tablecloths and waiters in uniform. A *trattoria* was usually a more basic, homely sort of place; the menu was often scrawled on a blackboard, and there were sheets of newsprint to cover the tables and on which to write the bill. An *osteria* was an unpretentious country or city hostelry, offering a few cold cuts of meat with some cheese, and maybe a simple pasta dish to accompany a glass of the local wine. However, that has all changed, and these days the choice of name for an establishment depends more on the tradition the place identifies with than price, decor or ambience. *Ristorante* is now a neutral, generic term that could apply to anything from a Michelin-starred gem to a seaside joint where mass-catering is the order of the day; and although there are *trattorie* and *osterie* that have existed for half a century, today the terms might as easily apply to the best restaurant in town. "*Trattoria*" often implies an interest in reviving and reinventing traditional dishes; whereas "*osteria*" tends to suggest an emphasis on sourcing the very best primary ingredients and wines, as promoted, for instance, by the **Slow Food movement**.

Visitors can consult the **Michelin Guides** for a wide selection of the best restaurants in the region.

Above left Restaurant table in the Parco Naturale del Monte San Bartolo **Above right** Caffè degli Specchi on Piazza dell Unita d'Italia, Trieste

Pizzerias

Pizzerias are found throughout Italy, but contrary to popular myth, it is only too easy to find doughy, substandard pizza. You have more chance of striking gold if you go to a pizzeria with a wood-burning oven (*forno a legna*), from which the pizzas should emerge bubbling, scorched and blistered. Pizzerias are almost always informal places, and pizza is usually only served in the evening (as it takes hours to get the oven hot enough). The classic accompaniment to pizza is a cold draught beer.

Cafés and Bars

At one end of the spectrum are grand cafés with chandelier-lit interiors and terraces fringing some of the most spectacular piazzas in Italy; at the other, modest local bars with 1980s colour schemes, steaming coffee machines and rustic plastic flowers. These unpretentious neighbourhood bars often have standing-room only and are places to come for breakfast, a quick toasted sandwich or a swift shot of coffee. Some have a few tables outside for a more leisurely breakfast or aperitif, though you should find time at least once on your trip to dawdle over a Campari soda and olives in a traditional pavement café watching life pass by.

Picnics

There is no better excuse for sampling local produce than a picnic. With that end in view, you will need to find a delicatessen (*alimentari*) where you can buy delicacies such as rosemary-spiked hams, mature gorgonzola, *speck* (smoked ham) and olives; a bakery (*il forno*); and a greengrocer (*fruttivendolo*) or market (*mercato*) packed with seasonal fruits and vegetables. Along with stall upon stall of the freshest fruit and vegetables, weekly markets also bring together local smallholders offering such things as home-cured cheeses and salamis. There are often stalls with specialities from the south of Italy too – capers, sun-dried tomatoes, mozzarella di bufala and spicy salami – which add a traditional touch. Less romantically, Italian supermarkets, including chains like Esselunga and Coop, stock very good-quality fresh produce as well as freshly baked bread.

Mountain regions often have picnic areas with massive outside grills – a great way of sampling a Chiavenna steak or a freshly caught red mullet. Around the lakes you will find free beaches (*spiaggia libera*) where you can settle on a grassy patch by the lakeside and enjoy your carefully chosen delights.

DIRECTORY

RISTORANTI, TRATTORIE, OSTERIE

Michelin Guides
guide.michelin.com

Slow Food movement
slowfood.it

PRICE CATEGORIES

The following price bands are based on a three-course meal for one, including a half-bottle of house wine, cover charge, tax and service:

inexpensive – under €30
moderate – €30–€50
expensive – over €50

Below far left Black truffles at the Sansepolcro market **Below left** Fruits on a Bolzano market stall **Below middle** Alfresco dining in Orvieto **Below middle right** Subterranean wine vault, Canonica a Cerreto, Chianti **Below** Display at a bakery and bar in San Casciano dei Bagni

Panoramic view of Isola Bella on Lake Maggiore

THE
ROAD TRIPS

TRIP 1

IN THE SHADOW OF THE ALPS
Turin to Castello di Rivoli

HIGHLIGHTS

Royal Turin
Admire the sweeping boulevards, elegant hunting lodges and pleasure palaces of this aristocratic city

Gourmet Piedmont
Taste the region's famous mushrooms and truffles and sample the rich, French-influenced cuisine

Strategic mountain passes
Walk in the footsteps of some of history's greatest armies – Hannibal, Augustus and Napoleon all marched through the Alps near Aosta

Paradise park
Explore Italy's first national park, the Parco Nazionale del Gran Paradiso, and see ibex, chamois, marmots and magnificent golden eagles

IN THE SHADOW OF THE ALPS

The rolling hillsides around Turin produce some of the world's most delectable wines and prized gourmet delicacies, such as white truffles and various kinds of cheese. Encircled by palaces and former hunting lodges and set against the amphitheatre of the snowcapped Alps, Turin is well-endowed with beautiful architecture and cutting-edge design. The tour then passes through the dramatic landscape of the Valle d'Aosta and the Gran Paradiso – the highest mountain entirely within Italy – to the spectacular *Monte Bianco* (Mont Blanc), Europe's loftiest peak, and to the towns at her feet.

Above Driving cows along the winding road from La Thuile to Col du Mont Cenis, *see p36*

ACTIVITIES

Ride up to the top of Turin's iconic Mole Antonelliana to view the towering mountains backing the city

Discover a wilderness paradise in Italy's first national park, the Gran Paradiso

Hike in the mountains and then take a chairlift or cable car from Courmayeur or La Thuile up to the highest peaks in Europe

Take the healthy waters in the thermal spa town of Pré-Saint-Didier

Follow in the footsteps of Hannibal and his elephants on the border between Italy and France

Below Stunning green farmland in the Valle d'Aosta, *see pp34–5*

TRIP 1: IN THE SHADOW OF THE ALPS 31

Above Remains of an aqueduct, part of the remarkable Roman ruins at Susa, *see p37*

PLAN YOUR DRIVE

Start/finish: Turin to Castello di Rivoli.

Number of days: 3–4, allowing half a day to explore Turin.

Distance: 470 km (292 miles).

Road conditions: Generally well-paved and signposted, but there is steep terrain in the Valle d'Aosta, which is often snowbound in winter; drivers are required to have winter tyres fitted and carry snow chains Oct–Apr.

When to go: Roads in the Alps are very dangerous in the winter. Stretches of the route between Pré-Saint-Didier and Col du Mont Cenis are closed during the winter months, when there is high snowfall. The best time to do this trip is between June and October.

Opening times: Shops tend to open Mon–Sat 9am–1pm and 4–7:30 or 8pm. Some shops are shut on Mon mornings or Wed afternoons, but city supermarkets often stay open for the siesta. Churches and museums are usually open 8 or 9am–noon and 4–7 or 8pm. Many museums are closed on Mondays.

Main market days: Turin: Porta Palazzo, Mon–Fri mornings and all day Sat; Aosta: Piazza Cavalieri di Vittorio Veneto, Sat (indoor Tue–Sat).

Shopping: Gourmet produce such as nougat, mushrooms and truffles, cheese made from mountain milk and, of course, wine. Other good buys include textiles in Biella and cuckoo clocks in Aosta and the mountain areas.

Major festivals: Turin: Cultural heritage week, Sep; Turin book fair, mid-May; Classical music festival, Sep; Slow Food fair, Oct (biannually); Luci d'Artista, Nov–Jan.

DAY TRIP OPTIONS

Those interested in **architecture** will find a host of **buildings** to explore in Turin with the works of Baroque architect Juvarra, and impressive **museums** and **churches**. Outdoor enthusiasts can take the **mountain air** in historic Aosta. See the fantastic **castle** at Fénis and enjoy the natural glory of the **Parco Nazionale del Gran Paradiso**. For full details, *see p37*.

VISITING TURIN

Parking
Parking is difficult and it is best to use an underground car park at Piazza Vittorio Veneto, Porta Nuova or Ciao Mario where you can use "Park & Ride".

Visitor Information
Piazza Castello/Via Garibaldi, 10122; turismotorino.org

Cable car to Basilica di Superga
Departs every hour from Sassi station in the Piazza Modena (Tram No.15).

WHERE TO STAY IN TURIN

Grand Hotel Sitea *moderate*
A luxury hotel, set right in the middle of the city's shopping area, offering elegant rooms and top-notch service.
Via Carlo Alberto 35, 10123; grandhotelsitea.it

Hotel Victoria *moderate*
Close to Via Roma and Piazza San Carlo, this resembles an English country house and has a garden for alfresco meals.
Via Nino Costa 4, 10123; hotelvictoria-torino.com

Ligotto Congress *moderate*
This city hotel with industrial-chic design features a rooftop jogging path from the film *The Italian Job*.
Via Nizza 262, 10126; nh-hotels.com

Below (clockwise from top left) The grand Piazza San Carlo; the Roman Palatine Gate; former bedroom in the Palazzo Madama; exterior of the Palazzo Madama in the Piazza Castello; dome of the Chiesa di San Lorenzo

❶ Palazzina di Caccia di Stupinigi
Piazza Principe Amedeo 7, Torino; 10042
Palatial, Rococo-style hunting lodge of the Savoys – a family from the Swiss Alps who went on to rule Italy. Its **Museo di Storia, Arte e Ammobiliamento** (Museum of History, Art and Interior Design) *(closed Mon)* has exquisite frescoes, chandeliers and marquetry. The *Sala degli Specchi* (Hall of Mirrors) holds a marble bath owned by Napoleon's sister, Paolina Borghese.

🚗 *From the hunting lodge, head southeast on Piazza Principe Amedeo to Viale Torino. Follow Corso Unione Sovietica to "centro". Park under Piazza Vittorio Veneto.*

❷ TURIN
Torino, Piedmont; 10100

With the Alps as a glorious backdrop, Turin (Torino) has squares, castles, palaces and boulevards fit for a king. Indeed, it was the first capital of the Kingdom of Italy (1861). Today, it is the country's design and contemporary art capital. And, for a taste of the *dolce vita*, Turin is a gourmet paradise and the birthplace of Italian cinema.

A three-hour walking tour
From Piazza Vittorio Veneto, walk up the Via Po to the town centre. Turn right into Via Montebello to reach the unmissable **Mole Antonelliana** ①. Topped by a 167-m (550-ft) spire, this edifice is a symbol of the city and home to the excellent **Museo Nazionale del Cinema** ① *(closed Tue)*. The Italian film industry was born in Turin, which was also the film production capital of the world (1906–16). The museum recreates the story of cinema with props and classic film clips, including the car chase in *The Italian Job*. Take the glass lift to the viewing platform on the spire for fabulous views of the city and the Alps. Next, turn right and then left into the wide Corso San Maurizio and left into the Giardini Reali. Continue through the park to the far corner and the Baroque **Palazzo Reale** ② *(closed Mon)*, once the official Savoy residence. The interior is graced with chinoiserie, gold, velvet and tapestries. Next door is the Piazza Castello,

Madonna and child, Palazzo Madama

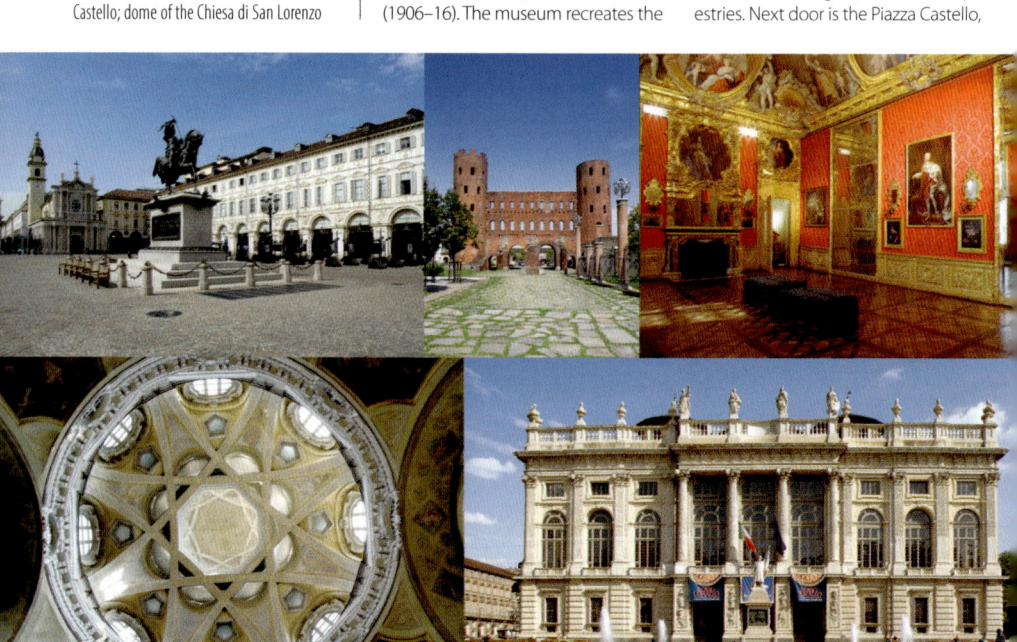

TRIP 1: IN THE SHADOW OF THE ALPS   33

Above Elegant colonnaded walkway along Via Roma, Turin

site of the Palazzo Madama, which houses the **Museo Civico d'Arte Antica** ③ *(closed Tue)*. Highlights here include Roman foundations in the basement, architect Filippo Juvarra's sinuous staircase and atrium, and *The Portrait of a Man* by Antonello da Messina (1476). Two of Turin's most atmospheric cafés are in the piazza – Mulassano and Baratti & Milano. On the western corner of the piazza is the **Chiesa di San Lorenzo** ④ *(open daily)*. The interior of this church is a Baroque fantasy of marble, stucco and gilding. It also has a replica of the *Sindone di Torino* (Turin Shroud), believed to be the sheet in which Christ's body was wrapped. Walk northwest from the piazza to the **Quadrilatero** ⑤ – the gridded area that recalls the old Roman settlement. The cobbled streets are full of bars, cafés, markets and churches. Return to Piazza Castello and walk down Via Roma and, near Piazza San Carlo, turn right into Via Accademia delle Scienze and the **Museo Egizio** ⑥ *(Egyptian Museum: closes early Mon)*. The collection includes papyri, a black statue of Ramses II (13th century BCE), sarcophagi and the tomb of Kha and Merit (c 1430 BCE), complete with vases of food and unguents for the afterlife.

🚗 From Piazza Vittorio Veneto, cross Ponte Vittorio Emanuele I and follow brown signs for Superga. Turn left onto Corso Casale, right at Strada Comunale di Superga, left at Piazzale Alberto Geisser and then on to Superga.

❸ Basilica di Superga
Torino, Piedmont; 10020

Spectacularly perched on a hill, this grand mausoleum *(open daily)* bears the tombs of over 62 members of the Savoy family and has a cloister with an Italian style garden. Duke Vittorio Amedeo engaged Juvarra to build the basilica in 1717 after defeating an invading French army in 1706. The funicular ride from Sassi station (just below) up to the basilica is always popular with children. A large plaque in the grounds commemorates the tragic loss of the Grande Torino football team, whose plane crashed into the hillside in 1949.

🚗 *Head west to pick up the SP590/ Via Torino, then go on SR11 through Chivasso to Cigliano. Next, take the SP593 to Cavaglia and SP143 to Biella.*

EAT AND DRINK IN TURIN

Il Barotto *moderate*
This informal restaurant specializes in cheese platters and cold cuts.
Via Baretti 8, 10125; ilbarotto.it

Plin & Tajarin *moderate*
A fun restaurant offering a creative menu of local specialities.
Via Goffredo Casalis 59, 10318; lnx.plinetajarin.it; closed Wed

Ristorante del Cambio *expensive*
Turin's most famous restaurant serves authentic *bollito misto* – a mix of cooked meats. Booking essential.
Piazza Carignano 2, 10123; delcambio.it

Above The Basilica di Superga, built to commemorate the liberation of Turin from the French

Above The fortress Il Melograno, Issogne, originally built in 1480

WHERE TO STAY

AOSTA
Duca D'Aosta Modern Retro Hotel
moderate
Set in the heart of the old town, this comfortable *albergo* has 60 rooms, decorated in retro 50s and 60s style, with French oak floors, stone showers and enamelled steel bathtubs, and a pleasant restaurant.
Piazza Narbonne 8, 11100; hotelducadaosta.com

AROUND AOSTA
Agriturismo Mont Rosset
inexpensive
This family-run *agriturismo* is located in a beautiful spot with valley views. It has six simply decorated rooms and a restaurant serving regional dishes.
Frazione Mont Rosset, Jovençan, 11020; mont-rosset.it; check website for closing periods

COGNE
La Madonnina del Gran Paradiso
moderate
A family-run, ECO hotel set in a panoramic position on the mountainside with its own spa. Its 30 rooms are clad in pine and there is a wood-burning oven in the restaurant.
Via Laydetré 7, 11012; lamadonnina.com; closed Apr–mid-Jun & Nov–mid-Dec

4 Biella
Biella, Piedmont; 13900
At the heart of "Textile Valley", Biella is famous as a major centre for high-quality wool and yarn production, and Italian designer names such as Zegna and Loro Piana have close links with the town. More than 50 factory outlets line the industrial approach roads – many of which are on the SS230 – look for *spaccio* on signs, meaning "outlets". There are outlets in Biella too. The town has a compact, attractive centre and highlights include the Renaissance basilica and cloister of **St Sebastian**, with lovely frescoes inside. A funicular goes up to the beautiful medieval village of Piazzo.

🚗 *Head southwest, then take the SP338/Via Ivrea and turn right onto the SP419. Fork right onto SP73, then continue north on the SP72 and the SS26 before turning off onto the SR4 to Issogne.*

5 Issogne
Aosta, Valle d'Aosta; 11020
The Valle d'Aosta is full of castles and medieval forts. Many were fortresses, while others were more palatial, such as **Issogne Castle** *(closed Oct–Mar: Mon)*. More château than fort, it is famous for the fountain in the courtyard, which has a pomegranate tree *(il melograno)* of iron. Restored over the years, the palace has frescoes of 15th-century street life, along with period furniture and artifacts. Nearby, the village of Champdepraz (just north on the A5) is the access point for the **Parco Naturale del Mont Avic** *(open Apr–Sep: daily; closed Oct–Mar:*

Mon; montavic.it), whose lakes, marshes and alpine bogs are home to many flower species, which attract clouds of butterflies.

🚗 *Go north, signposted Champdepraz, turn right at SR6, left at SS26 towards Aosta and follow signs to Fénis.*

Piedmontese fare
Local cuisine matches robust flavours with French flair, reflecting the area's relationship with the House of Savoy. The woods, especially near Alba, are truffle- and mushroom-rich and any dish with *salsa di tartufi bianchi* will be delicious. *Bagna cauda* is a warm dip made with oil, anchovies, garlic and cream. Blue gorgonzola is the best-known cheese – *dolce* (creamy) or *piccante* (crumbly). Look for soft cheeses, too, such as *caprino* (goat), *fontina* (cow) and *raschera* (a combination of cow's and either goat's or sheep's milk). Fondue *(fonduta)* is often made with *fontina* – delicious with Alba's white truffles.

6 Fénis
Aosta, Valle d'Aosta; 11020
The most famous of all the castles in the Valle d'Aosta is the **Castello di Fénis** *(open Apr–Sep: daily, Oct–Mar: Tue–Sun)*. Set on a grassy knoll, backed by a chestnut forest, it is every inch a fairytale medieval castle. Its origins date to the 13th century, but what is visible today is largely the 1340 creation of Aimone de Challant, who belonged to a noble family linked to the Savoys. The castle has a pentagonal layout and the keep is enclosed by a double perimeter wall, with watchtowers linked by a walkway. The

Above The remarkably well-preserved Castello di Fénis, watching over the Valle d'Aosta inner courtyard has a semi-circular staircase and wooden balcony, decorated with exquisite frescoes of St George killing the dragon and a group of wise men and prophets holding scrolls. There is also a small museum of local furniture inside.

🚗 Take the SR13, then turn left onto the SS26 west to Aosta. There is a car park at Piazza Arco d'Augusto.

❼ Aosta
Aosta, Valle d'Aosta; 11100
Named after Emperor Augustus, Aosta was once a mini-Rome in the centre of its own valley; today it is the regional capital. The triumphal Arco d'Augusto now sits on a traffic island and from it runs the Roman Via Sant' Anselmo, a pedestrian precinct. To the right, outside the city walls, is an impressive series of ancient church buildings around the **Collegiata di Sant'Orso** (open daily), dedicated to the patron saint of Aosta. Sant' Orso itself has a Gothic (15th-century) façade, a 12th-century Romanesque bell tower and an elegant cloister. At the end of the Via Sant'Anselmo, where all kinds of souvenirs can be purchased – from cuckoo clocks to local gourmet delights – is the Porta Praetoria, the two thick, arched walls forming the impressive stone entrance to the city. Inside, on the right, lie the remains of a Roman theatre. Just to the north, accessed through the Convento di San Giuseppe, is the **Amphitheatre** (open daily). In the old town, the Duomo in Piazza Giovanni XXIII dates from the 12th century and contains some of the best Christian art treasures from the area in the **Museo del Tesoro** (open weekends). Next to the Duomo is the Roman Forum with a supporting arcade (cryptoporticus).

🚗 Leave Aosta on the SS26 and bear left onto the SR47 after Sarre, heading south to Cogne.

❽ Cogne
Aosta, Valle d'Aosta; 11012
This is an excellent base for exploring Italy's first national park, the beautiful **Parco Nazionale del Gran Paradiso**. Originally a Savoy hunting reserve, 21 sq km (5,200 acres) were donated by King Vittorio Emanuele III in 1929 to form the present park. Today, it is home to the endangered ibex, as well as to numerous chamois, marmots, ptarmigans and golden eagles. Maps of the footpaths and routes are available from the visitor information centre (Via Bourgeois 34, 11012; 0165 740 40). A path meanders south to Valnontey, where the **Giardino Alpino Paradisia** (open Jul–Aug: daily) has a fine collection of more than 1,000 species of alpine flora. The best time to see these is from late-June to mid-July.

🚗 Head northwest on SR47, then turn left onto the SS26. Stay on SS26 till Chenoz and then continue straight in order to drive into Courmayeur.

Above left Near the Parco Nazionale del Gran Paradiso, Cogne **Above** Bikes – a favourite way to explore Aosta's national park

EAT AND DRINK

AOSTA

Vecchio Ristoro expensive
This Michelin-starred restaurant is centrally located and combines rustic charm with an elegant dining experience. The chef, Alfio Fascendini, is a master of innovation and seasonal specialities such as wild mushrooms. *Via Tourneuve 4, 11100; ristorante vecchioristoro.it; closed Sun & Mon*

COGNE

Lou Ressignon moderate
Well-established, family-run inn specializing in authentic Valdostano specialities. At weekends, music complements feasting. Also has rooms. *Rue des Mines 22, 11012; louressignon.it; closed Tue & Wed in low season, Nov*

Bar a Fromage expensive
Splendid little restaurant with a warm, intimate atmosphere where cheese is definitely king. Visitors can also buy some excellent produce in the shop. *Rue Grand Paradis 21, 11012; hotelbellevue.it; closed Thu in low season, 10 days after Easter & mid-Oct–Nov*

SHOPPING IN BIELLA

While there are many outlets just outside town, within Biella itself is **Fratelli Cerruti** (Via Cernaia 40; closed Sun), selling discounted men and women's classic clothes, and cashmere specialist **Piacenza1733** (Via Carlo Maggi; closed Sun & Mon)

Far left Glorious Romanesque fresco in Aosta's cathedral **Left** A salumeria (delicatessen) full of treats on Via Sant'Anselmo, Aosta

Above Climbers traversing an icy path in the mountains, Courmayeur **Above right** Museo Alpino Duca degli Abruzzi, Courmayeur

VISITING COURMAYEUR

Parking
There is a large car park by the cable car to Plan Checrouit, on the southern edge of town.

Visitor Information
Piazzale Monte Bianco 15, 11100; regione.vda.it/turismo

WHERE TO STAY

COURMAYEUR

Grand Hotel Royal e Golf *expensive*
Set on the main street of Courmayeur, this prestigious hotel is noted for its charm, good service and splendid views of Monte Bianco. There is a small wellness centre with swimming pool and solarium. There is also a very pleasant restaurant.
Via Roma 87, 11013; hotelroyalegolf.com

Hotel Auberge de la Maison *expensive*
Warm and welcoming, this homely mountain hotel and restaurant is rustically decorated. There are 33 individually designed rooms, together with a sauna, solarium and Turkish baths. The restaurant is noted for its excellent food and service.
Via Passerin d'Entreves 16A, 11013 (4 km/ 7 miles north of Courmayeur); aubergemaison.it; closed Nov–early Dec

⑨ Courmayeur
Aosta, Valle d'Aosta; 11100

In the majestic shadow of Monte Bianco (Mont Blanc), Courmayeur is a popular year-round resort and a joy to explore. The main hub, Via Roma, is traffic free and full of designer shops and gourmet gems. The **Museo Alpino Duca degli Abruzzi** *(Strada per il Villair 2; 0165 842 064; open daily, Wed pm)* tells tales of dramatic mountain rescues. Just north of Courmayeur at Entrèves, a cable car leads to Punta Helbronner – at 3,462 m (11,360 ft), it offers great views.

🚗 *Take the SS26 to Pré-Saint-Didier.*

⑩ Pré-Saint-Didier
Aosta, Valle d'Aosta; 07021

At just over 1,000 m (3,280 ft) high, the picturesque Pré-Saint-Didier is famous for its warm thermal waters. The spring is at a constant 36°C (98°F) at the point where the River Thuile forces its way through the narrow gorge into the Dora Valley. There is a well-known spa in the town, **Terme Pré-Saint-Didier** *(open daily; qcterme.com)*. The waters are said to have anti-inflammatory properties. Nearby is **La Thuile** (reached via the SS26). It is a pretty skiing and hiking town, and more of a family resort than chic Courmayeur. In summer, chairlifts allow access to heights of 2,400 m (7,900 ft) with scenic views and walking trails.

🚗 *Take the SS26, entering France on the D1090. Turn onto the D84, then take D902 past Val d'Isère at Lanslevillard, turning left on D115, followed by the D1006 signposted to Col du Mont Cenis (use the Fréjus tunnel in winter).*

⑪ Col du Mont Cenis
Lanslebourg-Mont-Cenis, 73480; France

Col du Mont Cenis (*Moncenisio* in Italian) is a 2,084-m (6,831-ft) high mountain pass in the Alps on the French–Italian border. It was an important invasion route and Napoleon I built a road there in 1810. It is also believed by some to have been Hannibal's pass when he marched his army and elephants over the Alps against Rome during the Second Punic War (218–203 BCE). The picturesque Lac du Mont Cenis is usually frozen until the end of May. The **Jardin Alpin** *(open daily)* has more than 120 flower species.

🚗 *Take the D1006 south. Enter Italy on the SS25, then take the SS24 from Susa to Exilles.*

⑫ Exilles
Torino, Piedmont; 10050

Overlooking the Valle di Susa, the little medieval town of Exilles is dominated by a splendid fort. **Exilles Fort** *(Via degli Alpini; forteexilles.it; open daily August; closed Jul–Sep)* is not only one of the oldest monuments in the valley, but also a great example of military architecture. A fort has kept watch over this passage between France and Italy since the 12th century,

Right Lac du Mont Cenis on a key invasion route in Italian history **Far right** The Italian skiing village of La Thuile

although what is visible today is mainly from the 19th century. It is said that from 1681–87, the "Man in the Iron Mask", a prisoner whose face and identity remain a mystery to this day, was incarcerated within these walls. Many have theorized as to his identity, most famously Alexandre Dumas, who postulated that he was Louis XIV's identical twin. Highlights include the Knights' Courtyard and the Staircase of Paradise leading to the Prison Courtyard. The fort's museum charts its long history and the story of Italy's alpine troops. From the roof there are splendid views of the upper Valle di Susa.

🚗 *Return back to Susa by heading northeast on the SS24.*

⓭ Susa
Torino, Piedmont; 10059

Known in Roman times as *Segusium*, Susa is a pretty mountain town. In the old town, at Piazza Savoia, the Porta Savoia gateway dates originally from the 4th century CE, although it was reconstructed in the Middle Ages. There is also a **Roman amphitheatre** *(open daily)*, aqueduct arches and the remains of some Roman baths. The remarkably well-preserved marble triumphal *Arco di Augusto* (Arch of Augustus) was built in the 1st century BCE by Gallic chieftain Cottius to commemorate the alliance with the ruling Romans. In the medieval historic centre, the Romanesque **Cattedrale di San Giusto** *(open daily)*, dating from the 12th century, has lovely frescoes and a fine campanile. The town is noted, too, for its shops full of gourmet delights.

🚗 *Head north, turn right onto SS25, signposted Avigliana, then Rivoli. Follow signs to car park at Castello.*

⓮ Castello di Rivoli
Rivoli, Piedmont; 10098

Set on a hill with splendid views, this castle was one of the Savoys' country residences. It is an imposing Baroque building bearing the classical French trademark style of master architect Filippo Juvarra. Inside, the **Museo d'Arte Contemporanea** *(closed Mon & Tue)* has works by Gilbert and George and Jeff Koons, while Maurizio Cattelan's stuffed horse is suspended from the ceiling – making a dramatic and inspiring contrast between modern and ancient. The museum often has excellent temporary exhibitions and there is a good café, as well as the highly acclaimed cuboid Combal. zero restaurant.

Above left The honeycomb façade of the 4th-century Porta Savoia, Susa **Above** The fort of Exilles, strategically located in the Valle di Susa **Below** In the Museo d'Arte Contemporanea, Castello di Rivoli

EAT AND DRINK

SUSA

Chez Zizi *inexpensive*
This shop offers free tastings and low-price local alcoholic beverages. Established in 1945, it draws customers from all over the area.
Corso Inghilterra 52, 10059; 0122 622 717; open daily

CASTELLO DI RIVOLI

Bistrot del Castello *expensive*
A centrally located restaurant situated right next to the Museo d'Arte Contemporanea. Try beautifully prepared meat and fish dishes here, such as octopus in a sea urchin sauce or aubergine rolls with Parmesan and tomatoes.
Via Gaspare Grandi 30, 10098; 011 958 7648; closed Mon

DAY TRIP OPTIONS

For visitors based in Turin, the first trip makes a good day out, while for those based in Aosta, the amazing mountain scenery is easy to explore.

Baroque architecture tour
In Turin ❷, see the beauty of the work of the great Baroque architect Filippo Juvarra (1678–1736) in the façade and staircase of the Palazzo Madama, as well as the other architectural and historical sights of the city. Then head out to the hunting lodge Palazzina di Caccia di Stupinigi ❶ and the Castello di Rivoli ⓮ – filled with thought-provoking modern art.

Head south on the SS23 to Stupinigi. Then take the E70 north (Tangenziale Sud) turning left onto the SP7 to Castello.

Art and castles in paradise
Based in Aosta ❼, take a trip to the fairytale castle in Fénis ❻. Next, head to Cogne ❽ to visit the Parco Nazionale del Gran Paradiso for an invigorating walk among breathtaking scenery.

Aosta is located on the SS26. For Fénis, take the SS26 and SR13. To reach Cogne, take the SS26 and then the SR47.

TRIP 2

IN THE LAND OF THE TRUFFLE

Barbaresco to Cuneo

HIGHLIGHTS

Kings of wine
Taste the nectar of the gods made from the Barolo and Barbaresco vineyards in the Langhe region

Gourmet delights
Linger over your meal in Bra, the home of Slow Food, and savour the famous white truffle of Alba

Mountain rides
Zigzag up the mountain pass from Sampeyre for spectacular views

Valley pastures
Stroll along the lush, wooded Valle Maira to the sound of sheep bells

Timeless Saluzzo
Take a tour of mellow Saluzzo's historic core, through frescoed Renaissance houses and palazzi

IN THE LAND OF THE TRUFFLE

Piedmont's attractions are diverse. The vine-braided hills of the Langhe yield velvety and elegant wines such as Barolo and Barbaresco – among Italy's most celebrated – while in the oak woods around Alba, keen-nosed hounds sniff out valuable musky white truffles. Villages in the area are dotted with fine restaurants (Bra was the birthplace of the Slow Food movement), which make the most of the bounty of hazelnut and chestnut groves, fruit orchards and mountain pastures. Castles and churches perch on hills; Occitan, the ancient Romance language of troubadors, is still spoken in the alpine valleys; and the dramatic mountain scenery is never less than enthralling.

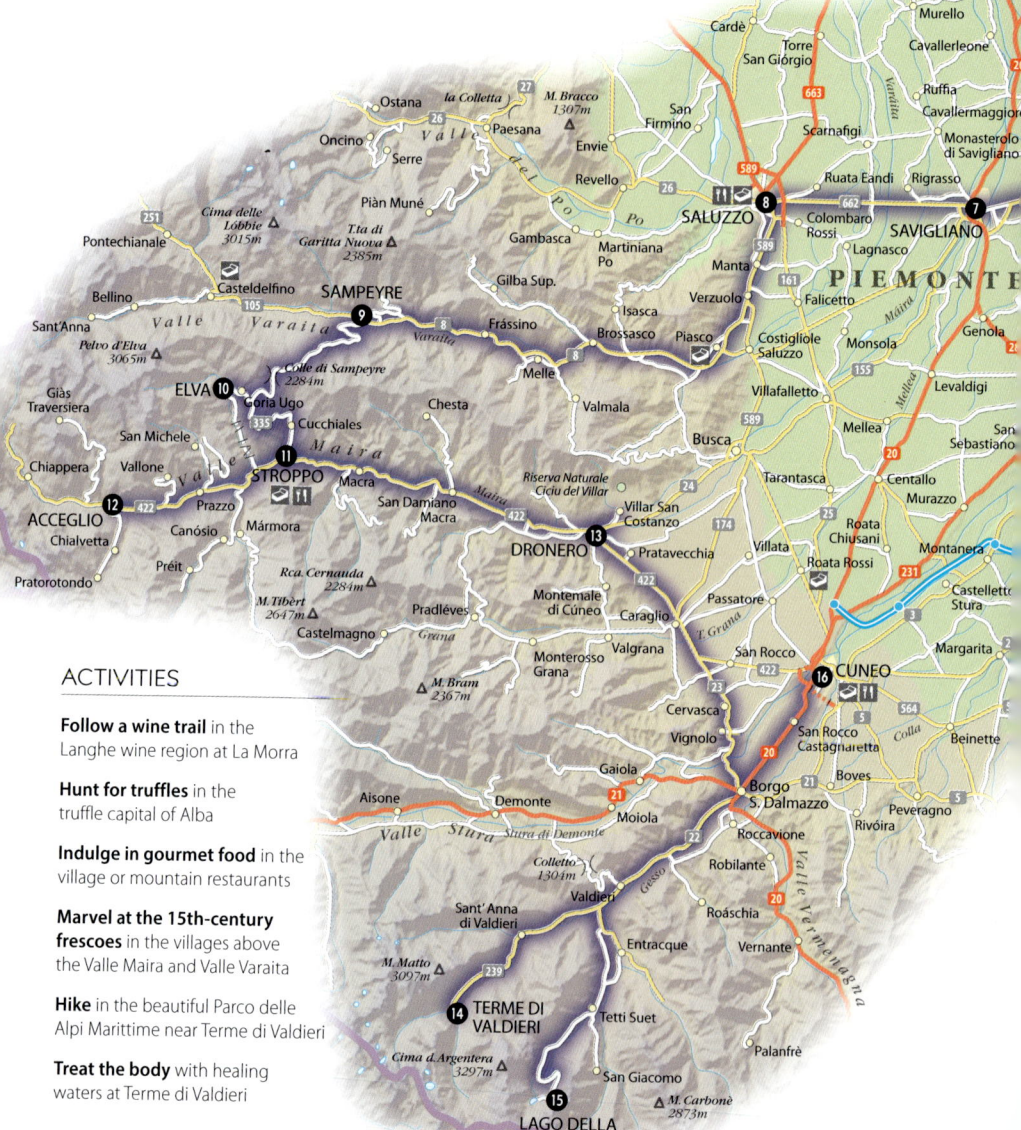

ACTIVITIES

Follow a wine trail in the Langhe wine region at La Morra

Hunt for truffles in the truffle capital of Alba

Indulge in gourmet food in the village or mountain restaurants

Marvel at the 15th-century frescoes in the villages above the Valle Maira and Valle Varaita

Hike in the beautiful Parco delle Alpi Marittime near Terme di Valdieri

Treat the body with healing waters at Terme di Valdieri

TRIP 2: IN THE LAND OF THE TRUFFLE   41

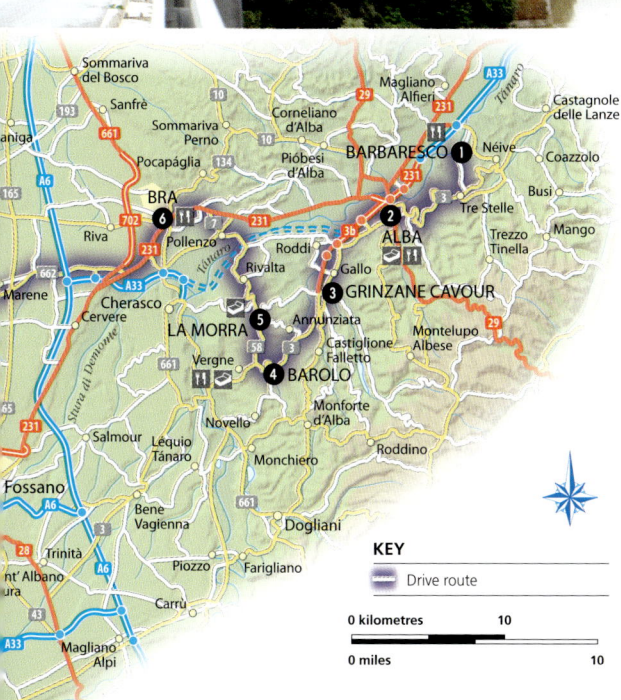

Above Abandoned brick bridge on the route to Bra, *see p43* **Below** Lofty mountain peaks of the Valle Maira near Elva, Stroppo and Acceglio, *see pp45–6*

PLAN YOUR DRIVE

Start/finish: Barbaresco to Cuneo.

Number of days: 3–4, allowing for a day in the Langhe region and a day each for Valle Varaita and Valle Maira.

Distance: Approx. 145 km (90 miles).

Road conditions: Roads are well-surfaced, but not always numbered. Rural routes are slow, winding and popular with motor bikers and cyclists at weekends. Mountain passes can be steep and mostly single track with few passing places. Roads from Saluzzo onwards may be impassable from Oct–May/Jun; only attempt these roads with snow chains, if experienced in driving in snow. Late autumn sees fog throughout.

When to go: Spring and autumn are best for travelling and wine festivals. The woods are most colourful in autumn; October is white truffle season in Alba:

Opening times: Shops tend to open 9am–1pm and 4–7pm Mon–Sat, with some closing on Mon morning. Churches are usually open 9am–noon and 4–7pm. Museum hours vary; those in smaller places close in the week's early part. Check ahead out of season.

Main market days: Alba: International White Truffle Festival (Oct–Dec); **Bra:** Fri; **Savigliano:** Piazza Santa Rosa, Tue & Fri; **Cuneo:** Piazza Galimberti, Tue.

Shopping: Alba is full of shops selling truffles and truffle-infused products – oil, pasta, purée – as well as hazelnut cakes and sweets. Cuneo is famous for chestnuts and Bra for its cheese.

Major festivals: Alba: Vinum (wine fair), late-Apr/May; Fiera del Tartufo Bianco (white truffle fair), Oct–Dec; Palio degli Asini (donkey derby), first Sun in Oct; **La Morra:** Mangialonga (food tour of vineyards), last Sun in Aug; **Bra:** Cheese fair, 3rd week of Sep, alternate years from 2013; **Cuneo:** Fiera del Marrone (chestnut fair), Oct.

DAY TRIP OPTIONS

Wine buffs will enjoy exploring the Langhe **vineyards** and **museums**, not to mention tasting the superior produce. **Outdoor enthusiasts** can head for the **pretty villages**, **valley greenery** and **mountain scenery** of the Valle Varaita. For full details, *see p47*.

Above Alba's main shopping street, Via Vittorio Emanuele II

WHERE TO STAY

AROUND ALBA
Villa La Meridiana Cascina Reinè *inexpensive*
A liberty-style villa with great views, set among vineyards and orchards a short drive east of Alba on Viale Cherasca. Truffle hunts can be arranged.
Località Altavilla 9, 12051; villalameridianaalba.it

AROUND BAROLO
Cà San Ponzio *inexpensive*
This farmhouse offers charming rooms and large breakfasts with delicious cakes. It's a good base for wine-country tours.
Via Rittane 7, 12060 Frazione Vergne; casanponzio.com

LA MORRA
Corte Gondina Boutique Hote *moderate*
Stylish and elegant, this hotel has fine antiques and furnishings, a lush garden and pool. Good breakfast too.
Via Roma 100, 12064; cortegondina.it

① Barbaresco
Cuneo, Piemonte; 12050
Barbaresco, overlooking the Tanaro river, makes a good introduction to the hilltop villages of the Langhe area, whose vineyards spill down the slopes in geometric patterns towards the rolling hills beyond. A stroll down Via Torino reveals characteristics typical of a wine-country village – a square 12th-century stone tower, one of a string of medieval watchtowers that once studded the region; a sundial (1999) illustrating the wine-making process painted over a whole wall of a house, and of course, the ubiquitous regional *enoteca* (wine bar), housed in the former church of San Donato.

🚗 **Follow SP3 south to Tre Stelle and continue along Via Rio Sordo to Alba. Cross the railway line into Viale Cherasca and take fourth exit into Corso M Coppino to a large parking place at Piazza San Paolo.**

② Alba
Cuneo, Piemonte; 12051
Alba rose to prominence in medieval times, when 100 brick towers reportedly dominated its skyline. Nowadays, there are only a few left around the Piazza Duomo, and the town stakes its claim to fame on the white truffle. During October and November, swarms of chefs and food enthusiasts descend on the town to sample its musky delights. It seems appropriate that the pink-brick **cattedrale** *(open daily)* is dedicated to San Lorenzo, the patron saint of chefs. On its façade, he is portrayed holding in his right hand the griddle on which he was martyred. Step inside the cathedral to see the lovely wooden choir stalls depicting still lifes and townscapes, inlaid in 1512 by Bernardino Fossati. The main street, Via Vittorio Emanuele II, is lined with shops selling truffles, oils, pastas, wines, cheeses and chocolates.

🚗 **Exit by Viale Torino to SP3bis, signed Barolo. Turn left at Gallo for Grinzane Cavour (signposted). Park by the castle.**

Slow Food
The region is known for its many food festivals. The pleasures of the table were held in high regard even before the Slow Food movement, which originated in Bra in 1986 in protest at the opening of a McDonald's near the Spanish Steps in Rome. The movement promotes traditional, local, seasonal and sustainable food. Piedmont restaurants serve their local delicacies with pride. Look for *bagna cauda* (hot dip) – an olive oil dip with anchovies and garlic, *fritto misto* (fried meats), *bollito misto* (boiled meats), *tajarin* (egg tagliatelle) and *agnolotti* (egg ravioli), the mountain cheese *castelmagno* and white truffles.

③ Grinzane Cavour
Cuneo, Piemonte; 12060
The magnificent 16th-century **Castello** *(closed Tue)* dominates Grinzane Cavour. It was once the home of Count Camillo Cavour, the town mayor for many years and a leading figure in the Italian Unification Movement of the 19th century. His bed, mayoral sash and

Below left Green rolling hills and vineyards around Barbaresco **Below right** The famous truffle castello at Grinzane Cavour, looming high over the village

some of his belongings are on show, as well as a barrel-maker's workshop and an 18th-century distillery. In November, the castle gains worldwide attention with its prestigious white truffle auction, when astronomical amounts of money – sometimes in excess of £100,000 for a single lot – change hands. More affordable for visitors are the fine wines and grappas for sale in the attached regional *enoteca*.

🚗 Follow SP3 southwest to Barolo and park in Piazza Colbert.

Above Road winding through the fertile vineyards around La Morra

④ Barolo
Cuneo, Piemonte; 12060
The highlight of this diminutive town is the **Castello dei Marchesi Falletti di Barolo** – the birthplace of Barolo, the "King of Wines". The vineyard has increased its reputation as a centre of wine production with its innovative interactive wine museum, **WiMu** *(open daily; from mid-Nov early closing, 6pm)*. Through five floors of the castle, visitors are enveloped in the history, art, food, music, films, literature and local traditions relating to the ambrosial liquid. The tour ends in the *tempio dell'enoturista* (Wine Tourist's Temple), where visitors can taste quality Barolo for themselves. There's an *enoteca* on hand for those who want to buy.

🚗 Take the SP3 and at the roundabout, take the first exit, SP58, to La Morra. Park in Piazza Martiri.

⑤ La Morra
Cuneo, Piemonte; 12064
La Morra is another town that focuses on wine, with plenty of atmospheric bars for tasting. A climb up through the narrow streets to the Piazza Castello is rewarded with superb views across wine country. Pick up a map for vineyard hikes at the **Cantina Comunale di La Morra** here, or from the tourist office. It's an easy 40-minute walk to the **Cappella del Barolo** *(open daily)* at Brunate, a deconsecrated little church that was painted in strikingly bold colours by American artists Sol Lewitt and David Tremlett in exchange for a supply of Barolo wine. Or, drive to nearby Annunziata, where the **Ratti Abbey and Wine Museum** offers guided tours and tastings.

🚗 On leaving La Morra take the left fork, follow SP58 and then SP7, following signs to turn left onto SS231 for Bra. Park in Piazza XX Settembre.

⑥ Bra
Cuneo, Piemonte; 12042
This lively town (named after *braida* – planting vines in rows wide enough for grain to grow in between) is known as the headquarters of the Slow Food movement. As a result, food is a vital part of any visit. Look for *salsiccia di Bra* (Bra sausage – a mixture of veal, pork, herbs and spices) on the menus of the excellent restaurants here. The tall church of **Santa Chiara** *(open daily)*, built in 1742, has a lovely Rococo interior and, in the words of its creator Bernardo Antonio Vittone, "a diaphanous dome" with an inner and outer shell, which creates wonderful plays of light. **Chiesa di Sant'Andrea** *(open daily)* is giddily Baroque, from its statue-topped façade to its altar packed with candles. Antique toys feature in the **Museo del Giocattolo** *(open Sun and by appointment; closed July & Aug)*.

🚗 Take SS231 and after 4 km (2.5 miles) turn onto SP662 westwards to Savigliano. Park in Viale del Sole or Viale Gozzano around the Parco Graneris.

Above left The exquisite dome of the Chiesa Santa Chiara, Bra **Above right** Atmospheric mist cloaking vineyards around La Morra

EAT AND DRINK

BARBARESCO
Antinè *expensive*
This restaurant serves delicious seafood. There's also a well-priced tasting menu. Booking advised.
Via Torino 16, 12050; antine.it; closed Tue, Wed & early Aug

ALBA
Piazza Duomo and La Piola *expensive*
Upstairs, the elegant Piazza Duomo comes under the Michelin-starred chef Enrico Crippa. On the ground floor, La Piola offers less expensive, rustic fare.
Pza Risorgimento 4, 12051; Duomo: piazzaduomoalba.it, closed Sun & Mon; Piola: lapiola-alba.it, closed Sun, Mon & 1st week in Sep

Other options
Check out **Tartufi Morra** *(Piazza Pertinace 3)* for truffle products and **Tartufi Ponzio** *(Via Vittorio Emanuele II 7A)* for hazelnut chocolate truffles.

AROUND BAROLO
Del Buon Padre *moderate*
In a quiet village, this place serves *fonduta Piemontese* (Piedmont cheese fondue) and beef braised in Barolo.
Via delle Viole 30, 12060 Vergne; buonpadre.com; closed Wed & Sun lunch

BRA
Osteria del Boccondivino *moderate*
A founding member of the Slow Food movement, this serves rabbit *tajarin* (thin tagliatelle) with butter and sage.
Via Mendicità Istruita 14, 12042; boccondivinoslow.it; closed Dec–Aug: Sun & Mon, Sep–Nov: Mon

Other options
Stock up on a Bra speciality, *ciuk* ("drunken" cheese aged in grape skins), from **Giolito** *(Via Monte Grappa 6)*.

Above Riverbed on the way to Sampeyre in the Valle Varaita **Above right** The historic centre of Saluzzo, with views across the valley

VISITING SALUZZO

Parking
Park in Piazza Garibaldi.

Tourist Information
Piazza Buttini 1, 12037; 0175 46 710; visitsaluzzo.it; closed Mon

WHERE TO STAY

SALUZZO AND AROUND

Castello Rosso *inexpensive*
Set on a hill amid parkland, this 16th-century castle offers a taste of luxury with spacious and colourful rooms. A good restaurant, pool and beauty treatments are also available.
Via Reynaudi 5, 12024 Costigliole Saluzzo (next to Piasco on SP1); castellorosso.com

Persico *inexpensive*
Friendly, modern hotel in the centre of town with simply furnished rooms. It has a good on-site restaurant.
Vicolo Mercati 10, 12037; albergopersico.net

❼ Savigliano
Cuneo, Piemonte; 12038

Despite losing out to Turin in the bid to be the capital of the Savoy kingdom, the citizens of Savigliano still built their triumphal arch (1585), which leads onto the broad, arcaded Piazza Santarosa – a good place for refreshments. Close by is the Baroque **Palazzo Taffini d'Acceglio** *(open Thu–Sun)*, which celebrates the exploits of Vittorio Amedeo I, Duke of Savoy, in a series of bold military frescoes, and has more decorative feminine rooms too. The **Museo Civico e Gipsoteca** *(open Sat & Sun)* contains sculptures by the 19th-century artist Davide Calandra, paintings and a reconstruction of an 18th-century pharmacy.
🚗 *Follow the signs for Saluzzo directly westwards on the SP662.*

❽ SALUZZO
Cuneo, Piemonte; 12037

Renaissance houses, churches, palazzos and a castle all spill down from Saluzzo's historic hilltop. Almost in France, the city was constantly changing hands between the French and the House of Savoy. On a walk through the narrow lanes and steep cobbled alleyways and steps up to the old town, it feels as though time has stopped here.

A 90-minute walking tour

From the car, walk up Via Ludovico II to Corso Italia, which cuts through a small piazza. To the left stands the late-Gothic **Cattedrale di Maria Vergine Assunta** ① *(open daily)*, whose façade has three round windows. The interior contains a beautiful polyptych by the 15th-century Flemish painter Hans Clemer (also known as the Master of Elva). The tourist office is further up on Via Martiri della Liberazione

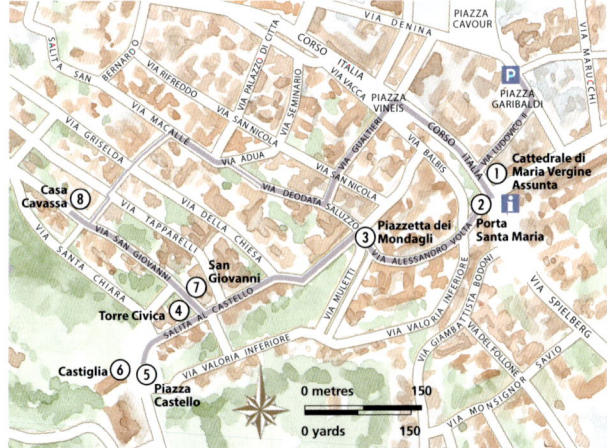

at Piazza Buttini. Cross Corso Italia and turn left through the **Porta Santa Maria** ② and follow Via Alessandro Volta, lined with porticoes, to **Piazzetta dei Mondagli** ③, where, at number 5, the 19th-century writer and leading figure of the Risorgimento, Silvio Pellico, was born.

Go up a steep flight of cobbled steps to Salita al Castello, past Renaissance houses with frescoes, loggias and terracotta decoration, and on to the **Torre Civica** ④ *(closed Mon–Fri)*, built in 1462. Climb up for marvellous views over the medieval rooftops to the mountains. At the top of the Salita are the **Piazza Castello** ⑤, the Fontana della Drancia (a favourite spot for newly married couples to be photographed), and the bulky **Castiglia** ⑥ with its formidable keep – once home to the marquises and later (until 1922) a prison.

Retrace your steps from the castle to see the brick church and the Romanesque bell tower of **San Giovanni** ⑦, begun in 1330. If the church is open, look in at the frescoes by Pietro da Saluzzo and, in the apse, the Cappella dei Marchesi, burial place of Ludovico II, who is ornately displayed as a medieval knight.

Continue along Via San Giovanni to the 15th-century palazzo, **Casa Cavassa** ⑧, which now houses the Museo Civico *(open 10am–1pm & 2–6pm Tue–Sun; tours 10am & 5pm)*. Originally the home of the Vicar General of the Marquis, Galeazzo Cavassa, it was restored by a devotee of the arts in the 1880s and filled with Renaissance art and antiques. There are also fine frescoes, friezes and coffered ceilings. Hans Clemer painted the *grisaille* (monochrome) frescoes of the *Labours of Hercules* on

Above Painted *trompe l'oeil* doorway in the heart of Saluzzo's old town

the courtyard arcades, and the exquisite *Madonna della Misericordia* altarpiece in Room 5. Don't miss the glorious panoramic view.

Go down steps to Via Deodata and Via Gualtieri and exit the walls at Piazza Vineis into Corso Italia (and the cathedral again). Head back along Viale della Liberazione to the car.

🚗 *Take SP589 to Verzuolo, then SP8 to Sampeyre. The road is slow, with some sharp bends. Park in Piazza della Vittoria.*

⑨ Sampeyre
Cuneo, Piemonte; 12020

The road follows and crosses the Varaita river as it winds its way through the Valle Varaita to the largest town in the area, Sampeyre, which is a popular base for summer hikes. Visit the tourist office Via Cavour for information. Along the way, leafy woods and lofty mountains frame the views. Of interest are the terracotta church of **Santi Pietro e Paolo** *(open daily)*, which has frescoes by the Biazaci brothers, and a small, but packed **Museo Etnográfico** *(open Jul & Aug: daily; Sep–Jun: reservations only)*. The more adventurous can drive up to the **Colle di Sampeyre**; the less adventurous can take the chairlift to the Sant'Anna valley. Either way, the view is dramatic and awe-inspiring. On the way to Sampeyre, stop at Piasco (look for the brown sign) to visit the **Victor Salvi Harp Museum** *(Jun–Sep: open 1st & 3rd Sun; Oct–May: closed Sat)*.

🚗 *Follow the signs for Elva, turning right onto the SP335 at Goria Ugo. The road is extremely steep and mostly single track with hairpin bends.*

⑩ Elva
Cuneo, Piemonte; 12020

There's plenty of space to stop and admire the awesomely rugged view from the southern side of the Colle di Sampeyre. Wood and rubble houses line the isolated valley at Elva, a village once famous for collecting and selling women's hair for wig-making. The 15th-century **Chiesa di Santa Maria Assunta**, decorated with animal and human heads on its exterior capitals, is adorned inside with a colourful series of frescoes by Hans Clemer.

🚗 *The SP335 is signposted to Stroppo. Park in the square by the church.*

Above The rugged Valle Maira seen from the road to Elva **Below** Stream cascading through the lush Valle Varaita

EAT AND DRINK

SALUZZO

Casa Pellico *moderate*
Located in the historic centre, this restaurant offers traditional Piedmontese dishes with an innovative twist. Dishes feature superb local ingredients, including Cuneo ham and a range of excellent cheeses. Good wine list, friendly service and a modern atmosphere.
Piazzetta dei Mondagli 5, 12037; casapellico.com; closed Mon

Locanda di Elva *moderate*
Located on the hamlet's town square, Locanda di Elva is a historic inn with a bar and restaurant. It serves a rustic, zero-mile, mountain pasture menu.
Borgo Serre 6; 12020; lalocanda dielva.it

Above left and right The pleasant townscape of Cuneo in Piedmont

VISITING DRONERO

Visitor Information
Piazza XX Settembre, 12025; 0171 9170 80

WHERE TO STAY

AROUND STROPPO

Locanda Spada Reale *inexpensive*
This typical mountain hotel features simple but comfortable rooms, each with a small terrace, and offers a scrumptious breakfast.
Via Vittorio Veneto 53, 12020 Frassino; 333 674 8872

CUNEO AND AROUND

Lovera Palace *inexpensive*
Elegant hotel with 40 rooms, central location and garage parking – a king and a pope have been past guests. It can organize truffle hunts in autumn.
Via Roma 37, 12100 Cuneo; palazzolovera.com

Tetto Garrone *inexpensive*
Surrounded by nut groves, this lovely farmhouse has large modern rooms, a courtyard garden of white flowers and a kitchen for the use of guests.
Via Campagna 45, 12100, Roata Rossi (Roata Rossi is signposted off SR589); tettogarrone.it; closed winter

Other options

For those who fancy a traditional spa hotel, the **Hotel Royal** at Terme di Valdieri opens from June to September. termerealidivaldieri.it

⓫ Stroppo
Cuneo, Piemonte; 12020

The Valle Maira is lined with leafy orchards, thick woods and lush pastures that tinkle with the sound of cow bells. Stroppo, the valley's capital in medieval times, has one church in its square and another jutting out dramatically on the spur above. This is the 12th-century **Chiesa di San Peyre**, which has a rocket-like bell tower and contains beautiful frescoes by the Master of Stroppo. To see inside, ask around for the key, then drive further up to park on a small patch of grass opposite the church.

🚗 *Take the slow SP422 west to Acceglio.*

⓬ Acceglio
Cuneo, Piemonte; 12021

At an altitude of 1,220 m (4,000 ft), Acceglio is the last town of the Valle Maira. During the 16th century, it was a stronghold of Calvinism, allowing the Huguenots to flee here over the nearby French border. Trees line the broad river, peaks loom above and the stone houses with their wooden roofs recall much earlier times. There are lovely walks leading to waterfalls and lakes from here (and from Chiappera, a little further on), but arm yourself with a good map before setting off.

🚗 *Take SP422 back through Stroppo and east to Dronero. Park in Piazza Capitano on the west side of town. For the Riserva Ciciu, take the SP24 towards Busca for 2 km (1 mile), then turn left at the crossroads for Villar San Costanzo and follow the signs.*

⓭ Dronero
Cuneo, Piemonte; 12025

Dronero, where the old men play *petanque* and you'll hear the Occitan language spoken, is home to the crenellated **Ponte del Diavolo** (Devil's Bridge), built in 1492 across the Maira river. It's a peaceful viewpoint over the vegetable gardens and trout ponds to the mountains beyond. Also of interest are the octagonal grain market and the **Museo Civico Luigi Mallé** *(open Sat & Sun)*, with displays on art, the town and art historian Luigi Mallé's life. Drive to the nearby **Riserva Naturale Ciciu del Villar** at Villar San Costanzo. Clustered in the woods, the *ciciu* ("puppets") are huge, eroded rocks with stone caps, up to 10 m (30 ft) high. They were left behind after the glaciers retreated. There are some great views and it is an excellent spot for a picnic.

🚗 *Follow SP422 to Caraglio, then the SP23 to Borgo San Dalmazzo and the SS22 towards Valdieri. Look for signs for Valdieri and Terme di Valdieri on SP22 which turns into the SP239. There is parking beyond the baths.*

Right Lago della Rovina, in the pristine environment of the Parco delle Alpi Marittime

⑭ Terme di Valdieri
Cuneo, Piemonte; 12011
This pleasant spot in the Valle Gesso was a popular summer retreat for Italian aristocracy in the 19th century. Set in the **Parco delle Alpi Marittime** (parcoalpimarittime.it), it's a good base for trips into the mountains – get a map from the visitor centre (open Jun–Sep: daily) or simply relax and take some of the algae or sulphur treatments. Wander through the **Giardino Botanico Alpino Valderia** (open mid-Jun–mid-Sep: daily), where the confluence of mountain and marine climates has produced over 400 plants species.
🚗 Retrace the journey here, turning right for Entracque before Valdieri. Bypass Entracque village by taking first right, signposted San Giacomo. Bear right at Ponte di Rovine for the Lago della Rovina. Park (paid) at Area di Sosta by the lake.

⑮ Lago della Rovina
Cuneo, Piemonte; 12019
The drive climbs gently through the mountains to the Parco dell'Argentura and ends at Lago della Rovina, popular with fishermen. It's impossible to miss the looming **ENEL hydroelectric pumping station** (tours available), the largest in Italy at Entracque. Take a gentle hike through the woods around the lake, or make a full day of it and head over the ridge to Lago del Chiotas and Lago Brocan. Look out for marmots, chamois and eagles.
🚗 Return to Valdieri on SP22 and continue to Borgo San Dalmazzo to

Above View of Dronero and its 15th-century Ponte del Diavolo

take SS20 to Cuneo. Follow signs for Torino to the roundabout just after the hospital. Take the third exit, go straight over the next roundabout into Lungostura Kennedy and park at the Piazza Foro Boario on the right.

⑯ Cuneo
Cuneo, Piemonte; 12100
The university town of Cuneo, wedged between the Gesso and Stura rivers, has a purposeful, bustling air and is a good base for exploring many parts of Piedmont. The historic area of town lies to the west of the wide 19th-century streets. The **Museo Civico** (closed Mon) traces local customs and costumes and displays prehistoric, Roman and medieval artifacts. Strolling through the town, look out for tempting displays of chestnut sweetmeats and Castelmagno cheese from the mountains.

EAT AND DRINK

STROPPO
Locanda Codirosso *inexpensive*
Offering views of the Maira Valley, this restaurant serves traditional dishes featuring locally sourced ingredients. Homemade dessert and craft beers. Booking advised.
Frazione Ruata Valle 8, 12020; codirosso.it; closed Dec–Apr

CUNEO
Osteria della Chiocciola *moderate*
The first-floor restaurant serves great specialities such as *ravioli ripieni di castagne* (ravioli stuffed with chestnuts) and *vitello tonnato* (veal in tuna sauce). It also has a great takeaway menu.
Via Fossano 1, 12100; osteriadella chiocciola.it; closed Sun

Pasticceria Arione *moderate*
The local delicacy is *Cuneesi al rhum* – a kind of bittersweet chocolate truffle made with rum. Ernest Hemingway stopped by to try it in 1954.
Piazza Galimberti 14, 12100; arionecuneo.it

DAY TRIP OPTIONS
It is possible to make a circular tour from Alba to appreciate the excellent food and wine of the Langhe vineyards and the hilltop villages. The stunning mountain scenery and wilderness is easily reached from Saluzzo or Cuneo.

Vineyard tour
Based in Alba ②, head for the wonderful wine museum WiMu at Barolo ④, which will set visitors up for La Morra ⑤, a town with great views over the rolling hills and vineyards. Take a walk through the glorious countryside from here. Then aim for the village of Barbaresco ①, another good vantage point, especially in the golden evening light, before returning to Alba.

🚗 From Alba take SP3 to Barolo, then SP3 and SP58 to La Morra. Head eastwards to Grinzane Cavour and pick up SP3 through Alba, aiming for Località Altavilla and Barbaresco, returning to Alba by SS231.

Mountain and valley greenery
Drive at a leisurely pace through the lovely Valle Varaita from Saluzzo ⑧, before reaching Sampeyre ⑨, where the Museo Etnografico is worth a visit. Drive on through spectacular mountain scenery to the villages of Elva ⑩ and Stroppo ⑪. Here, admire the frescoes in the churches before returning through the verdant Valle Maira and Dronero ⑬ and back to Saluzzo.

🚗 From Saluzzo take SP589 to Verzuolo, then SP8 through Piasco to Sampeyre. From here, head up to the Colle di Sampeyre and down on SP335 to Stroppo. Follow SP422 to Dronero, then SP589 to Saluzzo.

TRIP 3

SACRED MOUNTAINS AND ISLAND PALACES

San Carlone
to Varese

HIGHLIGHTS

Lakeside gem
Relax at the enchanting lakeside village of Orta San Giulio and explore its pretty island and Sacro Monte

Sacri Monti
Wander through small, tree-shaded chapels on the Sacri Monti (Sacred Mountains) and savour the quiet

Borromean Islands
From Stresa, island-hop by ferry, to tour the extravagant island palaces with their lakeside gardens and waterside restaurants

Lago Maggiore Express
Enjoy a day trip via boat across Lake Maggiore and on the private Centovalli railway to stunning alpine valleys and mountain towns

SACRED MOUNTAINS AND ISLAND PALACES

Popular in the 19th century as a stop on the Grand Tour, Lago Maggiore is a beautiful stretch of water reaching north into Switzerland. Nearby, little Lago d'Orta holds the bewitching village of Orta San Giulio with its magical island and laid-back atmosphere. The resort of Stresa, with its grand hotels, is the departure point for boats to the lavish palaces and gardens of the Borromean Islands. The area's temperate climate sets the gardens ablaze with camellias, azaleas and rhododendrons. Above this perfect setting, the steep hillsides are dotted with extraordinary 17th-century chapels forming the Sacri Monti (Sacred Mountains). Away from the lake, to the east, the little known town of Varese is a fine discovery, with its pretty centre, country walks and top-class art gallery.

Above Sailing in front of the terraced gardens of Isola Bella, see p53 **Opposite** People enjoying lunch at a lakeside restaurant next to Lake Orta see p52

ACTIVITIES

Explore the sleepy town of Orto San Giulio and catch a boat to its island

Stride up steep hillsides to marvel at the chapels and the views from the region's three Sacri Monti

Sail across the waters to the splendid palaces and gardens on the Borromean Islands

Walk or cycle up the Val Cannobina to picnic by the Sant'Anna gorge.

Enjoy a stroll past the colourful blooms in the gardens at Villa Taranto

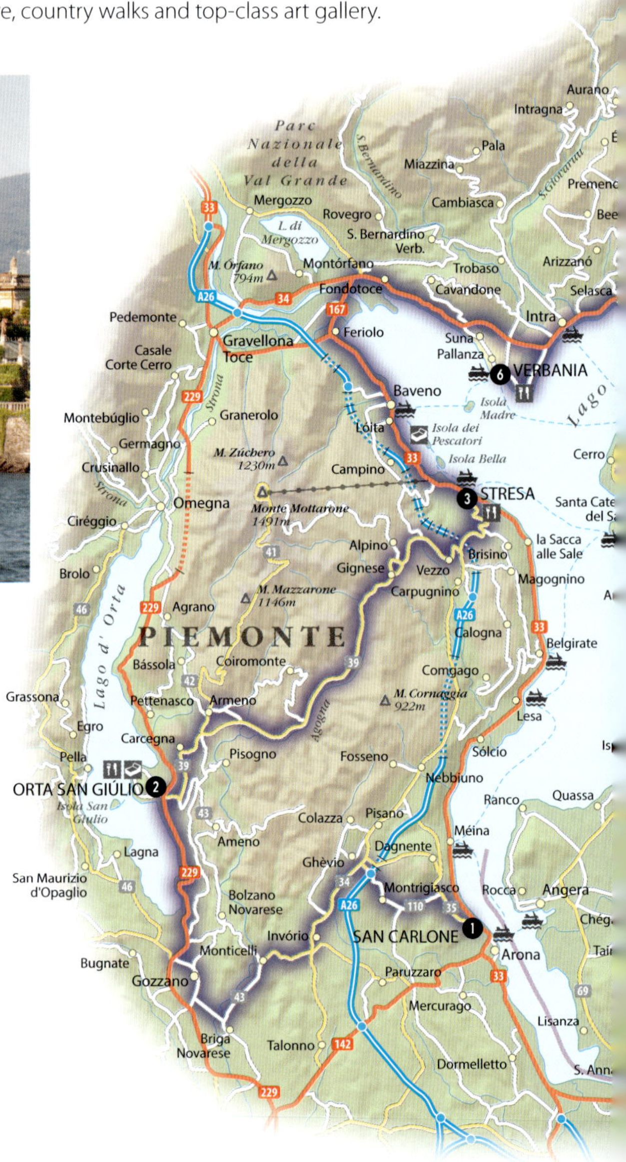

TRIP 3: SACRED MOUNTAINS AND ISLAND PALACES

PLAN YOUR DRIVE

Start/finish: San Carlone to Varese.

Number of days: 4–5 days, including a day on Lago Maggiore and a day's activity exploring the Val Cannobina.

Distance: Approx. 160 km (99 miles).

Road conditions: The higher roads can be steep and winding, and often have poor surfaces after icy winters. The lakeside roads are good, although winding, and they get very busy in summer, especially at weekends. Use snow chains in winter.

When to go: Easter–Jul and Sep are the best months to avoid the summer crowds. The villa gardens are at their best in late spring and early summer. Many hotels and restaurants close down for winter at the end of October.

Opening times: Shops tend to open Mon–Sat 9am–1pm and 3–7pm. Hours for villas vary – some are closed on Mon and most close early in winter.

Main market days: Arona: Tue & Fri; Orta San Giulio: Wed; Stresa: Fri; Cannobio: Sun am; Laveno: Tue am; Varese: Mon.

Shopping: Small boutiques sell turned wood, original paintings and hand-made jewellery in Stresa, Orta San Giulio and Cannobio. All villages have good *alimentari* (grocers) selling local salamis, cheeses, dried mushrooms and good Piedmont red wines.

Major festivals: Orta San Giulio: Firework festival, Jun; Stresa: Classical music festival, Aug–Sep; Camelia Festival, Apr or May.

DAY TRIP OPTIONS

Leave the car behind for the day and head for the famous **Borromean Islands by boat** from Stresa and explore them on foot; or opt for the **Lago Maggiore Express** – a trio of **ferry and mountain train trips** into neighbouring Switzerland. Alternatively, an attractive, circular route south and west from Stresa takes in the views, from the giant **statue of San Carlone**, the **pretty town** of Orta San Giulio and the **alpine pastures** between. For full details, see p55.

Above View across the rooftops of Stresa and over Lago Maggiore

VISITING ORTA SAN GIULIO

Parking
Use the car park by the tourist office (Via Panoramica). From here, a tourist train heads to the centre and Sacro Monte.

Tourist Information
Via Panoramica, 28016; distrettolaghi.it; closed Mon, Tue

WHERE TO STAY

ORTA SAN GIULIO
Leon d'Oro moderate
This family-run three-star hotel has en-suite rooms and a lakeside location.
Piazza Motta 42, 28016; albergoleondoro.it; closed Jan

STRESA
Hotel Verbano moderate
On the northernmost of the Borromean Islands, this romantic, 12-bedroom hotel is handsomely furnished. Once the last boat has gone, the island is all yours.
Via Ugo Ara 2, 28838 Isola dei Pescatori; hotelverbano.it

① San Carlone
Arona, Piedmont; 28041
Completed in 1698, one of Europe's highest statues rises 35 m (115 ft) above the town of Arona. It is a monument to the archbishop of Milan, Carlo Borromeo, an important figure in the Counter-Reformation. Climb up for superb views from inside the statue's head *(open Jul, Aug, Nov & Dec: daily; Sep, Oct, Apr & Jun: Wed–Sun; mid-March: Fri–Sun)*. 🚗 Turn west off S33 onto SP35 for Montrigiasco. Follow SP110 and SP34 through Invório and Monticelli to SP43. Follow signs to Gozzano till SP229. Turn right, heading north along the lake to Orta San Giulio.

② ORTA SAN GIULIO
Novara, Piedmont; 28016
Perched on a promontory, this medieval town, the jewel of Lago d'Orta, is a confection of frescoed, pastel-coloured houses lining a maze of romantic cobbled alleys and piazzas. The traffic-free centre makes exploring the island's intriguing nooks and crannies a delight.

A two-hour walking tour
From the car park and tourist office, walk south along Via Fava to the Moorish fantasy hotel **Villa Crespi** ① *(villacrespi.it)*. Follow the lakeside road to the main square, **Piazza Motta** ②, with cafés, shops and hotels and a weekly market held since 1228. The 16th-century town hall, **Palazzo della Comunità** ③, holds art shows and nearby **Rovera** *(Largo de Gregori 15; 0322 90123)* is a trove of local delicacies and wines. From the piazza, take a boat to **Isola di San Giulio** ④. Legend has it that, in 390 CE, Giulio, a Christian preacher, rid the island of its dragons and serpents and built the Romanesque Basilica di San Giulio *(open daily)* – his

Statue of St Francis of Assisi, Orta San Giulio

remains are in the crypt. The only street, Via del Silenzio, becoming the Via della Meditazione, leads past the Benedictine convent Palazzo dei Vescovi. The abbess has put up signs encouraging meditation on "the island within".
Back at Piazza Motta, take the Via Caire Albertoletti, a stepped lane past the late-Renaissance **Palazzo Gemelli** ⑤ and other elegant palazzi such as the **Casa dei Nani** (House of Dwarves) ⑥. Orta's oldest house, dating from the 14th century, this building takes its name from its four tiny windows. Passing by houses in a profusion of architectural styles, head up to the 15th-century Baroque church **Santa Maria Assunta** ⑦.

TRIP 3: SACRED MOUNTAINS AND ISLAND PALACES

LAGO MAGGIORE EXPRESS

For a scenic day trip, start from Stresa with a leisurely ferry ride (tickets at ferry stations and tourist offices) to the end of the lake and into Switzerland (passports are a must). Stroll through lakeside Locarno and hop on board the Centovalli express, a Swiss train that passes through stunning alpine scenery to Domodossola, Italy. There is time for a wander and a meal before catching the train back to Stresa *(lagomaggioreexpress.it)*.

From here, take Via Gemelli and turn left to the **Sacro Monte di Francesco** 8 *(open daily)*. Set on a hillside above the lake, with views to Isola di San Giulio, this is a devotional path with 21 chapels illustrating the life of St Francis of Assisi. Built between 1591 and 1750, the chapels contain 376 sculptures and 900 frescoes and alternate between Baroque and Renaissance styles. The restaurant here has a pretty, ivy-clad terrace. Return to the car park on the train.

🚗 **Leaving Orta San Giulio, cross the roundabout to follow narrow SP114 past the station. Turn left onto SP114, becoming SP39 later through Armeno. Drive over the hill, past small villages, and down the narrow lanes to Stresa.**

Sacri Monti

These devotional complexes are made up of a series of chapels, lining a path to the top of a mountain. The chapels illustrate the lives of Christ, the Saints or the Virgin Mary and were built in beautiful locations over the 16th and 17th centuries during the Counter-Reformation. There are nine such complexes across northern Italy, all UNESCO World Heritage Sites.

3 Stresa
Verbano-Cusio-Ossola, Piedmont; 28838

When the Simplon Tunnel opened in 1906, linking northern and southern Europe by rail, sleepy lakeside Stresa became a favourite of the European nobility. The town is now a sedate place with grand hotels, manicured gardens and a pedestrianized centre. It is beautifully located with stunning views up the lake to the Alps, and across to the famous treasures of the Borromean Islands. Take a ferry or boat taxi from the Stresa landing stage to reach the islands. **Isola Bella** *(open end Mar–end Oct)* has a grand Baroque palace with terraced gardens. Visit quieter **Isola Madre** *(open end Mar–end Oct)* for its 16th-century villa and extensive gardens, with splendid magnolias and camellias in spring. **Isola dei Pescatori**, also called Isola Superiore, is an erstwhile fisherman's village of narrow lanes and higgledy-piggledy houses, now given over mainly to restaurants.

A 5-minute stroll north of the centre of Stresa leads to the Lido, where a cable car ascends Monte Mottarone, stopping halfway at **Giardino Botanico Alpinia** *(closed Dec–Mar)*. There are walks at the summit and the 3-hour descent can be done on foot or by mountain bike.

🚗 **Take the lakeside SS33 northeast out of Stresa to Fondotoce. Continue along the waterside SS34 to Cannobio.**

Top Pretty Isola di San Giulio, a short boat ride from Orta San Giulio **Below** Statue of Carlo Borromeo, Arona **Below right** View from the cable car up Monte Mottarone, Stresa

VISITING STRESA

Parking
There is a large pay-and-display at Piazza Marconi by the ferry terminal.

Tourist Information
Piazza Marconi 16, 28838; stresaturismo.it

EAT AND DRINK

ORTA SAN GIULIO

Al Boeuc *inexpensive*
Away from the crowds, this cosy wine bar serves delicious Piedmontese cheese and *affettati misti* (cold cuts). Via Bersani 28, 28016; 339 584 0039; closed Thu

Villa Crespi *expensive*
This three-Michelin-starred restaurant, set in a Moorish-style luxury hotel, serves innovative Mediterranean cuisine. Via G Fava 18, 28016; villacrespi.it

STRESA

Il Clandestino *moderate*
Creative dishes using seasonal produce are beautifully presented here. The fish and seafood are particularly good. Via Rosmini 5, 28838; ristoranteil clandestino.com

⑤ Sacro Monte della SS Trinità di Ghiffa
Verbano-Cusio-Ossola, Piedmont; 28055
Set in a stunning position with views across the lake to the foothills of the Alps, the 17th-century complex on this sacred mountain is incomplete, with three main chapels and two smaller ones flanking the central sanctuary. They were built between 1605 and 1617 and contain depictions of biblical scenes, including the baptism of Jesus by John the Baptist, with God looking down from above.

🚗 *Return to SS34 and turn right towards Verbania. After 6 km (4 miles), once in Intra, follow signs to Villa Taranto, where there is a car park.*

Top Lago Maggiore and Verbania, ringed by forest-clad hills **Above** Ferry taking visitors across Lago Maggiore **Above right** Fresco at Varese's Sacro Monte

VISITING CANNOBIO

Parking
There are several well signposted pay-and-display car parks; Piazza Martiri della Libertà at the northern end is the largest.

Tourist Information
Via A Giovanola 25;
procannobio.it

VISITING VARESE

Tourist Information
Via Luigi Sacco 11, 21100;
varesecittagiardino.it

Funicular
sacromontedivarese.it/news/orari-funicolare-276.html

WHERE TO STAY

CANNOBIO

Pironi *moderate*
A friendly hotel in a 15th-century former monastery with comfortable rooms.
Via Marconi 35, 28822; pironihotel.it; closed Oct–Feb

Residenza Patrizia *moderate*
This modern hotel is near the beach.
Via Vittorio Veneto 37, 28822; 032 373 9713

AROUND VARESE

Al Borducan *inexpensive*
This is a historic antique-filled hotel set in a Liberty villa on the hillside.
Via Beata M Caterina 43, 21100;
hotelalborducan.com

④ Cannobio
Piedmont 28822
An attractive village close to the Swiss border, Cannobio is a relaxed holiday resort, popular with families. It has a good beach, a wide choice of watersports and plenty of cycle trails and hikes inland. Accommodation and restaurant options are dotted among the pretty, stepped lanes. The town is also known for a statue of the Virgin Mary said to have started bleeding in 1522. The **Santuario della Santissima Pietà** was built at the site in 1578.

🚗 *Head back on SS34 south to Ghiffa. Then turn right, following signs to Sacro Monte up steep lanes to the car park.*

Below Alfresco seating on one of the café-lined streets in Verbania

Val Cannobina
Explore the secluded Val Cannobina up to Traffiume and Orrido di Sant'Anna, a small gorge spanned by a Roman bridge. This pretty riverside path is an 8-km (5-mile) round trip and navigable on foot or by bike. Bikes and scooters can be hired from **Living Lake** *(Via Darbedo 5, 28822; 331 413 6998)*. There are many picnic spots and a restaurant *(see right)*.

⑥ Verbania
Verbano-Cusio-Ossola, Piedmont; 28922
Mussolini merged the villages of Suna, Intra and Pallanza under the Roman name for the lake, Verbania. This is an attractive town with narrow, shop-lined lanes in the centre. The key draw is the Botanical Gardens of **Villa Taranto** *(open mid-Mar–Oct)*. In 1931, capitalizing on the region's micro-climate, Neil McEacharn, a retired

Scottish captain, began landscaping a garden with species from around the world. The resulting 7 km (4 miles) of pathways meander through beds of dahlias, camellias and rhododendrons, past ponds with spectacular fountains and giant lily pads and lotus flowers.

🚗 Follow the road for 500 m (547 yards) to the Intra ferry station and catch the car ferry to Laveno. Take SP394dir (signposted Gavirate) out of Laveno to the roundabout in Fracce. Continue on Via Valcuvia, turning left up Via Sciareda into Casalzuigno.

Above Manicured garden at Villa Taranto, Verbania
Top right A cobbled street in Arcumeggia

⑦ Casalzuigno
Varese, Lombardia; 21030
Set in the chestnut-tree valley of Cúvia is the village of Casalzuigno, whose main attraction is the 15th-century **Villa della Porta Bozzolo** (closed Apr–mid-Sep: Mon–Wed, Oct–Dec: Mon & Tue, Dec–mid-Apr) and its 18th-century terraced gardens. The villa has frescoes, period kitchens and farm buildings.
🚗 Return to the main road, turning left onto SS394 and then left onto SP7, up the steep switchback to Arcumeggia.

⑧ Arcumeggia
Casalzuigno, Varese; Lombardia 21030
The stone houses and crumbling courtyards of this mountain village are decorated with 20th-century frescoes. Figurative works by artists such as Aligi Sassu and Remo Brindisi adorn the façades of some houses as part of an ongoing regeneration project that began in the 1950s.
🚗 Backtrack to the main road and head east on SS394, turning left to signposted Varese. Take SP62 southeast through Rancio Valcúvia and climb up the wooded Campo dei Fiori to Varese.

⑨ Varese
Varese, Lombardia; 21100
Nicknamed "The Garden City", Varese is a mix of early 20th-century villas and 17th-century Baroque buildings. At the heart of the town's centre is the Church of San Vittore and its 12th-century frescoed baptistry. To the north of town (well signposted and with its own car park), the 18th-century **Villa Panza** houses a fine collection of contemporary art with site-specific installations in the old stables and works by American artist Dan Flavin. There are also landscaped gardens and a good café. Follow signs north out of town along Via Virgilio and Via Prima Cappella to the **Campo dei Fiori** national park, once a hunting ground for the medieval dukes of Milan. From the park's ridge, the Via Sacra leads up the mountain past a series of 16th-century chapels, containing life-size scenes illustrating the Mystery of the Rosary. They form a **Sacro Monte** that culminates in the Baroque Santuario di Santa Maria del Monte and the village of Santa Maria del Monte. A 3-minute funicular (open Jun–Sep: Thu–Sun) whisks visitors up the mountain.

EAT AND DRINK

CANNOBIO
La Streccia *moderate*
Informal restaurant in a narrow alleyway, serving Piedmontese dishes featuring mushrooms and game.
Via Merzagora 5, 28822; ristorantelastreccia.it; closed Thu

VERBANIA
Il Milano *expensive*
The dishes at this waterside restaurant combine creativity and local traditions.
Corso Zanitello 2, 28922; ristorante milanolagomaggiore.it; closed Mon dinner & Tue

VARESE
Bologna *moderate*
This classic trattoria serves traditional fare; the *antipasto della casa* (mixed hors d'oeuvres) is a delicious meal in itself.
Via Broggi 7, 21100; albergo bologna.it; closed Tue & mid-Mar

AROUND VARESE
Al Cantinone *moderate*
Situated by the lake, this cosy restaurant serves local fish specialities and a great panna cotta.
Via Felice Cavallotti 32, 21016; 0332 535 706

DAY TRIP OPTIONS

Stresa is a good base for exploring the area. Chugging across the lakes on a ferry really should not be missed.

Lake Maggiore Express
A very reasonably priced round trip from Stresa ❸, on a scenic rail and ferry route exploring the valleys and towns on the Swiss–Italian border.

Borromean Islands
Catch a boat from Stresa ❸ to explore Isola Bella before moving on to Isola Madre for a picnic lunch, or Isola dei Pescatori for a meal of lake fish at one of the waterside restaurants. Aim to return to Stresa in the late afternoon, when the light on the water is particularly special.

Saints and swimmers
Enjoy sweeping views of the lake from the statue of San Carlone ❶, then head to Orta San Giulio ❷ for lunch. Catch a speedboat to its island and have a dip in the lake before driving to Stresa for dinner.

Take the SP114 on the return trip, followed by the SP39.

TRIP 4

COMO'S VILLAS AND VILLAGES

Como to Brunate

HIGHLIGHTS

Lakeside splendour
Enjoy the serene gardens and magnificent villas that have made Lake Como so famous

A change of view
Let someone else do the steering and see things from a different perspective on Lake Como's *traghetto* (ferry) service

Bella Bellagio
Visit the prettiest of the lakeside villages, set on the tip of a promontory with a scenic wooded hill behind it

Romance and panoramas
Explore romantic Varenna's exquisite villa gardens and climb up to Castello di Vezio for panoramic lake views

COMO'S VILLAS AND VILLAGES

Famed for the sparkling beauty of its water, romantic villas and serene lakeside gardens, Lake Como does not disappoint. The natural setting of thickly wooded mountainsides rising up from beside the lake has been drawing visitors since Roman times – the 19th-century Romantics were particularly attached to the area. This route includes ferry crossings, shore-hugging roads and country lanes with several leg-stretching jaunts up to panoramic viewpoints. Como, Bellagio, Varenna and other villages are perfect spots to pause and enjoy the water for an afternoon – or longer.

Above Appreciating the lakeside scenery from Bellagio, *see p61*
Opposite The winding road up to Santuario della Madonna del Ghisallo, *see p63*

ACTIVITIES

Go shopping for silk in stylish Como town

Walk up to the enchanting Sacro Monte di Ossuccio, high above the lake

Explore the fabulous lakeside gardens of villas Balbianello, Serbelloni and Melzi

Cycle or hike in the countryside around Menaggio where there are trails to suit all levels

Play a round of golf in the hills above Menaggio

Zigzag across the waters on a *traghetto* (ferry) for pure lake romance

See the stars at the astronomical observatory at Colma

TRIP 4: COMO'S VILLAS AND VILLAGES

KEY

▬▬ Drive route

PLAN YOUR DRIVE

Start/finish: Como to Brunate.

Number of days: 2–3 days, allowing half a day in Varenna.

Distance: Approx. 100 km (62 miles).

Road conditions: Roads are generally good, but with some tight bends on the narrow lakeside roads between Como and Menaggio and some steep, winding lanes after Bellagio. In summer, the lake roads can get very busy.

When to go: Visit Easter to July and during September to beat the worst of the summer crowds. Many of the gardens are in full bloom in May–June. Most lake hotels and restaurants close from the end of October until Easter.

Opening times: Shops tend to open 9am–1pm and 3–7pm Mon–Sat. Villa opening hours differ; some are closed on Mon and the gardens usually close early in winter.

Main market days: Como: Tue and Thu morning and all day Sat; Menaggio: 2nd and 4th Fri morning of month; Varenna: Wed.

Shopping: Como is famous for its high-quality silk, supplying Milan and the world's fashion houses. There are some outlets and factory shops around the town. Workshops in Bellagio produce ceramics, jewellery and leather goods. Stock up too on Valtellina red wines from the northern end of the lake.

Major festivals: Across the lake: Sagra di San Giovanni (fireworks and boat races), nearest Sat to 24 Jun; **Bellagio:** Festa Patronale San Giacomo (town's patron saint), 25 Jul. **Varenna:** Festa del Lago (recalls the attack by Como), 1st weekend in Jul.

DAY TRIP OPTIONS

Tire energetic **youngsters** with a tour of Como, a lakeside drive past **stately villas**, then **drive up** the Sacro Monte di Ossuccio before finishing at Menaggio lido. For a more restful time, take a **drive** on the quiet **backroads** away from the lake's bustle. Or make use of the **ferries** by crossing to Villa Balbianello, then back to explore Varenna with its **villas** and **castle**. For full details, see p63.

Above Colourful houses of Varenna looking over Lake Como Below left Church of the Madonna del Soccorso overlooking Menaggio Below right Inside the Church of the Madonna del Soccorso at the Sacro Monte di Ossuccio

VISITING COMO

Parking
Follow signs to a central multi-storey car park rather than look for an expensive roadside space with jacketed attendant.

Tourist Information
Via Pretorio, 22100; visitcomo.eu; closed Mon

WHERE TO STAY

COMO

Hotel Metropole Suisse *expensive*
Centrally located, this hotel offers well-furnished, comfortable rooms and scenic lake views.
Piazza Cavour 19, 22100; hotelmetropolesuisse.com

AROUND MENAGGIO

La Marianna *moderate*
This inviting family-run hotel has eight traditional rooms, most with lake views.
Via Regina 57, 22011 Cadenabbia di Griante (on SS340, 3 km/2 miles south of Menaggio); la-marianna.com

Villa Regina Teodolinda *expensive*
Set in lovely grounds, this carefully restored luxurious villa is serene and has a small swimming pool.
Via Vecchia Regina 58, 22010 Laglio (on SS340, 21 km/13 miles south of Menaggio); villareginateodolinda.com

BELLAGIO

Belvedere *expensive*
This hotel offers lake views, gardens, a pool, spacious rooms and parking too.
Via Valassina 31, 22021; belvederebellagio.com; closed Nov–Easter

① Como
Como, Lombardia; 22100

The comfortable provincial town of Como sits on the southern tip of the western arm of Lake Como. It is best enjoyed by wandering the cobbled, criss-crossing grid of narrow lanes, a reminder of its Roman origins, and by taking in the lake vistas from the promenade or on the hill above the town in Brunate *(see p63)*. An ancient silk-producing town, Como is a good place to shop for silk products.

In the main piazza, close to the harbour, the **Duomo** is a pleasing mix of Gothic and Renaissance styles with a Baroque dome. Next door is the medieval *broletto* (market hall) built in striped marble. Around the corner, the strong lines and functional style of the **Casa del Fascio**, completed in 1936 by architect Giuseppe Terragni, is one of the finest examples of Rationalist architecture in the country.

🚗 *From Como, head north on SS340, the lakeside road signposted for Cernobbio. Through the village and past the luxury hotel Villa d'Este, branch off onto the SP71 or Via Vecchia Regina.*

② Vecchia Regina: the SP71
Como, Lombardia

This narrow, winding road shows Lake Como in all its splendour. Running along the water's edge, the route weaves past private jetties, glorious retreats and splendid gardens built by European aristocrats and wealthy industrialists over the last few hundred years. Villa owners have included opera composer Vincenzo Bellini, fashionista Gianni Versace and, recently, Hollywood film star George Clooney. Most of the traffic takes the faster SS340, away from the lake, so drivers on this road are free to enjoy the views, stop to explore the little hamlets or peek into the celebrity-owned gardens.

🚗 *Rejoin SS340, just before Brienno, and continue north to Ossuccio. Turn left to the Santuario just after a bend in the centre of the village. Park at the end of the road in the little square at the bottom of the grassy footpath.*

③ Sacro Monte di Ossuccio
Como, Lombardia; 22016

Set in the folds of the hills above the lake, the Sacro Monte di Ossuccio is one of a series of UNESCO-recognized Sacred Mountains built across Northern Italy in the 17th century. Climb up through olive groves, past 14 chapels – each containing painted

life-size plaster figures in scenes from the Bible – to the Church of the Madonna del Soccorso. It is a wonderful retreat from the lakeside hustle and bustle, with superb views of the water at the top of the steep 1-km (half-a-mile) long path.

🚗 Follow the road back to the SS340 and continue north for 1 km (half a mile), then follow signs to the parking on the right.

❹ Villa Balbianello
Lenno, Como, Lombardia; 22016
One of many luxurious lakeside villas, the 18th-century Villa Balbianello *(open mid-Mar–mid-Nov: Tue & Thu–Sun)* stands on a verdant promontory with lovely views across the lake to the Grigne mountains. Paths lead down from the delightful loggia through beautiful terraced gardens to the water. Film buffs might recognize the location from *Star Wars: Episode II* (2000) and *Casino Royale* (2006), parts of which were filmed here. The house contains a small museum to its last owner, the explorer and mountaineer Guido Monzino and his Chinese, African and pre-Columbian art.

🚗 Continue north on the SS340 to Menaggio and its roadside, town-centre parking. The road gets very crowded on this section.

❺ Menaggio
Como, Lombardia; 22017
Lakeside Menaggio is more a working village than a resort. It is a great base for enjoying strolls, hikes and cycle rides in the surrounding area and there is even a good golf course – set up by four British visitors in 1907; the tourist office *(Piazza Garibaldi 3, 22017; 034 432 924; menaggio.com)* has maps and information and you can hire bikes from most hotels. In the village centre, **Piazza Garibaldi** offers some of the best restaurants and an attractive promenade leads down to the lido.

⛴ There is a ferry station in Menaggio for the **traghetto** to Bellagio (or return 3 km/2 miles on SS340 to Cadenabbia).

Above Palm-lined lakeside promenade, or *lungolago*, in the heart of Menaggio

❻ Bellagio
Como, Lombardia; 22021
On the tip between the two arms of Lake Como, pretty Bellagio has been attracting visitors for centuries. The village centre is a criss-cross of steep, stepped lanes lined with boutiques, hotels, restaurants and several villas and gardens. The 17th-century **Villa Serbelloni**, a Rockefeller institute, is closed to the public, but its formal terraced gardens can be visited on a guided tour *(open Mar–Oct: Tue–Sun)*. The Neo-Classical **Villa Melzi** *(open end Mar–Oct: daily)* has an orangery and a Japanese garden. From town, it's a half-hour stroll to the fishing hamlets, Loppia (west) or Pescallo (east).

⛴ Leave the car in Bellagio and catch one of the regular ferries to Varenna. Tickets available at the ferry terminal.

Above left Elegant Villa Balbianello, built in 1787 on Lake Como **Above centre** The imposing façade of Duomo di Como **Above** Como's Piazza San Fedele, the site of law courts in Roman times

VISITING BELLAGIO

Parking
The centre of Bellagio is car-free so use the spaces on the edge of the village. Limited free spots (green paint) are available around the communal gardens up the hill from the ferry station. Otherwise, the blue pay-and-display bays are the only option. Some hotels have special deals for parking.

EAT AND DRINK

COMO
Castiglioni Gastronomia *moderate*
This family-run delicatessen offers mouthwatering homemade pasta, salamis and cheeses, and serves a good-value lunch in a pretty courtyard. *Via Cesare Cantù 9, 22100; castiglionistore.com*

La Colombetta *expensive*
Simple, elegant dining rooms provide the backdrop for Sardinian-inspired fish specialities, often including homemade pasta, accompanied by good Italian wines. *Via Diaz 40, 22100; colombetta.it; closed Sun*

MENAGGIO
1976 Cavour *expensive*
Excellent food served in a relaxed and elegant atmosphere. The staff are helpful about the good wine list. *Largo Cavour 5, 22017; 0375 888 4751; closed Mon*

BELLAGIO
Silvio *expensive*
With magical lake views, feast on simple, refined meals based around the freshest fish – often caught by the owner Silvio or his son. *Via Carcano 12, 22021; bellagiosilvio.com*

Right The grandiose lakeside frontage of Villa Cipressi, Varenna Far right Varenna's village centre backed by a steep mountainside Below right Spectacular view of Lake Como from Castello di Vezio

VISITING VARENNA

Tourist Information
Via IV Novembre 7, 23829; varennaturismo.com

WHERE TO STAY

VARENNA

Hotel Du Lac *expensive*
Tucked in a quiet corner of the village, this comfortable hotel offers spacious bedrooms. There is a shaded waterfront bar and breakfast is served outside.
Via del Prestino 11, 23829; albergodulac.com

Hotel Milano *expensive*
This stylish hotel is centrally located, with a good restaurant, great lake views and charming owners.
Via XX Settembre 35, 23829; varenna.net

❼ VARENNA

Lecco, Lombardia; 23829

Set on the eastern shore of Lake Como and backed by steep mountains, Varenna is a sleepy fishing village that sparkles in the afternoon sun. The castle on the hillside above is said to be haunted by a 7th-century queen, Theodolinda, and in the 12th century, the village itself was involved in bloody wars with its bigger neighbour, Como.

A two-hour walking tour

The short ferry crossing from Bellagio is possibly the most romantic way to arrive in Varenna. Head uphill from the **ferry station** ① to the main road. Turn right and cross over to where the signposted path to the castle begins, next to the Hotel Ristorante Monte Codeno. A 15-minute walk up this very stepped mountain path leads to Vezio, an ancient hamlet of stone houses whose conquest by the Romans in 196 BCE is described by the Roman author Pliny the Younger. Follow the signs through tiny lanes, past the Piazza della Chiesetta di Sant'Antonio Abate, named for its tiny 16th-century church, and through an olive grove to the 13th-century **Castello di Vezio** ② *(open Mar–Oct: daily)*, which offers stunning views, lawns and ruined towers. The outdoor trattoria serves good, local specialities.

Return to the little piazza in front of the church, from where a panoramic path, called the Scabium, runs back

down to Varenna. From the church, turn right, if facing the church, and then right again after a 90-degree turn. Continue along, under a stone bridge, and take the signposted right fork downhill. A few minutes' steep walk or drive, accompanied by glorious views, leads to the main road into Varenna. Turn right and cross over to the luxuriant terraced gardens and museum at the 17th-century **Villa Monastero** ③ *(open hours vary, check website; villamonastero.eu)*, built on the site of a 13th-century Cistercian monastery. The rooms are grandly decorated and the garden's avenues and terraces are shaded by cypress, oleander and citrus trees.

Turn left out of the villa and pop into the splendid garden with its relaxing viewpoint at the hotel next door, **Villa Cipressi** ④.

Left out of Villa Cipressi leads into Varenna's main square, **Piazza San Giorgio** ⑤, with its 13th-century parish church and the 10th-century chapel of **San Giovanni Battista** ⑥, which has excellent frescoes. From here, head down into the grid of cool lanes to Varenna's waterfront cafés. Walk past the tiny harbour on the left and continue along the **walkway** ⑦ back to the ferry station and Bellagio.

🚗 Leave Bellagio on SP41 (see below), which winds for 5 km (3 miles) up to Magreglio. Park near the sanctuary.

⑧ Santuario della Madonna del Ghisallo
Bellagio, Lombardia; 22030
The Madonna del Ghisallo has been the patron saint of cyclists since 1949 and this sanctuary is a very popular destination for two-wheelers; it is often on the route of the annual Italy-wide cycle race, Giro d'Italia. Next door there is a specialist museum with bicycles and Giro-winners' pink jerseys, donated by Italy's cycling greats. From the Romeo Belvedere nearby there are unbeatable views of the eastern arm of the lake and the Grigne mountains.

🚗 *Continue south along the SP41.*

⑨ Valassina and Pian del Tiviano
Como, Lombardia; 22030
Crossing this rural corner of the lake takes drivers along winding lanes through chestnut woods and medieval hamlets. At **Colma**, there is an astronomical observatory with great views in three directions. Head towards the lake across the bowl of the Pian del Tiviano, which is carpeted with narcissi, lilies of the valley and bluebells in springtime. Here, the road switchbacks down to **Nesso**, a pretty lakeside village.

🚗 *Drive along SP41, turn right onto SP44 signed Sormano, carry on for 19 km (12 miles) till Nesso. At SP583 turn left to Como and continue for 16km (10 miles). Follow signs to the funicular and nearby car park.*

⑩ Brunate
Como, Lombardia; 22034
Catch the funicular up to Brunate *(every 15 min from 6am to 10:30pm; Jun–Aug: until midnight)* to finish the drive with some more spectacular views of the lake. The steep 6-minute ascent passes attractive 19th-century villas and their gardens to the summit where a small Art Nouveau resort offers a few restaurants and cafés as well as strategically sited places to drink in the lake views one last time.

Above Monument to cyclists at Santuario della Madonna del Ghisallo **Below** Steep alleyway between the houses of Varenna

EAT AND DRINK

VARENNA

Il Ristoro del Castello *inexpensive*
This informal alfresco restaurant serves lake fish, grilled meats and their own organic vegetables and olive oil. Reservation needed for evenings.
Via al Castello snc, 23828 Perledo, Lecco; open Mar–Nov: 10am–7pm daily; castellodivezio.it

Il Cavatappi *moderate*
Reservations are needed at this tiny, intimate place. The dishes are excellent and include local lake-fish specialities.
Via XX Settembre 8, 23829; cavatappi varenna.it; closed Jan–Feb: Wed, Mar–May & Oct–Dec

DAY TRIP OPTIONS
Several parts of this tour would make comfortable, varied day trips – with or without the car.

Villas and views
After exploring the lanes of Como ①, follow the lake road past lavish villas. Take a detour to walk up to Sacro Monte di Ossuccio ❸ for scenic views, before ending up in Menaggio ❺ for a swim at the lido.

Drive north from Como on SS340, branching off onto SP71 and up to the Sacro Monte di Ossuccio, then return via SS340 to Menaggio.

Back roads from Bellagio
Head away from the bustle of Bellagio ❻ on this back route to Como, which heads up to the Santuario della Madonna del Ghisallo ❽, dedicated to the patron saint of cyclists, before winding through wooded valleys to the lake road and back to Bellagio or Como ❶.

Leave Bellagio on SP41, take winding SP44 and then SS583 to reach Como.

Ferry-hopping tour
Leave the car in Bellagio ❻ and take the ferry (navigazionelaghi.it/biglietti-e-orari-lago-di-como) to Lenno/Villa Balbianello ❹. Return to Bellagio for lunch, then hop onto the ferry to Varenna town ❼ for Castello di Vezio.

TRIP 5

LOMBARDY'S GLACIAL VALLEYS
Bergamo to Erbusco

HIGHLIGHTS

Split-level Bergamo
Explore ancient lanes of the charming Upper Town, and the grand buildings and avenues of the Lower Town

Untouched valleys
Well away from the tourist trail, the Bergamasco and Brescian valleys are an insight into life in Lombardy through the ages

Low-key lakeside
Slow down to the gentle pace at quiet Lago d'Iseo – a world away from the international holiday resorts of the other northern lakes

Sparkling vintages
Sip the country's best fizzy wines among the vineyard-clad, gently rolling hills of Franciacorta

LOMBARDY'S GLACIAL VALLEYS

Many years ago, when Northern Italy's glaciers retreated to the Alps, they left behind a series of fertile valleys and pretty lakes backed by rugged hills. Strategically located cities such as Bergamo and Brescia have a long history as Roman, medieval and even Venetian strongholds. But there's evidence of much older human occupation up in the hills of the Val Camonica, where the rocks and caves are peppered with extraordinary prehistoric petroglyphs. Further down the valley, Lago d'Iseo is the perfect place to unwind, while the sparkling wines and hills of the Franciacorta provide relief from summer heat. Throughout the region, hearty pastas, polenta, salamis and cheeses are washed down with good table wines.

Above Bergamo's Upper Town, dominated by the Torre Gombito, see p68 **Below** Houses lining the banks of Lago d'Iseo, see p70

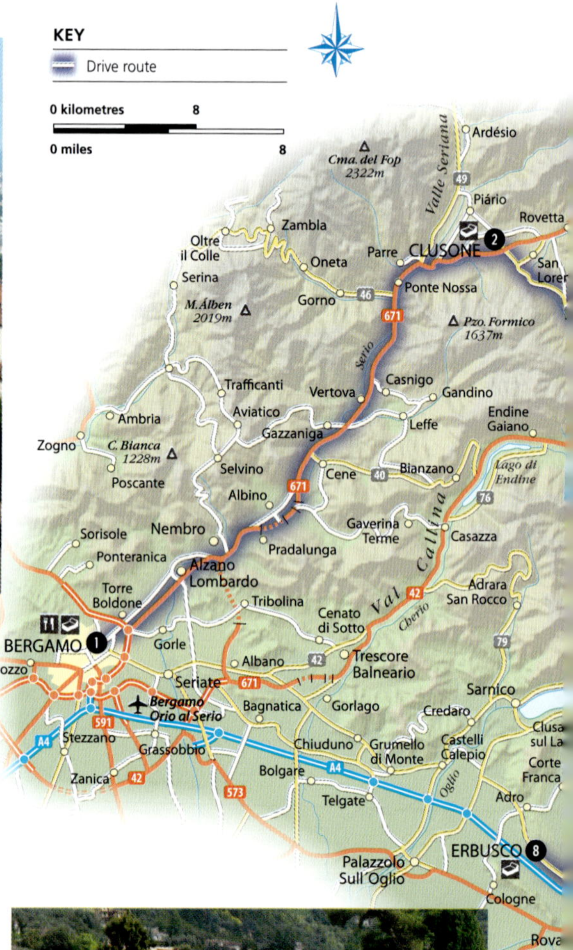

ACTIVITIES

Ride the funicular to Bergamo's Upper Town to uncover its history

Take a relaxing boat trip on the sparkling waters of Lago d'Iseo

Explore the Roman mosaics and other historic treasures in ancient Brescia

Tour the vineyards of the Franciacorta and sample its sparkling wines

Hike through the pre-alpine valleys and discover the prehistoric rock art

TRIP 5: LOMBARDY'S GLACIAL VALLEYS

Above Glacial mountain range along the Val Camonica, see p70 **Below** Lush Franciacorta vineyards near Iseo, see p70

PLAN YOUR DRIVE

Start/finish: Bergamo to Erbusco.

Number of days: 3 days.

Distance: Approx. 230 km (143 miles).

Road conditions: Light industry and heavy traffic mar the roads near to the cities, but the number of cars decreases further up the valleys. Roads will be busy on summer weekends. Tunnels should be taken with care.

Opening times: Shops tend to open 9am–1pm and 3–7pm Mon–Sat, although some shops in small villages are closed on Mon morning.

When to go: Spring and early summer see the alpine flowers at their best, while autumn is marked by wild mushrooms and wine festivals.

Main market days: Clusone: Mon; **Iseo:** Fri morning; **Lovere:** Sat morning.

Shopping: Look out for local produce such as (*formagella*) mountain cheese, (*casoncei, scarpinocc*) salami and pasta, as well as Franciacorta sparkling wines.

Major festivals: Bergamo: Sant' Alessandro, Sep; Santa Lucia, 13 Dec; **Brescia:** Mille Miglia vintage car race, 2nd week in Jun; **Erbusco:** Franciacorta festival, 2nd or 3rd weekend in Sep.

DAY TRIP OPTIONS

See the **medieval** and **Renaissance buildings** of Bergamo and then drive along **Val Seriana** to Clusone. Or, from Lago d'Iseo, spend time on Monte Isola for some **lakeside relaxation**, finishing with a trip to Zone to see the **stunning rock formations**. Explore the **wineries, vineyards** – and **wines** – of beautiful Franciacorta. For full details, see p71.

Above The spectacular dome in the Basilica di Santa Maria Maggiore, Bergamo

VISITING BERGAMO

Parking
On-street parking is hard to find in Bergamo's centre. Head for the underground car parks at Piazza della Libertà or Piazza della Repubblica, off Viale Vittorio Emanuele II. If you've got one, show a funicular ticket when paying, to get a discount on Sundays.

Tourist Information
There are guided walking tours (Apr–Oct: 3pm) and bicycles can be hired.
Città Bassa: Piazzale Guglielmo Marconi 12, 24121; 035 210 204. Città Alta: Via Gombito 13, 24129; visitbergamo.net

VISITING CLUSONE

Tourist Information
Piazza Orologio 23, 24023; visitclusone.it

Market day
On Mondays, the lanes are taken over by a market selling local salamis, cheese and fresh pasta. Smallholders from the hills nearby sell home-grown produce.

WHERE TO STAY

BERGAMO

La Valletta Relais *inexpensive*
This spick and span, family-run hotel on the hillside has pretty rooms.
Via Castagneta 19, 24129 Città Alta; lavallettabergamo.it

Gombit Hotel *moderate*
Set in a medieval tower in the heart of the Upper Town, this contemporary boutique hotel offers small, tidy rooms.
Via Mario Lupo 6, 24129 Città Alta; gombithotel.it

CLUSONE

Albergo Commercio e Ristorante Masci *inexpensive*
Simple, attractive rooms and a good restaurant in the village centre.
Piazza Paradiso 1, 24023; mas-ci.it

❶ BERGAMO

Bergamo, Lombardia; 24100

In the foothills of the Alps, prosperous Bergamo has an attractive Città Alta (Upper Town) whose Renaissance buildings and medieval lanes are encircled by impressive 17th-century Venetian walls. The medieval neighbourhoods and elegant avenues of the Città Bassa (Lower Town) are good for shopping and transport.

A three-hour walking tour

From the car park, turn right up the sweeping main road, Viale Vittorio Emanuele II, taking in the mix of attractive gated villas and 1930s Fascist architecture. Just around the bend is the **funicular** ❶ that takes visitors up to the Città Alta. Trundling up through the city walls and splendid palazzo gardens, this 7-minute ride ends near the medieval **Piazza Mercato delle Scarpe** ❷, once home to a shoe market. Follow Via Gombito, almost opposite, past the 12th-century **Torre Gombito** ❸, the only extant medieval tower of which there were about 20; this one marks the main crossroads of the Roman city. Continue up to **Piazza Vecchia** ❹, the city's Renaissance showpiece and site of the medieval Palazzo della Ragione (*temporary exhibitions: 3–7pm Mon–Fri; 10am–7pm weekends; closed Tue*). The piazza is lined with cafés and at its heart is the 18th-century Contarini fountain with white marble lions. Next to the palazzo, the Torre Civica bell tower rises 52 m (170 ft), offering splendid views of Bergamo and the countryside. The bells strike 100 times at 10pm, recalling an era when the gates would be closed for the night.

Pass under the arcade of the palazzo into Piazza del Duomo. The highlights here are the Romanesque church of Santa Maria Maggiore, with its opulent Baroque interior, and the funerary chapel Cappella Colleoni (1472), a Renaissance extravagance of twisted columns and pastel marble decorated with Giambattista Tiepolo's frescoes (1733).

Return to Piazza Vecchia, then turn left up Via Colleoni past boutiques. Head through the arch at Piazza Mascheroni into Piazza della Cittadella, once the heart of this military stronghold. Cross the courtyard to the gateway diagonally opposite, then turn left into **Colle Aperto** ❺ for views of the gardens and vineyards around the city walls. Head through Porta Sant'Alessandro to the upper funicular station.

Take the funicular up to the **San Vigilio** ❻ neighbourhood, ideal for a

Contarini fountain statue, Piazza Vecchia

Above left Façade of the Cappella Colleoni, Bergamo Above right View along Bergamo's funicular

TRIP 5: LOMBARDY'S GLACIAL VALLEYS   69

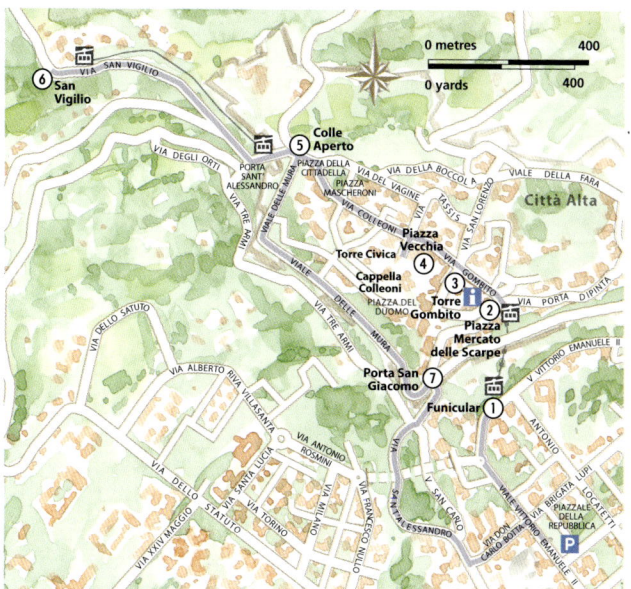

Above View of the Duomo and its Neo-Classical west façade from Torre Civica, Bergamo

drink with sweeping views across the city to the plains. Exit the funicular station and follow the road round to the left and on to the belvedere area, which has splendid views over 19th-century villas and gardens – the summer homes of wealthy Milanese. Rest here, then head down steep Via San Vigilio, keeping the funicular lines on the left. Turn left through Porta Sant'Alessandro to return to Colle Aperto. Here, catch the bus (line 1) to the car park or walk back along the lovely Venetian walls. To do the latter, head down Viale delle Mura, on the right, all the way to **Porta San Giacomo** ⑦, then take winding Via Sant'Alessandro down through a medieval neighbourhood to Via Don Carlo Botta, which leads left, back to Viale Vittorio Emanuele II and the car park at Piazza della Repubblica.

🚗 South of Bergamo, pick up the SS671 (signed Val Seriana) and follow signs to Clusone for 32 km (20 miles). On the roundabout after the small Fonti Pineta mineral water plant, follow signs to the centre and use one of the marked car parks.

❷ Clusone

Bergamo, Lombardia; 24023
High in the mill-lined Val Seriana, Clusone is an appealing medieval town of pastel-coloured houses and cobbled lanes rising up to the Piazza Orologio, where the frescoed and porticoed Palazzo Comunale sports a working astronomical clock from 1585. Still higher stands the Baroque **Basilica di Santa Maria Assunta**, with a 15th-century fresco of the *Triumph of Death* and a *Dance Macabre* next door; note the rich kings and bishops trying to bribe their way out of death.

🚗 Back at the roundabout, take the SS671 left towards Rovetta, then right onto SP53 to Lovere. Through Lovere, follow signs to Darfo Boario Terme on the SR55, then take the SS42 north up the Val Camonica to Capo di Ponte. At the roundabout at the village entrance, follow the brown signs to Naquane and Parco Nazionale delle Incisoni Rupestri over the railway line. Park by the 15th-century church. The park entrance is a 10-minute walk uphill.

Bergamo's polenta

The yellow cornmeal staple, polenta, features heavily on many of Bergamo's restaurant menus and has been enjoyed in the region for centuries. It can be served with salami, wild mushrooms, melted Taleggio cheese or roast veal. Or you might find it sliced and chargrilled along with a selection of fresh vegetables.

EAT AND DRINK

BERGAMO

Cooperativa Città Alta *moderate*
Hearty portions of local pasta, polenta and grilled meats are served here.
Vicolo Sant'Agata 19 (off Via Colleoni), 24129; ilcircolinocittaalta.it

Vineria Cozzi *moderate*
This is a classy *enoteca* (wine bar) with a stylish, good-quality restaurant attached.
Via Colleoni 22, 24129; vineriacozzi.it; closed Wed

Baretto di San Vigilio *expensive*
The views from this elegant restaurant create a romantic atmosphere.
Via al Castello1A, 24100; barettosanvigilio.it

Below Panificio Tresoldi, a bakery-patisserie in Bergamo's medieval Città Alta (Upper Town)

Above View of Sale Marasino, one of Lago d'Iseo's pretty villages **Top right** Sale Marasino's church, seen from the lake ferry **Above right** Iron Age rock carvings at Parco Nazionale delle Incisioni Rupestri

VISITING VAL CAMONICA

Tourist Information
Lungolago Marconi 2 c – 25049 Iseo (Bs); turismoval lecamonica.it

WHERE TO STAY

VAL CAMONICA

Casa Visnenza *inexpensive*
This comfy B&B is run by owners who are knowledgeable about local sights.
Via San Faustino 7, 25044 Cemmo di Capo di Ponte; casavisnenza.com; closed Mar–Nov: Mon –Fri

ISEO

La Tesa *moderate*
An organic farm in the hills above Iseo offering simple apartments and rooms.
Via Silvio Bonomelli, 25049 Colline d'Iseo; latesa.it; closed Jan–Feb

BRESCIA

Albergo Orologio *inexpensive*
A cosy boutique hotel in the town centre.
Via Cesare Beccaria 17, 25121; albergoorologio.it

ERBUSCO

L'Albereta *expensive*
Every comfort is catered for at this luxurious Relais & Chateaux hotel.
Via Vittorio Emanuele 23, 25030; albereta.it

❸ Val Camonica
Brescia, Lombardia; 25044

Scattered over the hillsides of the Val Camonica are thousands of stones inscribed with fascinating prehistoric rock carvings. Dating from Neolithic times through to the Iron Age, together they are recognized as a UNESCO World Heritage Site. One of the largest concentrations is found just outside Capo di Ponte. The **Parco Nazionale delle Incisioni Rupestri** *(open 8:30am–dusk Tue–Sun; parco incisioni.capodiponte.beniculturali.it)* is an attractive, open-air site littered with more than 100 carved boulders that can be explored over a couple of hours. Wonderfully evocative and dynamic, scenes portray hunts and funerals, boats, and people dancing, farming, fighting and worshipping.

🚗 *Return back down the SS42, forking right onto SP510 towards Brescia. After a series of tunnels, turn right onto the lakeside SP510bis, signed Lago d'Iseo. In Marone, just after the parish church on the right, take the poorly signed left turn to Zone SP32 (down the side of the Municipio building), then drive up the winding road to the car park at Zone.*

❹ The Pyramids of Zone
Brescia, Lombardia; 25050

Strange rock formations, resembling giant anthills, pepper the natural reserve around the village of Zone, high above Lago d'Iseo. Rain erosion of the area's moraine sand has created these extraordinary columns which are often topped by a granite boulder. At the entrance to the park stands the 12th-century **Chiesa di San Giorgio**, with frescoes of St George slaying dragons and the profile of Florentine writer Dante, who visited the area in the 14th century.

🚗 *Return to Marone via SP32, take SP510bis south to Iseo, which has several pay-and-display car parks.*

❺ Iseo
Brescia, Lombardia; 25049

The largest village on the eastern side of Lago d'Iseo, ancient Iseo was an important trading post before it was sacked by Federico I Barbarossa in the 12th century. Now a low-key resort, the semi-pedestrianized medieval village centre has an arcaded main square, stone lanes, a handful of decent restaurants and a lakeside promenade with views across the water to the wooded cliffs of the opposite shore. Ferries leave here for destinations around the lake, most notably to Monte Isola.

🚗 *Leave the car behind and catch a ferry across to Monte Isola.*

❻ Monte Isola
Brescia, Lombardia; 25050

The largest lake island in Europe, Monte Isola is 9 km (6 miles) around and more than 600 m (2,000 ft) high, topped by the Santuario della Madonna della Ceriola, with fabulous 360-degree views. Arriving is part of the fun, with lovely views of lakeside villages along the way. Stroll along

Above Passenger ferry cruising across Lago d'Iseo past stunning mountain scenery

the waterfront, or hire a bicycle and explore its tiny villages, stopping for a meal en route – strong legs are needed to get up to the Santuario.

🚗 From Iseo, take a right onto SP47bis to Ome, then SP46 to Rodengo-Saiano. Go through Gussago passing the church on the left and after the town centre take right. From here take the main road out of town and follow signs to Brescia, which has plenty of on-street pay-parking.

10am–6pm daily; bresciamusei.com) has fine Roman mosaics and medieval treasures, including a 4th-century bronze *Winged Victory*.

🚗 Retrace route back towards Iseo (follow signs to "Milan, Bergamo and Lago d'Iseo"), but turn left onto SP49, then follow signs to the autostrada that leads to the Strada del Franciacorta.

❽ Erbusco
Brescia, Lombardia; 25030
This village lies at the heart of a small, wine-producing area – known as Franciacorta – dotted with ancient religious buildings. The monasteries that cultivated this land in the Middle Ages were tax exempt, leading to the name Franciacorta. See franciacorta. wine/en/region/strada-franciacorta for information on drives and cycle rides through the idyllic countryside.

Franciacorta wines
The pleasant hills south of Lago d'Iseo have been a winemaking area for centuries. Attention turned to sparkling wines in the 1960s, and in 1995 the area was awarded the DOCG, in recognition of the quality of the sparkling wines made using the champagne method, involving a second fermentation in the bottle.

Above Small vineyard in Franciacorta, near Erbusco **Left** Ruined columns of the Roman Tempio Capitolino in Brescia

EAT AND DRINK

ISEO
Da Piccioli *moderate*
Try fried seafood and chips here.
Via Cristini, Marone, 25054; 338 734 6691

Osteria Il Volto *moderate*
This *osteria* blends traditional flavours of Brescian and Lake Iseo cuisines.
Via Mirolte 33, 25049; osteriailvolto.it; closed Mon, Tue & Wed

BRESCIA
La Grotta Antica Osteria *moderate*
Expect Brescian food – *casoncei* (salami-stuffed pasta) – in an elegant setting.
Vicolo del Prezzemolo 10, 25121; anticaosterialagrotta.it

WINERIES IN FRANCIACORTA

CA' DEL BOSCO
Via Albano Zanella 13, 25030 Erbusco; cadelbosco.com

CAVALLERI
Via Provinciale 96, 25030 Erbusco; 030 776 0217; cavalleri.it

BELLAVISTA
Via Bellavista 5, 25030 Erbusco; bellavistawine.it

FERGHETTINA
Via Saline 11, 25030 Adro; ferghettina.it

❼ Brescia
Brescia, Lombardia; 25121
Known for its arms industry and engineering factories, Brescia also has an attractive medieval centre and well-preserved Roman ruins. At the heart of the city is the broad, arcaded **Piazza della Loggia** with an imposing palazzo at one end and the Torre dell'Orologio opposite. Via dei Musei follows an ancient Roman road to the site of the forum, now Piazza del Foro, which is topped by the columns of the **Tempio Capitolino** from 73 CE. The nearby **Museo di Santa Giulia** *(open mid-Jun–Sep: 10am–7pm Tue–Sun, Oct–mid-May*

DAY TRIP OPTIONS
There are options for a city walk followed by a country drive, some lakeside relaxation or a wine tour.

Urban and rural exploration
Spend the morning on a walking tour of Bergamo ❶, enjoying funicular rides and architecture from the 12th to the 18th century. After lunch, enjoy the countryside of the Val Seriana on the way to medieval Clusone ❷.

Follow the drive's instructions, and back.

Monte Isola and the Pyramids
In Iseo ❺, stock up with picnic provisions before taking the ferry to Monte Isola ❻ to explore the island for most of the day. Cycle round the island, stopping to eat alfresco on the way. Return to Iseo in the late afternoon, then drive to Zone to see the extraordinary rock formations.

Take the ferry to Monte Isola; afterwards follow the SP510bis to Zone.

Romans and wine tasting
Explore Roman Brescia ❼, then enjoy a tour of the Franciacorta wine region. Head for Erbusco ❽ and visit a few of its wineries – perhaps on a bike.

Follow the drive's instructions to Erbusco. You may be able to hire a bicycle from a hotel or agriturismo.

TRIP 6

SWITCHBACKS AND LIMONAIE
Arco to Gargnano

HIGHLIGHTS

Lake Garda
Indulge in watersports at Riva del Garda, or visit the lemon-growing glasshouses along the lakeshore, where olive groves and citrus trees carpet the hillsides

Austrian heritage
Explore the Germanic heritage and cuisine of Lake Garda's northernmost towns, which were once part of the Austro-Hungarian Empire

Adrenalin-fuelled drives
Corkscrew through the Brasa gorge away from the lake into the wooded, alpine interior of the Tremosine

Enchanting Gargnano
Be charmed by this laid-back lakeside village and its peeling Art Nouveau villas and ancient churches

Panoramic view from Rocca Scaligera of Sirmione, flanked on both sides by Lake Garda

SWITCHBACKS AND LIMONAIE

Running along the northwestern shore of Lago di Garda, this route is for those who enjoy challenging drives. From the medieval village of Arco and the lakeside resort of Riva del Garda, the road skirts the lake before branching onto an exhilarating switchback – the eighth wonder of the world, according to British prime minister Winston Churchill – up to the comune of Tremosine. The climb through thick woodland brings breathtaking views and, at the end, a walk up to the Santuario della Madonna di Montecastello. The trip ends in dreamy Gargnano, set among olive groves and the *limonaie* (sheltered lemon groves) that give this shoreline its name.

Above The Torre Apponale on the Riva del Garda waterfront

Below View from Arco's castle
Opposite Narrow streets and brightly painted townhouses, Arco

PLAN YOUR DRIVE

Start/finish: Arco to Gargnano.

Number of days: 1 day.

Distance: Approx. 60 km (37 miles).

Road conditions: Roads are narrow and winding, and busy in summer. In winter, the switchbacks are impassable due to snow. The lakeside road plunges through galleried tunnels into dazzling sunlight.

When to go: Apr–Jun is ideal. Autumn, too, is pretty, but most places shut up shop from the end of Oct until Easter.

Opening times: Shops tend to open 9am–1pm and 3–7pm Mon–Sat. In villages, some are closed on Mon mornings.

Main market days: Arco: 1st & 3rd Wed; antiques market every 3rd Sat; Riva and Gargnano: 2nd & 4th Wed; Tignale: Tue.

Major festivals: Gargnano: Centomiglia Regatta, 1st weekend in Sep; Pieve: Easter Sunday.

❶ Arco
Trento, Trentino-Alto Adige
The **Castello** *(closed Jan: Mon–Fri)* atop the rocky outcrop looming over Arco was built in the 12th century, and the 30-minute wander up to it from the central Piazza 11 Novembre affords panoramic views. Arco became a popular winter retreat in the 19th century, when, as part of the Austrian Empire, its mild climate attracted Central European aristocracy. Explore the wonderful public gardens on Viale delle Palme and an impressive arboretum in the **Parco Arciducale Arboreto** *(closed for renovations; check gardatrentino.it for updates)*, which formed the grounds of the Habsburg Archduke Albert's winter palace.

🚗 *Follow the well-signposted SS45b for 6 km (4 miles) to reach the centre of Riva del Garda, from where the car parks are clearly signposted.*

❷ Riva del Garda
Trento, Trentino-Alto Adige; 38066
Always a strategic trading post, and part of the Venetian, then the Austro-Hungarian Empire until 1918, this fine lakeside resort of cobbled piazzas, stone buildings and atmospheric lanes is now a focus for watersports, with windsurfing and sailing opportunities galore. Offering beautiful views of Lago di Garda, the town's broad Piazza 3 Novembre is lined with porticoed buildings and watched over by the 13th-century **Torre Apponale**. To the west, above the waterfront, is the 12th-century **Bastione**, built by the Venetians in 1508, on Monte Rocchetta. The pleasant walk up to this ruined fortress is rewarded with sensational views over the lake.

🚗 *Leave Riva on SS45bis, heading south past Limone sul Garda, for about 17 km (11 miles). Take the second right turn for Tremosine up SP38.*

❸ Porto to Pieve: SP38
Brescia, Lombardia
When the SP38 opened in 1913, the German newspaper *Frankfurter Zeitung* dubbed it "the most beautiful road in the world". Linking isolated mountain communities with the lake, this exhilarating road switchbacks through narrow tunnels and wooded valleys, squeezing impossibly through the spectacular Brasa gorge and up to the green hills of Tremosine. The SP38 has been the setting for numerous car commercials, as well as breathtaking car chases in the Bond film *Quantum of Solace*.

🚗 *Follow SP38 for about 6 km (4 miles) from the lake to Pieve at the top of the mountain, where many village centre car parks are signposted.*

❹ Pieve di Tremosine
Tremosine, Brescia, Lombardia; 25010
One of the many hillside villages in the comune of Tremosine, Pieve has an attractive centre of stone-built houses. At 350 m (1,148 ft) above the lake, there are wonderful views across the sparkling waters to Monte Baldo opposite. The town's church has an 11th-century Romanesque bell tower but its main building, built later, is lit by Murano glass chandeliers, adding to its elegant Baroque interior.

🚗 *From the centre, head southwest out of town, following the signposted route to the next village, Arias, and then on towards Tignale.*

Above left Living on the edge in Pieve **Above** The Castello di Arco, high above the town

VISITING ARCO
Tourist Information
Viale del Palme 1, 38062; gardatrentino.it

VISITING RIVA DEL GARDA
Tourist Information
Largo Medaglie d'Oro 5, 38066; gardatrentino.it

VISITING PIEVE DI TREMOSINE
Tourist Information
Piazza Marconi 1, 25010 Tremosine; infotremosine.it, gardalombardia.com

WHERE TO STAY IN RIVA DEL GARDA
Restel de Fer *expensive*
Owned by the Menghelli family for more than 600 years, this farmhouse offers a handful of atmospherically furnished rooms. The locally sourced food in the restaurant is also excellent.
Via Restel de Fer 10, 38066; resteldefer.com; closed for renovations till 2025

EAT AND DRINK IN RIVA DEL GARDA
Osteria il Gallo *moderate*
This friendly, informal *osteria* in Riva centre serves hearty dishes of polenta, dumplings and homemade pasta, accompanied by good local wines.
Piazza San Rocco 12, 38066; 0464 556 200

Above left View over the Santuario di Madonna di Montecastello **Above right** Fresco in the Santuario di Madonna di Montecastello **Below** Boats at Gargnano's harbourside

VISITING GARGNANO

Tourist Information
Via Roma 5, 25084; gardalom bardia.com

WHERE TO STAY IN AND AROUND GARGNANO

Hotel Du Lac moderate
Superbly located on the lakeside, in a quiet corner of the village, this is the smaller of two neighbouring hotels run by the same family for three generations. Rooms have fine period furniture and there is a pretty terrace and pergola with panoramic views.
Via Colletta 21, 25084 Villa di Gargnano; hotel–dulac.it; closed Nov–Mar

Hotel Villa Sostaga expensive
On the hillside above Gargnano, this welcoming, family-run villa offers informal luxury in 11 handsomely furnished rooms. There are splendid views from the lovely grounds and pool. A well-priced restaurant (open to non-residents) serves memorable seasonal specialities.
Via Sostaga 19, 25084 Navazzo; villasostaga.it

⑤ Pieve to Tignale Road
Brescia, Lombardia
Driving through valleys of beech, ash and chestnut, past cool streams, alpine meadows and sheer mountain bluffs, it is easy to forget the bustle of the lake below. There are several viewpoints and picnic spots along the way.
🚗 Follow signs to Tignale. The roadside car park for the sanctuary is 1 km (half a mile) beyond the woodmill outside Prabione. To reach the sanctuary by car, follow signs on the road that descends to SS45bis.

⑥ Santuario di Madonna di Montecastello
Tignale, Brescia, Lombardia; 25080
This 17th-century sanctuary built over an ancient castle has an older chapel decorated with Renaissance frescoes. It is a peaceful spot, reached by a steep 20-minute walk that is rewarded with magnificent views and a small café (open Mar–Oct: daily). Extend the walk for another 20 minutes by following the path past the eremo (hermitage) up to the cross at the top of nearby Monte Cas.
🚗 Continue down the mountain to the lakeside road, the SS45bis. Turn right and head south to Gargnano, to the signposted, covered car park opposite the tourist office on the main road.

⑦ GARGNANO
Brescia, Lombardia; 25084
Perhaps the prettiest village on Lake Garda, Gargnano is a series of frazione (neighbourhoods) strung out along the waterfront between olive woods and secluded limonaie. The village is relatively untroubled by tourism and is perfect for a gentle wander or a lazy afternoon in the shade of an orange tree with dreamy lake views.

A two-hour walking tour
From the car park, walk down Via Roma away from the main road. The cloister of a 13th-century Franciscan monastery stands next to the Baroque **Church of San Francesco** ① just down on the right. The columns in the cloister are decorated with citrus fruits – a reference to the Franciscan introduction of lemon cultivation to the area. Legal wrangles keep the cloister closed to the public, but it is possible to peek inside by climbing the steps leading to the locked door just before the church. Continue down the lane to reach the pretty main square of Gargnano and its little marina. A building near the 16th-century **Palazzo Comunale** ②, displays cannonballs that were wedged into its walls during the 1866 War of Independence against Austria.

Head round the waterfront and east out of the square to Via Rimembranza to take in the 19th-century **Palazzo Feltrinelli** ③ on the right. Now part of the University of Milan, the palace was built by the paper and publishing magnates whose patronage can be seen throughout the village – in the hospital, the infant school and numerous family houses. The public **beach** ④ is a few minutes further along on the right in a grassy olive grove. The lane continues past several splendid Liberty (Italian Art Nouveau) villas,

notably the luxurious **Villa Feltrinelli** ⑤, now a top-class hotel, but formerly home to the Fascist leader Benito Mussolini and his family during the Republic of Salò *(see p83)*. Continue along the peaceful lane, past olive groves and occasional glimpses of the lake, to reach a large *limonaie* and the tiny Romanesque chapel of **San Giacomo di Calino** ⑥. This 11th-century church is one of the oldest on the lake. It is a peaceful place, with a 14th-century fresco of St Christopher on the lakeside wall, opposite the tiny shingle beach. This lovely spot is ideal for a picnic.

Return to the harbour in the village centre and take the lakeside lane round Hotel Gargnano, where the English novelist D H Lawrence spent a night in 1912. Continue along the walkways, past the waterfront villas and their boathouses, keeping the abandoned olive oil factory on the right. This scrubby path leads back to the car park, from where Via Donatore di Sangue branches off to the Escola Materna Feltrinelli, an infant school, on the left and the working *limonaie* on the right, on the other side of the main road (the SS45bis). The shady cobbled lane continues into the charming neighbourhood of **Villa** ⑦, which has a couple of hotels and a tiny picture-postcard port with a popular bar. Down at **Via Colletta 44** ⑧, a plaque declares that D H Lawrence lived here with his lover Frieda over the winter of 1912–13 while writing *Twilight in Italy*, an evocative piece on village life and the beauty of this area. Retrace your steps to the car.

Lemon Cultivation

In the 13th century, Franciscan monks founded a monastery in Gargnano and introduced citrus cultivation to the Lake Garda area. *Limonaie*, or purpose-built terraces for growing lemon trees, were introduced in the 17th century to protect the plants during the winter months. These skeletal structures have brick walls and terraced lines of narrow pillars. Citrus farming on a commercial scale had ended by the 20th century, because of blight and cheaper alternatives, but some *limonaie* are still open to the public.

Above Stone buildings of pretty Gargnano
Below right View of the Riviera di Limonaie
Below left Lemon souvenirs from the Riviera di Limonaie **Bottom left** *Limonaie* along the shoreline of Lake Garda

EAT AND DRINK IN GARGNANO

La Tortuga *expensive*
A Michelin-starred restaurant with a stylish dining room and knowledgeable staff. The wines here are well priced.
Via XXIV Maggio 5, 25084; ristorantelatortuga.it; closed Tue

Miralago *expensive*
This lakefront restaurant serves well-prepared fish and seafood dishes.
Via Zanardelli 5, 25084; 0365 71 209; closed Tue dinner

TRIP 7

FROM THE LAKE TO THE PLAINS

Salò to
Mantua

HIGHLIGHTS

Laid-back lakeside resorts
Relax in the low-key towns that line the lake with their pretty harbours, *belle époque* villas and fine shingle beaches – perfect for a quick dip

Wonderful wines
Sip the delicious light wines produced by the temperate climate and rolling hills of Cavaion Veronese, to the east and south of Lake Garda

Renaissance showpiece
Explore medieval and Renaissance Mantua whose elegant piazzas are dominated by the palazzos of power

Ruins with a view
Clamber the picturesque ruins of a 1st-century CE Roman villa in a charming olive grove at the very tip of Sirmione's promontory

Grotte di Catullo, ruins of a Roman villa at Sirmione, Lake Garda

FROM THE LAKE TO THE PLAINS

Exploring Lake Garda reveals the fascinating multilayered history of the region: the Romans enjoyed the natural spas on the lake's southern shore; the mighty Venetian Republic dominated the area during the 15th and 17th centuries; and the modern era of the 20th century dotted the lakeside with elegant *belle époque* resorts. Inland, it was the bloody battle for Italian independence that marked the wine-growing hills around San Martino, while Mantua was a centre of Renaissance power, as revealed by its rich art and architecture. This itinerary also showcases the different facets of this water-dependent region, from rice-covered plains to olive-grove and vineyard-clad hills. The route can also be linked with Trip 6 to Gargnano *(see pp76–7)* for a longer tour.

Above Salò overlooked by the bell tower of its cathedral, *see p82* **Below** Pretty harbour front with fishing boats at the resort of Bardolino, *see p83*

ACTIVITIES

Enjoy an open-air concert at Il Vittoriale in summer

Swim in Lake Garda from the shingle beach just south of Torri del Benaco

Immerse yourself in the thermal spa waters in Simione for some welcome relaxation

Climb the poignant memorial tower at San Martino della Battaglia

Sample fabulous local produce such as oil and wine from Bardolino, and tortellini pasta from Valeggio sul Mincio

Cycle among the picturesque rice fields – thankfully quite flat – around Mantua

Take a day trip to Venice by boat from Mantua

TRIP 7: FROM THE LAKE TO THE PLAINS

PLAN YOUR DRIVE

Start/finish: Salò to Mantua.

Number of days: 3 days.

Distance: Approx. 115 km (71 miles).

Road conditions: Lakeside roads get busy at weekends and in summer. The outskirts of the towns are lined by light industry but the roads are flat and well maintained.

When to go: Avoid the stifling summer heat on the plains by visiting in autumn, when the menus are full of pumpkin and chestnut dishes; spring is an attractive time, too. August sees the lake chock-a-bloc and the hotels close between Nov and Easter.

Opening times: Shops tend to open 9am–1pm and 3–7pm Mon–Sat, although in the small villages some will be closed on Mon morning.

Main market days: Sirmione & Torri del Benaco: Mon am; Lazise: Wed; Bardolino: Tue; Mantua: Thu am; San Martino della Battaglia: Sat am; Valeggio sul Mincio: 4th Sun of the month (antiques and bric-a-brac).

Shopping: Mantua has some small, attractive boutiques and wonderful delicatessens. Be sure to stock up on locally made olive oils and wines in Bardolino and around the Moreniche hills to the south of Lake Garda.

Major festivals: Bardolino: Festa dell' Uva (grape festival), Oct; Valeggio sul Mincio: Festa del Nodo dell'Amore (love knot or tortellini festival), 3rd Tue in Jun; Fiera di Valeggio (music and dance), 1st week in Jul.

DAY TRIP OPTIONS

Lake Garda has plenty for families, history buffs and activity addicts. Kids will love the varied and **macabre exhibits** at Il Vittoriale, followed by a **ferry ride**, **castle** visit and a **swim**. History buffs can start at Sirmione with **Roman** and **medieval remains**, before climbing the **memorial tower** at San Martino and finishing at the **gardens** of **pasta-loving** Valeggio sul Mincio. Mantua itself deserves a day: walk the **Renaissance city**, buy a **picnic**, then explore the countryside **on two wheels**. For full details, see p85.

VISITING SALÒ

Parking
There are pay-and-display parking sites around town, although the multi-storey car park on Via Brunati is the best bet.

Tourist Information
Piazza Sant'Antonio 4, 25087; rivieradeilimoni.it

VISITING TORRI DEL BENACO

Parking
The main car park is immediately opposite the ferry point on the south side of town. It is free out of season and pay and display at other times.

Tourist Information
Via Gardesana 815, 37010; comune.salo.bs.it

WHERE TO STAY

AROUND IL VITTORIALE

Hotel Villa Florida *moderate*
This hotel has small suites and apartments, plus gardens and a pool.
Corso Zanardelli 113, 25083; hotelvillaflorida.com; closed mid-Oct–Mar

Hotel Bolsone *expensive*
This secluded 15th-century manor house is set high above Lake Garda and has six rooms. No children under 12.
Via Panoramica 23, 25083; dimora bolsone.it; closed Nov–Feb

TORRI DEL BENACO

Garnì Onda *inexpensive*
All rooms here have balconies or terraces. A good breakfast is included.
Via per Albisano 28, 37010; garnionda.com; closed mid-Nov–Mar

Hotel del Porto *moderate*
Located lakeside, this hotel offers stylish rooms and even swisher bathrooms. Self-catering suites are also available.
Lungolago Barbarani 1, 37010; hoteldelportolagodigarda.it; closed Nov–Mar

SIRMIONE

Meublé Grifone *moderate*
Scenic lake views compensate for the simple rooms at this friendly hotel.
Via Bocchio 4, 25019; sirmione hotelgrifone.it; closed mid-Jan–mid-Mar

AROUND SAN MARTINO DELLA BATTAGLIA

Selva Capuzza *moderate*
Selva Capuzza has a winery, self-catering apartments and a good restaurant.
Agriturismo Borgo San Donino, 25015 Desenzano del Garda (just outside San Martino della Battaglia); selvacapuzza.it; closed mid-Jan–mid-Feb

❶ Salò
Brescia, Lombardia; 25087
An attractive and historic town, Salò basks in its own sunny bay on the western shore of Lake Garda. For more than 400 years it was the capital of the communities known as the Magnifica Patria, which were under Venetian domination until the Republic's fall in 1797. The town briefly came to the fore again during World War II when Hitler and Mussolini made it the capital of the Republic of Saló *(see opposite)*. Fronting the handsome lakeside promenade, **Lungolago Zanardelli**, is the porticoed 16th-century town hall, **Palazzo della Magnifica Patria**, not far from the unfinished Renaissance **Duomo**.

🚗 *Follow Via Trento (SS45bis) NE out of town through Gardone to a signed left turn to Il Vittoriale and car park.*

❷ Il Vittoriale degli Italiani
Brescia, Lombardia; 25083
The extravagant home and gardens of the poet and nationalist hero Gabriele d'Annunzio sprawl across the hillside above the *belle époque* resort of Gardone. A controversial figure, he was known for his affair with the actress Eleanor Dusé and, more famously, his fiery relationship with Mussolini, for whom he wrote the (meaningless) Fascist war cry "Eia, eia, eia! Alalà!" It is an egocentric place cluttered with the poet's possessions, which range from a gilded tortoise to the prow of the boat *Puglia*, which D'Annunzio commanded during World War I – and his own macabre mausoleum. Concerts are performed in the amphitheatre in summer.

🚗 *Return to the main road and turn left onto Via Roma (SS45bis). Continue into Toscolano-Maderno and catch the car ferry (traghetto), signed to the right.*

❸ Torri del Benaco
Verona, Veneto; 37010
The swallow-tail battlements of the **Castello Scaligero** guard the pretty little harbour at Torri del Benaco. The castle offers wonderful views from its towers and an engaging museum on olive cultivation and local fishing methods, as well as information about

Below left Café-lined harbour front at Lazise **Below right** San Severo church frescoes, Bardolino
Bottom Grotte di Catullo, ruins of a 1st-century CE Roman settlement with lake views at Sirmione

prehistoric rock carvings in the woods inland. It is also home to one of the oldest *limonaie*, or lemon tree glasshouses, on the lake. South of the village's network of quiet cobbled lanes lies a pleasant shingle beach.

🚗 *Take the main SR249 south to Bardolino. Parking in the centre is easy.*

❹ Bardolino
Verona, Veneto; 37011

This pleasant resort has a medieval warren of lanes and the frescoed 9th-century Romanesque **Chiesa di San Severo**. Away from town, the soft rolling hills of Cavaion Veronese are carpeted with vineyards and olive groves. The tourist office lists routes to oil and wine producers, and the **Museo del Vino** *(closed Nov–mid-Mar)* gives an insight into the history of these key local industries. Plus, the end products can always be sampled at the resort's many *enoteche* and restaurants.

🚗 *Take SP31 (Via Croce) out through the vineyards, turn right on Strada Villa. Carry straight onto Strada Tre Contrè, turn right onto SP31, through Calmasino, follow signs left to Lazise. Turn left for pay-and-display car parks.*

❺ Lazise
Verona, Veneto; 37017

A popular tourist town, Lazise's ancient centre is enclosed within beautiful **medieval walls**. Next to the small port stands the **Dogana Veneta**, the customs house used to tax goods on the lake during Venice's 400 years of rule. Next door, the small Romanesque church of **San Nicolò** holds 13th-century frescoes.

🚗 *Take SR249 south to Peschiera del Garda. Drive through the town centre, following signs to S. Benedetto/Sirmione. Park outside the walled town.*

Mussolini's Republic of Salò

In November 1943, Mussolini and Hitler made a last-ditch attempt to rally Fascist Italy against advancing Allied troops by establishing the Italian Social Republic of Salò. Villas and palaces on Lake Garda became ministries, while Mussolini and his family lived in Gargnano. The Republic limped on ineffectually until Italian liberation on 25 April 1945; three days later Mussolini was executed by partisans on Lake Como.

❻ Sirmione
Brescia, Lombardia; 25019

This historic town on a promontory jutting into the waters of Lake Garda is guarded by a mighty 13th-century castle, the **Rocca Scaligera**. The café-lined lanes lead north to the ruins of a 1st-century Roman villa, the **Grotte di Catullo** *(closed Mon)*, set among olive trees on the lake's edge. Visitors since Roman times have been drawn by the spa waters (tourist office has details).

🚗 *Follow signs south for Brescia, then follow signs to SP13 to Milan. The tower is just beyond the village.*

❼ San Martino della Battaglia
Brescia, Lombardia; 25010

A long spiral ramp leads up to the panoramic terrace at the top of this frescoed tower *(closed Sun)*, built in memory of those who died fighting during the Risorgimento, the movement for Italian unification. In 1859, during the wars of independence from Austria, these hills saw some of the bloodiest battles in history. On 24 June, during the Battle of Solferino, 40,000 men were killed or injured in one day. A Swiss businessman, Henry Dunant, witnessed the carnage and saw the local people helping the wounded, regardless of nationality. His suggestion of creating a neutral hospital corps to help during wartime led to the founding of the Red Cross in 1863. There is also an ossuary and a museum here, displaying love letters, bloodied uniforms and tattered flags.

🚗 *Follow SP13 to Pozzolengo, then SP18 towards Monzambano. Turn left onto SP74 (Strada Moscatello), then right onto SP19 (towards Volta Mantovana). Turn left onto SP3 to Vallegio sul Mincio.*

Above left Cafés and shops close to Piazza Vittoria, Salò's main square **Above right** Lake view from Il Vittoriale

EAT AND DRINK

SALÒ

Lerive Rock *expensive*
This restaurant in Hotel Bellerive serves dishes made from local ingredients.
Via Pietro da Salò 11, 25087; hotel bellerive.it; closed Nov–mid-Mar

TORRI DEL BENACO

Trattoria Bell'Arrivo *moderate*
By the little harbour, this trattoria is a cosy spot for tasty, good-value food.
Piazza Calderini 10, 37010; 351 603 5120; closed Tue

SIRMIONE

La Rucola 2.0 *expensive*
Enjoy the fish in this smart restaurant near the castle. Ideal for a treat.
Vicolo Strentelle 3, 25019; ristorantelarucola.it; closed Jun–Oct: Mon lunch, Sun; Oct–May: Fri lunch, Sun dinner, Thu

SAN MARTINO DELLA BATTAGLIA

Osteria alla Torre *moderate*
This friendly place offers old-fashioned cooking – try the homemade pasta.
Via Torre 1, 25015 ; osteriaalla torre.it; closed Thu

Above Colourful boats moored at Torri del Benaco on Lake Garda

VISITING MANTUA

Tourist Information
Piazza Andrea Mantegna 6, 46100; turismo.mantova.it

Bike and Boat Hire
To hire a bike for a day, register with a passport and leave a deposit at **Casa del Rigoletto** *(Piazza Sordello 4)*. Many hotels also have cycles for guests.

Lake and river cruises range from an hour's round trip to a day cruise to Venice. Contact the tourist office.

WHERE TO STAY

VALEGGIO SUL MINCIO

La Finestra Sul Fiume B&B *moderate*
This converted mill in an idyllic riverside location offers attractive suites and a spacious garden. Cycles can be hired nearby.
Corte Sega 2, 37067; lafinestrasulfiume.it

MANTUA AND AROUND

B&B Villa Ermanna *inexpensive*
Located just outside Mantua, this pleasant countryside house offers comfortable rooms and friendly service.
Str. Castelletto 24, 46100 Borgo Castelletto; 340 745 2743

Consorzio Agrituristico Mantovano *Moderate*
This cooperative coordinates many farmstay and B&B options across the fertile surrounding countryside.
Strada Chiesanuova 8, 46100; agriturismomantova.it

Casa Poli *moderate*
This minimalist boutique hotel, with small and comfortable contemporary rooms, is located a 10-minute walk from the city's central squares.
Corso Garibaldi 32, 46100; hotelcasapoli.it

Scaravelli *expensive*
Stay in airy, elegant rooms in a palace overlooking the square. A great mix of classic and contemporary styles.
Piazza delle Erbe 12, 46100; scaravelli.it

8 Valeggio sul Mincio
Verona, Veneto; 37067

On the western border of the Venetian empire, this sleepy town played a strategic role supported by its imposing 14th-century **Castello Scaligero**. In pretty riverside **Borghetto** the **Ponte Visconteo**, built by the Dukes of Milan in 1393, protected the edge of their territory. These days, Valeggio is more famous for tortellini, served in family-run restaurants all over town.

Close to the centre, the woodland, lawns and ornamental gardens of **Parco Giardino Sigurtà** are perfect for stretching your legs. Highlights include the tulips and irises in spring and the water lilies in summer.

🚗 *Follow SR249 to Roverbella. From the centre follow signs to Santa Lucia. Pass the left turn to Santa Lucia SS62 and turn right for Mantua. Overlook signs to the centre, follow signs to Padova, taking the "tangenziale nord" round to the SS10. Cross the bridge, head towards the Castello, turn right at the roundabout to the free parking along the town wall on Via Mincio.*

9 MANTUA (MANTOVA)
Mantua, Lombardia; 46100

Rising out of the rice fields around the River Mincio, Mantua (Mantova) is ringed on three sides by lakes awash with lily flowers in season. It's impossibly romantic, with cobbled lanes linking the piazzas, a clutch of Renaissance masterpieces of art and architecture and a comfortable, relaxed pace of life. In autumn, all the city's restaurants feature *ravioli alla zucca* (pumpkin stuffed ravioli) with sage butter.

A two-hour walking tour

Follow the city wall east from the car parks to Via San Giorgio, next to the castle, which leads into **Piazza Sordello** ①. The thin square is dominated on its eastern side by the sprawling **Palazzo Ducale** ② *(closed Mon)*. The largest palace in medieval Europe, it incorporates the 14th-century Castello di San Giorgio, churches, courtyards, gardens and the Palazzo del Capitano and Magna Domus. Once home to the ruling Gonzaga dynasty (1328–1707), the palace is a labyrinth of frescoed and mirrored rooms, the highlight being the *Camera degli Sposi* (the Married Couple's room) with frescoes by Andrea Mantegna (1474).

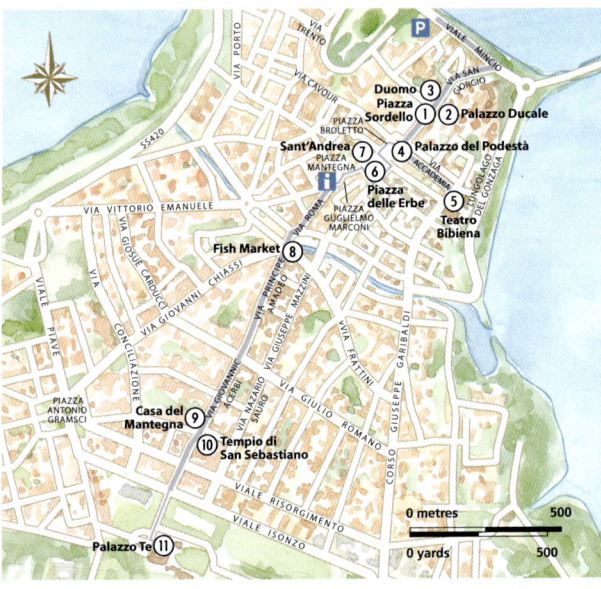

Above Fresco showing the Titans attacking Olympus, in the Palazzo Te, Mantua

Across the square, the **Duomo** ③ has an 18th-century façade and its interior was reconstructed from the Gothic original by Giulio Romano in 1545. Leave the piazza through the southern arch with the red-brick Torre Della Gabbia on the right, where people were punished by being hung in a cage and left to die. In Piazza Broletto, the façade of the 13th-century **Palazzo del Podestà** ④ has a statue of local Roman poet Virgil.

Duck left down Via Accademia to look into the 18th-century **Teatro Scientifico Bibiena** ⑤ (closed mid-Nov–mid-Mar: Mon; visit tourist office for concert details). Opened with a recital by Mozart in 1770, the theatre still performs work by Monteverdi, the Mantovan father of opera, and puts on productions of Verdi's opera *Rigoletto*, which is set in the city.

Return to the covered arcade on Piazza Broletto and head left past elegant shops into **Piazza delle Erbe** ⑥ and the 13th-century Palazzo della Ragione. The square is dominated by the Torre dell'Orologio with its astronomical clock dating from 1472. Visit Mantua's oldest church, the pretty 11th-century Rotonda di San Lorenzo, discovered in 1908 during the dismantling of the Jewish ghetto that had grown around it.

Round the corner, Piazza Mantegna holds more cafés and Mantua's most important church, **Sant'Andrea** ⑦, begun in 1472 by Leon Battista Alberti. Home to Andrea Mantegna's tomb, the barrel-vaulted interior houses two vases said to hold the blood of Christ.

Head south along Via Roma and across Piazza Marconi to the canal where, on the left, a small covered bridge is part of the **Fish Market** ⑧ built in 1536 by Giulio Romano. Fork left down Via Principe Amadeo, into Via Acerbi, where the temple-like **Casa del Mantegna** ⑨ was lived in briefly by the artist and now holds exhibitions. Across the road, the deconsecrated **Tempio di San Sebastiano** ⑩ is now a monument to Mantovans fallen in war.

Cross busy Viale Risorgimento to perhaps the city's greatest treasure, the **Palazzo Te** ⑪ (closed Tue), an island retreat for Federico Gonzaga and his mistress Isabella, designed by Giulio Romano and completed in 1535. The palace is a world of frescoes with a peaceful lawned garden. The *Sala di Amore e Psiche* is awash with erotic frescoes, while the Sala dei Giganti, with its paintings of falling columns, appears to be collapsing around you.

Head back in a straight line northeast on either Via Giovannic Acerbi or Via Nazario Sauro to the car park.

Above left Parco Giardino Sigurtà, Valeggio sul Mincio **Above right** Shady cafés and arcades in Mantua's Piazza delle Erbe

EAT AND DRINK

MANTUA AND AROUND

La Loggetta *inexpensive*
The fantastic ice-cream served here comes in a variety of flavours to reflect the seasons. It also serves vegan ice cream, milkshakes and granite.
Piazza Broletto 12, 46100; 037 640 3624

Due Cavallini *moderate*
Good-value, traditional cooking served by welcoming staff in a rustic dining room or walled summer garden. The *ravioli alla zucca* is highly recommended.
Via Salnitro 5, 46100; trattoriadue cavallinimantova.it; closed mid-Jul–mid-Aug & Tue

Dal Pescatore *expensive*
Set in a country house, a 40-minute drive from Mantua, this family-run restaurant – with three Michelin stars – serves unforgettable, innovative meals in an elegantly relaxed atmosphere.
Loc. Runate 15, 46013 Canneto sull'Oglio; dalpescatore.com; closed Mon & Tue

Il Cigno dei Martini *expensive*
In an elegant dining room overlooking a beautiful garden, well-judged cooking is matched by impeccable service.
Piazza d'Arco 1, 46100; ristoranteil cignomantova.it; closed Aug, Mon & Tue

---

DAY TRIP OPTIONS
Visitors are spoilt for choice when it comes to days out near Lake Garda.

Family day
Based in Salò ①, tour Il Vittoriale ②, then cruise across the lake on the car ferry to Torri del Benaco ③, where you can eat well, explore the village, play "King of the Castle" and have a dip from the village beach.

Follow driving instructions to Il Vittoriale and Torri del Benaco, and then back.

War and peace
Visit the Roman remains at Sirmione ⑥, then drive to San Martino della Battaglia ⑦ to climb the tower, a memorial to the war dead. Head to Valeggio sul Mincio ⑧, home of tortellini pasta and also the peaceful green spaces of Parco Giardino Sigurtà.

Follow driving instructions from Sirmione to San Martino and Valeggio, then return.

Town and country
Spend the morning exploring the majestic architecture of Mantua ⑨ – the Castello, palazzos and piazzas. Buy a picnic, then take the cycle path or a boat (visit the tourist office for routes). There are canals, rivers and pretty countryside to admire.

TRIP 8

THE HIDDEN VALLEYS OF THE ALTO ADIGE

Merano to Brunico

HIGHLIGHTS

Alpine hospitality, designer spas
Enjoy cosy alpine bars, hearty food and top-quality Alto Adige wines at traditional mountain inns; then, sweat it out in luxury at chic spa retreats

Churches, abbeys and castles
Enjoy wine tasting at Novacella Abbey; stroll among the frescoed Gothic cloisters of Bressanone cathedral; and admire the well-preserved bastion of Castel Tirolo

High-altitude challenge
Drive over the Passo di Monte Giovo (Jaufenpass) – the most northerly road pass in Italy – with stunning vistas of jagged mountains covered with a dusting of snow

Italian countryside with snowcapped mountains in the distance

THE HIDDEN VALLEYS OF THE ALTO ADIGE

A cheerful "Grüss Gott" rather than "ciao" is the greeting visitors will hear on this tour through Italy's South Tyrol. This fascinating borderland, passed back and forth between ruling powers down the years, is proud of its Germanic roots. The trip begins in the spa town of Merano – or Meran – and wends its way through secluded valleys where the traditional alpine way of life continues much as it has for centuries: cattle and sheep are led up to high pasture in summer, cheese is made in huts on the mountainside, and sweet hay is still cut by hand. After crossing the Monte Giovo/Jaufenpass, the route drops down to the Isarco (Eisacktal) valley for the Baroque splendours of the Abbazia di Novacella (Neustift) and the cathedral town of Bressanone.

ACTIVITIES

Soak in outdoor thermal pools and sunbathe below mountain peaks in Merano's state-of-the-art spa

Take a cable car to the 12th-century church of San Vigilio in a quiet mountain-top location above Merano

Go for a hike in the Parco Nazionale dello Stelvio near the Val d'Ultimo, or walk the high-altitude Adolf Munkel footpath in the Val di Funes

Learn how to smelt copper at a recreated Neolithic village near the Val Senales glacier

Shop for art and speciality foods in Bressanone's medieval arcades

Breathe in the smell of freshly cut hay on walks through velvety alpine pastures

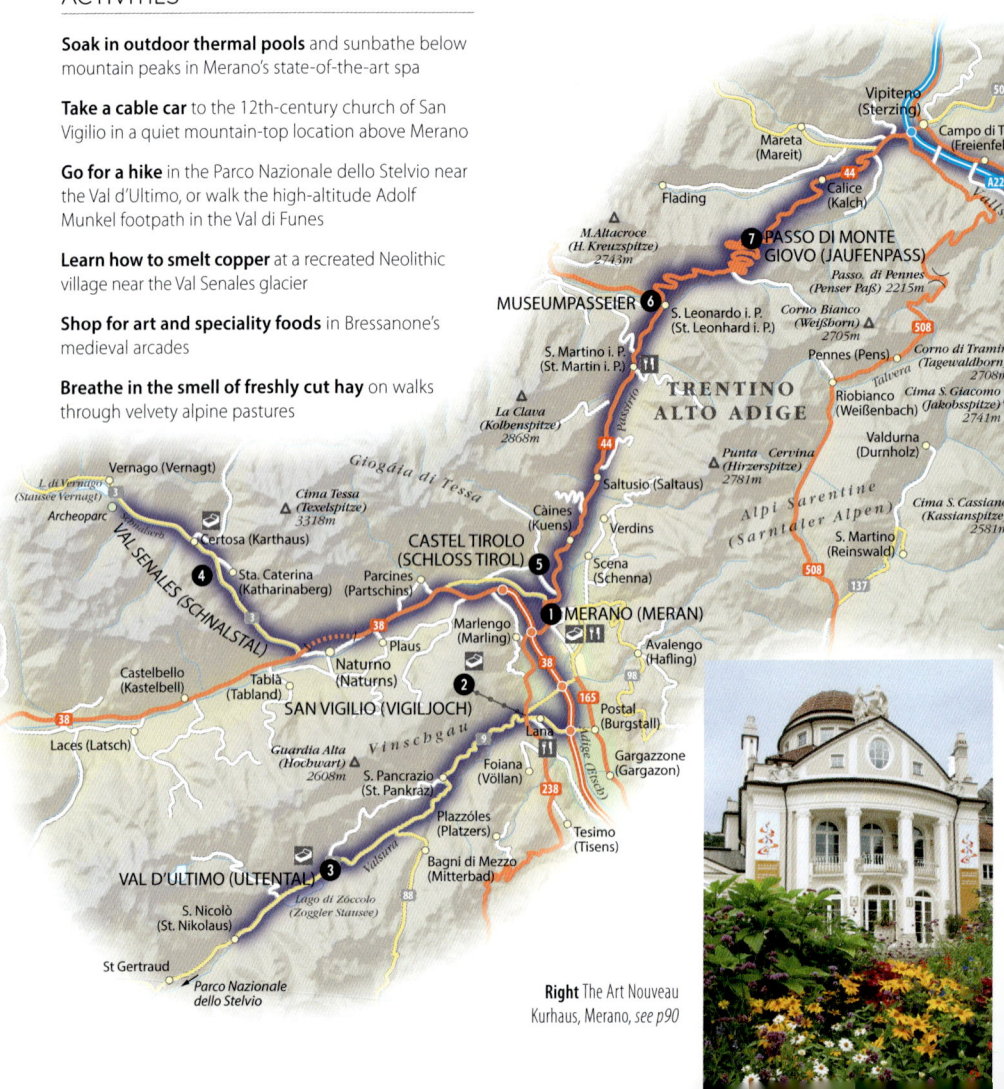

Right The Art Nouveau Kurhaus, Merano, see p90

TRIP 8: THE HIDDEN VALLEYS OF THE ALTO ADIGE 89

Above Vine terraces near the Abbazia di Novacella, *see p92*
Below Pretty houses in the spa resort of Merano, *see p90*

PLAN YOUR DRIVE

Start/finish: Merano to MMM Ripa at Brunico.

Number of days: 3, allowing half a day to explore Bressanone, and a visit to the thermal baths in Merano.

Distance: 290 km (180 miles).

Road conditions: The roads are well paved and well signposted. Mountain routes can be slow. The road to Monte Giovo is steep, with many switchback bends. Late snow may keep the Passo dell'Erbe/Wurzjoch closed into July.

When to go: Late Jun–late Sep is best, when the mountain passes and refuges are open, the summer hiking season is in full swing and cable cars are running. For tourist information, visit *suedtirol.info*.

Main market days: Merano: Fri & Sat; Bressanone: Mon; Brunico: Wed.

Shopping: Look for mountain cheeses and chutneys, *speck* (smoked ham), jams and preserves made from mirtillo berries, and quality Alto Adige wines. Interesting mountain products include *loden* (traditional jackets and hats made from wool felt) and crib figures from Bressanone.

Major festivals: Throughout the region: Törggelen (*see p94*) mid-Sep–Nov; **Merano:** Easter Monday horse races; Wine and food festival, Nov; **Bressanone:** "Treffpunkt" wine festival, end Jul; "Musik und Kirche" (classical music in churches), mid-Jul–mid-Sep; bread and strüdel market, Oct; International Mountain Summit, late Oct–early Nov; **Bressanone & Brunico:** Christmas markets, late Nov–early Jan; **Val di Funes:** Speck festival in late Sep to early Oct.

DAY TRIP OPTIONS

The drive can be broken up into day trips. Families can see the **castle** at Tirolo, then try **living like a Copper Age man** at the Archeoparc in Val Senales. Adults might prefer a Tyrolean **history museum**, a drive over a **mountain pass,** then a **soak** in a **spa**. Alternatively, stock up on an **alpine picnic,** **hike** on a **high-altitude trail**, then explore a **museum** about **mountain survival**. For full details, *see p95*.

Right Fresco of St Christopher on the exterior of Merano's Duomo **Right centre** The Church of San Vigilio, in a beautiful mountain setting **Far right** The quaint village of Unser Frau in the Val Senales **Below** View of Merano, beside the Passer river

WHERE TO STAY

MERANO (MERAN)
Terme Merano *moderate*
Stunning town-centre hotel designed by Matteo Thun with restful interiors. Rooms are spacious, with balconies.
Piazza Terme 1, 39012; hoteltermemerano.com

Vigilius Mountain Resort *expensive*
This luxury eco-spa, reachable only by cable car (15 mins from Lana), is a wonderfully relaxing place to stay. There's a fabulous quartzite-lined pool.
Monte San Vigilio (Vigiljoch), 39011 Lana; vigilius.it

VAL D'ULTIMO (ULTENTAL)
Arosea Life Balance *moderate*
This modern hotel offers understated luxury and sunny terraces. Some suites have outdoor saunas and showers.
Pracupola al lago 3551, 39016 St Valburga; arosea.it

Other options *moderate*
For farmhouse B&Bs offering spotless rooms, breakfasts from locally grown products, and often a pool and free Wi-Fi, visit *redrooster.it*

VAL SENALES (SCHNALSTAL)
Zur Goldenen Rose *moderate*
Wood-panelled, clean and snug rooms with wooden floors make this a good bolt-hole halfway up the Val Senales.
Karthaus 29, Senales (Schnals), 39020; goldenerose.it

❶ Merano (Meran)
Alto Adige; 39012

Tourists started flocking to Merano at the end of the 19th century, after Empress Elizabeth of Austria – known as Sissi – chose the town for her winter cure, and a resort of pastel-coloured Art Nouveau palaces and riverside promenades evolved. Sissi stayed at **Trauttmansdorff castle**, now home to interesting botanical gardens *(open daily)*. Take time to enjoy the town's landmark **thermal baths** *(open daily)*, designed by architect Matteo Thun, which opened in 2005. They offer thermal pools and treatments using mud, chestnuts and apples.

🚗 *From the centre, follow signs for Bolzano (Bozen), then signs for Lana. Follow the brown signs for Val d'Ultimo (Ultental) and the "Seilbahn" (cable car). Turn right and park at the cable car station in Lana.*

❷ San Vigilio (Vigiljoch)
Alto Adige; 39011

Step into the cable car at Lana and travel back in time to 1912, when it was built. It's the second oldest in Europe and climbs *(open daily)* in stately fashion to Vigilius Mountain Resort – an eco-resort built from larch that wraps around the mountain. From there, hop on a chairlift and soar above the larch woods of Monte San Vigilio (Vigiljoch), which has been a sacred place since prehistoric times. There's a café with panoramic views at the top, from where an uphill hike (15 minutes on Path 4) leads to the beautiful, simple Romanesque **Church of San Vigilio**, with 14th-century frescoes. Return on foot (1 hour; Path 3, then 34) or by chairlift to Vigilius – its restaurant (Ida) is a popular stop for hikers.

🚗 *Return to Lana. Follow the brown road signs for Val d'Ultimo (Ultental). Pass through San Pancrazio (Sankt Pankraz) to San Nicolò (Sankt Nikolaus) and the Lahnersäge Visitor Centre.*

❸ Val d'Ultimo (Ultental)
Alto Adige; 39016

The first part of the valley is the most dramatic, climbing steeply through orchards and vineyards, past signs for *waalwegs* (the ancient irrigation channels that make farming possible on the sunny, south-facing hillsides). The valley opens out into lush pastures dotted with traditional chalets topped by wooden roof shingles weighted with stones against stormy weather. Stop for refreshments at the village of San Pancrazio before heading on to San Nicolò and the **Lahnersäge Visitor Centre** *(open mid-May–Oct: Tue–Sat)* with its water-driven sawmill, just before the climb into the village of St Gertraud (1,519 m/ 4,984 ft), the starting point for hikes in the **Parco Nazionale dello Stelvio** *(stelviopark.bz.it)*.

🚗 *Return to Merano on SS38, skirting to west of town centre and turning west into Venosta (Vinschgau) valley. Soon after Naturno (Naturns) turn right and take the long, winding road into the Senales (Schnalstal) valley.*

Matteo Thun

Born in Bolzano, architect Matteo Thun has designed some groundbreaking buildings in Alto Adige, from the Vigilius resort, which won *Wallpaper* magazine's design award in 2004, to the spa complex in Merano. In the 1980s, with Ettore Sottsass and others, he cofounded the Memphis Group, which injected colour, humour and pizzazz into everyday design.

4 Val Senales (Schnalstal)
Alto Adige; 39020

Perched on a rocky outcrop, the little church of Monte Santa Caterina (Katharinaberg) is one of the few landmarks on the drive up the steep, wooded Senales valley. Many twists and turns lead to **Certosa (Karthaus)**, a village with a famous church and cloister, home to a silent order of monks from 1326–1725. Continue higher still to the **Archeoparc** *(Easter–Oct: open daily)* – a fascinating recreation of a late Neolithic village in an alpine landscape (1,500 m/4,921 ft) that was home to Ötzi the Iceman. The fascinating remains of this Copper Age man were found mummified in the glacier above the valley in 1991, and now rest in Bolzano *(see p100)*. At the Archeoparc, visitors can try their hand at archery, making fire, smelting copper ore, working a flint tool or baking bread in the typical domed ovens of 5,000 years ago.

🚗 Drive back down the valley and turn left to Merano. In the town centre, take SS44 and continue to Tirolo (Tirol). Parking is on the left, before the castle.

5 Castel Tirolo (Schloss Tirol)
Alto Adige; 39019

Such was the power of the counts of Tirol, who built their mountain eyrie in a strategic position on a hillside above Merano, that the whole region was named after them. Surrounded by lush forest, this huge 12th-century castle is well preserved and its keep, temple, knight's hall (an occasional concert venue) and refectory are all open to visitors. Within the complex is a **museum** *(open mid-Mar–mid-Nov: Tue–Sun)* of daily life in the Middle Ages, with interactive displays.

🚗 Continue north up the Val Passiria (Passeiertal) for 15 km (10 miles). Look out for the Sandwirt inn on the right, just before San Leonardo. The museum is next to it. Park outside the restaurant or in the car park left off the main road.

Andreas Hofer
An innkeeper and cattle dealer, Andreas Hofer (1767–1810) fought for the Tyrol's autonomy after it was ceded to Bavaria in 1805. He became a reluctant hero of the people after successful uprisings against Bavarian and Napoleonic troops. However, larger political forces overtook him and he was betrayed to the invaders. Napoleon supposedly gave the order to "give him a fair trial and then shoot him". He was executed in Mantua in 1810.

6 MuseumPasseier
Alto Adige; 39015

The Sandwirt inn was the birthplace of Andreas Hofer – the former stables next door are now a museum *(closed Mon)* in his memory. A short film (in Italian, German and English) tells Hofer's story, giving an insight into the Tyrolean fight for independence – always with a strong identity, Alto Adige is, to this day, an autonomous province. The museum reveals traditional alpine life via indoor displays and an open-air exhibition of wooden chalets, with barns and grain storage, a skittle alley, beehives, a communal oven, a mill for making loden (local felt fabric) and a schnapps still.

🚗 Continue into San Leonardo in Passiria (St Leonhard). Take a right, following the brown signs for the Passo di Monte Giovo (Jaufenpass).

EAT AND DRINK

MERANO

Trattoria Mainardo *moderate*
This simple trattoria is popular for its hearty, delicious dishes made with fresh ingredients. Lovely, cosy atmosphere and attentive service.
Via Mainardo 19, 39012; 0345 157 5412; closed Sun

Sissi – Andrea Fenoglio *expensive*
A one-star Michelin restaurant where renowned chef Andrea Fenoglio produces modern Italian cuisine with a regional bent.
Galileo Galilei 44, 39012; sissi. andreafenoglio.com; closed Mon & Tue lunch

AROUND SAN VIGILIO

Pfefferlechner *moderate*
A down-to-earth place dating back to 1297, where they brew their own beer, distil their own schnapps and produce their own smoked bacon and trout. Order the "Gupffleisch" in advance – neck of pork in schnapps, with bacon dumplings and white cabbage. Child-friendly, there's also a beer garden and playground outside and the medieval dining rooms overlook the stables.
St Martinsweg 4, 39011 Lana; pfefferlechner.it

AROUND MUSEUMPASSEIER

Trattoria Lamm *moderate*
In the main square of the village, the 17th-century Lamm inn prides itself on its simple Tyrolean dishes, such as homemade pasta, and a lovely strudel made with local honey.
Via Villaggio 36, 39010 San Martino in Passiria (just before MuseumPasseier); gasthaus-lamm.it; closed Sun eve & Mon

Below Twelfth-century Tirol Castle looks down on 13th-century Brunnenburg Castle

Above The road over the top of Italy at Passo di Monte Giovo (Jaufenpass)

VISTING BRESSANONE

Parking
Park off Via Brennero (Brennerstrasse) on the road from Novacella. Free parking (max. 2 hrs) just outside the pedestrian zone by the riverside at Stufles.

Tourist Information
Viale Ratisbona 9 (Regensburger Allee 9); brixen.org

WHERE TO STAY

ABBAZIA DI NOVACELLA
Pacherhof *moderate*
Near the abbey, this hotel makes its own wine from vineyards dating from the 11th century. Rooms have wooden floors and spacious bathrooms; some have balconies, and there's a huge pool.
Vicolo Pacher 1, 39040 Novacella; pacherhof.com

BRESSANONE AND AROUND
Ansitz zum Steinbock *inexpensive*
Beamed ceilings and white-washed walls characterize the uncluttered bedrooms in this imposing building, 18 km (11 miles) southwest of Bressanone, just beyond Chiusa (Klausen).
Vicolo F. v. Defregger 14, 39040 Villandro (Villanders); zumsteinbock.com; closed Jan

Elephant *expensive*
This hotel has an elegant touch of faded grandeur, and is centrally located. It also has a formal restaurant and more casual *enoteca* (wine bar).
Via Rio Bianco 4, Bressanone; hotelelephant.com

❼ Passo di Monte Giovo (Jaufenpass)
Alto Adige; 39010

Leaving the Passeier valley behind, there will be plenty of bikers and perhaps a few hardy cyclists for company on the ear-popping ascent to the Passo di Monte Giovo (2,094 m/ 6,870 ft). This is the most northerly road pass in Italy, giving access to stunning views of ridge after ridge along the Austro–Italian border. The big skies and saw-toothed peaks, with a dusting of snow even in summer, make it feel like driving over the top of the world. As the landscape opens out to high moorland, there are opportunities to stop for a coffee and admire the glorious views at makeshift roadside bars before making the long, winding descent to Vipiteno (Sterzing) in the Isarco (Eisack) valley.

🚗 Join A22 south towards Bolzano (Bozen)/Verona. Take Bressanone Nord (Varna) exit and turn right towards Bressanone. Exit from SS12, pass through Varna following brown signs for Quartiere Leone (Löwenhof), then take the road for Abbazia di Novacella on the left.

❽ Abbazia di Novacella (Neustift)
Alto Adige; 39040

In the 17th century, the Augustinian monks of Novacella commissioned a Weltwunder-Brunnen, a depiction of the Seven Wonders of the World, for their abbey, which had long been an important centre of learning in the Tyrol. In a moment of immodesty, they added their church to the picture as world wonder number eight. The abbey *(closed Sun)* offers a lot for the visitor to see, with its impressive bell tower and basilica, medieval cloister with 14th-century frescoes, its maze of painting-lined galleries, gardens and a library in which the monks still work. The complex, built in southern German Baroque style, is a great place to wander and enjoy: surrounded by vineyards, the abbey makes its own wine which can be sampled in the small tavern *(closed Sun)*, or bought from the shop.

🚗 Exit the abbey and take SS12 (not the motorway) into Bressanone. Park just outside the pedestrianized historic centre.

❾ BRESSANONE (BRIXEN)
Alto Adige; 39042

With its cobbled streets, medieval arcades and classic beer gardens, Bressanone (Brixen) seems like a busy metropolis after the quiet valleys earlier in the drive. Rich and powerful, Bressanone became an independent principate in the 11th century and its ruling bishops were constantly jockeying for power with the counts of Tyrol. Today, this attractive town is the artistic and cultural capital of the region.

A two-hour walking tour
This walk is best done Tue–Sat, when the shops and museums are open and the town is bustling. It begins in Piazza Duomo (Domplatz), the town centre.
Bressanone's cathedral, **The Dom** ① *(open daily)*, was built in the 10th century, rebuilt in the 13th century and rebuilt again, in lavish Baroque style, between 1745 and 1758, when its twin onion domes were added. The broad, vaulted nave is richly decorated in marble and stucco with a ceiling fresco of the *Adoration of the Lamb* by Paul Troger (1698–1762), an Austrian painter. Through the cathedral's right door is the Gothic **Kreuzgang** ② (cloister), with a series of richly frescoed vaulted archways painted between 1370 and 1510 by artists from Bressanone and Brunico (Bruneck).

Above Pedestrians wander the narrow streets of Bressanone's old town

TRIP 8: THE HIDDEN VALLEYS OF THE ALTO ADIGE   93

Return to Domplatz and turn into Piazza Parrocchia (Pfarrplatz), passing the **Pfaundlerhaus** ③ – a Gothic palazzo with a lavish Renaissance façade. At the crossroads, turn right into Via San Albuino (Albuingasse) and walk to Piazza Seminario (Seminarplatz) and the interesting 18th-century **seminary** ④ (now a theology college) with views of Plose mountain (2,500 m/8,200 ft) behind it. Backtrack via the riverside Vicolo della Ghiare (Griesgasse) to the Aquila (Adler) bridge, crossing the River Eisack into the **Stufels (Stufles)** ⑤ district, the oldest part of Bressanone, doing a loop past the Schutzangelkirche (church) and the theatre back to the bridge. Recross the river to the **Museo della Farmacia (Pharmaziemuseum)** ⑥ *(open 2–6pm Tue–Wed, 11am–4pm Sat; Jul & Aug: 11am–4pm & 2–6pm Mon–Fri & Sat).* This contains a fascinating collection of antique vials for lotions and potions, as well as ornate medical manuals covering 400 years of medical history. Re-enter the historic centre by the **Torre Bianca (Weissenturm) gate** ⑦ – the white tower is actually part of St Michael's parish church. At the cathedral, bear right into the **Portici Maggiori (Grosse Lauben)** ⑧, a shopping arcade that dates back to medieval times, but is now home to fashion and speciality food shops. Take a left turn into the small galleries of the **Portici Minori (Kleine Lauben)** ⑨, built in the 1400s, then continue along Vicolo Vescovado (Hofgasse) to the **Palazzo Vescovile (Hofburg)** ⑩ (Bishop's Palace), surrounded by a moat. The inner courtyard has Renaissance archways that lead to the Museo Diocesano (Diozesanmuseum) *(open daily, Nov & Feb–mid-Mar)*. The exhibits reveal just how powerful Bressanone's bishop-princes were: among the fine displays is a Byzantine silk cloak decorated with a stylized eagle, the personal emblem of Bishop Albuino – a gift from Emperor Henry II. Next to the palace is the **Giardino dei Signori (Herrengarten)** ⑪, a peaceful monastery-style garden growing vegetables, herbs and flowers.

🚗 *Follow the road for the highway, but before Chiusi's exit, turn left and follow the brown signs for Val di Funes (Villnöss).*

Above left The Abbazia di Novacella, set among vineyards **Above right** The Colossus, one of the Wonders of the World, Abbazia di Novacella

TYROLEAN FOOD SHOPPING

Located just the other side of the river to the Abbazia di Novacella, **DeGust** *(Zona Bsackerau 1 Löwecenter, Varna; degust.com; closed Thu & Sun)* sells well over 100 Italian artisan cheeses, including alpine styles such as the bittersweet blue cheese Golden Gel, matured in sweet grapes and wrapped in hay. There are also preserves, chutneys, salamis and South Tyrolean *speck* (smoked ham) for sale.

EAT AND DRINK

ABBAZIA DI NOVACELLA
Pacherhof *moderate*
The abbey *(see p92)* has four panelled *stube*, one of which is said to be the oldest in South Tyrol. The menu gives a modern spin on Tyrolean cuisine, using vegetables from the abbey's own garden. *Vicolo Pacher 1, 39040 Novacella; pacherhof.com*

BRESSANONE
Oste Scuro (Finsterwirt) *expensive*
Excellent local delicacies and a great atmosphere in this much-loved restaurant; good wine list, too. *Vicolo del Duomo 3, Bressanone 39042; finsterwirt.com; closed Sun & Mon*

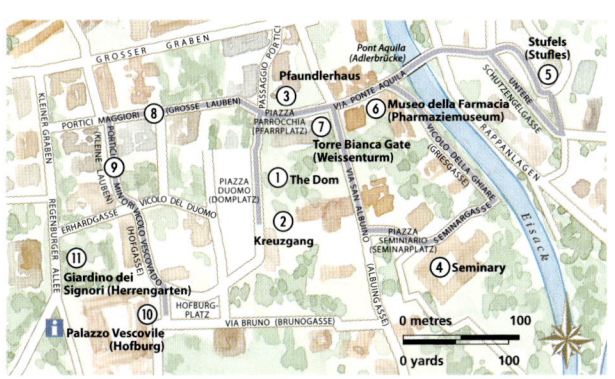

Above The church of Santa Maddalena, in an idyllic setting in the Val di Funes (Villnöss)

HIKING IN THE VAL DI FUNES

Kompass walking maps (1 cm : 500 m) are essential as they show footpaths, level of difficulty and the steepness of the terrain. Trails are simple to follow – red and white blazes painted on rocks and trees to keep walkers on the right path. Mountain refuges offer good food and drink en route.

WHERE TO STAY

AROUND VAL DI FUNES

Ansitz Ranuihof *inexpensive*
Once a hunting lodge, this farmhouse offers six comfortable doubles; breakfast includes milk and eggs from the farm. *San Giovanni 2, 39040 Val di Funes (Villnöss) (after Funes, veer south to San Maddalena then take the road to St Johann and Ranui); ranuihof.com*

Below Alpe di Zannes and Le Odle ranges with Geisler Spitzen

10 Val di Funes (Villnöss)
Alto Adige; 39040

A real gem of a valley, the spectacular Val di Funes is characterized by walls of grey saw-toothed peaks – the Puez Odle (Puez Geisler) mountains – rising above the lush, green rolling meadows that open out after Funes. It's a beautiful part of the drive for a gentle walk, or to spend a half-day on a more ambitious hike such as the Adolf Munkel path – a five-hour circular trail that starts and ends in Zannes (Zanser Alm) at the head of the valley *(see suedtirol.info; Kompass map 55)*. The path climbs to 2,000 m (6,560 ft) at one point, giving panoramic views, and there are huts or *rifugi* en route for revitalizing refreshments.

🚗 *From Funes, take SP163 uphill to the signposted Kopfel Joch pass. There, turn right onto SP29 to the Passo dell'Erbe (Würzjoch). Park at Ütia de Börz inn.*

11 Passo dell'Erbe (Würzjoch)
Alto Adige; 39030

This road pass reaches more or less the same giddy heights as some of the more famous Dolomite passes, but is one much less commercialized and the view of the mountains on the approach is sensational. Alta Via 2, one of the high-level trans-Dolomite footpaths, crosses the road between Kopfel Joch and Würzjoch, so parking and having a half-hour or so walk in either direction will give a flavour of hiking these high trails. A visit to the Ütia de Börz inn at the pass is recommended – the food is good and it is also a fabulous base for a few days hiking (half-board and minimum three-day stay preferred).

🚗 *From the pass, descend to San Martino (St Martin) in Badia, passing Ciastel de Tor. Turn left onto the SS244 towards Brunico. Follow the signs for Brunico centre and the MMM Ripa. Park at the castle.*

Törggelen

An old South Tyrolean tradition, the Törggelen season roughly coincides with the arrival of the new season's wine *(Oct–mid-Nov)*. It's a time when people go for hikes and gather to feast on local specialities before the onset of winter. The name comes from the Latin word *torquere*, to turn or squeeze – referring to pressing grapes to make wine. Some say the tradition came from wine merchants visiting the wine growers to try the new wine – after the tasting, they would be given a feast. A typical Törggelen spread involves *speck* or sausage, roast chestnuts and breads.

TRIP 8: THE HIDDEN VALLEYS OF THE ALTO ADIGE

Reinhold Messner
Mountaineer Reinhold Messner grew up in Val di Funes (Villnöss) and learned to climb with his father. Messner thought the usual "siege" techniques used on mountaineering expeditions were disrespectful to the environment and pioneered the alpine style of climbing – using minimal equipment – in the Himalayas. He is famous for making the first solo Everest ascent without oxygen and was the first man to climb all 14 of the world's peaks over 8,000 m (26,250 ft). He founded a mountain museum at five locations in the South Tyrol, including one that opened in 2011 in Brunico (Bruneck).

⓬ MMM Ripa at Brunico (Bruneck)
Alto Adige; 39031

The main market town of the Val Pusteria (Pustertal), Brunico (Bruneck) grew around the castle built in 1250 by the Prince-Bishop of Brixen, Bruno of Wullenstätten, and flourished thanks to its position on the trade route between Venice and Germany. In 2011, Reinhold Messner opened the doors to this fifth part of the Messner Mountain Museum Ripa – inside the Castello di Brunico *(open mid-May–Oct, Tue–Sun)*. The display is a tribute to the mountain peoples of the world who have made their homes at the very margins of where it is possible to live – Sherpas, Indios, Walser, Mongols and Hunzas.

Above left Houses from the 16th and 17th centuries, Brunico **Above right** Castello di Brunico, home to the Messner Mountain Museum Ripa **Below left** Cycling on the Alta Pusteria bike path near Brunico (Bruneck)

EAT AND DRINK

AROUND PASSO DELL'ERBE
Maso Runch *moderate*
Just east of Badia, this restaurant is popular for its hearty six-course menu. After rustic appetisers, expect homemade ricotta and spinach ravioli, pork shin with sauerkraut, local wine to drink and apple strudel for dessert.
Runch 11, 39036 Pedraces; masorunch.it

Hotel Lech da Sompunt *expensive*
Try spit-roasted *porchetta* (suckling pig), fondue and fresh trout from their pond. Other specialities include *canederli* (dumplings) and *Kaiserschmarren* (sweet cranberry pancake).
Str Sompunt 36, 39036 Pedraces; lechdasompunt.it; closed 7 Apr–10 Jun, Oct & Nov

DAY TRIP OPTIONS
To break up the tour into day trips for adults and children, use either Merano or Bressanone as a base.

Ice Man adventure
Children will enjoy travelling from Merano ❶ and visiting the castle and interactive museum at Castel Tirolo ❺. Next, it's off to the Archeoparc in Val Senales ❹ to discover how Ötzi the Ice Man lived. Enjoy dinner at Pfefferlechner in Lana *(see p91)*, with its adventure playground and animals as well as great food and beer brewed on the premises.

Take SS44 north from Merano, turn left to Tirolo. Return to Merano, access Val Senales via SS38, picked up just outside Merano. Lana is also close to Merano – follow SS238 for Bolzano/Bozen/Lana.

Tyrolean treats
Plunge into the Tyrolean past at the MuseumPasseier ❻, then head up to "drive over the roof of Italy" and enjoy a high-altitude coffee or drink at the Passo di Monte Giovo ❼. Return to Merano ❶ to explore the botanical gardens of Trauttmansdorff Castle. Finish off the day with a relaxing splash in the thermal pools at Merano's beautiful spa complex.

Access all from the Passiria/Passeier valley road (the SS44).

Taste of the mountains
Stock up on an alpine picnic at the bustling Saturday farmers' market in Bressanone ❾ or DeGust in Varna *(see p93)* and hit the high-level trails in the Val di Funes ❿ or do a bit of the Alta Via 2 footpath from Passo dell'Erbe ⓫. Head on to the mountain museum at Brunico ⓬ to learn about real mountain living.

Follow the driving instructions from Bressanone to Val di Funes, Passo dell'Erbe and Brunico. Return via SS49.

TRIP 9

CLASSIC DOLOMITES TOUR

Bolzano to
Alpe di Siusi

HIGHLIGHTS

Famous road passes
Negotiate exhilarating hairpin bends and switchback roads that wind like ribbons around the Dolomites

Michelin-starred hotspots
Dine at top-class restaurants on dishes made from the finest local produce

Time-travel experience
Visit Ötzi – the remains of a 5,000-year-old Ice Man in Bolzano's archaeological museum – and follow the trail of dinosaurs in the Bletterbach gorge

Award-winning wine producers
Stop for tastings along the Strada del Vino, in the oldest wine region of the German-speaking world

CLASSIC DOLOMITES TOUR

This itinerary is for those who like heights: it offers switchback roads, chairlift and cable car rides – and dizzying haute cuisine. A popular skiing and hiking area, there are exceptional hotels and restaurants in this province, which has more Michelin stars than any other in Italy. The route crosses the most famous passes of the Dolomites, a range of limestone mountains raised skywards 250 million years ago when Africa collided with Southern Europe. Bring hiking boots; it's worth getting out of the car and walking, not least for a glimpse of history. Some trails lead along the World War I front line, where Italian and Austrian troops dug themselves into the mountains to survive. In 1919, after war ended, this German-speaking region – known as South Tyrol – became a part of Italy.

ACTIVITIES

Taste the superb wines of the Alto Adige on the Strada del Vino

Walk back in time to the last Ice Age in the gorge at the Geoparc Bletterbach

Ride up in a chairlift and hike in the Catinaccio mountains, and enjoy delicious hearty food in a mountain refuge

Drive over the roof of Italy across the stunning Pordoi, Falzàrego, Valparola and Gardena passes of the Dolomites

Climb through World War I galleries blasted into the rock at Lagazuoi and view wartime memorabilia at the Tre Sassi fort

Catch the *enrosadira*, when the Dolomites glow in the rays of the setting sun

TRIP 9: CLASSIC DOLOMITES TOUR   99

PLAN YOUR DRIVE

Start/finish: Bolzano to Alpe di Siusi.

Number of days: Approx. 4–5.

Distance: 219 km (136 miles).

Road conditions: The roads are pretty good. Routes over mountain passes are narrow with steep turns and can be busy. The A22 motorway can get heavily congested with long queues of traffic near tolls – leave plenty of time to get to and from airports. Beware speed limit of 110 kmph (68 mph), lower than on other Italian motorways.

When to go: May to Oct (some cable cars only operate mid-Jun–mid-Sep). Early or late snow may close the passes – look for signs on the approach roads or call 0471 200 198.

Main market days: Bolzano: fruit and vegetable market at Piazza Erbe (Obstplatz), Mon–Sat; **La Villa:** last Thu of month; **Corvara:** 2nd & last Sat of month; **Ortisei (St Ulrich):** Fri.

Shopping: Look for local wine, liqueurs and grappas, wild honey, cheeses and salami; *loden* (traditional felt jackets and hats); fruit compôtes and preserves; and *kräutersalz* (salt and herb mix).

Major festivals: Across region: Törggelen *(see p94)*, mid-Sep–Nov; **Bolzano:** Transart (festival of contemporary culture), Sep; Christmas market, late Nov–23 Dec; **Appiano (Eppan):** medieval horsemanship, Whitsun, late-May to early Jun; **Castelrotto (Kastelruther):** Spatzen folk festival, Jun & Oct; Christmas market in Dec; **Val Gardena (Gröden) & Alta Badia:** Ski World Cup events, Dec.

Above The limestone peaks of the Dolomites as seen from Marmolada, *see p102* **Below** Typical valley scenery on the Strada del Vino, *see p101* **Below left** Wall painting on the side of a Bolzano "Torgglhaus", or restaurant, *see p100*

DAY TRIP OPTIONS

Using Bolzano as a base offers family day trips exploring an **archaeological museum**, enjoying a **picnic** then going on a **hike** to look for **dinosaurs** in a **gorge**, before admiring the **frescoes of dwarves and giants** in a **castle**. Adults may prefer a **wine tour** (including a visit to a **wine museum**) through famous **wineries** of the Alto Adige, enjoying a **gourmet lunch** along the way. For full details, *see p103*.

Above Statue of Walther von der Vogelweide in Piazza Walther (Waltherplatz), Bolzano

VISITING BOLZANO (BOZEN)

Parking
Park in Piazza Walther (Waltherplatz), on Via Laurin or outside the train station (in the Central Parking facility).

Tourist information
Via Alto Adige 60, 39100;
bolzano-bozen.it

WHERE TO STAY

BOLZANO
Greif *expensive*
This central, 500-year-old inn is now a chic 33-bedroom haven filled with original art and Biedermeier furniture.
*Piazza Walther, 39100;
greif.it*

AROUND GEOPARC BLETTERBACH
Krone *moderate*
This 16th-century, friendly, family-run village inn has an excellent restaurant.
*Dorfplatz 3, Piazza Principale, 39040 Aldino (Aldein);
gasthof-krone.it*

❶ BOLZANO (BOZEN)
Alto Adige; 39100

In a valley at the junction of the Talvera and Isarco rivers, Alto Adige's main town has changed hands several times over the centuries. In the Middle Ages it was controlled by the Counts of Tirol, then by the Bishops of Trento; next it passed to the Habsburgs, then to Bavaria and Austria. Although it was given to Italy at the end of World War I, there's still a real Germanic feel to the town centre.

A two-hour walking tour
Via Laurin connects the train station to the start of the walk at **Piazza Walther** ①. Passing the statue of Walther von der Vogelweide (1170–1230), a German poet of the Middle Ages, head to the Gothic **Duomo** ② *(open daily)* with its elaborate steeple and lozenge-pattern roof. A short walk leads to the **Chiesa dei Domenicani** ③ *(open daily)*, with Gothic frescoes from the Giotto school and fine 15th-century frescoes by Friedrich Pacher in the cloister (separate entrance). Head up Via Goethe-Strasse to the food market on **Piazza Erbe (Obstplatz)** ④. On one corner stands the fountain of Neptune (1745), known as Gabelwirt (Innkeeper with a Fork) – walk past this and head up Via dei Francescani (Franziskanergasse) to the **Convento dei Francescani** ⑤ *(open Mon–Sat)*, dating to the first half of the 14th century. Inside is one of Bolzano's finest treasures: a superb Gothic wooden altar carved by Hans Klocher.

Detail of a fresco from Bolzano's Gothic Duomo

Backtrack a little to the top end of the market and take a left into the road named after **Dr Joseph Streiter** ⑥ – a mayor of the town in the mid-19th century – here are shops selling vintage clothes, chocolate and accessories. Continue to Via dei Bottai (Bindergasse) and turn right to **Piazza Municipio (Rathausplatz)** ⑦, lined with beautiful Rococo stucco façades. Another right turn leads down **Portici (Lauben)** ⑧, a porticoed shopping street with oriel windows and elegant Baroque floral plasterwork.

Continue along Via Museo to the **Museo Archeologico** ⑨ *(open 10am–6pm Tue–Sun)*. The prize exhibit here is Ötzi – the remains of a man in his 40s from the Copper Age, preserved in the ice of the Alps on the Italian–Austrian border. There's a video reconstruction of how Ötzi may have met his end in 3500 BCE. Cross the River Talvera (Talfer) to the arch on **Piazza Vittoria (Siegesplatz)** ⑩, commissioned by Mussolini in 1928. Return back over the bridge,

carrying straight on to Piazza del Grano, then turn right back to Piazza Walther.

🚗 From central Bolzano, follow signs for Funivia (cable car) di S Genesio and for Castel Roncolo. Turn right, crossing the river to the car park. Walk up the steps (slippery when wet) to the castle.

❷ Castel Roncolo (Schloss Runkelstein)
Alto Adige; 39100
Pier Paolo Pasolini filmed his version of Boccaccio's (1313–75) bawdy tales *The Decameron* (1971) in this 13th-century castle *(closed Mon)*. The secular frescoes are some of the best in the world. Images of giants and dwarves, the legendary lovers Tristan and Isolde and the world of chivalry were painted to impress in the 14th century – the castle was part of the Vintler family's bid to be accepted into noble society.

🚗 Return to Bolzano centre, cross the Ponte Druso and go straight. Take SS42 for Appiano (Eppan) and Strada del Vino (Weinstrasse). Turn right to Caldaro. Park in the wine centre car park or in the blue boxes outside the town centre.

❸ Strada del Vino (Weinstrasse)
Alto Adige; 39052
Although it's one of the smallest wine regions in Italy, Alto Adige produces more DOC wines than any other. This section of the drive follows part of the South Tyrolean Wine Road. Start at Caldaro's **Winecenter della Cantina** *(open daily)*, with wines for any budget. More tasting opportunities are on offer at the wine bar/visitor centre, **Punkt** *(closed Mon)*, on the main square. Enjoy, too, Caldaro's 16th-century Uberetsch architecture, which mixes Gothic and Renaissance styles.

🚗 Follow Strada del Vino (Weinstrasse) through Termeno (Tramin) and Magre

(Magreid), then take the minor road to the station and cross over A22 and River Adige. Turn left onto SS12 to Egna (Neumarkt) and turn right through the village. Turn right onto SS48 towards Val di Fiemme. After two sharp bends follow signs left for Aldein (Aldino). Turn right after village and park at the Geoparc.

❹ Geoparc Bletterbach
Alto Adige; 39040
Geology fans can see how the Dolomites were formed, epoch by epoch, as well as spot the tracks of prehistoric reptiles by walking the length of this 8-km (5-mile) fossil-packed gorge *(admission charge)*, which has carved its way down the mountain since the last Ice Age. The **Geopath** is for experienced walkers (with hiking boots); an easier 30-minute forest path from the visitor centre gives views into the canyon.

🚗 Descend via Aldein (Aldino) to SS48. Turn left to Cavalese in the Val di Fiemme. Park in the main square.

❺ Val di Fiemme
Trentino; 38033
The focus of Cavalese's town centre is the **Magnifica Comunità**, a medieval palazzo *(open Jul–Sep: daily)* frescoed with images of San Vigilio. This was once the summer palace of the Bishops of Trento, who used to stay here to escape the summer heat. Stay for a coffee or lunch before carrying on along SS48 to Tésero. This is known for its **Chiesa di San Rocco**, frescoed with activities not allowed on a Sunday, such as drinking and playing dice.

🚗 From Tésero, take the minor road (not SS48) to Predazzo, then before Moena take a deviation to the right. Head past Lago di Soraga and return to SS48. Drive through Pera di Fassa and park at the Vajolet chairlift station.

Above left Magnifica Comunità, Cavalese's historic parliament building **Above right** Vines on the slopes above Lago di Caldaro, on the Strada del Vino **Below** Bustling market on the Piazza Erbe, Bolzano

EAT AND DRINK

BOLZANO

Ca' de Bezzi (Batzenhäusl) *moderate*
This 600-year-old inn offers mixed plates served in cast-iron pans. Good wine.
Via A Hofer (Andreas-Hofer-Strasse) 30, 39100; batzen.it

Franziskanerstuben *moderate*
This homely restaurant offers a mix of Italian and Tirolean dishes.
Via dei Francescani 7, 39100; franziskanerstuben.com; closed Tue

STRADA DEL VINO

Ansitz Pillhof *expensive*
The best wines from South Tyrol are on display in the *enoteca* (wine shop) here; try by the glass at the bar or in the bistro.
Via Bolzano 48, 39057 Frangart, Appiano (Eppan) (on SS42 south of Bolzano); pillhof.com

Restaurant Ritterhof *expensive*
This restaurant serves locally sourced dishes with an imaginative twist and has a good wine list.
Weinstrasse 1/A, Kaltern, 39052; restaurant-ritterhof.it; closed Sun dinner & Mon

Zur Rose *expensive*
In this Michelin-starred restaurant, find seafood and flavours from across the country. The cellar is well-stocked.
Via Josef Innerhofer 2, 39057 San Michele, Appiano (Eppan); zur-rose.com; closed Sun, Mon & Thu lunch

VAL DI FIEMME

El Molin *expensive*
Great *stuzzichini* (snacks), a superior pizzeria and even Michelin-starred food.
Piazza Cesare Battisti 11, 38033 Cavalese; alessandrogilmozzi.com (book for lunch); closed Mon & Tue & Wed lunch

Above left Mountain scenery behind Corvara
Above centre Lago di Fedaia, near Canazei **Far right** Hiking in the Dolomites at Marmolada
Below The glacier on top of Marmolada

WHERE TO STAY

VAL SAN CASSIANO

Garni Ai Pini *inexpensive*
A family-run guesthouse with sauna.
Strada Glira 4, 39036; ai-pini.it; closed Easter–early Jun, Oct & Nov

Aman Rosa Alpina *expensive*
Understated luxury at this spa hotel.
Strada Micurà de Rü 20, 39036 San Cassiano in Badia; rosalpina.it

Chalet Susi *expensive*
Simple chalet with well-presented apartments.
Via Sotsas 4, 39036 La Villa; chaletsusi.it; closed Easter–mid-Jun, Oct & Nov

CORVARA

La Perla *expensive*
Luxury hotel with exceptional food.
Strada Col Alt 105, 39033; hotel-laperla.it; closed Apr–mid-May & mid-Sep–Oct

ALPE DI SIUSI (SEISER ALM)

Cavallino d'Oro *moderate*
A 700-year-old inn with 40 rooms.
Piazza Kraus 1, 39040 Castelrotto; cavallino.it

Romantik Hotel Turm *expensive*
Superb spa hotel with great food.
Piazza Chiesa 9, 39050 Fie allo Sciliar; hotelturm.it; closed first 2 weeks Apr & early Nov–21 Dec

6 Val di Fassa
Trentino; 38039

Popular with skiers, Val di Fassa's classic sight is the **Rosengarten mountain range** (Catinaccio in Italian). A chairlift *(mid-May–early Nov)* climbs from Pera to Ciampedie at 2,000 m (6,562 ft), where it's possible to walk among the peaks. An easy one-hour forest trail (Path 540) leads from Ciampedie to the Gardeccia refuge – perfect for a lunch stop.

🚗 *Continue on SS48 to Canazei, and begin the signposted ascent to the Passo Pordoi. Bear right on SS48 up a series of steep switchbacks to Passo Pordoi, which has ample free parking.*

> **Rosengarten (Rose garden)**
> Ladin legends are part of an epic oral tradition. One has it that the dwarf King Laurin, angry when his beloved Princess Similde was taken away from him, put a spell on his rose garden so that no one would see it again by day or night – but he forgot to include dawn and dusk – when the sun gives the mountains their rosy glow.

7 Passo Pordoi
Alto Adige; 38032

For the best views of glacier-topped Marmolada (3,246 m/10,650 ft), take the cable car *(open late Jun–mid-Sep)* from Passo Pordoi (2,239 m/7,346 ft) up to **Sass Pordoi**. Alternatively, stretch the legs for half an hour or so along the Viel del Pan ("trail of bread") – an old grain-smuggling route which begins at the pass behind the Albergo Savoia (hiking boots essential). Once back in the car, descend through a series of steep switchbacks to pretty **Arabba**. Carry on along the Livinallongo valley, passing the 11th-century Andraz castle, which once defended the iron ore mines and foundries producing swords for export across Europe.

🚗 *Descend on SS48 through Arabba and Livinallongo; climb to the Passo di Falzàrego. Park at the cable car station.*

8 Lagazuoi (Lagació)
Veneto; 32043

A cable car whisks passengers up from Passo di Falzàrego to Lagazuoi at 2,778 m (9,114 ft) in just three minutes *(early Jun–Oct)*. A short walk uphill leads to the Lagazuoi refuge, a large café/restaurant with stunning, far-reaching views of most of the Dolomites. In World War I, Austrian troops gained a bird's-eye view of the Passo Valparola from the exposed Kaiserjäger path to the northwest. Visitors with walking boots and a head for heights can turn right from the cable car station and head down the rock-cut steps that lead to the wartime galleries, blasted into the heart of the mountain (rent helmets/torches at the entrance). This exciting descent lasts about 90 minutes and is a hit with older children. Alternatively, return to the pass by the cable car.

🚗 *Turn left towards Passo di Valparola and drive for a few minutes to the Museum of the Tre Sassi Fort.*

9 Tre Sassi Fort
Veneto, 32043

Built in 1897 by the Austro-Hungarian army to defend the Passo Valparola (2,168 m/7,113 ft), this fort was opened as a museum *(open mid-Jun–end Sep: daily)* in 2003 to commemorate the 1914–18 war, with the entrance now guarded by "soldiers" in full uniform. Once home to a garrison, the fort now exhibits poignant memorabilia, letters, photographs and films showing the harsh, icy conditions that the soldiers on both sides fought under during a conflict that saw tens of thousands die.

🚗 *Descend to Val San Cassiano.*

⑩ Val San Cassiano
Alto Adige; 39030
This is a lovely part of the Alta Badia, where footpaths lead through lush pastures from Capanna Alpina into the mountains of the **Fanes-Sennes-Braies Natural Park** – site of many Ladin legends. In this quiet valley, look for chamois, capercailies and eidelweiss. There are also traditional *vila* settlements – wooden homes with a galleried hayloft, built around a central square with a fountain, drinking trough and communal bread oven – a merging of sociable Roman customs with those of the more isolated Rhaetian and Bajuvares peoples centuries ago.
🚗 Continue to La Villa (Stern). Turn left for Corvara.

Ladin country
The third language in this region, after Italian and German, is Ladin – a combination of Latin, Celtic and Rhaetian. During the Roman Empire, Ladin territory ran from Switzerland to the Adriatic Sea, but a Germanic culture from Bavaria took precedence around 400 CE. There are about 30,000 Ladin speakers in the Dolomites today and it is used in public administration. There are TV and radio programmes in Ladin, as well as the newspaper *Usc di Ladins*.

⑪ Corvara
Alto Adige; 39033
In 1930, mountain guide Franz Kostner saw the potential of Corvara as a ski resort and built Italy's large lift to Col Alt (1,980 m/6,496 ft). He then set up the first ski school and made the valley accessible to cars. The town is still unspoilt and is the centre of the Ladin-speaking area. A trip up Col Alt is worth it for the restaurant and views at the top.

🚗 From Corvara, follow signs for the Passo Gardena (Grödner Joch). Park at the bar/restaurant at the top.

⑫ Passo Gardena (Grödner Joch)
Alto Adige; 39033
This route has outstanding views of moorland and mountain, with a café at the top at 2,121 m (6,959 ft). The descent leads into the **Val Gardena (Grödnertal)** and the villages of Selva (Wolkenstein), Santa Cristina (Sankt Christina) and Ortisei (Sankt Ulrich), which throng with skiers in winter but are relatively peaceful in summer.
🚗 Descend on SS243 and turn right onto SS242. At Ortisei (St. Ulrich), turn left for Castelrotto (Kastelruth). Go straight on to Siusi (Seis). Park at the cable car for a walk or drive past Fié allo Sciliar (Völs am Schlern), then turn left to Prösels.

⑬ Alpe di Siusi (Seiser Alm)
Alto Adige; 39040
The route runs below the Alpe di Siusi plateau at 2,000 m (6,560 ft) *(closed to traffic 9am–5pm, unless staying in a hotel on the mountain)*. The road is flanked by hay meadows, while above looms Sciliar (Schlern) mountain, symbol of the Dolomites, topped by two peaks. In early summer, the wild flowers are stunning – take the cable car from Siusi (Seis) to the pastures around Compaccio (Compatsch) to see them. From Siusi, continue past the onion-domed St Konstantin church to Fiè allo Sciliar. Carry on to forbidding **Castel (Schloss) Prösels** *(Apr–Oct: guided tours May–Oct)*, built around 1500 by the Lords of Völs – witch hunters, friends of Emperor Maximilian and owners of salt mines near Innsbruck.

Above The pretty ski resort of Corvara, a good base for a trip up Col Alt

EAT AND DRINK

VAL SAN CASSIANO
Rifugio Scotoni *expensive*
Accessible only on foot, walk to this popular mountain hut for its wood-fire cooked mixed grills.
Alpe Lagazuoi 2, 39036 La Villa in Badia (1-hour's hike on Path 20 from Capanna Alpina, off the San Cassiano valley road); scotoni.it; open early Jun–early Oct

St. Hubertus *expensive*
Come here for Michelin-starred dishes.
Strada Micurà de Rü 20, 39030 San Cassiano; 0471 849 500; closed Tue

CORVARA
Rifugio Col Alt *expensive*
Enjoy dishes such as pasta with venison ragù or oysters with champagne.
rifugiocolalt.it; closed Apr–mid-Jun & mid-Sep–early Dec

AROUND PASSO GARDENA
Stüa Catores *moderate*
Try the deer ravioli with bilberry butter.
Via Sacunstr. 49, 39046 Ortisei; stuacatores.com; closed Tue

DAY TRIP OPTIONS
To break up the tour into day trips, use Bolzano as a base. Families will enjoy a look into the area's past. Adults will enjoy the wine tour – but may want to do it in a tour group minibus – contact suedtiroler-weinstrasse.it.

Family time-travel
Visit the Museo Archeologico at Bolzano ❶ to learn about Ötzi and life in the area in the Copper Age. Pick up a picnic in Bolzano, then drive to Geoparc Bletterbach ❹ to search for dinosaur fossils. Enjoy lunch, then set off to Castel Roncolo ❷ for a classic castle with lively frescoes.

From Bolzano, take SS12 south to Ora, pick up SS48 east, turning off left to Aldino, then Bletterbach. Return the same way, passing through Bolzano, then taking SS508 north.

Wine tour
From Bolzano ❶, drive the Strada del Vino ❸ to Caldaro to visit its wine centres and plan which wineries to visit. Head to Tramin, then Cortaccia, Magre, Egna and Ora. Enjoy tastings and lunching at a winery restaurant.

Follow the drive's directions for the Strada del Viño, but stay on the SS12 at Ora, returning to Bolzano.

TRIP 10

MOUNTAINS AND LAKES
Laghi di Fusine
to Trieste

HIGHLIGHTS

Stunning scenery
Visit the national parks and pretty mountain villages
in the Alpi Giulie

Cultural capital
Wander past the palazzos and loggias of Udine,
the historic capital of Friuli

Borderland vineyards
Explore the low-lying hills, dotted with vineyards,
farms and country inns, close to Slovenia

Roman remains
Admire the remains of the Roman town of Friuli,
now the most important archaeological site
in northern Italy

Imperial grandeur
See the ruins left in Trieste by the Romans,
and the grand palazzos and coffee houses
left by the Habsburgs

MOUNTAINS AND LAKES

Bordering Austria and Slovenia, Friuli-Venezia Giulia has a rich and complex history, reflected in its patchwork of languages and ethnic groups. The northern area around Tarviso – part of the Austro-Hungarian Empire till World War I – boasts stunning alpine scenery, complete with braided rivers, pristine lakes and the high peaks of the Alpi Giulie. Towards the south, these mountains give way to the fertile hills and plains of Friuli. Dotted with castles, this land, home to winemaking and ham-curing, has the charming city of Udine as its capital. To the east, near the Slovenian border, are two of Italy's most important fine-wine regions: Colli Orientali and the Collio. Closer to Gorizia, the stark, dramatic uplands of the karst plateau drop down to the Adriatic and the Neo-Classical city of Trieste.

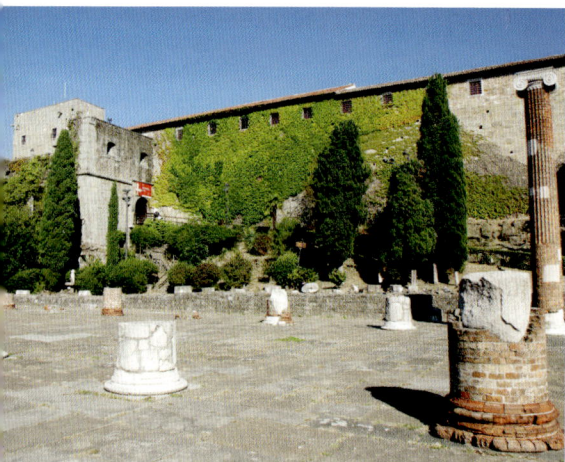

Above Remains of the colonnaded Roman Forum in front of the medieval Castello di San Giusto, Trieste, *see p113*

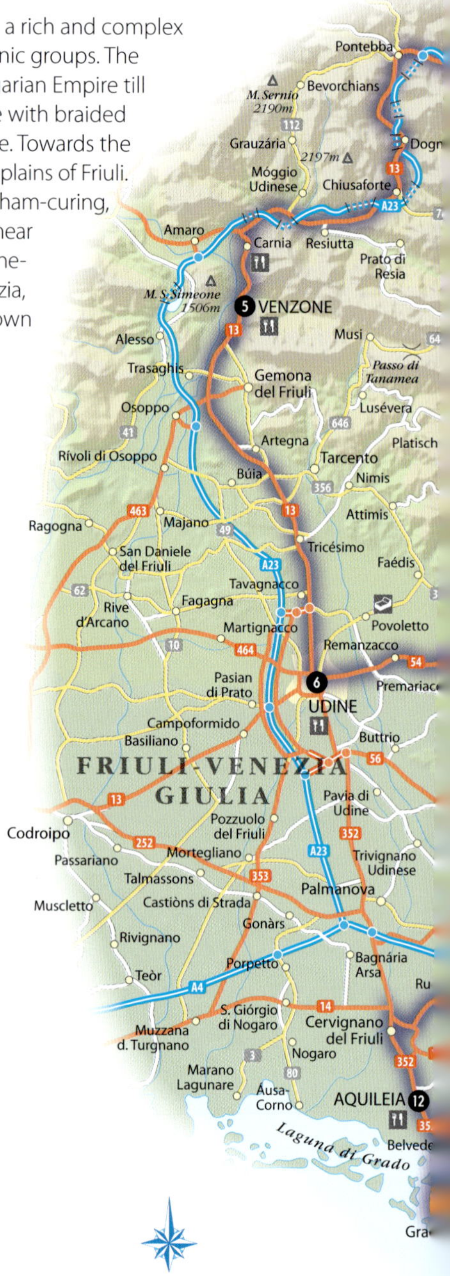

KEY

Drive route

0 kilometres 10

0 miles 10

ACTIVITIES

Walk the loop of the Laghi di Fusine

Hear the call of the wild with some dog-sledding in Tarvisio

Cross-country ski or snow shoe in winter – or walk in summer – in the pristine countryside around Valbruna

Ascend to the spiritual heights of Monte Lussari by cable car

Scare yourself with the mummies in the Duomo, Venzone

Wander through the charming small town of Cividale del Friuli, with its 8th-century Tempietto Longobardo

Take a walk in the footsteps of Austrian poet Rainer Maria Rilke, along the cliffs at Duino

Spend a day exploring in Trieste's "museum quarter"

TRIP 10: MOUNTAINS AND LAKES

Above Early autumn colours of the lakeside woodlands around the Laghi di Fusine, see p108

PLAN YOUR DRIVE

Start/finish: Laghi di Fusine to Trieste.

Number of days: 5 days, including half a day for Udine; 1 day for touring the wine regions and a day in Trieste.

Distance: 270 km (168 miles).

Road conditions: The road to the Laghi di Fusine is easy to drive as most of the alpine routes are wide. Signage is good but scarce around Gorizia and on small vineyard roads. Snow chains are obligatory in winter.

When to go: The Alpi Giulie's autumn hues are glorious, while winter offers endless opportunities for skiing. Udine and the wine regions are best visited Apr–Nov. Maritime Trieste can be mild – but also windy – at any time of the year.

Opening times: Shops tend to open 9am–1pm and 4–7:30pm Mon–Sat (some food shops are shut Mon and Wed afternoon, all other shops are shut Mon morning). Church and museum hours vary, but are usually 9am–noon and 4–7 or 8pm. Many museums are closed on Monday.

Main market days: Tarvisio: Sat am; Udine: Via Zanon, daily; Via Redipuglia, Sat; Cividale del Friuli: Sat; Cormòns: Fri; Trieste: Tue–Sat.

Shopping: Look out for salt-cured, air-dried hams and salami throughout the region, and grappa and wines from the Collio and Colli Orientali.

Major festivals: Tarvisio: Krampus (St Nicholas Eve), Dec; Udine: Friuli DOC food and wine, Sep–Oct; Cividale: Palio di San Donato (medieval festival), late Aug; Trieste: Barcolana regatta, Oct; Palio di Trieste: Carnevale, late Jan–mid-Feb across Friuli.

DAY TRIP OPTIONS

From Tarvisio, take **cable cars** to hilltop **churches** and **walk** in the mountains. Explore ancient **castles** and **towns** rebuilt after earthquakes. See the **Roman ruins** in Aquiléia. Drive around the **vineyards** of the Collio, before visiting **lively** and **cultured** Trieste. For full details, see p113.

Above The picturesque hamlet of Valbruna, in the shadow of the Alpi Giulie

GETTING TO LAGHI DI FUSINE

From Tarvisio, take the SS54 east through Fusine in Valromana and then the small Via dei Laghi on the right about 3.5 km (2 miles) to the two lakes.

WHERE TO STAY

TARVISIO

Edelhof *moderate*
At the edge of a forest, this grand residence has 17 rooms and a restaurant.
Via Diaz 27/29, 33018; hoteledelhof.it

VALBRUNA

Valbruna Inn *moderate*
This cosy village inn has rooms that look from flower-decked balconies on to the Alpi Giulie.
Via Alpi Giulie 2, 33010; valbrunainn.com

MALBORGHETTO

Casa Oberrichter *inexpensive*
A hotel housed in a wood-beamed 15th-century palace with a restaurant.
Via Superiore 4, 33010; casa-oberrichter.com

AROUND UDINE

La Faula *moderate*
Set in idyllic countryside, this working farm offers nine characterful rooms.
Via Faula 5, Ravosa di Povoletto, 33040 Udine (A23 exit Udine Nord in direction of Tarvisio. From SS13 Pontebbana drive towards Povoletto-Cividale. At roundabout, turn right to Povoletto); faula.it

❶ Laghi di Fusine
Udine, Friuli-Venezia Giulia; 33018

The two lakes of Fusine, the Lago Inferiore and the Lago Superiore, occupy a glacial basin set amid dense forests of red fir trees, framed by curving hills and a crown of alpine summits. The colours of the mirror-like surfaces of the lakes vary, as the seasons and light change. And in autumn, the forests are ablaze with intense hues. Walk a circuit of the lakes on the Sentiero del Rio del Lago.

🚗 *Head north onto the SS54, and then turn left, following the sign to Tarvisio. Parking in Tarvisio can be tricky as it gets extremely busy – use on-street parking, which is best at the northern end of town.*

❷ Tarvisio
Udine, Friuli-Venezia Giulia; 33018

In the far northeast of Friuli-Venezia Giulia, where Italy, Slovenia and Austria meet, Tarvisio flies the flags of the three border communities. The town is charming and very alpine-oriented – the local hero is Julius Kugy, who climbed the Alpi Giulie (Julian Alps) in the early 1900s. Ski outlets, hotels and smart food shops line the main street.

Alpine sports such as skiing, snowboarding, dog-sledding and walking are the main attractions, so visit the Tourist Office *(Via Roma 14, 33018; 0428 2135; tarvisiano.org)* for information on these and other outdoor activities, including a programme of guided walks. Enjoy the village ambience and the daily market in Piazza Mercato.

🚗 *Take the SS13 in the direction of Udine, and turn left onto Via Saisera and follow signs for Valbruna.*

❸ Valbruna
Udine, Friuli-Venezia Giulia; 33010

This delightful alpine hamlet in the Val Canale opens on to a beautiful world of mountain meadows and forests – habitats for roe deer and a myriad of birds. Throughout the year, Valbruna is the place for nature lovers. A network of walking trails leads into the valley, to mountain peaks and to the **Santuario Monte Lussari**, located at an altitude of 1,790 m (5,872 ft) *(open Jun–early Sep: daily)*. The walk to the sanctuary takes about 3 hours; or you can take the cable car from neighbouring Camporosso. In winter, the plains of Valbruna transform into a fabulous cross-country ski domain right alongside the village, with a huge network of trails extending through the upper Val Saisera.

🚗 *Take Via Salsera to return back to the SS13 and turn left to Udine, then turn left to reach Malborghetto.*

❹ Malborghetto
Udine, Friuli-Venezia Giulia; 33010

The main street of Malborghetto is tucked along the edge of a valley that is skirted on both sides by a ridge of mountain peaks. A sign points out the village's two main historic sights – the 13th-century **Santa Maria della Visitazione** *(open Tue–Sun)* on the town hall square near the Municipio or town hall and, down the street, the

Above Hotels with geranium-festooned balconies near the centre of alpine Tarvisio

Above Fresco from the Duomo di Sant'Andrea Apostolo, Venzone

17th-century **Palazzo Veneziano**, which houses the **Museo Etnográfico** *(closed Mon)*, an ethnographic museum with displays on geology, prehistory, ethnology and forestry.
🚗 *Return to the SS13, following directions to Udine. After 43.5 km (27 miles) turn left signposted for Venzone. Park outside the walls or near Piazza Municipio.*

⑤ Venzone
Udine, Friuli-Venezia Giulia; 33010
The medieval town of Venzone prospered due to its position on an old trading route linking the Veneto to Carinthia (Austria), Kranjska Gora (Slovenia) and Bavaria. In 1976, an earthquake killed 3,000 people and destroyed most of the town's buildings. However, the citizens rallied and rebuilt them with care, skilfully renovating many medieval treasures – the town is now a historic monument. Admire the walls, tower and old gate, the **Porta San Genesio**, as well as the loggia on **Piazza Municipio**, whose excellent museum has pictures and displays of Venzone before and after the earthquake. The 14th-century **Duomo di Sant'Andrea Apostolo** *(open daily)* is a noteworthy Romanesque-Gothic edifice whose interior is adorned with frescoes. Also of interest is the Duomo's chapel, **Cappella di San Michele**, which contains mummified corpses. On the other side of the SS13, visit Bordano and its delightful **butterfly house** *(open Mar–Oct: daily)*, home to more than 400 species of butterfly.
🚗 *Continue south on SS13 to Udine.*

⑥ Udine
Friuli-Venezia Giulia; 33100
Midway between the mountains and sea, Udine is a small powerhouse of art, architecture and gastronomy. Start out from **Piazza della Libertà**, referred to as the most beautiful Venetian square on dry land – the city was conquered by Venice in 1420 – and ringed by fine 15th–17th-century buildings whose façades are an elaborate lacework of arches and porticoes. Among these are the Venetian-Gothic **Loggia del Lionello** and the Renaissance **Loggia di San Giovanni**. The **Torre dell'Orologio** (clock tower), where the main castle gate once stood, is part of another portico. From here, take the path to the old route, whose **Civici Musei di Udine** *(closed Mon)* houses valuable frescoes in the Galleria d'Arte Antica.
Piazza Matteotti, with its 1543 fountain, is the heart of the city's elegant café and shopping zone – reached by the old market street, Via Mercatovecchio. Lastly, pass in front of the Palazzo del Comune and head to the Piazza del Duomo to see the Latin cross-shaped **cathedral** *(open daily)*, whose foundations date to 1335. Masterful 18th-century frescoes by Tiepolo can be seen in the **Museo Diocesano** *(open daily)*, housed in the Palazzo Arcivescovile (Archbishop's Palace).
🚗 *Take the SS54 northeast following signs for Cividale del Friuli.*

Below Statue of Heracles in the beautiful Piazza della Libertà, Udine Below right The decorated window of a lavender shop in Venzone

EAT AND DRINK

TARVISIO

Tschurwald *moderate*
An interesting mix of Austrian and Italian food is on the menu here: homemade pasta, polenta with local cheese sauce and game dishes in season.
Via Roma 8, 33018; 0428 405 34; closed Thu

MALBORGHETTO

Locanda Aquila Nera *moderate*
This friendly, family-run restaurant specializes in local cuisine, including *cjalcons* (dumplings) and various types of gnocchi.
Via Bamberga 31, 33010; 0428 600 10

VENZONE

Locanda al Municipio *moderate*
This restaurant in the heart of Venzone is famous for its fish-based dishes and seasonal homemade pasta.
Via Glizoio di Mels, 33010; 340 587 5355; closed Mon

AROUND VENZONE

Hotel Ristorante Carnia *expensive*
This highly feted restaurant is bright and contemporary, with a menu based on seafood and classic Friulian dishes.
Via Canal del Ferro 28, 33010 Carnia (6 km/4 miles north of Venzone on SS13); hotelcarnia.it

UDINE

La Ciacarade *moderate*
This wood-beamed restaurant has a handful of tables plus a long bar. Enjoy smoked trout, cheese fritters with onion and *prosciutto cotto d'oca all'arancio* – orange-flavoured goose prosciutto.
Via S Francesco 6/A, 33100; 338 422 9658; closed Sun dinner

Above left River Natisone, Cividale del Friuli **Top right** Statues in the Tempietto Longobardo, Cividale del Friuli **Above right** Piazza Paolo Diacono, site of a market in Cividale del Friuli

WHERE TO STAY

CIVIDALE DEL FRIULI

B&B Dai Toscans *inexpensive*
This central B&B has a stylish interior and serves up a delicious breakfast.
Corso Giuseppe Mazzini 15/1, 33043; daitoscans.it

Locanda al Pomo d'Oro *inexpensive*
Located in the centre of town, this modest hotel still serves its original purpose of providing travellers with shelter, tasty food and good wine.
Piazza San Giovanni 20, 33043; alpomodoro.com

Locanda al Castello *moderate*
A 20-minute walk from the centre, this family-run inn offers old-fashioned charm with the amenities and services of a luxury hotel.
Via del Castello 12, 33043; alcastello.net

CORMÒNS

Agriturismo Domus Rustica *inexpensive*
Set in bucolic vineyards just 2 km (1 mile) outside Cormòns.
Via Sottomonte 75, 34071 Brazzano; 0481 602 88

Albergo Ristorante Felcaro *moderate*
A fine, antique-filled villa with a sauna, pool and tennis courts.
Via S Giovanni 45, 34071; hotelfelcaro.it

❼ Cividale del Friuli
Udine, Friuli-Venezia Giulia; 33043

Set on the banks of the River Natisone, Friuli traces its name and origin to a Roman fortification that was built here in 53 BCE and christened Forum Julii by Julius Caesar. In 568 CE, it became the capital of the feudal Duchy of Lombard and later, like much of this region, fell under the dominion of the mighty Venetian Republic. The town contains treasures from all of these epochs concentrated around its historic centre and the eclectic 15th–17th-century cathedral, **Santa Maria Assunta**, in the Piazza del Duomo. Take the cobbled lane through the oldest section of town, past 14th-century houses, to the 8th-century frescoes and reliefs at the **Tempietto Longobardo**. From the chapel, there are wonderful views of the Ponte del Diavolo and the aquamarine River Natisone. Nearby, the 16th-century Palazzo dei Provveditori Veneti attributed to the master architect Andrea Palladio houses the **Museo Archeologico Nazionale** *(closed Mon)*. From the museum, take the main street, Corso Mazzini, up to the Piazza Paolo Diacono with its pretty fountain and a myriad architectural styles.

🚗 *Take the SR356 south, follow the signposts for Prepotto, travelling on SP53 and SP48.*

❽ Colli Orientali
Friuli-Venezia Giulia

It is worth taking some time to explore this lovely, hilly vineyard area between Cividale del Friuli and Cormòns. Several Indigenous grape varieties – rarely found elsewhere – are grown here. Look out for the perfumed red Schioppettino and delicately sweet Picolit, which can yield a dessert wine of great finesse. At Prepotto, there are two vineyards that offer a taste of these exceptional wines – **Vigna Petrussa** (*Via Albana 47, 33040 Prepotto; 043 271 3021; vigna petrussa.it*) and **Le Due Terre** (*Via Roma 68/B, 33040 Prepotto; 043 271 3189; schioppettinodiprepotto.it*).

🚗 *Continue on the small wine road via Dolegna del Collio, Venco and Brazzano to reach Cormòns.*

❾ Cormòns
Gorizia, Friuli-Venezia Giulia; 34071

Cormòns was part of the Habsburg Empire from 1497 to 1918, and its architecture and statue of Maximilian I in Piazza della Libertà are testimony to its historical inheritance. The town still toasts the Austrian Emperor Franz Joseph (1830–1916) on his birthday (Aug 18). The ruins of the Castello di Cormòns can be seen on the slopes of nearby Monte Quarin.
Today this small town, surrounded by vineyards, is the capital of the Collio wine business. The **Franco Toros** (*Loc. Novali 12, 34071; 0481 613 27; vinitoros.com*) is a must-visit for wine lovers. Cormòn's long main street, lined with palaces and noble residences, loops around from the Piazza XXIV Maggio, home to the **Palazzo Locatelli**. This Palladian-style edifice houses an *enoteca* (wine shop), which showcases and serves local produce and wines. Maps of wine routes are available here.

🚗 *Take Via Roma/SR409, turn right towards San Floriano in Localitá Zegla.*

❿ Collio: Strada del Vino
Gorizia, Friuli-Venezia Giulia; 34170

Collio is the colloquial name given to the sloping Isonzo hills to the north of Gorizia. Wedged between Cormòns and the Slovenian border, this narrow strip of land is a pleasant patchwork of vineyards, orchards and, more recently, olive groves. Follow the network of tiny roads forming the signposted

Strada del Vino e delle Ciliegie (Wine and Cherry Route). Between the mountains and sea, the microclimate and "ponka" soils (marl, clay-limestone) help create many celebrated DOC white wines – Pinot Grigio, Friulano, Ribolla Gialla and Malvasia Istriana. Maps, available by the roadside on the way out of town and in tourist brochures, mark out the wineries with tasting rooms. Pay close attention to the maps and signposts, as a wrong turn could lead to Slovenia.

Follow signs to Russiz – where the vineyards are spread across the hillsides. The splendid estate of **Villa Russiz** *(Via Russiz 4–6, 34070 Capriva del Friuli; 0481 800 47; open daily)*, founded in 1869 by French Count Theodore de la Tour, was one of the first wineries in Friuli to use French vine varieties. The villa has tasting rooms, a park, a chapel and a small mausoleum whose tiled cupola perches above rows of vines. The count's wife had the mausoleum built for him in 1894.

From Russiz, continue towards Capriva del Friuli, stopping at **Castello di Spessa** *(open daily)*. This medieval castle was altered in the 1880s and is now the centrepiece of a huge complex containing a winery, a golf course and a hotel.

🚗 *From Zegla, turn right towards Capriva del Friuli, cross Capriva's centre, turn right and after the railway station turn left onto SR56 to Gorizia.*

⑪ Gorizia
Friuli-Venezia Giulia; 34170

The 11th-century **Castello di Gorizia** *(closed Mon & Tue)* hilltop district is an enclave of medieval architecture: the castle has glorious views. The nearby quarter of Santo Spirito is home to the Gothic **Chiesa di Santo Spirito** and the **Musei Provinciali** *(closed Mon)*, which houses displays on World War I and regional history. In the mesh of medieval, Baroque and 19th-century architecture in the town below, there are walkways along the River Isonzo and villas such as the **Palazzo Coronini-Cronberg** *(closed summer: Mon & Tue)*, which is set in magnificent parklands.

🚗 *Take the SR351 to Gradisca d'Isonzo and continue to Cervignano del Friuli. From here, take the SR352 to Aquileia.*

Top Hillside vineyards along the wooded Strada del Vino **Below left** The main square in Cormòns **Below right** The 11th-century Castello di Gorizia

EAT AND DRINK

CIVIDALE DEL FRIULI

Al Monastero *moderate*
Set in an old monastery, this restaurant offers classic Friulian dishes, including top-quality hams and salamis and a good choice of homemade pasta and meat dishes. Desserts include *strucchi* (fruit- and nut-filled pastries).
Via Ristori 9, 33043; almonastero.com; closed Sun eve & Mon

Osteria Trattoria Alla Speranza *expensive*
This historic bar and *osteria* serves traditional fish dishes with a modern twist. The blackboard menu is complemented by a good wine list.
Piazza Foro Giulio Cesare 15, 33043; 0432 731 131; closed Mon

AROUND COLLI ORIENTALLE

Al Cjant dal Rusignul *expensive*
This attractive country restaurant is renowned for its homemade pasta, mushroom and game. Good wine list.
Via Mernico 2, 34070 Mernico-Dolegna del Collio (just east of Prepotto); ferrucciosgubin.it; closed Mon–Wed

CORMÒNS

Trattoria Al Cacciatore *expensive*
A local landmark, this upmarket restaurant prepares traditional dishes with great finesse using the best local ingredients.
Via Subida 52, 34701; lasubida.it; closed Tue & Wed

AROUND CORMÒNS

Al Giardinetto *moderate*
In a friendly atmosphere, try regional dishes such as goulash and sweet gnocchi with a plum sauce.
Via Matteotti 54, 34071 Cormons; 0481 60 257; closed Mon & Tue

VISITING TRIESTE

Parking
Narrow streets and a one-way system make driving in Trieste difficult. There are few car parks, although many hotels have undercover parking (at extra cost). Park in the car park on Riva Nazario Sauro or on-street in the residential area between the historic centre and the cathedral/castello. Check that it is not a tow-away zone. There is a big paid parking area in Molo IV and one near the station.

Tourist information
Via dell'Orologio 1, angolo Piazza dell'Unità; 0403 478 312; turismofvg.it

WHERE TO STAY

TRIESTE
Hotel Albero Nascosto *moderate*
This small, charming hotel is part of a project for the restoration of the historic centre of Trieste. It has been beautifully renovated using the best quality materials and crafters.
Via Felice Venezian 18, 34124; alberonascosto.it

Hotel Miramare *moderate*
Near the Castello di Miramare, this adults-only hotel is modernist and minimalist. Rooms have sea-facing terraces and high-tech facilities. There is also a beach bar and restaurant.
Viale Miramare 325/4, 34136; hotelmiramaretrieste.it; closed mid-Nov–mid-Mar

⑫ Aquileia
Friuli-Venezia Giulia; 33051

Founded as a Roman colony in 181 BCE, Aquileia was the Roman capital of Friuli and is now northern Italy's most important archaeological site. The attractive ruins include Roman houses, a forum and an impressive ruined harbour. What was once a great town with a population of 200,000 is now home to a mere 3,500 people who live by tending their vineyards or catering to the tourists who come to marvel at the mosaics. The best of these are in the **basilica**, whose extraordinary floor mosaic of 700 sq m (837 sq yards) is the largest early Christian mosaic in the West. Take a circular walk on the Via Sacra to visit the excavations and the **Museo Archeologico Nazionale** *(closed Mon; museoarcheologicoaquileia.beni culturali.it)*, a treasure trove of Roman artifacts, bas-reliefs and sculpture.

🚗 *Take the SR352 south to Grado, then the SP19 towards Monfalcone. In Monfalcone, take the SS14 to Duino.*

⑭ TRIESTE
Trieste, Friuli-Venezia Giulia; 34100

Once the third city of the Austrian-Habsburg Empire, after Vienna and Prague, Trieste is now a cluster of Roman, eclectic-style, Art Nouveau and Neo-Gothic architecture. From the bay and waterfront promenades to the top of San Giusto hill, Trieste retains an international atmosphere among the salty breezes washing in from the Adriatic.

⑬ Duino
Trieste, Friuli-Venezia Giulia; 34100

The star attraction here is the **Castello di Duino** *(open daily, winter: Sat & Sun; castellodiduino.it)*, which has played host to many illustrious guests in its time, notably the Austrian poet Rainer Maria Rilke (1875–1926). Do not miss the glorious gardens and the bunker constructed in 1943. To complete the visit, take the panoramic 2-km (1-mile) long Rilke walk along the clifftops.

🚗 *Take the coastal SS14 to Trieste.*

A two-hour walking tour
From the car park, head up Riva 3 Novembre towards **Piazza dell'Unità dell'Italia** ①. The grand sweep of façades includes the 1870 Palazzo Comunale, Palazzo del Governo, Palazzo del Lloyd Triestino – the shipping company's headquarters – and Casa Stratti, home to Caffè degli Specchi, an 1839 coffee house.

Visit the Tourist Information Office for maps, before heading northeast, through the small Piazza Verdi to the bottom of Corso Italia, the main road referred to locally as "Corso". Cross over and take the small Via Cassa di Risparmio to Via G Mazzini. Turn left and rejoin the waterfront avenue Riva 3 Novembre: on the corner is the Neo-Classical **Chiesa Greco-Ortodossa di San Nicolò** ②. Continue along to the picturesque, warehouse-lined strip of

Far left The clifftop Castello di Duino **Above centre** The 18th-century Canal Grande in Trieste **Above right** Caffè degli Specchi in Trieste's Piazza dell'Unità dell'Italia

the **Canal Grande** ③: dug in 1756 to allow ships to unload inside the city. The canalside **Via Rossini** ④ is lined with restaurants, bars and markets, leading to Piazza Ponterosso. James Joyce's statue adorns the bridge. The Irish writer lived in Trieste for over a decade. Cross the bridge to the Piazza Ponterosso and head for the church, the **Chiesa di San Spiridione** ⑤, a Neo-Byzantine Serbian Orthodox church. Take Via Dante Alighieri back to the Corso Italia, and cross over to the gaping pit of the **Teatro Romano** ⑥, a Roman amphitheatre built by Emperor Augustus around 30 BCE.

The steps alongside the Teatro lead to the **Tor Cucherna** ⑦, the ruins of a medieval tower, with fantastic views from the street above. From here, take the Treppe Giuseppe Rota stairway for the final climb up to the hilltop of San Giusto. Named after one of the city's patron saints, this area has Roman relics, medieval churches, public gardens and viewpoints. The piazza around the **Monumento ai Caduti** ⑧, a World War I memorial, is a popular romantic spot with terrific views. Carry on through the colon-naded **Foro Romano** ⑨ and on to the 14th–16th-century **Castello di San Giusto** ⑩ (open daily). Across Piazza delle Cattedrale stands the Gothic stone lacework and trilobite arches of the **Cattedrale di San Giusto** ⑪, a fusion of two 15th-century churches – hence its asymmetrical façade. Look to the right of the rose window for two huge cannonballs wedged into the wall. Head downhill on Via della Cattedrale into suitably windy Via della Bora (Northeast Wind Street) and on to the **Arco di Riccardo** ⑫, a crumbling Roman gateway from the 1st century BCE. Turn right and trace the walls of the Chiesa Santa Maria Maggiore perched on a ledge over the old town – alongside the small **Basilica di San Silvestro** ⑬. A wide stairway leads down to the Via del Teatro Romano. Cross the street and head back to Piazza dell'Unità past the pretty square of Piazza Piccola. Museum lovers may wish to see the unofficial museum quarter – near Piazza Hortis – with three museums (closed Mon): the Civico Museo di Storia ed Arte e Orto Lapidario (archaeology), the Civico Museo di Storia Naturale (natural history) and the Civico Museo Sartorio (art and culture). Return to the car park via Via F Venezian.

EAT AND DRINK

AQUILEIA

La Capannina *moderate*
This restaurant specializes in seafood dishes, in a setting next to Roman ruins.
Via Gemina 10, 33051 Aquileia; 0431 91 019; closed winter: Wed

DUINO

Sardoc *moderate*
Robust cuisine such as *jota* (a thick cabbage, beans and potato soup), followed by veal shanks and strudel.
Fraz. Precenico 1/B, 34013 Duino-Aurisina; sardoc.eu; closed Mon & Tue

TRIESTE

Bracerie Venete *moderate*
This steakhouse offers a unique take on traditional dishes.
Via della Madonnina 5, 34131; bracerievenete.com; closed Sun

Osteria da Marino *moderate*
This tavern serves Mediterranean staples such as mozzarella with tomatoes and Ligurian olives.
Via del Ponte 5, 34100; osteriadamarino.com

DAY TRIP OPTIONS

The incredibly varied landscape gives a choice of three enjoyable day trips.

Alpine village tour
From Tarvisio ②, walk a loop of the Laghi di Fusine ①, then on to Valbruna ③, stopping to take the cable car from Camporosso to Monte Lussari, and finish in Malborghetto ④.

Take SS54 east to reach the lakes, then SS13 west to the other alpine villages.

Archaeological sites
See the beautiful piazza and frescoes of Udine ⑥, then drive to Aquileia ⑫ to see its fantastic Roman remains and enjoy a delicious lunch. Finish the day at the architectural jewel of Trieste ⑭.

Take SS352 from Udine to Aquileia. Continue on SS352, left onto SS14 all the way along the coast to Trieste.

Vineyards to the coast
From Gorizia ⑪, visit Russiz and Collio ⑩ winding through vineyards and stopping for a tasting on the way to Cormòns ⑨. Then its off to Trieste ⑭ and the coast for an afternoon walk around the city and perhaps an evening's entertainment.

Roads in the wine area are narrow and winding: use the SS55, then the A4 (E70) to Trieste to save a little time.

TRIP 11

THE VENETO PLAIN
Verona to Venice

HIGHLIGHTS

Romantic Renaissance city
Soak up the atmosphere in beautiful Verona, the setting for Shakespeare's tale of hapless love, *Romeo and Juliet*

A Baroque garden masterpiece
Wander around Valsanzibio's strictly ordered hedges, lawns and paths, virtually unchanged since the 1670s and set in idyllic countryside

An ancient city, full of young life
Visit Padua's Basilica di Sant'Antonio, the university where Galileo taught and a medieval marketplace – all infused with the buzz of student life

Timeless city of bridges
Explore magical, waterborne Venice, where the grand palaces, churches, museums and squares are joined by a labyrinth of alleyways and canals

THE VENETO PLAIN

The great Veneto plain is dotted with some of Italy's most magnificent cities and impressive fortified medieval towns, filled with priceless artworks and architecture. These cultural treasures are further enhanced by their exquisite natural setting among the rolling Euganean Hills, the lush Riviera del Brenta and the Venetian Lagoon. Meandering roads lead to rustic-style restaurants and spa resorts that have been popular since Roman times. Padua's world-class art and serene churches and gardens bustle with youthful excitement, thanks to its student population. The winding Riviera del Brenta is a natural and architectural delight, famous for its Palladian villas – country homes for the Venetian nobility. The trip's conclusion is magical Venice, its Grand Canal lined with palaces. Although it's busy with visitors year round, it is simply unmissable.

ACTIVITIES

Experience the thrill of live opera in Verona in the wonderful Roman arena (arena.it)

Ramble or ride on the pathways and cycle tracks in the lovely Euganean Hills

Find peace and spiritual calm during an overnight stay at the Abbazia di Praglia

Take a leisurely boat trip on the Riviera del Brenta and admire its architectural wonders (ilburchiello.it)

Go island hopping in Venice's lagoon

Left Cyclists negotiating the winding streets of Arquà Petrarca, see p119

TRIP 11: THE VENETO PLAIN 117

Above Driving through the Euganean Hills, see p118

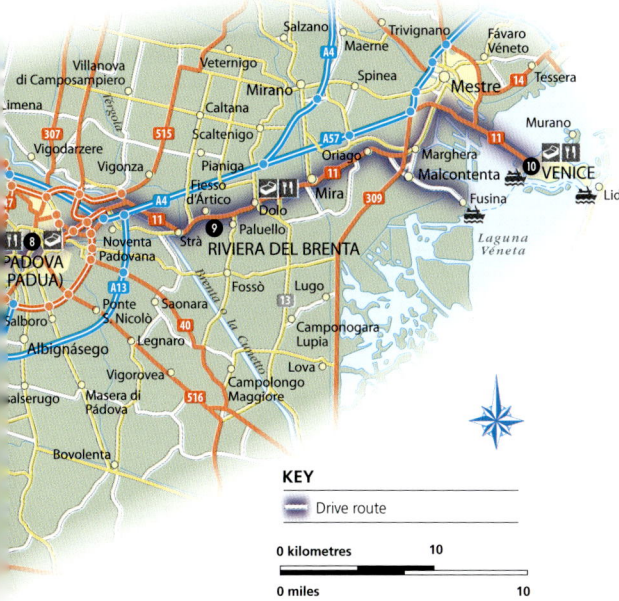

KEY
— Drive route

Above View across Prato della Valle in Padua, see p119

PLAN YOUR DRIVE

Start/finish: Verona to Venice.

Number of days: 4, allowing a full day for the Euganean Hills, half days for the smaller towns and a full day for Venice.

Distance: Approx. 153 km (95 miles).

Road conditions: A mix of hilly and flat roads makes for easy-to-medium drives.

When to go: Visits are feasible year round, though spring (Mar–May) and autumn (Sep–Oct) are best for more pleasant temperatures. The foothills and plain can get hot during Jul–Aug, while fog is not uncommon in winter.

Opening times: Shops tend to open 9am–1pm and 3–7pm Mon–Sat. Villa opening hours differ; some are closed on Mondays and the gardens usually close early in winter.

Main market days: Montagnana: Thu; **Este:** Sat; **Padua:** Mon–Sat; Venice: Mon–Sat.

Shopping: Look out for ceramics in Este, local delicacies (wine, honey or *giuggiole* – the jujube fruit) in the Euganean Hills and handicrafts (glass, paper, jewellery) in Venice.

Major festivals: Verona: opera season Jun–Aug (arena.it); Montagnana: antiques market, every 3rd Sun Sep–June; Palio dei 10 Comuni (medieval horse race and pageantry festival), Aug–Sep (palio10comuni.it); **Venice:** Carnival, Feb–Mar; Film Festival, Aug–Sep; Regata Storica, 1st Sun in Sep; Biennale Art, Apr–Nov bi-annually (labiennale.org).

DAY TRIP OPTIONS

Those with an interest in the performing arts will love a day in **Verona** with Juliet's **famous balcony** and an amphitheatre, home to **open-air opera**. Magical **Venice** rewards lovers of art – modern as well as classical – with a wealth of **museums**, **galleries** and **churches** full of priceless works. A foray into the Euganean Hills will delight lovers of **rural landscapes**, **elegant gardens** and **pretty abbeys**. For full details, see p121.

Above left The Castello di San Pietro, on a hill above Verona Above centre Giardini Dell' Arena, in the heart of Padua Above right Padua's 13th-century Basilica di Sant'Antonio

VISITING VERONA

Visitor Information
Via Leoncino 61, 37100; 045 806 8680; turismo.comune.verona.it

WHERE TO STAY

VERONA

Hotel Torcolo *inexpensive*
This charming, family-run place is in a quiet street, but close to the arena.
Vicolo Listone 3, 37121; hoteltorcolo.it

Hotel Aurora *moderate*
This hotel has a lovely roof terrace overlooking the central square.
Piazzetta XIV Novembre 2, 37121; hotelaurora.biz

MONTAGNANA

Hotel Aldo Moro *moderate*
This hotel provides top service, spacious rooms and a good breakfast.
Via G Marconi 27, 35044; hotelaldomoro.com; closed 2 wks Jan & 1–20 Aug

ESTE

Agriturismo Barchessa *inexpensive*
Four self-catering apartments make up this 18th-century villa.
Via Cappuccini 5, 35042; agriturismobarchessa.com

ARQUÀ PETRARCA

Alloggio Franciscus Agriturismo *inexpensive*
These are country-style rooms in restructured farm buildings.
Via Vallesselle 20, 35032; alloggiofranciscus.it

PADUA

Albergo Verdi *moderate*
A central hotel with bright rooms.
Via Dondi dell'Orologio 7, 35139; albergoverdipadova.it

❶ Verona
Veneto; 37100
Top of most visitors' list is the shrine **Juliet's House** (*Casa di Giulietta, Via Cappello 23*), the so-called home of the tragic heroine of Shakespeare's drama. Close by is the **Roman arena**, where crowds once gathered to watch gladiator action and, today, enjoy open-air opera. Over the river are the Renaissance **Giardino Giusti** (1580), and the **Museo di Storia Naturale** (*closed Mon*), with displays of fossilized crocodiles and palm trees. Climb up to **Castello di San Pietro** for glorious views of the city. West of the centre, **San Zeno Maggiore** (1138) is a superb example of Romanesque architecture.

🚗 *Leave on SR11 east (signed Venezia) across river Adige. At San Bonifacio, turn right to SP7 signposted for Arcole, Cologna Veneta and onto Montagnana. Follow signs to "stazione" and car park.*

❷ Montagnana
Veneto; 35044
Before entering the town, wander along the grassy moat to admire the sturdy, redbrick castellated walls and 24 defensive towers erected by the town's rulers between the 14th and 18th centuries. All four massive gateways lead to the main square and 15th-century **Duomo**, which holds works by Renaissance masters Paolo Veronese and Giorgione. Be sure to try the local prosciutto and, perhaps, the *stracotto d'asino* (donkey stew).

🚗 *From the car park, turn right along the walls. Around the corner, turn right at the traffic lights on the SR10 (towards Padua). At a medieval tower on the right, turn left into Via Augustea. At the crossroads, turn right into Via Schiavin to car park No.3 (Castello), in Via Vigo di Torre, just past the Tourist Office.*

❸ Este
Veneto; 35042
Once the capital of the pre-Roman Veneti, Este was absorbed into the Roman Empire before being razed to the ground by Attila the Hun. The town rose again under local nobility, the Signori d'Este, who constructed its imposing **castle** (*closed Tue*). In 1405 it came under the protection of the Venetians. The **Museo Nazionale Atestino** (*closed Mon*) has evidence of this turbulent history. Este also has a tradition of fine porcelain, especially good-quality, hand-decorated pieces.

🚗 *Carry on along the walls to a roundabout and take 2nd right onto SP6. Follow signs for Baone, then SP21 into the Euganean Hills.*

Statue at the Casa di Giulietta, Verona

❹ Euganean Hills
Veneto
The Colli Euganei is an area of beautiful rolling hills cloaked in woods full of wild boar and deer. The volcanic origins of these hills means fertile soil for crops and vines, and quarries that yielded the trachyte used for paving the streets of Venice. Wildflowers abound and there are special pockets, such as Monte Ceva, where mini prickly pears grow. Rewarding walks abound (for maps of routes – in Italian – visit parcocollieuganei.com). At the foot of the hills are spa resorts such as Abano and Montegrotto Terme.

🚗 Once in the hills, follow one of many signs to Arquà Petrarca along winding roads. Follow sign for "Arquà Alta: centro storico" up the hill to the car park.

⑤ Arquà Petrarca
Veneto; 35032
This utterly charming town – with steepish, paved streets leading past Venetian-Gothic stone palaces – is named after the medieval Italian poet Petrarch, who spent his final years here. Visit his lovely house, **Casa di Petrarca** *(closed Mon)*, which has his mummified pet cat on display. Shops sell *giuggiole* (the jujube fruit) steeped in liqueur as well as local wines.

🚗 Head in the direction of Padua on the SP16 and, 2 km (1 mile) on, branch left onto the SP25 for Valsanzibio. Park outside the villa's entrance.

⑥ Valsanzibio
Veneto; 35030
Spend an afternoon exploring these exquisite Baroque gardens *(open Mar–Nov; valsanzibiogiardino.com)* created in 1669 for the Venetian noble Zuane Francesco Barbarigo on shady terraces that appear to grow out of the hillside. Fountain after fountain is draped with Classical allegorical statues, and water games amuse young and old alike, as does a maze of box shrubs. The house, **Villa Barbarigo**, is of a simple design compared to the gardens.

🚗 Continue north on SP25 to Galzignano Terme. Turn left at a T-junction and left again onto SP99, then right for the winding ascent of Monte Venda, the highest Euganean Hill. Then carry on the descent into Torreglia, head left (towards Padua), turn left to Tealo, and follow signs for Praglia.

⑦ Abbazia di Praglia
Teolo, Veneto; 35037
This pretty Benedictine **abbey** *(closed Mon; praglia.it)*, set in gorgeous countryside, was founded in the 11th century and renovated in the 15th and 16th centuries. A monk-led tour reveals how the brothers restore ancient books and grow herbal products for sale along with cosmetics and honey. It is possible to stay here overnight.

🚗 Drive north to SP89, turn right to join SS250. Through Tencarola, head into Padua (around SR47), right on Via Castelfidardo, then right on Via Cernia, and left to park at Prato della Valle.

⑧ Padua (Padova)
Veneto; 35100
There's plenty to see here, from the **Prato della Valle** – Italy's largest square – to the country's second-oldest university, the **Palazzo del Bo**, founded in 1222 and visited on a fascinating guided tour *(daily)* that takes in Galileo's rostrum and a 16th-century anatomy theatre. A short stroll away is **Piazza delle Erbe**, where a market *(Mon–Sat)* is held. Nearby, too, is the **Duomo**, partly built to a plan by Michelangelo, and frescoed **baptistry**. Don't miss the gardens of the **Orto Botanico** *(closes winter 5pm)*, close to the **Basilica di Sant'Antonio**, a major destination for pilgrims. Padua's major art attraction is the **Cappella degli Scrovegni** *(cappella degliscrovegni.it; advance booking essential)*, with Giotto's lyrical 14th-century frescoes of Bible stories – a masterpiece of Western art.

🚗 Backtrack a little and follow signs to the "tangenziale" northeast. After the IKEA exit, follow signs for Venezia and SR11, turn left and follow signs to Stra.

Above Cappella degli Scrovegni, Padua, Giotto's masterpiece **Below left** Prato della Valle, Padua, Italy's largest square **Below right** The thickly wooded Euganean Hills

VISITING PADUA

Tourist Information
Galleria Pedrocchi, 35100; turismopadova.it

EAT AND DRINK

VERONA

Antica Bottega del Vino *expensive*
Try the *risotto all'Amarone*, a rice dish with the robust local Amarone wine.
Via Scudo di Francia 3, 37121; bottegavini.it

MONTAGNANA

Il Ristorante Aldo Moro *expensive*
Here, mouthwatering dishes include *tortellini con zucca* (pumpkin-filled pasta) and *oca al forno* (baked goose).
Via G Marconi 27, 35044; ristorantealdomoro.com; closed Mon

TEOLO

Trattoria le Banchine *moderate*
Enjoy homemade ravioli and delicious regional specialities in a beautiful countryside setting.
Via Costanzo 7, 35037; lebanchine.it; closed Mon & Tue

ARQUÀ PETRARCA

La Montanella *moderate*
Try the *risotto alla quaglia* (quail) and *papera alla frutta* (duck baked with fruits) followed by dessert.
Via dei Carraresi 9, 35032; montanella.it; closed Mon–Wed

PADUA

Ristorante Antico Brolo *moderate*
The signature food here is *Fantasia di baccalà*, a special salt cod dish.
Corso Milano 22, 35139; anticobrolo.it; closed Thu lunch

Above Grand Canal and the Church of Santa Maria della Salute, Venice

VISITING VENICE

For information on getting to and around Venice, see hellovenezia.it. It is possible to tour the other islands in the lagoon, such as Murano, Burano and Torcello, by waterbus.

Tourist Information
Giardini ex Reali, San Marco; veneziaunica.it

SHOPPING IN VENICE

For handmade paper, visit Rivoaltus *(Ponte di Rialto, 11 San Polo, 30125)* or pick up Venetian velvet slippers at Pied à Terre *(Sottoportego di Rialto, San Polo 60, 30125; it.piedaterre venezia.com).* For a unique African slant on Murano beads, visit Collection Muranero by Niang Moulaye *(Salizada del Pignater 3545, 30122 Castello).*

WHERE TO STAY

RIVIERA DEL BRENTA

Hotel Villa Ducale *inexpensive*
Enjoy the waterside elegance at this villa, set in gardens just beyond Dolo.
Riviera Martiri della Libertà 75, 30031 Dolo; villaducale.it

VENICE

Fujiyama B&B *moderate*
Find minimalist calm in this small but central hotel above an Asian tea house.
Calle Lunga San Barnaba 2727A, 310123 Dorsoduro; fujiyamavenice.it

Palazzina Grassi *expensive*
Relax in the luxury of a Venetian palazzo set on the glorious Grand Canal.
Ramo Grassi 3247, San Marco; palazzinagrassi.com

⑨ Riviera del Brenta
Veneto; 30039

The Brenta canal is lined with a number of splendid, elegant villas in Neo-Classical and Renaissance styles. Owned by Venetian nobility from the 1300s, they are a window into a long-vanished lifestyle. Just across the River Brenta, off the main road (SR11) and set in lush parkland, the grandest is the magnificently porticoed **Villa Pisani** *(Via Doge Pisani 7; 049 502 074; closed Mon; villapisani.beniculturali. it),* which has a wonderful maze, and frescoes by Tiepolo. Just before the Marghera industrial build-up, fork right across the canal for Malcontenta (the villa's nickname), then follow signs to **Villa Foscari**, designed by Andrea Palladio in 1555 *(041 5470 012; open Apr–Oct: Tue–Sun; lamalcontenta.com).* For more villas, see turismovenezia.it.

🚗 *From Villa Foscari, follow the river southeast to Fusina. Park and catch the ferry to Venice. Or, return to SR11 and pass through Marghera, then cross the causeway to Venice. Park at Tronchetto (to the right) or Piazzale Roma (straight on). Take a* vaporetto *into the city.*

⑩ Venice
Veneto; 30100

A whole city floating on a lagoon, Venice is a magical combination of grand palazzos, magnificent churches and ordinary houses amid a network of age-old alleyways and canals. Museums and art galleries attest to the city's glorious past, when it was a wealthy superpower. A stroll through some of the quieter *sestieri* (districts) is the best way to gauge the pulse of this unique city.

A four-hour walking tour

From Tronchetto or Piazzale Roma, catch a *vaporetto* (waterbus) down the Grand Canal and alight at **Rialto Mercato** ①, the commercial heart of the city since medieval times, with pioneer private banks such as the Bancogiro, dating back to 1157. It is now a wine bar with a great canalside terrace. Nowadays, Rialto is the site of a lively market *(open 7:30am–1pm Mon–Sat).* Close by is the most famous of the city's 350 bridges, the 16th-century **Ponte di Rialto** ②. Spanning the Grand Canal at its narrowest point, the bridge is lined with craft shops and jewellers.

Take the canalside walkway **Riva del Vin** ③, where wine was once unloaded. This is a perfect place to enjoy the bustling activity on the Grand Canal – Venice's 3.5-km (2-mile) principal artery for goods, gondolas and all. Turn right into

Above left The Danieli Palace, one of Europe's most famous hotels *Above centre* Gondolas on Venice's Grand Canal *Above right* One of the arcades around Piazza San Marco, Venice

Rio Terà San Silvestro. This is San Polo, Venice's smallest district, crammed with craft ateliers and shops, jewellers and glassmakers. Following signs for Ferrovia, turn left through Campo San Aponal and onto **Campo San Polo** ④. This spacious square once hosted bullfights, but is now a favourite with local kids, who zoom about on their bikes. During Venice's prestigious Film Festival, it is transformed into a huge open-air cinema.

Pass the church and cross Ponte San Polo to wind through the maze of alleys from Campo San Tomà to **Campo dei Frari** ⑤. This square is mostly taken up by the towering brick Basilica di Santa Maria Gloriosa dei Frari, the final resting place of the Renaissance composer Claudio Monteverdi. Keep left to Sotoportego San Rocco and over **Rio de la Frescada** ⑥ into Dorsoduro. Turn left along Crosera San Pantalon, then right, to cross the bridge to **Palazzo Foscari** ⑦, possibly the birthplace of the great Doge Francesco Foscari (r.1423–57). Continue through the peaceful square **Campiello dei Squelini** ⑧ to Ca' Rezzonico, a Gothic palace with the **Museo del Settecento Veneziano** ⑨

(closed Tue). Cross Ponte San Barnaba and the eponymous square, and take Calle della Toletta to the **Gallerie dell'Accademia** ⑩ *(closed Mon pm)* in Campo della Carità. This former Palladian convent holds a priceless collection of 15th–18th century paintings by Titian, Carpaccio, Giorgione and Bellini. Italy's leading gallery of early 20th-century art is nearby, after San Vio – the **Peggy Guggenheim Collection** ⑪ *(closed Tue)*. Peggy's former home, the Palazzo Venier dei Leoni, houses key works by Giacometti, Picasso and Pollock, as well as a sculpture garden and terrace on the Grand Canal. From here, it is a short walk via Campo della Salute to the old customs warehouse, renovated by Japanese architect Tadao Ando into the gleaming **Punta della Dogana** ⑫ *(closed Tue)*. It now features contemporary works from the collection of François Pinault. Take the *vaporetto* from La Salute across to Venice's famed **Piazza San Marco** ⑬ and Doges' Palace. If time allows, head out to the lagoon's islands of Murano, Burano or Torcello by *vaporetto*, otherwise return to Piazzale Roma or Tronchetto.

EAT AND DRINK

RIVIERA DEL BRENTA

Bacaro dei Storti *moderate*
This lovely restaurant specializes in fish dishes. Great wine pairings and beer selection.
Via Giuseppe Mazzini 13, 30031 Dolo; 0415 640 298

Osteria da Caronte *moderate*
Enjoy traditional cuisine with a refined touch at this riverside restaurant.
Via Dolo 29, Paluello di Stra, 30030 Dolo; osteriadacaronte.it; closed Tue eve & Wed

VENICE

Bar alla Toletta *inexpensive*
A humble snack bar frequented by locals. Try the traditional Venetian *tramezzino* (sandwiches) here.
1191 Dorsoduro, 30123; 0415 200 196

Osteria L'Orto dei Mori *expensive*
An inventive Sicilian chef provides an innovative take on local dishes.
Campo dei Mori 3386, 30121 Cannaregio; osteriaortodeimori.com; closed Tue & Wed

DAY TRIP OPTIONS

Verona and Venice deserve at least a day's exploration, and the pretty Euganean Hills merit a day trip, too.

Performing arts in Verona

In Verona ①, start at Piazza dei Signori and Dante's statue. Head to nearby Juliet's House and then cross the River Adige to the Teatro Romano – where the Bard's plays are still performed. Walk along the river to the Ponte Scaligero footbridge. Cross back over and carry on to the Roman arena, now a venue for open-air opera.

Venice's canalside treasures

Take a *vaporetto* down Venice's ⑩ Grand Canal to the Punta dell Dogana, then walk to the Peggy Guggenheim Collection for modern art, before admiring the medieval works in the Gallerie dell'Accademia. Lunch in a backstreet *osteria*, then wander slowly to the Ponte di Rialto. Cross over and walk to Piazza San Marco to see the Basilica and Doges' Palace. Hop on a *vaporetto* to get back to the car park.

Green delights

From Este ③, drive into the Euganean Hills ④, through the vineyards, up to pretty Arquà Petrarca ⑤. Move on to Valsanzibio ⑥ and its Baroque garden. Lunch around Monte Venda, then on to Abbazia di Praglia ⑦.

Follow the drive's instructions to the Abbey, then return via SP89 and SP247.

TRIP 12

DOLOMITES TO VENETO HILLS
Cortina d'Ampezzo to Treviso

HIGHLIGHTS

Alpine wonders
Explore the magnificent Dolomites, which crown the fashionable resort of Cortina d'Ampezzo

Renaissance towns of the foothills
Visit superb Renaissance Feltre, utterly charming Asolo and laid-back Bassano del Grappa, set among rolling hills

Scenic war memorial
Ascend to the sombre memorial at Monte Grappa – a key battleground of World War I in a spectacular setting

Gourmet food
From Treviso's radicchio and tiramisù to Monte Grappa's fiery spirit and asparagus, enjoy treats galore

Mountains overlooking a charming resort in Cortina d'Ampezzo

DOLOMITES TO VENETO HILLS

Rising to breathtaking heights in the far north of the Veneto region are the inspiring Dolomites mountains – elegant pale towers soaring above emerald meadows ablaze with brilliant wildflowers. Resort towns such as Cortina d'Ampezzo serve visitors in glorious summer as well as in winter, when the ski slopes are buzzing. This leisurely trip touches on traditional villages in picturesque spots that have inspired centuries of artists, including Titian. A thrilling bonus is majestic Monte Grappa (1,775 m/5,823 ft), all but unknown to overseas visitors. At the lower altitudes, walled towns nestle into the rolling foothills, cloaked with vines and woodland. The trip concludes in delightful Treviso, proud home of tiramisù and red chicory.

Above Detail of the façade of the historic cathedral at Asolo, *see p129*

Above Dramatic landscape of the tree-covered Dolomites mountains, *see pp126–7*
Below right View of the bridge designed by Palladio, Bassano del Grappa, *see p128*

ACTIVITIES

Go mountain walking or rock climbing on clearly signed routes in the Dolomites at Cortina d'Ampezzo

Clamber through World War I trenches at the Cinque Torri

Hike through the Parco Nazionale Dolomiti Bellunesi near Belluno and Feltre

Explore the solemn memorial to the fallen of World War I at Monte Grappa

Eat a bowl of creamy tiramisù in quiet Treviso, the place where it was invented

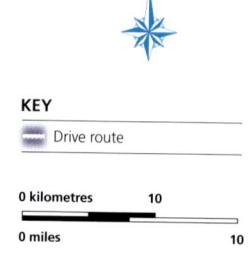

KEY

Drive route

0 kilometres 10
0 miles 10

TRIP 12: DOLOMITES TO VENETO HILLS | **125**

PLAN YOUR DRIVE

Start/finish: Cortina d'Ampezzo to Treviso.

Number of days: 4 days.

Distance: 270 km (168 miles).

Road conditions: Fairly hilly and, on occasion, mountainous and winding.

When to go: Jun–Oct for outdoor activities, though the plains can get hot Jul–Aug. Winter brings snow and skiing to the mountains, so carry snow chains. Main roads are kept clear but mountain roads may be closed.

Opening times: Shops tend to open 9am–1pm & 4–7:30pm Mon–Sat (food shops can be shut Mon & Wed after noon). Church and museum hours vary, but are usually 9am–noon & 4–7 or 8pm. Many museums are closed on Mon.

Main market days: Cortina d'Ampezzo: Tue & Fri; **Belluno:** Wed; **Feltre:** Tue & Fri; **Bassano del Grappa:** Thu & Sat; **Asolo:** Sat; **Treviso:** Mon.

Shopping: Look for ceramics at Bassano del Grappa and cheese around Feltre and Monte Grappa.

Major festivals: Feltre: Palio (medieval pageantry), 1st week in Aug; **Bassano del Grappa:** Mestieri in Strada (street market), Sep; **Asolo:** Incontri Asolani (chamber music), Aug–Sep.

DAY TRIP OPTIONS

Nature lovers can concentrate on the scenic Ampezzo valley with a **walk**, spectacular **mountain views** and a visit to the home of a **grand master**. From Treviso, enjoy a Renaissance tour starting at the **pretty town** of Asolo, then on to the **walls** of Feltre, the **palazzos** of Belluno and the **garden** at Nevegal. For full details, see p129.

Above Cortina d'Ampezzo, nestling below the dramatic Dolomites Below View of mountains, forests and a lake from Pieve di Cadore

VISITING CORTINA D'AMPEZZO

Tourist information
Corso Italia 81, 32043; dolomiti.org/it/cortina/ufficio-informazioni

WHERE TO STAY

CORTINA D'AMPEZZO

Meublé Montana *moderate*
A friendly hotel in the centre of town, close to shops, restaurants and transport. Corso Italia 94, 32043; cortina-hotel.com; closed May, Nov

❶ Cortina d'Ampezzo
Veneto; 32043

Chic Cortina, a leading winter ski resort, was part of the Habsburg Empire from the 16th century until after World War I and is today a charming mix of Tyrolean and Italian. The pretty town is set in a natural amphitheatre formed by the breathtaking crags and spires of the Dolomites, whose lower slopes are cloaked in thick forest and lush, flower-filled meadows. The central pedestrian street, the Corso, is lined with smart boutiques. Winter brings crowds of jet-set skiers, but during the summer months, Cortina is an excellent base for walkers and climbers with its many chairlifts and cable cars. Information on walks is available from the tourist office.

🚗 *From town, drive up SR48 for Passo di Falzarego. Park at Bai de Dones café.*

❷ THE CINQUE TORRI
Belluno, Veneto; 32043

The leisurely chairlift ride to the Cinque Torri rock towers ends with spectacular views of Cortina d'Ampezzo nestled within its crown of Dolomites peaks, a stunning backdrop to an open-air World War I museum. Close to the Austrian–Italian border, this area was a key strategic location, heavily fortified by both sides. After exploring the trenches and gun emplacements, take the lovely woodland track – sturdy walking shoes are recommended – back to the road. Two mountain huts *(rifugi)* provide café facilities in summer.

A three-hour walking tour
From **Bai de Dones** ❶, take the Cinque Torri *seggiovia*, or chairlift (10am–5pm daily), up to **Rifugio Scoiattoli** ❷ (2,225 m/7,300 ft), which boasts a magnificent terrace facing the Tofane-Lagazuoi range, northwest of the valley. Close at hand are the jagged rock teeth of the Cinque Torri (Five Towers), rising from earthy gums. Once off the chairlift, turn immediately left and take the

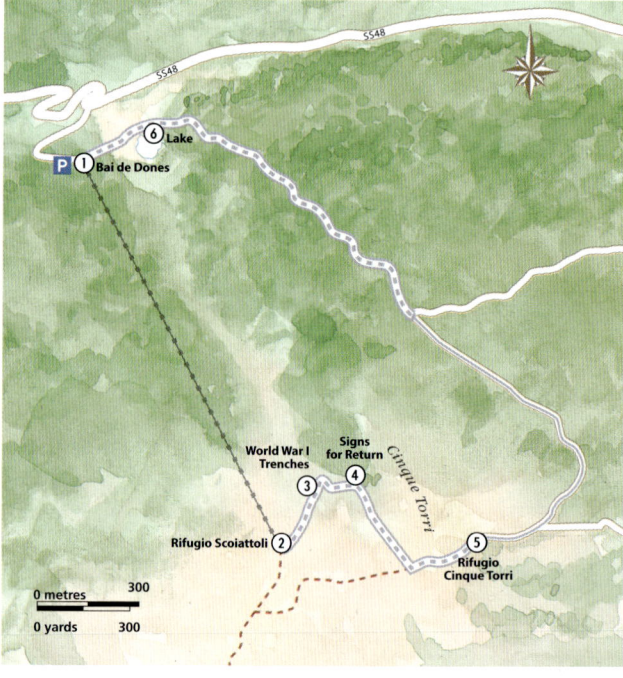

path downhill into the trench on the slope, brightly flowered in summer. Signs point out rest areas, observation points and artillery positions. At the end of the first line of **World War I trenches** ③, turn right to go down the reconstructed timber steps, which conclude at a covered area. Fork right and immediately left again. A little way up the hill, veer right to the **signs for return** ④ indicating the route back up to Rifugio Scoiattoli. Approaching the rifugio, take the left fork along the grassy ridge towards the foot of the dramatic rock towers, whose sheer cliff faces attract many climbers. Continue on the path to the **Rifugio Cinque Torri** ⑤. A quiet road leads downhill to the northeast, offering views of the majestic Sorapiss mountain. The way forks left and enters shady conifer woods where squirrels and roe deer are not uncommon. About 20 minutes further on, when the path veers right, follow the northwest road signed Bai de Dones. This pretty route meanders amid alpenrose shrubs and pine trees, before reaching a small **lake** ⑥. Close by are the café, chairlift and car park.

🚗 Leave Cortina d'Ampezzo on SS51, go past Zuel and onto Dogana Vecchia, the old customs point between the Habsburg Empire and Italy. San Vito is the next main town.

Outdoors in the Dolomites
A UNESCO World Heritage Site, these spectacular mountains in the far northeast of Italy are a superb destination for skiing in winter and climbing and trekking in the summer. Aided climbs known as *vie ferrate* criss-cross the sheer rock faces and a network of paths link *rifugi*, or mountain huts, which provide refreshments in the summer season.

③ San Vito di Cadore
Veneto; 32046
Dramatic Monte Antelao, at 3,264 m (10,709 ft) the highest mountain in the eastern Dolomites, rises over the village of San Vito di Cadore, while breaks in the trees afford inspiring views of the Pelmo massif. Further along the SS51, at Valle di Cadore, the **Chiesa di San Martino** occupies a high promontory, the site of an ancient castle. Near the valley floor is the covered wooden **Ponte di Rualan**.

🚗 Continue through Tai di Cadore, taking SS51bis to Pieve di Cadore.

④ Pieve di Cadore
Veneto; 32044
Pieve di Cadore stands at the foot of the Marmarole mountain range. A **statue** in the main square recalls its native son Titian, the foremost painter of the 16th-century Venetian school. His pretty home, **Casa di Tiziano** *(open May–Sep; closed till June 2025 for restoration)*, is now a small museum.

🚗 Head back towards Tai di Cadore and branch left onto SS51 past Longarone. Exit for Ponte nelle Alpi and follow signs for Belluno "centro". Follow signs for Nevegal and from Piazzale Nevegal, take the way indicated for Faverghera. The car park is located at the top.

⑤ Nevegal
Belluno, Veneto; 32100
On an elongated ridge marking the end of the mountains and the start of the Veneto Plain, this tiny village is surrounded with dairy farms and ski slopes. A 30-minute walk from the car park leads to the **Giardino Botanico delle Alpi Orientali** *(open mid-Jun–mid-Sep; closed Sep–Jul: Mon)*.

🚗 Return to Piazzale Nevegal and return to SP1. Across the river, fork right for Belluno "centro". Follow signs to the Lamboi car park and take the escalator (scala mobile) to town centre.

Top Dramatic cloud-topped Dolomites above the Pieve Valley **Above left** Statue of the artist Titian, favourite son of Pieve di Cadore **Above right** View of a mountain village in the Dolomites **Below** Casa di Tiziano, Titian's home in Pieve di Cadore

EAT AND DRINK

CORTINA D'AMPEZZO

El Zoco *moderate*
Top Italian cuisine and excellent wines.
Loc. Cademai 18, 32043; 0436 860 041; closed Mon

Ristorante Tivoli *expensive*
Refined Italian cuisine with one Michelin star and a superb panoramic terrace.
Loc. Lacedel 34, 32043; ristorantetivoli.it; closed Mon & Tue lunch, Easter–Jun & Oct–Nov

NEVEGAL

Ristorante La Casera *inexpensive*
Offers rustic food such as deer ragù and polenta with sausage and cheese. Booking advised.
Via Faverghera 751, 32100; 0437 908 180; closed Mon & Tue

WHERE TO STAY

BELLUNO

Albergo delle Alpi *inexpensive*
Furnished with all mod cons, this hotel, built on the site of a historic inn in the town centre, also has a good restaurant.
Via Jacopo Tasso 13, 32100; dellealpi.it

FELTRE

Via Paradiso 32 *moderate*
This comfortable modern hotel in the town centre has three suites and serves local delicacies at breakfast.
Via Paradiso 32, 32032; viaparadiso32.it

MONTE GRAPPA

Villa Scalabrini *inexpensive*
A comfortable hotel at the foot of the Verdugo mountains. Rooms are clean and tastefully furnished.
Via G.B. Scalabrini 3, 31017 – Crespano di Pieve del Grappa (Tv); villascalabrini.it

BASSANO DEL GRAPPA

Hotel Al Castello *inexpensive*
This traditional inn has cosy rooms and is well placed for sightseeing.
Via Bonamigo 19, 36061; hotelalcastello.it

ASOLO

Albergo Al Sole *moderate*
This is a captivating 16th-century villa with mod cons, near the main piazza.
Via Collegio 33, 31011; albergoal sole.com; closed Jan

TREVISO

Leoni di Collalto Palace *moderate*
Housed in a 15th-century building, this hotel offers a relaxing stay.
Via Collalto 13, 31100; leonidicollalto.com

SHOPPING IN THE VENETO

In Monte Bassano, look for fine cheese such as Morlacco and Bastardo del Grappa in **La Casera** (*Viale Monte Grappa 84; 0424 30 716*).

For hand-decorated ceramics in Bassano del Grappa, try **L'Arte della Ceramica** (*Via Angarano 21; 0424 503 901*); or taste the wide range of grappa and liqueurs at **Osteria Grapperia Nardini** (*Ponte Vecchio 2; nardini.it*).

Gourmet goodies such as potted *radicchio rosso* (red chicory) abound in Treviso, especially at **Bottega del Baccalà** (*Via S Parisio 15–17; fermi-treviso.com*).

Right View of Bassano del Grappa from its famous wooden bridge **Top** Boating on one of Treviso's many tree-shaded canals

⑥ Belluno
Veneto; 32100

Backed by the soaring Schiara massif, pretty Belluno, the provincial capital, is worth a visit for its grand squares, such as **Piazza del Mercato** (also known as Piazza delle Erbe), lined with splendid Renaissance palaces and home to an elegant 15th-century fountain. Nearby, the 16th-century **Duomo** has a Baroque campanile that affords excellent views in all directions. The town's **Museo Civico** is worth visiting for its paintings by local 16th–18th century masters.

🚗 *Head back to SP1 and turn right to Feltre, past Trichiana and Mel. After Lentiai, fork right on the SS50 to cross the River Piave towards Feltre. Follow signs for "centro", then "centro storico", circling the town to the car park. Yellow signs direct pedestrians into Feltre.*

⑦ Feltre
Veneto; 32032

This charming walled Renaissance town comes alive in mid-Aug for its colourful Palio horse race and medieval pageantry festival. Only 3 km (2 miles) away is **Pedavena**, known for its brewery. It is also the gateway to the wild Vette Feltrine mountain range, part of the Dolomiti Bellunesi National Park, where there are spectacular walks to be enjoyed (*dolomitipark.it*).

🚗 *Leave Feltre on the SS50, towards Bassano, then turn left at Cáupo following signs for "Monte Grappa" on the scenic SP148 as it winds its way up the northernmost flank of the mountain. Drive on past Osteria Forcelletto and take the fork to SP149 to Cima Grappa.*

⑧ Monte Grappa
Veneto; 36061

Towering over the edge of the vast Veneto plain is 1,775-m (5,823-ft) high Monte Grappa. The peak is home to **Cima Grappa**, a monumental terraced *ossario*, a poignant memorial to the Italian and Austrian troops whose bones rest there. Lush meadows now cover the World War I battlefields. On a clear day, the views extend all the way to the Adriatic coast and Venice.

🚗 *Return to SP148 and turn left for the zigzag descent to Romano d'Ezzelino. Turn right onto SP74 and follow signs for "centro". Park on Viale Fosse by the town walls.*

⑨ Bassano del Grappa
Veneto; 36061

With a charming, traffic-free centre, Bassano is well-known for ceramics, fiery grappa spirit and the prized white asparagus (in spring). For some wonderful rooftop views, climb the 43-m (141-ft) high **Torre Civica**. Straddling the River Brenta is the landmark bridge **Ponte degli Alpini**, designed by Andrea Palladio in 1571 (rebuilt in 1948), from which there

Far left Road leading to Belluno **Left centre** Delightful Belluno with its Duomo and Baroque campanile **Below** Flowers adorning houses in the pretty hillside town of Asolo

EAT AND DRINK

FELTRE

Osteria Crash *moderate*
A fun and friendly *osteria* with an excellent selection of wines and beers.
Via Paradiso 46, 32032; 0439 81 169; closed Mon & Sun eve

MONTE GRAPPA

Osteria Forcelletto *inexpensive*
Hearty country fare and views over the Valsugana to the Asiago plateau.
Via Feltre 46, 32030; 320 700 9298

BASSANO DEL GRAPPA

Antico Ristorante Cardellino *moderate*
Try the *baccalà alla Vicentina*, a local cod speciality.
Via Bellavitis 17, 36061; ristorantecardellino.it; closed Thu

B38 *moderate*
Refined restaurant whose specialities include pheasant.
Viale delle Fosse 1, 36061; bonotto.it

ASOLO

Antica Osteria Al Bacaro *moderate*
Enjoy *spezzatino* (stew) and *baccalà* (salt cod) at wooden trestle tables.
Via R Browning 165, 31011; albacaroanticaosteria.it; closed Wed

TREVISO

Locanda Ponte Dante *moderate*
Set close to the river, this restaurant serves delicious stews and sardines.
Piazza Garibaldi 6, 31100; locanda pontedante.com; closed Sun eve & Mon; Jul & Aug

Toni del Spin *moderate*
Try the *pasta e fagioli* at this trattoria.
Via Inferiore 7, 31100; ristorante tonidelspin.com; closed Mon lunch

---

are impressive views of the town. The **Museo Civico** *(closed Tue)* contains works by 19th-century sculptor Canova. In Piazza Garibaldi stands the 11th-century Romanesque-Gothic **Chiesa di San Francesco**.
🚗 *Leave on Viale Venezia (SP248) for Asolo, turning left for "centro" after 16 km (10 miles). Park at Piazza Garibaldi.*

⑩ Asolo
Veneto; 31011
This beautiful hillside town has long attracted poets (Robert Browning), aristocrats (Caterina Cornaro, 15th-century queen of Cyprus) and travellers (Freya Stark). A visit should start at **Piazza Garibaldi**, its fountain fed by underground aqueducts that once filled the Roman baths. Just across the main street stands the venerable **Cattedrale**. Pass through a city door on Via Collegio and walk uphill to the 14th-century fort, **La Rocca** *(open Sat & Sun)*, for views over the town and lush countryside.
🚗 *Return to SP248 and drive through Montebelluna towards Conegliano. Turn right at the roundabout before Venegazzu onto SR348 and follow signs straight to Treviso. Take the first turn-off for "centro" and park at Viale Battisti.*

⑪ Treviso
Veneto; 31100
This walled market town-cum-city on the River Sile is scored with waterways from the long-gone days of canal navigation. Stroll east along the banks to a poignant "barge cemetery", where the old timber craft were sunk when road transport took over. The lively fish market has its own island, modelled by Venetian architect Carlo Scarpa (1906–78). One of Treviso's claims to gastronomic fame is that it invented the classic Italian dessert tiramisù; it also purports to be the home of *radicchio* (red chicory) and *pasta e fagioli* (pasta/bean soup).

DAY TRIP OPTIONS

Choose between the wonders of nature and the human-made splendour of the Renaissance.

Painterly landscapes
Using Cortina d'Ampezzo ❶ as a base, do a little shopping before heading up to the Cinque Torri ❷. Work up an appetite climbing to see the views – if painting isn't an option, take a photo.

Lunch at a mountain hut, then drive to San Vito di Cadore ❸, with more photo opportunities at the Ponte di Rualan. Drive on to Pieve di Cadore ❹ to see the place of Titian's birth.

Follow the drive's instructions.

Renaissance tour
From Treviso ⑪, head to pretty Asolo ⑩, the "pearl of the province", then on to walled Feltre ❼ with its historic Renaissance centre. After lunch, drive to Belluno ❻ to explore its grand palazzo-lined squares, 16th-century Duomo and Renaissance paintings.

Take the SP55, then the SS248 to Asolo. Retrace route back on SS248, then take SS348 to Feltre. Take the SS50, then SP1 to Belluno. To return quickly, take SS50 north to A27. Take this south to Treviso.

TRIP 13

THE PO DELTA
Ferrara to Ravenna

HIGHLIGHTS

Courtly capital
Explore Ferrara's Renaissance palazzos, medieval churches and magnificent castles, built by its powerful d'Este rulers

The mighty Po
Follow Italy's longest river as it heads to the sea over rich alluvial plains, reclaimed since Roman times

The lagoons of Comacchio
Discover these superb wetlands, an important sanctuary and breeding ground for migrating water birds

Byzantine majesty
Feast your eyes on splendid Ravenna – the last great capital of the Roman Empire – rich in glittering mosaics

THE PO DELTA

The massive River Po winds across its expansive delta in large, lazy arcs, now somewhat tamed by reclamation. It is the largest flood plain in Italy, and easy to explore. This trip starts at Ferrara and then wanders through rich agricultural lands, along the massive, protective river banks to wild wetlands of superb natural beauty with excellent cycling paths and well-marked walking trails. After the ancient forest of Mesola, the beauty of the Pomposa monastery, the busy fishing village of Porto Garibaldi and the fascinating town of Comacchio, the journey ends with the world's greatest Byzantine treasures in the charming city of Ravenna.

ACTIVITIES

Catch a fish with local fishers in Porto Garibaldi; and stay overnight on board a traditional fishing boat

Photograph the birdlife of the Valli di Comacchio at sunset, including the migrating flamingos

Take a class in mosaic-making and learn the ancient Byzantine art of designing with glass in Ravenna

Ride a bicycle across the Valli di Comacchio – the delta is very flat here and perfect for cycling

Hike in Il Bosco della Mesola, the last forest in the delta, and look out for fallow and red deer

Take a dip at a sandy-beached lido along the delta coast from Porto Garibaldi

Left Ferrara's Loggia of the Merchants, Piazza Trento Trieste, *see p134* **Above right** Mudflats and reed beds in the wildlife haven Valli di Comacchio, *see p138*

TRIP 13: THE PO DELTA

PLAN YOUR DRIVE

Start/finish: Ferrara to Ravenna.

Number of days: 2–3 days.

Distance: Approx. 240 km (150 miles).

Road conditions: Generally excellent.

When to go: Summer is best, with clear skies and good beach weather. The Po valley around Ferrara and the coast is prone to fog in winter.

Opening times: Most museums open 10am–6pm, with small museums often only open on weekends outside the summer months. Churches are usually open 7:30am–noon and 3–7:30pm.

Main market days: Ferrara: Mon & Fri; Ro & Comacchio: Wed; Argenta: Thu; Ravenna: Mon & Thu pm on Piazza Della Resistenza; Mesola: Sat.

Specialized markets: Ferrara: Antique Market, 3rd Sun of month (except Aug); Ravenna: Antique and Handicrafts Market, 4th weekend of month.

Shopping: Modern mosaic gifts and all tools and requirements for making mosaics are available in Ravenna.

Major festivals: Ferrara: Buskers Festival, last week in Aug; Ferrara Palio di San Giorgio (medieval horse race and pageantry), last Sun in May; Ferrara Hota: Air Balloon Festival, 3rd week in Sep; Porto Garibaldi: Festa della Madonna del Mare (boat festival and celebration), Jun; Comacchio: Sagra dell'Anguilla (eel festival), first 3 weekends in Oct; Ravenna: Ravenna Festival (music, drama and dance; *ravennafestival.org*) May–Jul.

DAY TRIP OPTIONS

Architecture enthusiasts will enjoy the **frescoes**, **duomo** and **castle** in Ferrara, one of the **delta's oldest buildings** in the Po Delta at Argenta and more **mosaics** and **great architecture** in Ravenna. Nature-loving families can head to the Valli of Comacchio to enjoy the **waterbirds** and pristine **delta** environment and visit the **eel factory** at Comacchio. Next, they can visit the coast for a **swim** at a lido or carry on to Il Bosco della Mesola to see the **deer**. For full details, *see p139.*

❶ FERRARA

Ferrara, Emilia-Romagna; 44121–44124

The d'Este dynasty ruled over Ferrara from the 13th to the 16th century, enriching it with a splendid castle, medieval architecture and fine Renaissance palaces. This stroll leads through the oldest part of the city to the sombre, moated castle at its centre, Castello Estense.

Above A narrow alley through the historic centre of Ferrara

VISITING FERRARA

Getting to Ferrara
From the A13 toll road, take exit Ferrara Nord onto Via Eridano/SP19. The nearest airports are Bologna and Venice.

Parking
Centro Storico, Via Darsena

Bicycle hire
Rent-a-bike Ceragioli *(Piazza Travaglio 4, 44121; 339 405 6853)*

Tourist Information
Castello Estense, 44121; ferraraterraeacqua.it

WHERE TO STAY

FERRARA AND AROUND

Hotel Ferrara *inexpensive*
This central hotel combines a sleek modern style with a characterful old building – some rooms have views onto neighbouring Castello Estense. Bicycles available for rent.
Largo Castello 36, 44121; hotelferrara.com

Lama di Valle Rossa *inexpensive*
This *agriturismo* (farm stay) just 7 km (4 miles) from the historic centre of Ferrara, serves generous breakfasts and offers bicycles for hire. Exit Ferrara Sud from A13 Bologna-Padova, follow the signs to Bologna for about 4 km (2.5 miles), turn left at the sign "Marrara – S. Bartolomeo" and drive up Via Sgarbata for 3 km (2 miles) more.
Via Sgarbata 103, 44124; lamadivallerosa.it

Hotel Touring *moderate*
Set in the town centre and offering excellent value for money, this 1950s hotel has quiet rooms, excellent staff and parking permits for a small fee.
Viale Cavour 11, 44121; hoteltouringfe.it

A two-hour walking tour

From the car park on Via Darsena, enter the city to the right of the 17th-century Porta Paola. Cross Piazza Travaglio diagonally right to the busy shopping street Via San Romano. Cross Via Ripagrande/Carlo Mayr and turn right on **Via Volte** ①, one of the oldest parts of the city. The archways once joined the river warehouses on the right to the merchants' houses on the left. At the end, turn left, then right into Vicolo Granchio. Go straight on, in a series of doglegs, into Via Carmellino and Via Borgo di Sotto.

This leads to the **Oratorio dell'Annunziata** ②, with superb frescoes, including a 15th-century fresco by the school of Pisanello. Continue into Via Scandiana – on the right is the **Chiesa di Santa Maria in Vado** ③. In 1171 a priest celebrating mass broke the host, which sprayed blood over the vault above the altar, confirming the miracle of the Eucharist.

On the left is **Palazzo Schifanoia** ④ *(closed Mon)*, which belonged to the d'Este family and is now home to a museum containing artifacts from the d'Este court as well as some of the most significant 15th-century fresco cycles in Italy showing court life, zodiac signs and Roman gods.

Return past the oratory, turn right at Via Pergolato, then left at Via Savanarola past **Casa Romei** ⑤, a fine example of a Ferrerese nobleman's house, combining medieval and Renaissance elements.

Turn left at Via Terranuova, then right into Via Mazzini past the **Synagogue** ⑥ *(closed for renovations until further notice)*. On the left of Via Mazzini is the Ghetto. In 1492, Ercole I gave shelter to Jews fleeing persecution in Spain. When d'Este power waned, the community was gated in 1627 and closed in 1859. Now a charming area, it was the setting for Giorgio Bassani's 1962 novel, *The Garden of the Finzi-Continis*.

Detail from the façade of Ferrara's Duomo

Via Mazzini opens into a series of squares in the city's heart. On the right of Piazza Trento Trieste is a Renaissance bell tower, attributed to Leon Battista Alberti (1404–72), and the medieval Loggia of the Merchants. Facing west is the Duomo, the magnificent 12th-century **Basilica di San Giorgio** ⑦.

Below Statue of Niccolò III d'Este (1383–1441), the Marquess of Ferrara, outside the Palazzo Municipale **Below right** The glassy waters of a peaceful wooded pond near Il Mulino del Po

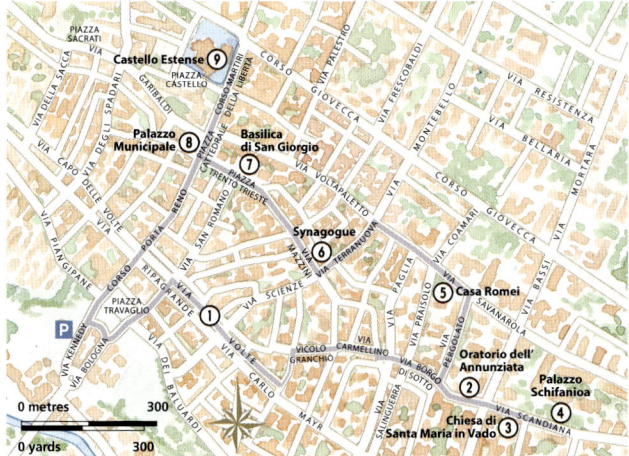

(open daily). The lower part of the façade is Romanesque while the intricately carved upper part was built later in Gothic style.

Directly opposite is the **Palazzo Municipale** ⑧, a 12th-century d'Este residence remodelled in the 16th century to house the City Hall. To the right, above an arch designed by Leon Battista Alberti, is a statue of Niccolò III d'Este on horseback; to the left, seated on a column, is his son Borso.

Turning right up Corso Martiri della Libertà, the last column on the left has marks from when the River Po burst its banks, flooding the city. Nearby is the statue of the Ferrarese Dominican monk Girolamo Savonarola, a leader of Florence whose passionate sermons started the Bonfire of the Vanities in 1497, when all "sinful goods" were taken from the city's houses and burned.

Surrounded by a moat is the symbol of Ferrara, the **Castello Estense** ⑨ (closed Tue), built in the 15th century to protect Niccolò II d'Este against his own people. As d'Este rule became established, the castle grew into a fine home with terraces and frescoed apartments. Return to the car park.

🚗 Leave Ferrara on Via Pomposa, towards Copparo – turn left into Via Pontegradella, then left into Via Caretti, and right into SP2. Just before Corlo, take 1st left onto SP14 (towards Ro). At Ro follow signs to "Centro Storico", left at Via Dazio, follow signs for Area Golenale del Po – Mulino sul Po. Park in the designated area. Walk over the embankment to the park.

Cycling in the Po Delta

Geographically the whole area of the Po Delta is very flat, making it ideal for exploring on a bike. The tourist office (Piazza San Francesco 7, 35404; turismo.ra.it) has maps and route maps as well as information about bike hire in the city. Check with your hotel if they offer free bikes for guests.

Scenic routes include the Destra Po Route, part of the Eurovelo cycle routes from Athens to Cadiz. Most locals are keen cyclists, and many hotels and guides offer biking tours.

② **Il Mulino del Po**
Ro, Ferrara, Emilia-Romagna; 44030

This small parkland with picnic areas and bicycle hire, on the banks of the river near the Polesella bridge, featured in a 1940 novel by Riccardo Bacchelli, Il Mulino del Po (The Mill on the Po), evoking the harsh realities of life on the river. There is a small museum in the barge/houseboat that was used in a 1949 film of the book. The tethered barge was manoeuvred into midstream, where the force of the water turned the waterwheel it carried, grinding the corn. The tall mooring poles are an indication of how high the river flows when in flood.

🚗 Returning to Ro, take 1st left onto Via Vallalbana/SP24, following signs to Berra. At Canova, turn left into Via Brusantina Pampano/SP12 to Ariano. At Piazza Garibaldi turn left to SP11 to Mesola. Use car park on Viale Roma.

EAT AND DRINK

FERRARA

Caffetteria Ristorante Schifanoia inexpensive
This small pavilion has been turned into a delightful garden café by artist Simone Bavia.
Palazzo Schifanoia, Via Scandiana 21, 44121; 340 617 8870; open Tue–Sun lunch only

Leon d'Oro inexpensive
Almost a Ferrara institution, this central café and pasticceria opposite the Duomo is famous for its pampapato, a nutty, nougat-style sweet dipped in chocolate.
Piazza della Cattedrale 8, 44121; leondoroferrara.it; closed Wed

Cà d'Frara moderate
As you would expect in a restaurant in Via del Gambero (Prawn Street), Cà d'Frara serves seafood, but also homemade pasta specialities such as cappellacci di zucca (pumpkin pasta).
Via del Gambero 4, 44121; ristorante cadfrara.it; closed Tue, Wed & Thu lunch

Osteria Del Ghetto moderate
In the heart of the Jewish ghetto, this small osteria has a typically local menu: try the cosciotto di maialino in porchetta – ham-wrapped roast pork with fennel.
Via della Vittoria 26, 44120; osteriadelghetto.it; closed Mon

L'Oca Giuliva expensive
A small restaurant with an excellent wine cellar. Try the splendid salama da sugo, a spicy sausage in ragù sauce. Booking advised.
Via Boccanale di Santo Stefano 38/40, 44121; ristorantelocagiuliva.it; closed Tue

IL MULINO DEL PO

Il Mulino sul Po moderate
This rustic restaurant, situated on a floating fishers" barge, serves all-you-can-eat, cafeteria-style dishes.
Via Marconi, 45030 Giaretta; ilmulinosulpo-ristorante.it; open Wed–Sun lunch, Fri & Sat dinner

Above The Castello Estense, or castello di San Michele, in Ferrara

Top right The impressive redbrick Treponti Bridge, Comacchio **Below left** Boats in the harbour at Porto Garibaldi **Below right** Detail of the façade at the Abbazia di Pomposa

VISITING COMACCHIO

Consorzio del Parco Regionale del Delta del Po
This office provides information on bike hire, boat tours and walking trails throughout the Po Delta.
Corso Mazzini 200, 44022; parcodeltapo.it

WHERE TO STAY AROUND IL BOSCO DELLA MESOLA

L'Oasi di Valle Canneviè-Porticino/ Hotel Rurale Canneviè *inexpensive*
Combining tourism and wildlife preservation, this mini eco-park near the Lido di Volano is run in conjunction with the Province of Ferrara and offers accommodation with a restaurant and bar as well as guided tours (in Italian) of the surrounding wetlands. Also offers bicycles for hire.
Via per Volano 45, 44021 Codigoro; oasicannevie.com; tours: Mar–mid-Nov; closed mid-Nov–Feb

❸ Castello di Mesola
Ferrara, Emilia-Romagna; 44026
One of the last *delizie* (pleasure lodges) built by the Ferrara dukes, the Castello di Mesola was part of a huge hunting estate. Building started in 1578, creating a central block with four towers surrounded by a semi-circular porticoed courtyard. The former stables and granary now contain bars, a restaurant and a local produce shop. The filmic nature of the setting was used by director Mario Soldati for his 1954 film *La Donna del Fiume*, with Sophia Loren.

🚗 Head east on Via 25 Aprile, then right at Strada Statale Romea/SS309. Fork left to Bosco Mesola and Gigliola, turning left and following the signs to Bosco della Mesola and car park.

❹ Il Bosco della Mesola
Ferrara, Emilia-Romagna; 44026
Once an extensive forest, only 1,000 hectares (4 sq miles) of Il Bosco della Mesola (*parcodeltapo.it*) remain and are now under the protection of the Corpo Forestale. Explore the forest on foot or by bicycle (hire available near front gate) along the 1.5 km (1 mile) of paths. These lead through an attractive setting of English oak, holm oak and pine, inhabited by the shy red deer of Mesola, the only native population of red deer in Italy.

🚗 Return to Gigliola, then turn left at Via Vecchia Corriera and right at Strada Giralda Centrale, continuing to Abbazia di Pomposa and car park.

❺ Abbazia di Pomposa
Via Pomposa Centro, 12, Codigoro Ferrara; 44020
This superb Romanesque abbey was first established in the 7th century, and by 1001 it had been made a royal abbey by Emperor Otto III. However, after several centuries of decline, the last monks left Pomposa in 1671. The abbey was built in the style of a basilica, with a central nave and an aisle on each side, using material salvaged from other sites. The two carved roundels came

Below Fishers unloading the day's catch at Porto Garibaldi

Above The square-turreted 16th-century Castello di Mesola

from Ravenna. The complex is an architectural delight – the 48-m (157-ft) bell tower, or campanile, is typical Lombard Romanesque. The interior is covered with frescoes of biblical scenes by Bolognese masters and the floor was created in the 11th and 12th centuries by Venetian crafters.

In the 11th century, the monk Guido d'Arezzo is said to have invented modern musical notation while teaching music here.

🚗 *Head south on Loc. Lovara/SS309, turn left at SP54 to Lido di Volano, then right at Strada Panoramica Acciaioli. At Porto Garibaldi, fork left on Via Cacciatori, then left into Via Florido Braga, right at Via Volturno to the port.*

6 Porto Garibaldi
Ferrara, Emilia-Romagna; 44029

Named in honour of the Risorgimento hero Giuseppe Garibaldi (1807–82), who landed here during his flight from the Austrians in 1849, this busy fishing port has several sandy beaches, perfect for a dip in the Adriatic. The **Lido delle Nazioni**, **Lido di Pomposa**, **Lido degli Scacchi** and the **Lido degli Estensi** are all accessible from here by ferry for foot or bicycle passengers.

The town also has one of the largest fishing fleets in the Adriatic, with boats leaving the Magnavacca Canal early in the morning and returning later to unload their catch. It's easy to charter a boat for a fishing trip from the harbour.

🚗 *Head west on Via Giacomo Matteotti, which becomes Strada Provinciale di Comacchio/SP1. At Comacchio, turn left at Via Trepponti/SP1 and follow the road around the town. Turn right at roundabout to Corso Giuseppe Mazzini and ample parking.*

7 Comacchio
Ferrara, Emilia-Romagna; 44022

This picturesque town has derived its prosperity from many centuries of fishing, salt harvesting and catching eels from the nearby lagoon. Founded by the Etruscans and annexed by the Romans, who built a canal to deepen the lagoon, Comacchio went on to prosper under the Goths, Lombards, Venetians and finally the Papal States. The historic centre is divided by canals with ten brick bridges. The **Trepponti Bridge**, built in 1634, has five staircases and five semi-circular arches and crosses five different canals. It's also possible to visit the eel pickling factory, **La Manifattura dei Marinati** (*Corso Mazzini 200; open daily*).

🚗 *Continue along Corso Mazzini, past La Manifattura dei Marinati, turn left, then right into Via Spina/SP1, left at Strada Poderale Belfiore, crossing the canal, straight onto Via Arsa and Via Anita in Loc. Fosse, passing Via Agosta along the edge of the lagoon, then turn left on Via Martinella Rotta and park in a layby for the view.*

Above left A canal traversing the colourful Comacchio houses. **Above right** The elegant 14th-century bell tower at the Abbazia di Pomposa **Below** One of the well-tended sandy beaches at Porto Garibaldi

EAT AND DRINK

CASTELLO DI MESOLA
Ristorante Al Castello *moderate*
Set within the walled courtyard of the castle, this trattoria puts on a good show for locals and visitors alike. Try steamed asparagus with cheese and truffles, pasta with venison ragù, and fried chicken pieces covered with sesame seeds.
Piazza Umberto I 9, 44026; 0533 993 088; closed Mon & Tue

IL BOSCO DELLA MESOLA
Locanda del Bosco *moderate*
This restaurant serves a robust menu of typical local dishes based on meat, fish or game on offer according to the season. Choose from homemade Pappardelle with wild boar, chargrilled steak Florentine or mutton.
Via Forconcelli 2, 44026; locandadelbosco.it

ABBAZIA DI POMPOSA
Corte Madonnina *moderate*
An *Azienda Agricola* (farm business), just south of the abbey, selling its own wines directly to the public. The adjoining farmhouse serves typical cuisine: salama da sugo (medieval sausage), pumpkin ravioli and eels.
SS Romea (Località per Volano 1), 44021 Pomposa; cortemadonnina.it; closed Mon

Above Flamingos feeding on the wetlands, Valli di Comacchio **Above right** Sumptuous mosaic inside Ravenna's Basilica di San Vitale
Below Frescoed nave in the Basilica di Sant'Apollinare Nuovo, Ravenna

VISITING RAVENNA

Tourist Information
Ravenna's tourist offices sell a **combined ticket** that includes entry to: the Basilica di Sant'Apollinare Nuovo, the Neonian Baptistry, the Basilica di San Vitale and the Mausoleum of Galla Placidia. A clear map is provided with the ticket.
Piazza San Francesco 7, Ravenna; turismo.ravenna.it

WHERE TO STAY

ARGENTA

Villa Reale *inexpensive*
Conveniently located in the town centre, this simple hotel is housed in a beautiful villa and offers friendly service and clean, well-equipped rooms.
Viale Roiti 16/A, 44011; hotelvillarealeargenta.net

RAVENNA

Hotel Centrale Byron *inexpensive*
This budget hotel is in the historic centre and offers basic, but clean and comfortable facilities. There is parking in a nearby private garage.
Via IV Novembre 14, 48121; hotelsravenna.it

Santa Maria Foris *moderate*
Set in a comfortable, restored villa in the historic centre, this hotel offers pleasant, modern rooms.
Via Giuseppe Pasolini 61, 48121; villaforis.it

Albergo Cappello *expensive*
A superb Renaissance palazzo only a few steps from Piazza del Popolo – some rooms and suites have period furnishings with elegant frescoes.
Via IV Novembre 41, 48121; albergocappello.it

⑧ Valli di Comacchio
Ferrara, Emilia-Romagna; 44022

The lagoons of Comacchio are wetlands of international importance and the centrepiece of the Parco Delta del Po *(parcodeltapo.it)*, which covers an area of 3,500 hectares (14 sq miles) and stretches from Chioggia to Comacchio. It was designated a World Heritage Site in 1999. Large raised banks divide the lagoons, providing flat paths perfect for cycling along, and here and there stand the remains of fishing lodges and small salt pans. The shallow, brackish waters are an ideal habitat for more than 300 species of water birds. Species that can often be sighted include flamingoes, avocets, spoonbills, shelducks, black-winged stilts, slender-billed gulls and Mediterranean gulls. Visitors can also view the lagoon by boat or from walking trails.

🚗 *Return along Via Martinella Rotta. Turn left at Via Valle Umana, at Anita turn right on Via Fossa dei Socialisti and left on Via Pagana that leads to Longastrino. Turn right at Via Molinetto/SP10, which curves left. Turn right at Via Giovanni Amendola/SS16, which continues to Argenta.*

⑨ Argenta
Ferrara, Emilia-Romagna; 44011

As the mouth of the Po Primario, the old River Po, silted up, channels were cut to the sea. One of these became known as the River Reno. On its northern bank lies quiet Argenta, an ideal spot for bird-watching forays to the **Campotto Oasis**, three small lagoons south of the town. Just by the oasis stands the **Parish Church of San Giorgio** *(Via Cardinala)*. Built in 569, it is one of the oldest buildings in the delta. Although the church is rarely open, its portal of Roman marble is worth a look. Further south, on the same road, is the excellent **Museo delle Valli** *(closed Mon; vallidiargenta.org)*. Traditional life in the delta, land reclamation and local wildlife are well covered by its displays and bicycles are available to hire for an excursion around the lagoon.

🚗 *From Argenta, turn right into Via Nazionale Ponente/SS16 for 36 km (22 miles). Take the exit for Ravenna Centro, follow Via Faentina/SS253, then go left at Circonvallazione San Gaetanino. Turn sharp right at Via Don Giovanni Minzoni, fork right, then turn left into car park at Largo Giustiniano.*

10 Ravenna

Ravenna, Emilia-Romagna; 48100

From 402 CE until 476, Ravenna was the capital of the Western Roman Empire and remained the capital of Byzantine Italy until the 8th century. The city's importance in the early Christian era endowed it with monuments and lavishly decorated churches – eight buildings have been listed by UNESCO. But Ravenna is a living city and not just an architectural museum – its piazzas and historic monuments are linked by streets bustling with local life, which can be explored using the bike hire services found throughout the city. The octagonal **Basilica di San Vitale** (open daily), built 527–48, is the only major church from the period of Emperor Justinian I to survive virtually intact. Its colourful mosaics are the height of Byzantine splendour – look for the emperor portrayed with court officials, and on the opposite wall, the Empress Theodora. Within the complex is the small building of the **Mausoleo di Galla Placidia** (included in group ticket), regarded as the best preserved of the mosaic monuments, and the **Museo Nazionale di Ravenna** (separate ticket), in the cloisters, with

Above The exterior of the Byzantine Basilica di San Vitale, Ravenna

14th-century frescoes of Santa Chiara and a collection of fabrics, ivories, coins and icons. Nearby Via Cavour is a fine shopping street, which leads to Piazza Andrea Costa and the **covered market** (morning only) selling flowers, fish, meat and cheese and all manner of fresh local produce. Via IV Novembre leads straight to elegant **Piazza del Popolo** with its two Venetian-style columns with saints Apollinare and Vitale perched on top. Behind is Palazzo Communale and to the left, Palazzo Veneziano, built when Ravenna was part of the Venetian Republic in the 15th century. The archway in Palazzo Veneziano leads to **Via Cairoli**, a narrow shopping street with Liberty-style shop façades.

The **Basilica di Sant'Apollinare Nuovo** (combined ticket), in Via di Roma, has a cylindrical bell tower and some of the largest Byzantine mosaics (6th century). Directly opposite, Via Negri leads into Largo Firenze and the side door to the **Basilica di San Francesco**, its 10th-century crypt full of water with fish swimming over the 5th-century mosaic floor. Leave by the front door into Piazza San Francesco. Through the garden to the right is the Neo-Classical **Tomb of Dante** (open daily; free entry) – the Italian poet died here in 1321. In Piazza Duomo stands the last of the combined ticket sites: the late 4th- or early 5th-century **Neonian Baptistry**. The octagonal building contains delightful Greco-Roman influenced frescoes. From here, Via Cavour runs towards the imposing 16th-century **Porta Adriana**. Left at Via Barbiani is the **Domus dei Tappeti di Pietra** (open daily, entry through San Eufemia), the site of a Roman villa and beautiful Byzantine mosaics.

Above Free yellow bicycles available for tourists in Ravenna

EAT AND DRINK

ARGENTA AND AROUND

Oasi *moderate*
Bar/trattoria closest to the Museo di Valli. Enjoy picnic lunch in the park.
Via Vallesanta 6, 44011; 0532 808 017; open Wed & Thu lunch, Fri–Sun lunch & dinner

Ristorante Patuelli *moderate*
Situated opposite the parkland south of the museum, this place serves superb chargrilled eel and other local delicacies.
Via Cardinala 11/A, 44011 Campotto; 0532 808 314; closed Mon & Tue

RAVENNA

Gustavo Bizantino *inexpensive*
Busy self-service buffet with great fresh food minutes from the covered market. Pile your plate with delicious bread, grilled vegetables and fresh salads.
Via Angelo Mariani 12, 48121; gustavoitaliano.it; open Tue–Sun lunch

Osteria dei Battibecchi *moderate*
This place has a small but tasty menu of homemade lasagne, pork hot pot with cardoons, and caramelized figs.
Via della Tesoreria Vecchia 16, 48121; 0544 219 536

Enoteca Ca' de Vèn *moderate*
This bar/restaurant, set in a historic palazzo near Dante's Tomb, is a Ravenna institution – try the *piadina* and *crescioni* (filled Italian flatbreads).
Via Corrado Ricci 24, 48121; cadeven.it; closed Mon

DAY TRIP OPTIONS

Adults will enjoy Ferrara and Ravenna's historic buildings, while the watery, wildlife-filled Po Delta and the beach will keep young families busy.

Art and architecture
At Ferrara ❶, spend half a day seeing the city's frescoes and Renaissance architecture, then head off to Argenta ❾ to visit one of the delta's oldest buildings and lunch in the countryside. Next explore the churches and Byzantine mosaics in Ravenna ❿.

The SS16 joins all these stops.

The natural world
From Ravenna ❿, pack a picnic and set off early to Valli di Comacchio ❽, to spend a couple of hours watching the water birds on the lagoon. Carry on to Comacchio ❼ to visit the eel pickling factory, then head off to Porto Garibaldi ❻ for lunch on the beach. Drive north to the woods of Bosco della Mesola to glimpse the shy deer, or just stay on the beach.

Head north from Ravenna on SP1, turning left at Cruser following signs to Comacchio. Retrace drive instructions to Porto Garibaldi, then head up along the coast to Bosco Mesola.

TRIP 14

THE AZURE COAST TO THE PO VALLEY

Genoa to Portovenere

HIGHLIGHTS

Magnificent palazzos
Explore the grand historic palaces and the dark tangle of ancient alleyways in vibrant Genoa

Ham, violets and fine art
Discover the architectural and artistic gems amid the gourmet delights of historic and affluent Parma

Golfo dei Poeti
Take in the exquisitely framed views of the sea at beautiful Portovenere where Lord Byron once swam

Apennine scenery
Zigzag around the mountains and through the untouched countryside of the tree-clad Apennines

THE AZURE COAST TO THE PO VALLEY

At the western end of the Riviera di Levante, Genoa, the capital of Liguria, is a dynamic, multilayered city, with the extra spice of being a working port. Built on the wealth of merchants, it's a city of glittering Baroque churches, of 16th- and 17th-century palazzos and of fish and oranges spilling out of dark alleyways. At the eastern end of the Riviera, literary La Spezia, the naval capital of Liguria, is big sibling to pretty Portovenere, and gateway to the Cinque Terre. Inland, above the farms and unspoilt Apennine countryside, affluent Parma and Reggio Emilia take well-deserved pride in what they have produced – fabulous art and architecture and the famed prosciutto and Parmigiano.

Above Basilica San Prospero and Piazza San Prospero, Reggio Emilia, *see p146*
Below right Cattedrale di San Lorenzo, Genoa, *see p144*

KEY

― Drive route

0 kilometres 15
0 miles 15

ACTIVITIES

Explore Genoa, Europe's largest medieval centre, and climb the hills above for a panoramic overview

Take a boat from Portovenere for the sparkling Golfo dei Poeti (Gulf of Poets) and the lovely islands of Palmária, Tino and Tinetto

Sample the delights of the Po Valley – from the freshest of fish on the coast to the renowned Parmigiano and prosciutto from Parma

Go hunting for mushrooms in the Apennines

Cycle around the historic sites of Parma at a leisurely pace

TRIP 14: THE AZURE COAST TO THE PO VALLEY

PLAN YOUR DRIVE

Start/finish: Genoa to Portovenere.

Number of days: 4–5, allowing a day for Genoa, a trip to Parma and time to enjoy La Spezia and Portovenere.

Distance: Approx. 325 km (200 miles).

Road conditions: Mountain roads are twisting and slow, and the coast road is winding and busy in summer.

When to go: Genoa is good to visit in winter. It gets full during the Boat Show in Sep, and some places close for Aug. The interior mountains are accessible all year, although snow chains may be needed in winter. The coast gets busy in Jul & Aug.

Opening times: Major museums open 9am–7pm Tue–Fri and from 10am Sat & Sun. Some museums and churches close early afternoon. Shops may close all day Sun and Mon am in smaller towns, and open 9am–12:30pm and 3:30–7:30pm on other days (large shops are open all day). Some of Parma's shops close Thu pm.

Main market days: Genoa: Mon–Sat; Parma: Mon–Sat; Reggio Emilia: Tue & Fri; La Spezia: Fri.

Shopping: In Genoa, look for pesto, *trenette* (short linguini) and *trofie* (pasta twists); in Langhirano, prosciutto and *culatello* (hams) and, in the mountains, porcini mushrooms. Parma is justly famous for its ham, cheese and Parma violets. Reggio Emilia's shops also sell Parmigiano-Reggiano cheese.

Major festivals: Genoa: Holy Week processions, Easter; Festival Musicale del Mediterraneo (concerts at the port), Jul & Aug; International Boat Show, 2nd week in Sep; La Spezia: Palio del Golfo (rowing race), 1st Sun in Aug; Parma: Festival del Prosciutto, Sep; Palio (medieval sports), Sep; Verdi Festival, Oct; Portovenere: Festa della Madonna Bianca (religious procession), mid-Aug.

DAY TRIP OPTIONS

It takes a full day to see the sights in the **museums**, **churches** and **palazzos** in Genoa. Then, drive along the **coast** to visit the port of La Spezia and romantic Portovenere with its **castle**, **grotto** and **islands**. For full details, see p147.

Above Picturesque scenery en route to Langhirano, *see p145*

Above The huge arch of medieval Porta Soprana, the main entrance to Genoa

VISITING GENOA

Parking
The main car park is under Piazza della Vittoria, where bus tickets for the city can be bought. The centre is closed to traffic.

Tourist Information
Via Garibaldi 12; visitgenoa.it; open daily

WHERE TO STAY

GENOA

Cairoli *inexpensive*
Contemporary art inspires the bright and fresh rooms in this palazzo hotel, with an outdoor terrace and small gym. Garage parking is available.
Via Cairoli 14/4, 16124; hotelcairoligenova.com

Cristoforo Colombo *moderate*
Colourful and elegant rooms in the historic part of the city. In summer, breakfast is served on the roof terrace.
Via Porta Soprana 27, 16123; hotelcolombo.it

Domus Victoria *moderate*
This charming, centrally located B&B features a pleasant terrace and spacious rooms, including family options.
Piazza della Vittoria 15, 16121; 328 704 2913

Hotel Continental Genova *moderate*
A beautiful Art Nouveau hotel offering elegant rooms and a large breakfast.
Via Arsenale di terra 1, 16126; hotelcontinentalgenova.it

① GENOA (GENOVA)

Genoa; 16100

Surrounded by hills and looking out to sea, proud Genoa was transformed in the 16th and 17th centuries, when its merchants commissioned grand palazzos in what was then named "Strada Nuova" (New Street) – now called Via Garibaldi, it is a UNESCO World Heritage Site and three of the palazzos are world-class museums. For great views of the historic centre, take the lift to the neighbourhood of Castelletto.

A three-hour walking tour

Start from the De Ferrari metro station and follow Via Dante to the two towers of the **Porta Soprana** ①, a gate in the 12th-century walls that separates the historic from the modern city. The Vico Dritto di Ponticello leads past the **Chiostro di Sant'Andrea** ②, a ruined 12th-century cloister that was once part of a Benedictine monastery. **Casa di Cristoforo Colombo** ③, the supposed boyhood home of Christopher Columbus, is next door. Return to Porta Soprana and turn left into Via Ravecca, past the bell tower and cloisters of the 13th-century Chiesa di Sant'Agostino, now the **Museo di Sant'Agostino** ④, with works by Giovanni Pisano (1250–1315) and Antonio Canova (1757–1822). The museum fronts **Piazza di Sarzano** ⑤, so long, that it was once used for jousting and rope-making.

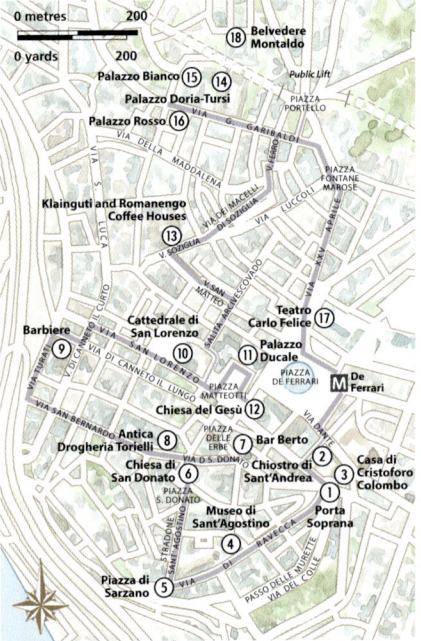

Stradone di Sant'Agostino leads to the Romanesque **Chiesa di San Donato** ⑥ with an octagonal campanile, a rose window and, inside, striped columns and a painted ceiling. Follow Via San Donato round the church to Piazza delle Erbe, with a full range of bars, including lively **Bar Berto** ⑦ (1904), decorated with tiles from Albisola. Walk back past the church to Via San Bernardo and look for the **Antica Drogheria Torielli** ⑧, filled with all kinds of herbs and spices.

Via San Bernardo leads to arcaded Via Turati. Turn right and keep going until the sign for Vico dei Caprettari is on the right. Look in (or get a haircut) at the **Barbiere** ⑨, to admire the Art Deco ornamentation. The alleyways here have an enticing mix of shops.

Turn left into Via di Cannetto then right into Via San Lorenzo with its striped 12th-century **Cattedrale di San Lorenzo** ⑩, flanked by two lions. Look inside for the Renaissance Cappella di San Giovanni Battista, once home to St John the Baptist's ashes. Carry on to Piazza Matteotti and the 16th-century **Palazzo Ducale** ⑪. Look inside for exhibitions. For some Baroque pomp, continue to the right of Piazza Matteotti and the **Chiesa del Gesù** ⑫, full of coloured marble, gilt stucco and frescoes. Take Salita Arcivescovado, turn left onto Vico San Matteo, then right to Via Soziglia for a drink and a cake in coffee houses **Klainguti** or **Romanengo** ⑬, dating from the 1800s. A left turn at the end of Via Soziglia onto

Vico del Ferro leads to Via Garibaldi and its great palazzos. Step inside **Palazzo Doria-Tursi** ⑭ for the beautiful courtyard and double marble staircase and view the stucco work. The **Palazzo Bianco** ⑮ has wonderful paintings by Filippino Lippi, Veronese and Caravaggio, as well as Dutch and Flemish masters Rubens, Van Dyck and Memling. The **Palazzo Rosso** ⑯ has paintings, furniture and 17th-century frescoes. Continue to Piazza Fontane Marose and Via XXV Aprile, passing the 19th-century **Teatro Carlo Felice** ⑰, home of Genoa's opera house.

If there's still time, take the Liberty-style lift from Piazza Portello, off Via Garibaldi, up to **Belvedere Montaldo** ⑱ for sweeping views. If staying longer in Genoa, take time to explore the port area.

🚗 *Follow signs to motorway A12 east to the Chiavari exit, signed Parma, then SP225 to Carasco. Take SP586, then turn right onto SP26bis. Continue up the Passo del Bocco and take the SP3 through Bedonia. Follow signs for A15 on SP523. After railway bridge, turn right for Berceto. Park in Piazza San Giovanni. For Corchia, follow signs to Corchia.*

② Berceto
Parma; 43042

The road to Berceto climbs through the Apennines and chestnut, beech and oak forests to the Valle del Taro, which is porcini mushroom country. Quiet Berceto, with its stone houses and cobbled streets, has changed little since it was an important stop on the Via Francigena. Its main attraction is the Romanesque **Duomo di San Moderanno**, which has a 12th-century lunette of the Crucifixion.

Tucked away in chestnut groves a little west of Berceto, the charming village of **Corchia** dates back to the 13th century. Everything here is made of stone. For 400 years the village depended on its nearby mines, which only closed in 1943.

🚗 *Take SP15 to Calestano, then follow signs for Langhirano, turning right onto SP61. Continue for 17 km (10.5 miles), then turn left onto SP665.*

③ Langhirano
Parma; 43100

It is a lovely drive through Calestano, where the countryside opens out into green terraced meadows, vines and orchards. The next town, Langhirano, is dedicated to the curing of air-dried ham; its many factories open their windows to what is said to be a perfect combination of sea and mountain air. The **Museo del Prosciutto** *(open weekends)* in the Foro Boario, a former cattle market, tells the history and process from pig to plate.

🚗 *Take SP665 to the signposted Castello di Torrechiara and car park.*

④ Castello di Torrechiara
Parma; 43010

This impressive castle *(closed Mon)* was built in the 15th century for defence, as can be seen from the three rings of walls and four square towers, and also as a family residence. There is a series of vivid 16th-century frescoes: the *Salone degli Acrobati* (Acrobats' Room) shows gymnasts in a human pyramid on the backs of lions and the *Camera d'Oro* (Golden Room) tells the love story between Count Pier Maria Rossi, for whom the castle was built, and his lover, Bianca Pellegrini.

🚗 *Take SP665 to Parma. Use a free car park off the tangenziale (ring road). Buy a ticket from machine for bus to centre.*

Above top The port of Genoa, facing the Ligurian Sea **Above left** Mural of St George slaying the dragon on the town hall, Genoa **Above right** The spectacular Castello Torrechiara, near Langhirano **Below left** The picturesque village of Calestano

SHOPPING IN TORRECHIARA

Buy prosciutto, salami and Parmigiano at **Salumeria da Gardoni** *(Piazza Leoni 5, 43010; 0521 355 119)*.

EAT AND DRINK

GENOA

Antico Forno Patrone *inexpensive*
Near the Porta Soprana, try the great artisanal focaccia and other Genovese specialties.
Via Ravecca 72r, 16128; 0102 511 093; closed Sun

Il Cadraio *moderate*
Traditional Genoese specialities served in a cosy, rustic trattoria. Great wine list.
Vico dietro il coro della Maddalena, 26r, 16124 Genoa;ilcadraio.it

Da Rina *expensive*
This restaurant, overlooking the Porto Antico, serves fish dishes and antipasti.
Mura delle Grazie 3r, 16128; ristorantedarina.it

AROUND BERCETO

Bar Pizzeria Iasoni Nadia *inexpensive*
Try pizzas, local game and mushroom dishes at this small trattoria.
Corchia 43042; 0525 61 814; closed Mon

La Pergola *moderate*
This restaurant puts mushrooms to the fore – expect porcini risotto and wild mushroom soufflé.
Via Garibaldi 19, 43041 Bedonia; ristorante-lapergola.it

Above left Boats in La Spezia's harbour
Above right Piazza Prampolini, Reggio Emilia Below Statue of the 16th-century artist Parmigianino in Piazza Santa Maria della Steccata, Parma

ACTIVITIES IN PARMA

Explore the car-free centre of town by hiring a bike from one of the **Punto Bici** *(infomobility.pr.it)* pick-up and drop-off points in the city. For tours of prosciutto and Parmigiano factories with tastings, try **Food Valley Gourmet Tours** *(Viale Frati 38D; foodvalley travel.com)*.

WHERE TO STAY

PARMA

Hotel Torino *moderate*
This comfortable hotel, furnished in modern style, is right in the historic centre and has garage parking.
Borgo Angelo Mazza 7, 43121; hotel-torino.it

REGGIO EMILIA

Albergo delle Notarie *moderate*
In the heart of the city, this hotel has views of the cathedral, a good restaurant and parking.
Via Palazzolo 5, 42121; albergo notarie.it

LA SPEZIA

Hotel Firenze e Continentale *moderate*
This large hotel, with an attractive marble and wood interior, offers stylish and comfortable accommodation with good views.
Via Paleocapa 1, 19122; hotelfirenzecontinentale.it

PORTOVENERE

Belvedere *moderate*
This family-run hotel offers a terrace overlooking the sea, rooms with balconies and on-site parking.
Via Garibaldi 26, 19025; belvedereportovenere.it

5 Parma
Parma; 43100

Seductive Parma is a treasure house of art and architecture, and a store of gastronomic delights. The 11th-century **Duomo** reflects both aspects. It is home to works by two sons of Parma – Parmagianino (1503–40) and Correggio (1489–1534), who painted the *Assumption* (1534) in the central cupola, and at the main entrance is the earliest known bas-relief of the slaughter of a pig. Next door, the 13th-century octagonal baptistery, by architect and sculptor Benedetto Antelami (c 1150–1230), is a confection of pink and white Verona marble. Don't miss the decorative interior.

Stroll over the green lawn to the vast Palazzo della Pilotta, built by the Farnese family and housing several museums. A visit to the **Galleria Nazionale** *(open Tue–Sun)* allows a closer look at works by Parmagianino, Correggio and others. Here, too, is the **Museo Archeologico Nazionale** *(open Tue–Sun)* and the wooden **Teatro Farnese**, inaugurated in 1628, when the auditorium was flooded to recreate a *naumachia* (naval battle). The three-tier auditorium has a revolving stage, the first in Italy.

The **Museo Glauco Lombardi** in Via Garibaldi is testament to Maria Luigia, who became Duchess of Parma in 1815 after Napoleon's abdication, and was a famous fan of Parma violets. Her dresses, jewellery, family portraits and watercolours are all on show.

🚗 *From the tangenziale (ring road) take SS9 to Reggio Emilia. Park in the centre at Caserma Zucchi on Viale Isonzo.*

6 Reggio Emilia
Emilia Romagna; 42100

As affluent as its neighbour Parma, if less glamourous, Reggio Emilia is a pleasant town to visit, with two large, lively central squares. Piazza Prampolini holds the **Duomo**, topped by a brick octagonal lantern tower, its Romanesque upper half in contrast to the 16th-century marble lower half, where Adam and Eve appear in the lunette over the doorway. In the same square, in 1797 the **Palazzo del Capitano del Popolo** flew the red, green and white tricolour that was later – in 1848 – to become Italy's national flag. It's a brief walk along the colonnaded street to Piazza San Prospero and the Baroque **Basilica San Prospero**, its façade busy with statues of saints, and guarded by six pink Verona marble lions. The profuse displays of sculpture, natural history and archaeology in the antique glass cases of the **Musei Civici** are a work of art in themselves. Don't miss the fine black and white medieval mosaics in the entrance hall.

🚗 *Take SS63 south towards La Spezia. At Aulla, join SS62 and follow signs for A15 to La Spezia and the road by the port. Turn right on Viale Amendola and park in Piazza d'Armi (2nd left).*

TRIP 14: THE AZURE COAST TO THE PO VALLEY

7 La Spezia
La Spezia, Liguria; 19100

With its mild climate and stunning position at the head of the Golfo della Spezia, backed by mountains, it's easy to see why Byron, Shelley, George Sands and D H Lawrence all loved the area. Nowadays, it is a thriving port and Italy's chief naval base, and it's still a treat to take a boat out into the bay. Standing back from the palm-fringed Giardini Pubblici along the sea front is Piazza Chiodi, site of the naval Arsenale from the 1860s. Next to it is the grand **Museo Tecnico Navale** *(open daily)* with model ships, figureheads and submarines. Wide boulevards lead to the centre and the modern market in Piazza Cavour with its wavy roof. Close by, the **Museo Amedeo Lia** *(closed Mon)* has first-class enamels and ivories, Roman bronzes and works by Tintoretto, Cranach and Canaletto. Next door, the **Museo del Sigillo** has the world's largest collection of seals, including Chinese jade and Art Nouveau objects by René Lalique.

🚗 *Take SP530 to Portovenere. Park on the main road before the village.*

8 Portovenere
La Spezia, Liguria; 19100

Dependent on fish in Roman times, when it was known as Portus Veneris (Port of Venus), Portovenere is still a typical Ligurian fishing town, with tall ochre and pink tower houses rising up from the small harbour. A walk along the harbour front and up the marble steps leads to the striped Genoese-Gothic **Chiesa di San Pietro**, stunningly sited on the tip of the rocky promontory that borders the western side of the Golfo dei Poeti. Alongside is the **Arpaia Grotto**, or Byron's Grotto, where a plaque on the wall commemorates the poet's swim to Lerici. Windows in the wall provide perfectly framed views of the Cinque Terre. Turning back towards the town, steep alleyways lead up to the chunky 16th-century **Castello Doria**, with more stunning views, and then back down to the main Via Capellini, a run of little bars, restaurants and boutiques. If time allows, take a boat from the port to explore one of the lovely islands nearby – Palmária, Tino or Tinetto.

BOAT TRIPS AND FERRIES
For information on passenger boats between La Spezia and Portovenere, Isola Palmária and the Cinque Terre, visit **Consorzio Marittimo Turistico** *(5 Terre, Via Don Minzoni 13, 19121 La Spezia; navigazionegolfodeipoeti.it)*.

WHERE TO EAT

PARMA
Enoteca Fontana *inexpensive*
This restaurant, popular with locals, serves wine by the glass from an extensive wine list (the Lambrusco is good). Snacks feature local specialities.
Strada Farini 24/A, 43121; 0521 286 037; closed Sun

Gallo D'Oro *moderate*
Rabbit and horsemeat feature on the menu here apart from classic Parma dishes, a variety of salads and stuffed pastas. It is located in the historic centre.
Borgo della Salina 3, 43121; gallodororistorante.it

LA SPEZIA
Il Ristorantino di Bayon *expensive*
Stylish and intimate restaurant with the accent on fish. Enjoy Palmária mussels and *trofie* (tightly twisted pasta) with shrimps and almonds. Booking advised.
Via Felice Cavallotti 23, 19121; ilristorantinodibayon.it

AROUND PORTOVENERE
Locanda Lorena *expensive*
It takes a boat trip to reach this excellent seafood restaurant on the Isola Palmária, but it's well worth it. They also have rooms.
Via Cavour 4, 19025 Isola Palmária; locandalorena.com; closed Wed & Nov–Feb

Above Portovenere's harbour, with its pastel-coloured tower houses **Left** Fishing boat in the sea beneath Castello Doria, Portovenere

DAY TRIP OPTIONS
Genoa easily deserves a day to itself for exploration and from there you can head down the coast to La Spezia and a boat trip to Portovenere.

Medieval Genoa
Simply spend the whole day in Genoa 1, investigating the maze of alleyways that make up the medieval centre, the Baroque jewel of San Gesù and the magnificent Cattedrale di San Lorenzo before discovering the artistic treasures of the palazzos. Stop for a coffee at Pasticceria Klainguti and be sure to end the day with a seafood supper.

Big port and little harbour
From Genoa 1, enjoy the coastal road to La Spezia 7, stroll the port's pleasant boulevards, take in some maritime history, then hop on a boat to lovely Portovenere 8 and soak up the wonderful views of the Cinque Terre from the Chiesa di San Pietro.

For La Spezia from Genoa, choose between SP1, which gives good views of the coast until Sestri Levante, or the quicker A12/E60 motorway, which gives a journey time of 1.5 hours.

TRIP 15

THE LIGURIAN COAST AND APENNINES

Camogli to Riomaggiore

HIGHLIGHTS

Parco Nazionale delle Cinque Terre
Explore the five exquisite villages of this UNESCO World Heritage Site in a dramatic setting on the Ligurian coast

Fruits of the forest and sea
Sample the freshest seafood and enjoy produce such as pestos, chestnuts and honey from Apennine farms

Peaceful Parco dell'Antola
Hike among the wooded hills, dotted with lakes and ancient villages, in this overlooked part of Liguria

Jewel of the Riviera
Enjoy lovely Portofino, squeezed between turquoise waters and the lush greenery of its promontory

THE LIGURIAN COAST AND APENNINES

Sparkling waters lap the Ligurian coast. Beach resorts, tiny fishing harbours, hidden coves and exquisite Portofino all vie for attention with the famous five villages of the Cinque Terre, where colourful mosaics of houses tumble down steep cliffs to the sea. Inland lies a landscape of ancient hamlets and shady dry-stone terraces of vines, olives and aromatic basil. In contrast, the Ligurian Apennines are a world apart – one of medieval castles and agricultural villages set among lakes, meadows and chestnut forests, where sheep graze peacefully and horses are still used to log timber.

Above Typical tower houses of the Cinque Terre, Manarola, *see p158*

ACTIVITIES

Hike or cycle along the *sentieri* – trails – in the stunning Parco Nazionale delle Cinque Terre

Enjoy a panoramic picnic at the Santuario di Montenero above Riomaggiore

Taste the speciality of Vernazza – honey-coloured *sciacchetrà*, a sweet dessert wine

Surf the waves or laze on the beach at Levanto

Take a boat trip from Camogli for coastal views of San Fruttuoso, Portofino and the Cinque Terre coast

Play a round of seaside golf at Rapallo

Explore Lago di Brugneto amid beech and chestnut woods

TRIP 15: THE LIGURIAN COAST AND APENNINES

Above The popular Monterosso al Mare beach, Cinque Terre, see p156

PLAN YOUR DRIVE

Start/finish: Camogli to Riomaggiore.

Number of days: 4–5, allowing one day each for the coast and the interior and 2 days for the Cinque Terre.

Distance: Approx. 182 km (113 miles).

Road conditions: Roads are slow, narrow, twisting, often very steep and sometimes single track with infrequent passing places. If you choose to visit the Cinque Terre by car rather than by public transport, arrive early in the day to be sure of a parking place. There are no petrol stations in the Cinque Terre.

When to go: Coastal resorts get very crowded Jul–Aug and roads may be impassable. Spring and autumn are cooler and less busy. Autumn makes for the best colour in the interior.

Opening times: Shops close 1–4pm; some in the main towns open on Sundays. Churches and museums hours vary, but are usually open in the mornings until 1pm and from 4–7pm. Museums are usually shut on Mondays.

Main market days: Bonassola: Thu; Levanto: Wed; Monterosso al Mare: Thu; Vernazza: Tue.

Shopping: Look for *sciacchetrà* (sweet wine) in the Cinque Terre, *castagnaccio* (chestnut cake), virgin olive oil, pesto, honey and Limoncino liqueur.

Major festivals: Camogli: Stella Maris (sea procession), 1st Sun in Aug; Sagra del Pesce (fish festival), 2nd Sun in May; **Levanto:** Festa del Mare (in honour of San Giacomo), late Jul; **Monterosso al Mare:** Sagra dei Limoni (lemon festival), late May; Torneo di Noci (walnut tournament), Sep; **Manarola:** Presepe di Manarola (Manarola Nativity), Dec; **Pentema:** Presepe di Pentema, Dec–Jan.

DAY TRIP OPTIONS

It's easiest to reach the Cinque Terre by **train** – once there, walk **La Via dell'Amore** (The Love Trail) from Riomaggiore to Manarola for views of **pretty villages** and **harbours**. Enjoy the **cable car** and **coastal delights** of Sestri Levante. Get away from it all in the **Apennines**, exploring Torriglia's **castle** and **walking** around Lago del Brugneto. For full details, see p159.

Right Beachgoers in Abbazia di San Fruttuoso **Below right** Rapallo castle, built in the 16th century to ward off pirates **Below left** Colourful façades on Camogli's beachfront promenade

WHERE TO STAY

CAMOGLI

La Camogliese *moderate*
Friendly, family-run 3-star hotel with balconies overlooking the sea, right in the centre of town.
Via Garibaldi 55, 16032; lacamogliese.it

Villa Rosmarino *expensive*
Chic villa high above Camogli, with six very contemporary, art-filled rooms, with terrace, pool, garden and views. Children under 8 not allowed.
Via Figari 38, 16032; villarosmarino.com

PORTOFINO

Eden *moderate*
Set a little way back from the piazzetta, this is the most affordable hotel in town, with a charming garden and restaurant.
Via Dritto 18, 16034; hotel-portofino.com

RAPALLO

Italia e Lido *inexpensive*
Enjoy the private beach and dining terrace at this historic promenade hotel next to the castle.
Lungomare Castello 1, 16035; italiaelido.com

TORRIGLIA

Hotel della Posta *inexpensive*
Built in the early 1900s, this central hotel is simple, but well furnished.
Via Matteotti 39, 16029; 010 944 050

Below The picturesque harbour settlement of Portofino

① Camogli
Genoa; 16032

Steeped in seafaring tradition and once rivalling Genoa in naval power, the town acquired its name, Casa Mogli (house of wives), because the menfolk spent so much of their time at sea. The *case torri*, the colourful houses up to seven storeys high, threaded with steep alleyways that are the hallmark of the fishing villages of the Levante coast, are stacked up from the picturesque harbour. During the *Sagra del Pesce* (fish festival) in May, the harbour is the scene of a festive fry-up when thousands of fish are cooked in a giant 5-m (15-ft) pan and distributed free to the crowds. The 12th-century **Dragonara Castle**, set on a rocky promontory, separates the busy harbour from the beach, and the **Museo Marinaro** (closed Mon), full of models of ships, paintings and naval instruments, recalls the town's glorious maritime past.

🚗 For San Fruttuoso, take a boat from Camogli (along the coast, or walk about 3 hours in each direction).

② San Fruttuoso
Genoa; 16030

The boat from Camogli chugs round the Golfo del Tigullio to the ancient Benedictine **Abbazia di San Fruttuoso**, straddling a sandy cove; originally, boats would have moored under its arches. Sights include the 11th-century church, topped by a tiled cupola, the cloisters, and the 16th-century watchtower. The other attraction, visitable by glass-bottomed boat, is a larger than life-size bronze statue of **Cristo degli Abissi** (Christ of the Deep), sunk out in the bay in 1954, hands raised in blessing for those who work on or under the sea. There are beachside cafés, bars and swimming, but no road access.

🚗 Head north out of Camogli to Via Aurelia/SS1, then turn right. Fork right onto the SP39, then right again onto SP227 along the coast to Portofino. Park in the multi-storey car park.

③ Portofino
Genoa; 16034

Even those without a luxury yacht anchored in the enchanting harbour can appreciate how Portofino earned its reputation as one of Italy's most romantic spots. Window shopping at Missoni or Dior and people-watching from a waterside café may be a draw for many, but for the most gorgeous views, walk to **Castello Brown** (closed Nov–Mar: Mon–Fri), up in the pines on the peninsula. Montague Yeats Brown, the British consul, gave his name to this 16th-century castle when he lived here in the 1890s. From here, walk on to the **Faro**, the old lighthouse at the Punta del Capo. Art lovers should visit the **Museo del Parco** (closed winter: Tue), overlooking the harbour, which displays intriguing modern sculptures.

🚗 Take the SP227 north to Rapallo. Park along the seafront or at the car park on Via Milite Ignoto.

④ Rapallo
Genoa; 16035

The grand hotels and villas lining Rapallo's Lungomare still recall the 19th-century aristocrats and literati, among them Max Beerbohm and Ezra Pound, who were attracted by the town's inviting climate and location. Along the shore, past the ruined 16th-century castle jutting out into the sea, the ochre Villa Tigullio houses the **Museo del Merletto** (open Sat & Sun), where drawers full of lace reflect the town's past history of lace-making. In the centre, the **Museo Gaffoglio** (closed mid-Dec & May) holds an eclectic collection of Meissen porcelain, 19th- and 20th-century pastoral paintings and exquisite Fabergé pieces. For the best view of the area, take a ride up the *funivia* (cable car) from Piazza Solari to the striped and pinnacled **Santuario di Montallegro** (1559), which houses a Byzantine icon said to possess miraculous powers.

🚗 Take the SS1 towards Genoa and, from Recco, turn right onto SP333. At Gattorna, take SP21 to Torriglia. Park in the main square.

⑤ Torriglia
Genoa; 16029

A 30-minute drive on a steep and twisting road leads from the coast up to the chestnut forests, lakes and villages of the Ligurian Apennines. Verdant in spring and summer, and glorious in autumn, this is a much less-visited area than the coast. Torriglia's main sight is its castle, perched high above the town. The domain of the Fieschi from the mid-14th century, then the Doria family from the 16th to the 18th centuries, it is now in ruins. The area is known for its porcini mushrooms and *canestrelli* biscuits.

🚗 Take the uphill road north to SP15-1 and turn left and left again, following brown signs to Pentema. Park at the road's end for the top of village or follow signs to Pezza for the lower part.

Above The small fishing village of Camogli **Below** The ruins of Torriglia castle, set among woods

WHERE TO EAT

CAMOGLI AND AROUND

La Cucina di Nonna Nina *moderate*
Whether dining in the blue and white rooms or outside in the garden, visitors will enjoy the best of Liguria's cuisine.
Via Molfino 126, 16032 Località San Rocco (from Camogli take SP1 towards La Spezia, then turn right); lacucina dinonnanina.com; closed Wed

La Bossa di Mario *expensive*
Wine bottles line the walls of this small enoteca (wine bar), which has a daily-changing menu featuring dishes such as stuffed anchovies, rabbit or a fish ravioli.
Via della Repubblica 124, 16032; la bossa.it; closed Wed & open lunch Sun

PORTOFINO

Ö Magazin Bistrot *expensive*
An ideal spot on the water for watching the world go by. Be prepared to wait for a table. Try the ragù with pasta.
Calata Marconi 34, 16034; omagazin.it

RAPALLO

Osteria Ö Bansin *moderate*
Long-established restaurant in the old town with an accent on fish and good-value fixed-price lunches.
Via Venezia 105, 16035; trattoriabansin.it; closed Mon

TORRIGLIA

La Taverna dei Fieschi *moderate*
After admiring the Bakelite radios, try dishes that celebrate local porcini mushrooms, chestnuts, wild boar and *canestrelli* (biscuits).
Via Magioncalda 30, 16029; 010 945 1041

PARCO DELL'AVETO

This is an important protected area of mountain peaks, beech woods and glacial lakes, famous for its large number of insectivorous plants. The park office in Borzonasca can supply maps and information about walks and hikes in the area.
Via Mallè 75A, Borzonasca 16041; 0185 343 370; parks.it/parco.aveto

WHERE TO STAY

PENTEMA

A o Soâ B&B *inexpensive*
Enjoy a relaxing stay at this country villa with elegantly furnished rooms and a large, lush garden.
Via Broglio 11, 16010 Savignone; savibed.com

AROUND FONTANIGORDA

Due Ponti *inexpensive*
The peaceful location – surrounded by pines, with the River Trebbia lapping at the bottom of the garden – makes this a welcoming hotel. It has a good restaurant and bikes are available.
Via Nazionale 2, 16023 Loc. Due Ponti (3 km/2 miles before Loco on SP45); hoteldueponti.com

BORZONASCA

Il Bosco di Campo Marzano *moderate*
This old farmhouse has garden views and a great pool. The rooms are spacious, and the common area includes a shared kitchen for the use of all guests.
Via Campomarzano 5, 16041; ilboscodicampomarzano.it

SESTRI LEVANTE

Hotel Suisse *inexpensive*
Modern, clean hotel within easy walking distance of the Baia del Silenzio beach.
Via Dante 88, 16039; 0185 42 253

Villa Agnese *moderate*
On the outskirts of town, this modern and eco-conscious hotel has light, airy rooms and a relaxing garden. Expect organic produce for breakfast.
Via alla Fattoria Pallavicini 1A, 16039 (close to Sestri Levante exit of A12); hotelvillaagnese.com

Hotel Helvetia *expensive*
This charming luxury boutique hotel provides classic Riviera style with a panoramic outdoor pool and spectacular views of Sestri's Bay of Silence.
Via Cappuccini 43, 16039; hotelhelvetia.it

6 Pentema
Genoa; 16029

Still very much the isolated mountain village it has always been, Pentema clings to the hillside, stone houses and sheds fronting steep cobbled streets and steps. At Christmas, the village is much visited for its *presepe*, which consists of more than the Christmas crib. Yellow numbers painted on the walls direct pilgrims on a journey through more than 40 life-size tableaux, reflecting all aspects of 19th-century village life and crafts, culminating in the Nativity scene. Many of these can actually be seen all year round.

🚗 *Head back towards Torriglia until meeting SP15-1, then turn left towards Propata. Turn right just before a tunnel, following signs to Lago del Brugneto and park near the dam.*

7 Lago del Brugneto
Genoa; 16025

Lush terraced meadows, groves of hazelnut, beech and chestnut and horse-logged wood are hallmarks of the **Parco dell'Antola** (*parcoantola.it*), which encompasses the arms of Lago di Brugneto. An artificial lake constructed in 1959 to provide water for Genoa and Piacenza, the lake makes a good stopping point for a peaceful and undemanding walk (see website for suggestions). A wooded path, following old mule tracks, skirts the arms of the lake close to the water, while other trails lead to waterfalls and an old mill.

🚗 *From the lake, follow signs for Montebruno, turning left at SS45. Carry on along SS45, signed Piacenza, turn right onto SP17 after Loco, then turn left onto SP18 to Fontanigorda. There is plenty of parking available.*

Below The Baia di Silenzio and the harbour at Sestri Levante **Bottom left** The peaceful, wooded countryside around Lago del Brugneto **Bottom right** One of Fontanigorda's 13 pineapple-topped fountains

Far left Typical stone houses in the mountain village of Pentema **Middle left** The river that feeds Lago del Brugneto **Left** Hans Christian Andersen's favourite beach at Sestri Levante

WHERE TO EAT

SESTRI LEVANTE
Cantina del Polpo *moderate*
There's plenty of fish on the menu, but there are other options, too, such as *trofie* (or *trofiette*) *al pesto* (twisty pasta), *torte di verdura* (vegetable pie), plus excellent local wines and grappas.
Piazza Cavour 2, 16039; cantinadelpolpo.it

Balin *expensive*
Try gazpacho with shrimp, tuna tartare and many other creative fish dishes at this fine restaurant set on the beach.
Viale Rimembranza 33, 16039; 349 947 2695

8 Fontanigorda
Genoa; 16023
It is easy to while away half an hour or so here, walking the cobbled streets in search of all 13 of the pineapple-topped fountains for which this small, red-roofed mountain village is famous. The fountains are dedicated – aptly enough for a place with an abundance of water – to the Mater Dolorosa (Our Lady of Sorrows). The Baroque church of **Santi Antonio e Jacopo** has a decorative red-and-gold interior and impressive barley-sugar columns.

Follow the sign for Casoni on SP17, then SP48, drive over the Passo di Fregarolo and turn right at SP586 for Borzonasca, where the Abbazia di Sant/Andrea di Borzone (3 km/2 miles east of the village) is signposted along SP49. For Borzonasca, park in Piazza Garibaldi by the church.

9 Borzonasca
Genoa; 16041
After a spectacular journey over the 1,203-m (3,950-ft) Passo di Fregarolo, Borzonasca's main attraction is the **Abbazia di Sant'Andrea di Borzone** (open daily), a short drive east of the town. Standing in peaceful isolation and guarded by a 600-year-old cypress tree, the Benedictine complex was founded in the 12th century on an earlier 9th-century Lombard building, and is characterized by its rows of blind brick and stone arcading. The bell tower was probably originally an ancient watchtower. In the town itself, shops sell local honey, San Stè cheese, and, in season, hazelnuts; and the Aveto Park office provides information about hikes in the area.

Take SP586 for Carasco and follow signs for Chiavari onto SP225, then turn left on SP1 for Sestri Levante.

10 Sestri Levante
Genoa; 16039
Danish author Hans Christian Andersen enjoyed his visit here in 1833 so much that the town named the sandy beach **Baia delle Favole (Bay of Fairy Tales)**. On the other side of the peninsula along which this popular resort clusters, lies the more intimate **Baia di Silenzio**, with its fleet of fishing boats and colourful houses. Close by, the **Galleria Rizzi** recreates a palazzo interior of the 19th century, including works of art such as still lifes by the Baroque painter Felice Boselli. Lively Via XXV Aprile/Corso Colombo is packed with interesting shops and restaurants, and the Hotel dei Castelli on the hill offers refreshments and panoramic views of both bays.

Take SP1 towards La Spezia until Passo del Braco, then turn right onto SP332, then SP64 for Bonassola. Park along the seafront.

Below Borzonasca, the closest village to the Benedictine Abbazia di Sant'Andrea di Borzone

Right The curving bay of Levanto, flanked by two wooded headlands

WHERE TO STAY

LEVANTO

A Durmí *moderate*
Beautifully appointed, bright and airy rooms around a quiet courtyard garden that has plenty of relaxing shady spots. Mini apartments are also available.
Via Viviani 12, 19015; adurmi.it

Palazzo Vannoni *moderate*
Colourful frescoes and antiques fill the rooms of this lovely 19th-century palazzo. Ample breakfasts are served under a pergola in the garden.
Via Marconi 4, 19015; hotelpalazzovannoni.it

MONTEROSSO AL MARE

La Spiaggia *moderate*
This family home-turned-hotel on the Monterosso seafront is at a walking distance from the old town centre.
Via Fegna 98; 19016; laspiaggiamonterosso.com

Porto Roca *moderate*
Soak up the sea views from the beautiful verandas, terrace and garden of this luxurious hotel, set on the headland and with a private beach below.
Via Corone 1, 19016; portoroca.it; closed Nov–Mar

CORNIGLIA

Cecio 5 Terre Rooms *inexpensive*
Located just 2 km (1 mile) from the beach, this guesthouse offers lovely views and comfortable rooms with family options.
Via Serra 58, 19018; cecio5terre.com

Below The village of Corniglia, set on 100-m (330-ft) high cliffs

⓫ Bonassola
La Spezia; 19011

A little quieter than Sestri Levante, the town of Bonassola shelters behind its sea wall, on top of which a boardwalk stretches the length of the dark, sandy beach. In the town centre, the **Chiesa di Santa Caterina** has a sumptuous Baroque interior with two stunning processional crosses of intricate silverwork. Paintings of ships hang on the walls – ex-votos from thankful sailors. On a cliff west of the town, the **Cappella della Madonnina della Punta** beckons for a sunset walk.

🚗 *Follow signs for Levanto. There is a large car park next to the tourist office on the seafront.*

⓬ Levanto
La Spezia; 19015

With the best beach in the area – long and sandy – and good opportunities for kayaking and surfing, Levanto is a destination for lovers of the outdoors. It's also a good entry point for the Cinque Terre. However, the historic centre provides plenty to see as well. The medieval walls, the **Castello di San Giorgio** *(closed Mon & Tue)*, **Torre dell'Orologio** and the pretty **Loggia del Commune** all date back to the 13th century. But perhaps best of all is the lovely **Chiesa di Sant'Andrea**, a beautiful example of Ligurian Gothic with its striped, green serpentine and white Carrara marble façade and delicate lacy rose window.

🚗 *Take SP43 past the train station, then SP370, which finishes with a steep descent to Monterosso. Park at the seafront, or on Via Roma.*

> **Walking in the Cinque Terre**
>
> As well as the famous **Sentiero Azzuro (Blue Trail)**, which connects all five villages, there are numerous well-marked trails linking the shrines and hilltop hamlets of the **Parco Nazionale delle Cinque Terre**. Some of these trails can be covered by bike or on horseback. Pick up maps, bus and train timetables, and information on the Cinque Terre card (required to access the trails) from information points or tourist offices at the train stations. The park's website, parconazionale5terre.it, is also a useful source of information.

⓭ Monterosso al Mare
La Spezia; 19016

Monterosso is the first of the five Cinque Terre villages encountered when approaching from the west, and the only one to be built on the flat. A tunnel hewn out of rock

connects the long, sandy beach of the new town, **Fegina**, to the older part, where a huge modern statue of Neptune (14 m/45 ft), nicknamed "Il Gigante", stands in front of the harbour. Here, too, in Piazza Garibaldi, is the 13th-century serpentine and white marble striped **Chiesa di San Giovanni**, complete with rose window. Climb the hill to the **Convento dei Cappuccini** (1622) and its **Chiesa di San Francesco** for excellent artworks – *Crucifixion* by Van Dyck, *La Veronica* by Strozzi and two good pieces by Luca Cambioso.

🚗 *Take SP370, then a series of right turns onto Vernazza. There is a car park outside the village.*

Above Narrow alleyway in Corniglia, typical of all the Cinque Terre towns

⑭ Vernazza
La Spezia; 19018

Regarded by many as one of Italy's most perfect villages, Vernazza's pastel- and earth-coloured houses, strewn with washing, crowd the little piazzetta that fronts the natural harbour. Take time here to watch the locals fishing close to the stacks of striated rocks and the bobbing fishing boats. The harbourside **Chiesa Santa Margherita d'Antiochia** (1318), distinguished by its octagonal bell tower, is unusual in having its door on the eastern (altar) side. Perched on top of the rocky promontory, the watchtower of the **Castello Doria** was built in the 15th century, as were many others along this coast, to ward off marauding pirates.

🚗 *Head out of town on SP63 and follow SP61 and SP30 to Corniglia. Park before you get to the village.*

⑮ Corniglia
La Spezia; 19018

Compact Corniglia, the only Cinque Terre village not directly on the sea, sits high on a cliff amid terraced vineyards and olive groves. Less busy than its counterparts, it makes for a peaceful stroll through the boxy houses and eclectic mix of attractive gift, clothes and food shops lining the main Via Fieschi. Looking seaward from the dark and narrow alleyways, the Santa Maria Belvedere offers the chance to admire the dramatic, jagged edge of the coastline. To get to the beach or the train station, descend the famous **Lardarina**, the broad zigzag path of nearly 400 steps, from where a coastal trail connects with Manarola.

🚗 *Head back on SP30, then turn right onto SP61 and right again onto SP51. At roundabout after Groppo, take SP59 to Manarola. Park outside the village.*

Below The harbour and the Chiesa Santa Margherita d'Antiochia at Vernazza

Left The popular sandy beach at Monterosso al Mare

EAT AND DRINK

LEVANTO
Taverna Garibaldi *inexpensive*
Popular with locals and set on a bustling street, this place specializes in pizzas of all varieties as well as prawns and *bresaola* (air-dried beef).
Via Garibaldi 57, 19015; 0187 808 098

Da Rino *moderate*
Sit outside and watch the local street life as you sample minestrone soup or simple seafood linguine.
Via Garibaldi 10, 19015; 0187 813 475; open eves only

VERNAZZA
Ristorante Pizzeria Vulnetia *moderate*
Popular place serving good fish dishes – try the marinated anchovies or linguine – as well as pizzas and pastas.
Piazza Marconi 29, 19018; 0187 821 193

Belforte *expensive*
This place serves creative dishes, best eaten on the cliffside *terrazzo con vista* (terrace with view) at sunset.
Via Guidoni 42, 19018; ristorante belforte.it; closed Tue

CORNIGLIA
A Butiega *inexpensiveþ*
Stock up on picnic supplies: sandwiches and seafood antipasti are on offer at this tiny deli.
Via Fieschi 142; 19018; 0187 812 292

Enoteca Il Pirun *moderate*
After sampling a glass or two of the local wine in this cosy wine bar, head upstairs for a bite to eat.
Via Fieschi 115, 19018; 0187 812 315

Above Manarola, a classic Cinque Terre village of pastel-coloured houses set by the sea

WHERE TO STAY

MANAROLA

Ca' d'Andrean *inexpensive*
Family-run hotel in a typical Cinque Terre tower house in the upper village. It has spacious modern rooms and a courtyard garden with fragrant lemon trees.
Via Discovolo 101, 19017; cadandrean.it

La Torretta *expensive*
This chic and peaceful hotel has an elegant and eclectic style. The hot tub with a view, airy rooms and subtle lighting make for a pampering stay.
Vico Volto 20, 19010; torrettas.com

RIOMAGGIORE

Hotel Due Gemelli *moderate*
A comfortable hotel with sea views, rooms with balconies and a lovely breakfast. Free parking for guests.
Via Litoranea 1, 19017; duegemelli.it

16 Manarola
La Spezia; 19010

Manarola's pink- and ochre-washed houses and narrow streets cascade down to its tiny harbour, where an old-fashioned crane winches the boats in and out of the water. The little **Sciacchetrà Museum** *(open Mar–Oct daily)* gives a good insight into the making of the eponymous local amber-coloured wine. From the Gothic **Chiesa di San Lorenzo** (1338), with its ornate rose window and separate square bell tower, previously an ancient lookout, there's a pleasant walk up through the vineyards and down to the classic viewing point at **Punto Bonfiglio**. At Christmas time, the hills above the village are decorated with prettily illuminated Nativity scenes – *presepe* – all made from recycled materials.

🚗 *Return up SP59, then take SP370 at the roundabout. Next, turn right onto SP32 to Riomaggiore. Park at the top of the village, paying at the booth.*

17 RIOMAGGIORE
La Spezia; 19017

Named after the Rio Major (Main River) that now flows underground between houses clinging to the steep-sided ravine, Riomaggiore is a good place to start walking the Cinque Terre trail. There are great views on the climb to the 14th-century Santuario di Montenero.

A two-hour walking tour
This walk offers a quick tour of the village before the hard climb begins. From the car park at the top of the village, head down Via Santuario and turn first right along Via Pecunia to the **Chiesa di San Giovanni Battista** ①. Founded in 1340, its lovely rose window and Gothic doorways are a result of 19th-century remodelling and, inside, the graceful, two-toned, grey arches frame a life-size wooden crucifix by Baroque sculptor Anton Maragliano. Head down the broad steps to the bustling **Via Colombo** ②, where the river roars underfoot, and continue past the coloured houses, little shops and boats parked on the road near the harbour. On the right, there's a blue-lit tunnel towards the train station; walk through it to find one of the many **murals** ③ by Silvio Benedetto that decorate the village. This one depicts the building of the *muretti a secco* (dry-stone walls) that form the Cinque Terre terraces.

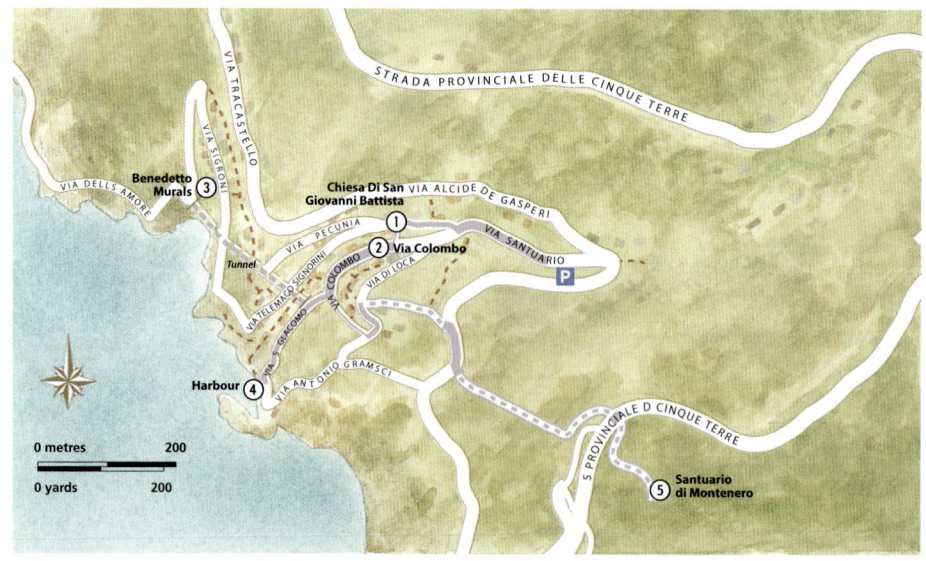

TRIP 15: THE LIGURIAN COAST AND APENNINES

Left Pretty Riomaggiore, built over the Rio Major **Below left** Dramatic rock formation, at Riomaggiore **Below right** Small shrine to the Madonna, by a doorway in Manarola

EAT AND DRINK

MANAROLA
Alla Marina *moderate*
Sit outdoors and watch the walkers and swimmers as evening falls, while having local treats – mainly seafood.
Via Lo Scalo 16, 19017; 0187 958 512; closed Mon

RIOMAGGIORE
Osteria La Torpedine *moderate*
This restaurant serves the day's catch, as well as fried squid and pasta with clams. Friendly service and great attention to wine pairings.
Via Gramsci 25, 19017; 0187 920 692; closed Tue

Fuori Rotta *expensive*
A creative restaurant, Fuori Rotta is perfect for special occasions. It serves well-presented fish specialities.
Via Signorini 48, 19017; ristorante fuorirotta.com; closed Wed

At the end of Via Colombo, a subterranean passage emerges at the **harbour** ④. Stop here to take in the views; admire the boys jumping off the rocks and look back at the houses tumbling higgledy-piggledy down the cliff. Then, follow the path to the left to see the little beach before returning through the tunnel to Via Colombo. Now the climb begins. Take the steps up Via Gramsci, and go round a children's playground to Via di Loca, past some handy seats. More steps, signed Santuario di Montenero, lead past terraces filled with rows of pepper and basil plants.

Go around the cemetery to the main Manarola to Riomaggiore road, where the views begin to open up – it's also the start of Sentiero 3a, marked by red and white stripes. Cross the road, then turn right, taking the concrete steps on the left-hand side up through vineyards and scrub to the gleaming white **Santuario di Montenero** ⑤, set among the pines. At 341 m (1,120 ft), there are great views along the coast in both directions. Walk past the restaurant to spot the little cog railway – *trenino del vino* – used to take workers and grapes up and down the terraces at harvest time.

Energetic hikers can carry on to the Colle del Telegrafo (making a 9-km/6-mile round trip in total). To get back to the car, descend to the road, then follow it down to Riomaggiore. There is a bus service, but stop by the visitor information office for a timetable first.

Above Fishing boats in the clean waters of Riomaggiore's harbour

DAY TRIP OPTIONS

The coastal towns of Levanto, Sestri Levante and Camogli all make good bases for day trips.

Cinque Terre experience
Starting from Levanto ⑫, get a flavour of the upper and lower Cinque Terre by exploring the pretty village and harbour of Manarola ⑯, then walk the easy Via dell'Amore trail to Riomaggiore ⑰. From here, hike up through the terraces of vines to the Santuario di Montenero.

From Levanto, the easiest option is to take the train, which stops at all five Cinque Terre villages.

Golfo del Tigullio
Enjoy the Golfo del Tigullio from Sestri Levante ⑩, exploring Rapallo ④, where you can spend time on the beach and take a cable-car ride. Then continue round to the little gem of Portofino ③, before returning.

From Sestri Levante take SP1 to Rapallo, then SP227 to Portofino, and back. Or, relax and take one of the boats that ply the coast from town to town.

Explore the Ligurian Apennines
From Camogli ①, drive through the chestnut and beech woods to the castle at Torriglia ⑤, then head to the timeless village of Pentema ⑥. For exercise, the nearby Lago del Brugnello ⑦ is good for a walk.

From Camogli, take SP333 to Gattorna, then SP21 to Torriglia. The SP15-1 runs from Pentema to Lago del Brugneto.

TRIP 16

SANCTUARIES AND FORESTS
Fiesole to Anghiari

HIGHLIGHTS

Great Benedictine abbey
Wander around the Abbazia di Vallombrosa along heavily forested trails of beech and firs

Historic castles
Conquer the ruined Castello di Romena and climb the tower of the splendid Castello di Conto Guidi

Pristine forests
Visit the best-preserved forests in all Italy, the Parco Nazionale delle Foreste Casentinesi, home to wild animals such as wolves, boars and mouflon (mountain sheep)

Holy sanctuary
Visited by St Francis and one of the holiest places of the Franciscan monks, the medieval Santuario della Verna is set in an untouched forest

SANCTUARIES AND FORESTS

A thousand years ago, followers of the early Christian faith retreated from the everyday world of men and established monastic communities deep in Italy's forests. Their aim was to live a life of poverty, commune with nature and listen to the word of God resounding in the silence. While protecting the forests, the monasteries grew: some retained a sublime simplicity, others were decorated with great works of art. Forests such as Casentino and Vallombrosa are now national parks and part of Italy's natural heritage. This trip takes in sophisticated Fiesole, the Hermitage of Camáldoli, the castle town of Poppi and the La Verna Sanctuary, and visits Michelangelo's birthplace and the beautiful town of Anghiari overlooking the Upper Tiber Valley.

Above Benedictine monks at the Santuario della Verna, see p168

ACTIVITIES

Take a hike in the Casentino Forest among pine woods, beech and maple trees

Ride a bike along the River Arno as it approaches the town of Stia

Enjoy a picnic in the unspoiled Forest of Vallombrosa (Valley of Shadow)

Learn Italian at Poppi's cultural institute – or take a class in stone masonry

Visit a Roman amphitheatre in the middle of the town of Fiesole

Listen to heavenly organ recitals and Gregorian chants at the La Verna Sanctuary

Below The ancient town of Anghiari, rising above the surrounding vines and fruit trees, see p169

TRIP 16: SANCTUARIES AND FORESTS

Above Walking down a trail in the Casentino Forest, *see p167*

PLAN YOUR DRIVE

Start/finish: Fiesole to Anghiari.

Number of days: 2–3 days.

Distance: Approx. 140 km (87 miles).

Road conditions: Generally excellent.

When to go: Summer is best, with plenty of festivals and concerts. In spring, the weather can be changeable but often good. Autumn sees the forests change colour, but winter is not recommended. Many mountain passes close as do many restaurants and hotels, and travel can be difficult.

Opening times: Most museums open 10am–6pm (small museums only on weekends outside the summer). Monasteries and sanctuaries observe the religious calendar and churches usually open 9am–noon and 3–7pm. Sundays and major religious feast days are likely to be busy.

Main market days: Fiesole: Sat; **Stia:** Tue; **Pratovecchio:** Fri; **Poppi:** Sat; farmers' market, Tue; **Anghiari:** Wed.

Major festivals: Fiesole: Estate Fiesolana (music and arts), Jun–Sep; **Vallombrosa:** church music, Jun; **Poppi:** Il Gusto dei Guidi (food and wine), Aug; **La Verna:** Festival of Organ Music, Jul & Aug; **Caprese Michelangelo:** Festa della Castagna (chestnut festival), Oct. **Anghiari:** Festa dei Bringoli e di San Martino (pasta festival), Nov.

Shopping: The monks at Vallombrosa and La Verna sell products such as liquors, jams and CDs of monastic music. In Anghiari, buy oils, soap and creams from the medieval olive oil mill of Ravagni; nearby Bussatti make textiles on looms left by Napoleon's retreating troops.

DAY TRIP OPTIONS

There's lots for families to do here, from conquering **castles** with **towers** and **dungeons** to touring the villages' main squares. Or explore the **Roman ruins** of Fiesole – the **amphitheatre** and **museum**, then enjoy a **picnic** and **walk** in the forest of Vallombrosa. Adults may enjoy exploring the many ancient **churches**, **sanctuaries** and **monasteries** of the area. For further details, *see p169*.

① Fiesole
Firenze, Toscana; 50014

This important Etruscan, then Roman, town was conquered by Florence in 1125. Its position in the hills above the Renaissance city and clear air induced the Medicis to build a villa here. At the town centre, Piazza Mino da Fiesole is overlooked by 14th-century **Palazzo Pretorio** with its handsome double loggia. The **Duomo di San Romulo di Fiesole** has an impressive polyptych by Bicci di Lorenzo (1373–1452) depicting stories of St Nicholas. Nearby, the **Area Archeologica** (closed winter: Tue) contains a superb Roman theatre and baths from the 1st century BCE. Evidence of the Etruscans is still obvious from the city walls (Via della Mura Etrusche) and the tombs in Via del Bargellino. For sumptuous views of Florence, take Via San Francesco, by the side of the Duomo, up to the convent, which stands on the site of the original Roman acropolis.

From the centre of town, Via Vecchia Fiesolana leads to the hamlet of San Domenico, home to two important churches. **Badia Fiesolana** (Via della Badia dei Roccettini 9; closed Sun & public holidays) is a rare example of the Romanesque style in Tuscany. The abbey was consecrated in 1032 and dedicated to the martyred bishop, St Romulus. Its serpentine and marble façade was retained during 15th-century restorations attributed to architects Brunelleschi and Michelozzo. The interior, and the convent next door, show the rational style of the early Florentine Renaissance and use of the local grey stone, *pietra serena*. Nearby, the 15th-century **Chiesa di San Domenico** contains works by the locally born Renaissance painter and monk Fra Angelico (c 1395–1455).

🚗 **Head back down the hill onto SP53 towards Florence. Follow signs for SS67 autostrade to Pontassieve. Follow the brown signs for Vallombrosa, via Pelago on SR70, then right onto SP83, then onto Via Vallombrosana (SP85). Turn right to the Abbey. Park on Via San Benedetto.**

VISITING FIESOLE

Take the SS65 from Firenze. Turn right onto Via Salviati and follow signs to Fiesole.

Tourist Information
The tourist office *(Via Portigiani 3/5; fiesoleforyou.it)* is next to the Area Archeologica. The three museums around the Roman theatre can be visited on one ticket and cover prehistory to the Renaissance.

WHERE TO STAY

FIESOLE

Villa San Michele *expensive*
Part of this Renaissance villa is attributed to Michelangelo. Expect total luxury.
Via Doccia 4, 50014; villasan michele.com

ABBAZIA DI VALLOMBROSA

Grand hotel Vallombrosa *inexpensive*
This large hotel has simple rooms and is an excellent base for trekking.
Via G. Carducci 2, 50066; vallombrosa lberghi.com

Above The green serpentine and white marble façade of Badia Fiesolana **Below** Consuma Pass, a route through the Tuscan Hills west of Poppi **Below right** Piazza Mino da Fiesole bathed in sunlight

② ABBAZIA DI VALLOMBROSA
Vallambrosa, Firenze, Toscana; 50066

Founded in 1036 by a Benedictine monk, the Vallombrosa Abbey has a large monastery, church, cloister, tower, sacristy and kitchens. Its first monks lived as hermits in primitive conditions and the woods around are dotted with their chapels and holy places. This walk is a good way to understand something of their way of life and history.

A one-hour walking tour

Pick up a free map and audio guide from the **Centro Visitatori** ① *(Via San Benedetto 1; open Apr–Oct: daily)*. Walk back down Via San Benedetto and turn right into the road that runs in front of the monastery. There is a large gate to the abbey, **Church** ② and ancient pharmacy. The church *(vallombrosa.it; open daily)* was remodelled in the 17th century and has a rich Baroque interior. The *trompe l'oeil* ceilings are a perfect example of the style. Exit the abbey complex to the right. The road turns round to the left and runs into an elegant avenue of trees. On the right is a small **Fish Pond** ③, still well

TRIP 16: SANCTUARIES AND FORESTS

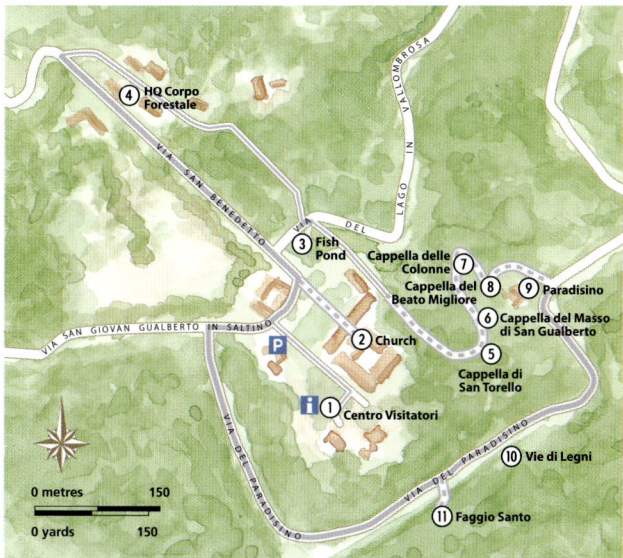

Above Grassy remains of the 1st-century BCE Roman theatre, Fiesole **Below** Aerial view of Abbazia di Vallombrosa, set within the forest

EAT AND DRINK

FIESOLE

Perseus Fiesolano *moderate*
Rustic decor and simple food are combined with great atmosphere, especially on summer evenings when booking is recommended. *Piazza Mino 9R, 50014; casatrattoria.com/perseus-fiesolano; closed Sun dinner*

La Reggia degli Etruschi *expensive*
Excellent Tuscan cuisine is served in this large restaurant with panoramic views over Florence. Enjoy wine tasting in the *enoteca* (wine bar). *Via San Francesco 18, 50014; lareggiadeglietruschi.com; closed a week in Aug*

ABBAZIA DI VALLOMBROSA

Archimede *moderate*
This restaurant uses vegetables straight from the owner's farm. The Tuscan dishes include *ribollita* (bread and vegetable soup), mixed grills and meat and fowl roasted on a spit. *Loc. Ponte Casalino, 50066; ristorantearchimede.it*

stocked with fish, which was a useful food source for the monks. Follow Via San Benedetto downhill; on the right are the well-ordered Giardino Botanico (Botanic Gardens) and, at the bottom of the hill, the chalet-like **HQ Corpo Forestale** ④. At this point, turn hard right. The path runs up the hill between some buildings of the Corpo Forestale. Pass the open area to the left, where an old saw mill once stood, to a pretty picnic spot where water flows into the old public washing basin from the pond above. With the pond to the right, take the track straight uphill, marked Scala Santa. At this point, the path becomes steeper and the irregular stonework makes sensible shoes preferable.

Once past the confines of the monastery, the path turns sharp left over a stone bridge to a small chapel, the **Cappella di San Torello** ⑤. This is one of four chapels set in beautiful woodland, the others being **Cappella del Masso di San Gualberto** ⑥, **Cappella delle Colonne** ⑦ and, after a sharp right turn, **Cappella del Beato Migliore** ⑧. To the left of the last is a stone staircase leading up to the road and the **Paradisino** ⑨. This complex was originally a group of monks' cells clustered around the small church. As the monastery's fame grew and more visitors arrived, it became a type of hotel. It is believed that the English poet John Milton stayed here, as he mentioned Vallombrosa in his poem, *Paradise Lost*. The terrace offers splendid views – on a clear day – all the way to Florence's Duomo.

Across the road from Paradisino is a gushing fountain of ice-cold water. The road slopes down towards the abbey and soon reaches an open area and a rough stone path leading up to the woods. Beside it are steep, stone-lined cuttings forming artificial avenues called **Vie di Legni** (Wooden Roads) ⑩. These avenues once criss-crossed the mountains and were used to drag giant tree trunks to the Arno to be floated down to Florence.

Further on, to the left, is the chapel **Faggio Santo** (The Holy Beech Tree) ⑪, the holiest place here. The abbey's founder, St Gualberto, is said to have arrived in a snowstorm and rested beneath the tree. When he awoke, it had sprouted leaves to protect him from the elements. The tree is still there. A 10-minute walk leads back to the abbey complex and the car park. There is a good bar with toilet facilities above a large village green.

🚗 **Turn right along winding Via del Lago in Vallombrosa (to Consuma). Turn right signposted Passo della Consuma at Via Casentinese/SR70, then left at SP74. Follow the brown signs to Castello di Romena. Follow the road to the car park.**

WHERE TO STAY

STIA AND AROUND

Hotel Falterona *inexpensive*
In the historic centre of town, this refurbished hotel, set in a Renaissance building, offers a comfortable and relaxed atmosphere. Rooms are beamed and some have frescoed ceilings.
Piazza Bernarndo Tanucci 85, 52017; albergofalterona.com

Monastero Santa Maria della Neve *inexpensive*
Set in the historic centre and run by Dominican nuns, this guesthouse offers basic but comfortable rooms. Rules of the order apply (10pm curfew).
Piazza Landino 25, Pratovecchio 52015 (southeast of Stia on SP310); monasterodomenicane.org

Borgo Tramonte *moderate*
Simple, clean, rustic-style rooms in a large, restored, 18th-century farmhouse on the edge of the Casentino Forest. Enjoy the nearby walking trails, mountain biking and horse riding.
Loc. Papiano, 52017; borgotramonte.it

CAMÁLDOLI AND AROUND

Monastery of Camáldoli *inexpensive*
Run by Benedictine monks, this hotel offers peaceful stays within the monastery – rules apply (11pm curfew).
Camaldoli Monastery, 52014; camaldoli.it; closed Jan & Feb

I Tre Baroni *expensive*
This resort in Moggiona, on the road to Camáldoli, is a combination of hotel rooms and apartments scattered through the village. The decor is period and the place is relatively relaxed.
Via di Camáldoli 52, 52014 Moggiona di Poppi; itrebaroni.it

③ Castello di Romena
Pratovecchio, Arezzo, Toscana; 52015

Dating from the 10th century, this **Castello** *(open Jul–mid-Sep: daily, Mar–Oct: Fri–Sun; closed Nov–Feb)* once had three central towers and 11 smaller ones reinforcing the walls. Set on the highest defensive point of the Casentino valley, the castle is thought to have been visited by the poet Dante (c 1265–1321) – who mentions it in his *Divine Comedy* – after his exile from Florence. The castle still has its keep, central tower with drawbridge, prison tower and Piazza d'Armi, where the army was trained. Cypresses mark the position of the walls and there are fabulous views of the valley below.

The delightful **Pieve di San Pietro di Romena** is nearby – head back down the tree-lined avenue and take the track on the left. At the T-junction, turn right onto SP73 and into the car park. The earliest reference to this church was in 1054 and the current building dates to 1152. There is evidence of an earlier building from an Etruscan or Roman cult. The simple Romanesque semicircular apse faces east towards Jerusalem and the three naves, pillars with Lombard Christian capitals referring to fertility rites, and unadorned interior evoke a spiritual calm and tranquillity. There is also a picnic area looking out over the valley towards Poppi.

🚗 *Turn right onto SP74 towards Stia, then right onto Via Fiorentina/SP73 into Pratovecchio. After the piazza, turn left into Via Garibaldi, then Via Roma to "Centro Stia". Don't take SP556, keep straight, then right onto Via Edmondo De Amicis. Take first left, under the arch, and park in Piazza Bernardo Tanucci.*

④ Stia
Arezzo, Toscana; 52017

The pretty, historic town of Stia nestles between the River Staggia and the nascent River Arno, which runs down the Casentino valley and on to Florence. The town developed in the 11th century under the jurisdiction of the Guidi Counts from Poppi, who ruled over the area from the 11th–15th centuries. Stia prospered down the centuries due to its excellent woollen cloth production, an industry that continues to this day. The centre of town is set around Piazza Tanucci

Top The ruins of Castello di Romena, above the Casentino valley **Right** Piazza Tanucci's centrepiece, the Fontana dei Serpenti, Stia **Far right** The charming Romanesque Pieve di San Pietro di Romena, Castello di Romena

Above left Eremo di Camáldoli, founded by San Romualdo *Above centre* The Casentino Forest, where the monks sought isolation *Above right* Façade of the Romanesque Pieve di Santa Maria Assunta, Stia

with the Fontana dei Serpenti and the **Pieve di Santa Maria Assunta**, a Romanesque church with a splendid *Annunciation* by Bicci di Lorenzo (1414). There's also a shop selling the famous local Casentino cloth.

🚗 *At lower end of Piazza Tanucci turn left before the bridge onto SP310, back to Pratovecchio, turn left onto Via Monte/SP72, then left onto Via Appennino/SP72. Turn left to stay on SP72 (signed Eremo di Camáldoli), then join SP69 to the hermitage.*

The Casentino Forest

This vast forest provided the wood used to build the great fleet of the Medicis and, today, the **Parco Nazionale delle Foreste Casentinesi, Monte Falterona e Campigna** *(parco forestecasentinesi.it)* is still one of the most prized forests in Europe. The forest is an important sanctuary for the Apennine wolf, wild boar, deer, and mouflon (mountain sheep).

❺ Camáldoli
Arezzo, Toscana; 52010

Italian monks sought to understand God better by withdrawing from the world to a life of contemplation in the forest. The **Eremo di Camáldoli** *(camaldoli.it)* was one of the hermitages founded by the Benedictine monk San Romualdo (c 953–1027), son of the duke of Ravenna. He established a community of five cells with a small oratory here in c 1024. Only 14 monks remain, cut off from visitors, but Romualdo's original austere cell is still visible. The Church of the Hermitage (c 1220) underwent an astonishing Baroque transformation in the late 16th century, giving it grand frescoes and elaborate cornices. Look out for the fine altarpiece of the Madonna by Andrea della Robbia (1435–1525).

Nearby, along Località Camáldoli, lies another interesting monastic complex, run by the same order as the hermitage. The **Monastery of Camáldoli**, however, maintains closer community contact. At the centre of the hamlet is a large hostel, a monastery, and a church with major works by the late-Renaissance artist Giorgio Vasari (1511–74). Don't miss the Antica Farmacia (1543) – an old pharmacy – with walnut cabinets.

Camáldoli is also home to the **Foreste Casentinesi Visitor Centre** *(open spring & summer)*, which has good maps of the area, making it the perfect starting place for exploring the park's 600-km (373-mile) network of paths on foot, horseback or by bike.

🚗 *Head south along SP67 towards Poppi. At the junction with Via Roma/SR70 turn right, then left onto Piazza Garibaldi/SP65. Cross the bridge and turn left into Piazza 4 Novembre, then follow round to Piazza Gramsci and park.*

EAT AND DRINK

STIA
La Rana da Filetto *moderate*
A simple (and rather hidden) restaurant serving hearty Tuscan specialities such as *ribollita* (meat and vegetable soup), wild boar, deer meats and bruschetta with wild game patés. Great value.
Loc. Tirasasso, 52017; 0575 504 505

CAMÁLDOLI
Albergo Ristorante Camáldoli di Tassini *moderate*
This guesthouse has been looking after travellers for years. Rustic fare includes delicious *acquacotta* (literally "cooked water") – a hearty Tuscan soup, *ravioli all'ortica* made with ricotta and nettles, and roasted wild fennel.
Loc. Camáldoli 13, 52010

Below A glade at Camáldoli in the Casentino Forest

Above The medieval walled town of Anghiari, decked with flags **Above right** The birthplace of sculptor Michelangelo, Caprese Michelangelo

WHERE TO STAY

POPPI

Albergo Casentino *inexpensive*
The only hotel in the historic centre of Poppi fronts onto the piazza with comfy rooms, a garden and restaurant.
Piazza della Repubblica 6, 52014; albergocasentino.it

CAPRESE MICHELANGELO

Terra di Michelangelo *inexpensive*
This *agriturismo* is a complex of stone farmhouses, apartments and rooms offering daily and weekly rates.
Loc. San Polo 70, 52033; terradimichelangelo.com

Il Vigno *moderate*
A rustic collection of restored farm buildings with rooms and apartments at daily or weekly rates. Mountain bikes and trail maps available.
Loc. il Vigno 262, 52033; agriturismoilvigno.eu

Below The Santuario della Verna, where St Francis of Assisi once stayed

⑥ Poppi
Arezzo, Toscana; 52014

The historic heart of this castellated town rises majestically above the modern commercial centre. Poppi was the seat of power of the Guidi Counts until they picked the wrong side in the 1440 war between Florence and Milan. Fortunately, the splendid 12th-century **Castello dei Conti Guidi** *(open daily)* remains, with its magnificent tower, mullion windows, battlements and stone staircases. Other highlights include the colonnaded **Piazza Amerighi**, and the 17th-century hexagonal **Chiesa di Madonna del Morbo** with a *Madonna and Child* by Filippino Lippi (1457–1504).

The church, dedicated to the Virgin, was built in gratitude for the end of the plague, which hit Poppi and the Casentino area very hard. A walk around Poppi is a great way to experience an Italian medieval town, and its alleys and squares are also perfect for kids to blow off steam.

🚗 *Cross back over the Arno to Piazza Garibaldi, then turn right at SR70 towards Santuario della Verna/Via Bibbiena SR71. On SR71, keep left onto Viale Michelangelo, then a sharp left onto Viale Luigi Gori/SS208 all the way to La Verna. From the car park it's a 5–10-minute walk to the Sanctuary.*

Della Robbia
La Verna and the Casentino is home to terracotta masterpieces of the Della Robbia sculptors. Luca della Robbia (1400–82) perfected a white majolica with a blue background, and yellow and green glazes to protect the works from the elements. Andrea della Robbia (1435–1525) created the masterpieces *The Crucifixion* and *The Assumption* in the Basilica Maggiore at La Verna.

⑦ La Verna
Arezzo, Toscana; 52010

One of the holiest sites in Italy, **Santuario della Verna** *(laverna.it)* is a monastic community that developed around Saint Francis of Assisi (1182–1226) who spent 40 days in retreat here in 1224. While in La Verna, he developed stigmata – the wounds of Christ appeared on his body. Count Orlando of Chiusi gave La Verna to Francis as a retreat for contemplation and built him the chapel Santa Maria degli Angeli, the nucleus of the convent. The sanctuary appeals to believers and non-religious alike as its impressive views, pristine woods and fascinating collection of buildings and the stories associated with them are compelling.

TRIP 16: SANCTUARIES AND FORESTS 169

🚗 Head southeast on SP208, turn right onto Via Roma/SP60, then left onto SP54 to Caprese Michelangelo. Turn left at Via Capoluogo, go up the hill and park.

⑧ Caprese Michelangelo
Arezzo, Toscana; 52033a

This small mountain town is best known as the birthplace, in 1475, of Michelangelo Buonarroti, one of the greatest artists of all time. His father, a government functionary, worked here briefly, but soon after the boy's birth, the family returned to Florence. It is said that the artist returned here frequently, but there's little evidence of his presence. In the remains of the castle there's a small **museum** *(open 10am–1pm & 3–5:30pm Sat & Sun; capresemichelangelo.net)* for those who wish to pay homage.

🚗 Head south on SP47 to Anghiari. Follow SP43, avoiding signs for Centro, then turn right up Corso Giacomo Matteotti to the car park. Walk via the tunnel to the elevator up to town centre.

⑨ Anghiari
Arezzo, Toscana; 52031

The unquestionable antiquity of this medieval citadel gives it a special charm and its knot of ancient lanes and piazzas is pleasant to wander round. It was of strategic importance because of its position on the trading routes between the Adriatic and central Italy. Impressive sections of its 12th- and 13th-century walls remain intact, containing several gateways and even old churches. Apart from a reputed visit by Thomas Beckett in the 12th century, Anghiari is most famous for the battle in 1440, when the Florentine Medicis defeated the superior forces of the Visconti Milanese. **Palazzo della Battaglia** *(open daily, winter: closed Tue)*, in the central Piazza Mameli, has scale models of the battle. The town's main square, Piazza Balduccio, has a statue of Garibaldi and has been a market area for 800 years.

DAY TRIP OPTIONS
Younger kids will love the castles, while older ones would enjoy Roman sights, a picnic and a forest walk. The more spiritual will enjoy the quiet forest holy places.

Castellos
From Stia ④, visit the ruins of Castello di Romena ③, then drive on to the well-preserved Castello dei Conti Guidi in Poppi ⑥. For a final treat, have gelato at Paradice *(Piazza Garibaldi 5/6, Poppi).*

From Stia, take the SP della Scarpaccia to Castello di Romena. Take SP73 to SR70 to Poppi. Return on SR70, SP310.

Romans and a forest walk
Based at Fiesole ①, spend some time shopping for a picnic. Then tour the Roman sights and museums, climbing up to the acropolis. Drive to Abbazia di Vallombrosa ② and enjoy a picnic there, with the abbey's jam, then work off the food with a walk in the woods.

Follow the drive's directions, then return the same way.

COURSES IN POPPI

Centro di Cultura Italiana Casentino
This cultural centre runs courses on the Italian language and seminars on opera, cooking and even stone masonry.
Piazza Amerighi 1, 52014; 0575 529 774; parlital.it

EAT AND DRINK

LA VERNA
Refettorio del Pellegrino *inexpensive*
Visitors can expect a wholesome, set-price three-course meal, including a glass of wine. Takeaway lunches also on offer for an affordable price.
Santuario della Verna, 52010; laverna.it; open daily, lunch & dinner

CAPRESE MICHELANGELO
Il Cerro *moderate*
This family-run restaurant pays great attention to local produce and wines.
Via Il Cerro 120, 52033; ristorante ilcerro.it; closed Mon & Tue

Il Rifugio *moderate*
Expect hearty mountain food such as homemade pasta with local truffles and mushrooms, and roast meats.
Loc. Lama 367, 52033; ilrifugio ristorante.eu; closed Wed

ANGHIARI
Da Alighiero *moderate*
Enjoy superb homemade pastas with porcini, Chianina veal with rosemary, and semifreddo with pistachios.
Via Garibaldi 8, 52031; ristorantealighiero.it; closed Tue

Ristorante La Nena *moderate*
A cosy restaurant with attention to detail on classic Tuscan dishes.
Corso Matteotti 10/14, 52031; ristorante nena.it; closed Mon

Top left Small shrine in the pristine woodland around La Verna **Left** The imposing tower of Castello dei Conti Guidi, Poppi

Secluded retreats
Based at Poppi ⑥, see its *Madonna and Child*, then shop for picnic supplies. Drive to Camáldoli ⑤ to tour the monastery and then picnic at the hermitage. Next, stop at Stia ④ to see its Romanesque church and then visit the delightful church at Castello di Romena ③.

From Poppi, head north on SP67 and SP69 to Camáldoli. SP72, SP310 to Stia. SP della Scarpaccia, then left to Romena. Take SP73 to SR70 back to Poppi.

TRIP 17

VAL D'ARNO AND THE CHIANTI HILLS

Ponte Buriano
to Volpaia

HIGHLIGHTS

Landscapes of Leonardo
See the ancient bridge and Le Balze scenery that so captivated Leonardo da Vinci that he put them in his paintings

Chianti Classico
Enjoy the rolling hills and neat vines that make Chianti one of Europe's most delightful winemaking areas

Soft stone villages of Chianti
Explore some of Italy's most beautiful small towns, producing excellent wine and the highest quality olive oil

The art of Nature
Explore the modern sculpture gallery at Pievasciata, where artists display their works in a natural park

VAL D'ARNO AND THE CHIANTI HILLS

Many of the mystical landscapes that glow in the paintings of Leonardo da Vinci can be seen in a little known part of Tuscany between the right bank of the River Arno and the Pratomagno mountain range. Crossing the Arno, the road soon leaves the industrial flatlands and rises into the delightful countryside of the Chianti. This area is most famous for the light red wine it produces that is the perfect match for a bowl of delicious pasta. Like the wine, the people of the area are generous and easygoing, and the light on the landscape has inspired painters and poets, while the local produce are specialities to be savoured.

ACTIVITIES

Photograph the brilliant autumn colours in Chianti as the vine leaves turn gold against the silver-green of the olive trees

Get married in Greve, where the Comune conducts the ceremony and there are villas and restaurants in abundance for guests and gourmets

Take a Tuscan cooking class in Chianti and learn about the local food that accompanies the wine

Hire a bike and follow the path of the "Eroica" bike race along the back roads of Chianti

TRIP 17: VAL D'ARNO AND THE CHIANTI HILLS

Above Looking towards the church of Santa Croce in Piazza Matteotti, Greve in Chianti, see p174

Below Country villa and autumn vines in the Val d'Arno
Left A traditional majolica platter in Castellina in Chianti, see p175

PLAN YOUR DRIVE

Start/finish: Ponte Buriano to Volpaia.

Number of days: 2–3 days.

Distance: 100 km (62 miles).

Road conditions: Roads are generally good and well signposted. In winter the Chianti roads can be icy and snow chains may be needed on some roads.

When to go: Chianti has a definite season, May–Oct, and at other times of the year many restaurants and amenities close. Autumn is less crowded and the changing colour of the leaves is beautiful.

Opening: Major museums are open 8:30am–7:30pm and often close Mon. Small museums often only open on weekends outside the summer months. Hours for churches vary but they are generally open 7:30am–noon and 3–7:30pm. Shops open 10am–1pm and 4–8pm and close Sun and Mon mornings.

Main market days: Loro Ciuffenna: Mon; Pian di Scò, Greve in Chianti and Castellina in Chianti: Sat; Radda in Chianti: 4th Mon of month.

Major festivals: All over: Cantine Aperte (tasting day at wineries), last Sun in May; Calici delle Stelle, night of San Lorenzo (wine-tasting in the piazzas), late Jul or early Aug; San Martino, cantinas open for tasting of the new wine, 1st & 2nd week Nov. **Greve:** Chianti Classico Wine Festival, 1st weekend in Sep.

Shopping: The area is famous for wines and olive oil. Wine shops and most vineyards have the capacity to ship locally and internationally.

DAY TRIP OPTIONS

Using Greve in Chianti as a base, drive through **pretty hamlets** along the Via Sette Ponti, picking up a **picnic** on the way to Ponte Buriano **Natural Reserve**, ideal for a **walk**. Wine lovers can stay at Castellina in Chianti to enjoy a **wine tasting**, tour a **vineyard** and explore **cellars** in Chianti wine towns. History buffs will enjoy **medieval town halls** and **churches**, **castles** and **Etruscan finds**, then contrasting this all with a walk around an outdoor **modern sculpture park**. For full details, see p177.

Above The Neo-Romanesque Church of San Salvatore, Castellina in Chianti

GETTING TO PONTE BURIANO

From A1 Florence-Rome, take Arezzo exit. Pass under Viale Don Minzoni, then left towards Bibbiena. At roundabout, take Via Sette Ponti/SP1 to Ponte Buriano. Cross bridge, through town, turn left and left again. Park near the river on the right.

WHERE TO STAY

AROUND PONTE BURIANO
Antico Borgo Frosini moderate
This old stone country house with a large pool is perfect for a relaxing stay.
Loc. Pratantico 57, 52100; 0575 335 297 172

Fattoria La Lama moderate
A small hamlet made up of three houses and a barn in the middle of the countryside.
Chiani 63/A, 52100; 0575 363 612; fattorialalama.it

BORRO
Il Borro expensive
Rent an 18th-century villa or a simple apartment. The staff are very helpful.
San Giustino Valdarno, 52020 Loc. Borro 1; ilborro.com

VIA SETTE PONTI
Villa Belpoggio inexpensive
Only 2 km (1 mile) from Loro Ciuffenna, this historic house in luxurious gardens has comfortable rooms and suites.
Via Sette Ponti Ponente 40, 52024 Loro Ciuffenna; villabelpoggio.com

CASTELLINA IN CHIANTI
Palazzo Squarcialupi moderate
In the historic centre, this large hotel has comfy rooms, a pool and a terrace.
Via Ferrozzola 1, 53011; palazzosquarcialupi.com

Right Typical Le Balze sandstone landscape near Piantravigne Far right The famous seven-arched bridge of Ponte Buriano

❶ Ponte Buriano
Arezzo, Toscana; 52100

With its seven beautiful arches crossing the River Arno, the 13th-century Romanesque Ponte Buriano is the start of an ancient pilgrim route, the Via Sette Ponti. The bridge also marks the start of a regional natural reserve that runs along the river to the dam at Penna. These wetlands are key nesting grounds for migrating birds – find out about trails through the reserve from the **visitor centre** *(by the bridge; 393 53089; parks.it)* at Ponte Buriano. The bridge itself has not changed since Leonardo da Vinci visited it in the late 15th century, when he was so taken by its beauty he put it in the background of his *Mona Lisa*.

🚗 *Head northwest along Via Sette Ponti/SP1, through Castiglion Fibocchi. At San Giustino Valdarno, turn left for Borro. Follow signs to the car park.*

❷ Borro
Arezzo, Toscana; 52028

In the medieval era, this tiny clutch of houses could only be reached by a drawbridge spanning a deep gully. Today, this hamlet has been fully restored by the Ferragamo family (of the Florentine fashion house), and now houses artisans' workshops. The automated *presepe*, or **nativity scene** *(open daily)*, which rather surprisingly includes Pinocchio, was created by the local priest.

🚗 *Return to Via Sette Ponti/SP1 and turn left at Loro Ciuffenna, park in Piazza Vittorio Emanuele II. Return to SP1 and carry on before turning left onto Strada Comunale di Piantravigne to town. Return to SP1 to Pian di Scò. In town, turn right into Viale Alessandro Volta/SP1 and use car park on right.*

❸ Via Sette Ponti
Arezzo, Toscana; 52024, 52028, 52026

A series of pretty villages mark the defensive points on the Via Sette Ponti (Road of the Seven Bridges), with views over the lake basin of the Balze. In tiny **Loro Ciuffenna**, visit the Romanesque Pieve di San Pietro a Gropina, with a carved stone pulpit and capitals, and the ancient Tuscan mill.

Further along the SP1, **Piantravigne** perches perilously amid the towering sand and limestone pinnacles of Le Balze. The final stop, the parish church of Santa Maria in **Pian di Scò**, with its imposing bell tower, still has a simple Romanesque interior, largely unaltered since the 12th century.

🚗 *Leave on SP87 to Figline Valdarno. At roundabout, take 2nd exit onto Via Francesco Petrarca/SS69. Turn left at Via Nicolò Copernico/SP16 to Greve in Chianti. Follow signs to car park.*

❹ Greve in Chianti
Florence, Toscana; 50022

At the heart of town, **Piazza Matteotti's** irregular architecture reveals Greve's prosperity in the Middle Ages, as the wealthy merchants were required to pay for their own *loggias* (porticoes) – now filled with shops, bars and restaurants. The statue in the piazza is of local explorer Giovanni da Verrazzano (1485–1528), the Italian who sailed to North America. Chianti is a top cycling destination and the Eroica Trail is well signposted and suitable for all levels. Bikes can be hired from Officina Ramuzzi *(Via Italo Stecchi 23, 50022 Greve in Chianti; 055 853 037; ramuzzi.com)*.

🚗 *Take SR222 south to Castellina in Chianti. Park to the south of the town centre on Via 4 Novembre.*

⑤ CASTELLINA IN CHIANTI

Siena, Toscana; 53011

The rolling hills of the Chianti have always separated Florence and Siena, the two great Tuscan rivals for power. Barely touched over the centuries, the fields and vineyards remain as they were when they were first carved out by oxen. The towns, too, have changed little and reflect the intense respect of their residents for traditional values.

Above Busy bric-a-brac market in Greve in Chianti

A one-hour walking tour

Start from the car park with views east across the fields of Chianti. At the top of the steep entry ramp, join the main road that skirts the town. Follow this to the left, then on the right, and on the corner of Via delle Mura, is **Enoteca Poggio Amorelli** ①, below a castle-like bastion – taste its wines or arrange a vineyard visit. Continue along Via delle Mura up the hill to the Rocca della Comune. Walk past Remembrance Park on the left, with valley views, and turn right into **Piazza della Comune** ②, dominated by the huge Rocca built by the Medici to defend against Siena. The entire town was once fortified, but most of the walls and the gates are long gone. Left of the tower is the **Museo Archeologico del Chianti** ③ *(open Apr–Oct: daily)*, which contains

The black cockerel insignia of Chianti

mostly Etruscan exhibits from the area. Head out of the square to the right past the trattoria La Torre. Take Vicolo della Rocca downhill to the main street, Via Ferruccio, which can get busy in summer. Directly opposite is the Renaissance **Palazzo Squarcialupi** ④, now a fashionable hotel and the wine store Fattoria La Castellina *(0577 740459; lacastellina.it)*. Tastings and tours can be organized here. Over the road is a classic butcher's shop, **Macelleria Stiaccini** ⑤. Try a delicious *panino con la finocchiona* (fennel salami sandwich). Slightly further up the hill is the **Tourist Office** ⑥ *(open Apr–Oct: Mon–Sat)* for information on wineries and Etruscan tombs. If more refreshment is needed, the Chianti Bar, further uphill, provides simple snacks and wine by the glass. At the top of the street is the **Church of San Salvatore** ⑦, which was rebuilt after World War II. It contains a fresco, *Madonna Enthroned*, by the pre-Renaissance artist Lorenzo di Bicci (1373–1452). Return to Via Ferruccio and take the path to the left leading into **Via delle Volte** ⑧. This medieval enclosed walkway runs parallel to Via Ferruccio and was used for defensive and religious purposes. To the left, slit windows provide glimpses of the countryside, and to the right some of the old cellars have been turned into workshops and restaurants. The walkway finally returns to Via Ferruccio, close to the car park.

🚗 Head south, turn left at Via del Mandorlo to SP102, then on to Vagliagli. Fork left to Monteliscai. At Via dei Ponti/SS408 turn left, then left again to Strada Comunale di Catignano. Turn left to Pievasciata, then left on Via del Campana to the sculpture park.

PRODUCE IN THE VAL D'ARNO

Zolfino beans and Valdarno chicken – both local delicacies – as well as olive oil and Vin Santo can be bought from **Fattoria Casamora** *(Via di Casabiondo 5, 52026 Pian di Scò; 055 960 046; casamora.it)*. For homemade yoghurt and cheeses, try **La Capanna del Sole** *(Loc. Casamona, 52024 Casamona; capannadelsole.it)*. Call before visiting.

EAT AND DRINK

AROUND PONTE BURIANO

Pizzeria Grand Prix Motor Pub *inexpensive*
A simple pizzeria that also serves delicious pasta dishes.
Loc. Indicatore 25C, 52100; 0575 368 882

BORRO

Osteria del Borro *expensive*
A romantic setting, this place specializes in seafood and meat – superb gourmet treats from an open kitchen.
Frazione 52, 52024 San Giustino V.no; osteriadelborro.it

VIA SETTE PONTI

Ristorante La Torre *moderate*
Located inside a medieval tower. The fish dishes here are a highlight.
Via Alighieri 20, 52024 Loro Ciuffenna; 055 917 2032; closed Mon

GREVE IN CHIANTI

Da Verrazzano *expensive*
Enjoy Tuscan treats such as *ribollita* (bread and vegetable soup), *panzanella* (tomato and bread salad) and good wine on a splendid terrace overlooking the piazza.
Piazza Matteotti 28, 50022; ristorante verrazzano.it; closed Mon

CASTELLINA IN CHIANTI

Antica Trattoria La Torre *moderate*
Tuck into good traditional food in the central piazza.
Piazza del Comune 15, 53011; anticatrattorialatorre.com

Above Radda in Chianti, once the capital city of Chianti Above right Volpaia, known for its blooming flowers in early summer

COOKERY COURSES IN CHIANTI

Preparing food can be as much fun as drinking the wine that goes with it, and at **Tenuta Casanova** (*Loc. Sant'Agnese 20, 53011 Castellina in Chianti; tenuta casanova.it*) they show how to do both with gusto and finesse. Or learn to prepare traditional Tuscan recipes in the grand **Castello di Vicchiomaggio** (*Via Vicchiomaggio 5, 50022; Greve in Chianti; vicchiomaggio.it*).

WHERE TO STAY

AROUND CHIANTI SCULPTURE PARK

Dievole *expensive*
The rooms in this 18th-century villa-turned-wine resort are stylish and breezy.
Loc. Dievole 6 (fraz. Vagliagli); 53019 Castelnuovo Berardenga; dievole.it

AROUND CASTELLO DI BROLIO

Villa di Sotto *inexpensive*
This simple B&B, about 2 km (1 mile) south of Brolio, offers genuine Italian warmth and hospitality on the edge of the sweet village of Villa a Sesta.
Via di San Caterina 30, 53109 Villa a Sesta; villadisotto.it

AROUND RADDA IN CHIANTI

Badia a Coltibuono *moderate*
This once Romanesque abbey, surrounded by two acres of forested land, offers peace and quiet amid lush Italian gardens. The former monk quarters are now a lovely frescoed lounge.
Loc. Badia a Coltibuono, 53013 Gaiole in Chianti; coltibuono.com

VOLPAIA

Pieve Aldina *expensive*
Located on the wine route that connects Florence to Siena, this stunning Tuscan country retreat provides easy access to charming lesser-known villages.
Chianti Crossing, 53017 Radda in Chianti; lesdomainesdefontenille.com

Wine tasting in Chianti
Vineyards are working enterprises, so try to book in advance for tours and tastings. Large operators usually have staff on hand, but smaller ones may need to call someone who can speak English. However, driving around, visitors will see "*cantina aperta*" signs, which indicate that the vineyard is open for tasting and buying wine. There is usually a small charge for a tour and tasting and this often includes snacks.

6 Chianti Sculpture Park
Pievasciata, Siena, Toscana; 53010

This contemporary sculpture park (*open daily; chiantisculpturepark.it*) is in a superb setting of macchia scrub, holm oak and pine trees. The one-hour trail visits 25 site-specific works by Italian and international artists, such as William Furlong's *Off the Beaten Track*: stainless-steel cubes that emit sounds of city life as you pass. Built in May 2004, the park was the inspiration of Rosalba and Piero Giadrossi, who are often at the nearby gallery La Fornace.

On leaving the park turn left (north). Drive 3 km (2 miles) on a dirt track. Turn right, then left onto SP408. Turn right towards Castelnuovo Berardenga; fork right, staying on SP484. Park on the left, opposite the Fattoria Castello Di Brolio.

7 Castello di Brolio
Siena, Toscana; 53013

This small village is surrounded by an enormous vineyard and castle with the same name that date back to the 10th century and have been owned by the Ricasoli family since then. Although it's now part of Siena, the castle (*closed Mar–Nov: Mon–Wed*) was a Florentine stronghold that was demolished by the Sienese army, then completely rebuilt in the 16th century. Baron Bettino Ricasoli (1809–80), who played a key role in the Unification of Italy and was twice Italy's prime minister, gave it its current mock-medieval style in the 19th century. There is still evidence of a mortar attack from World War II on the western wing. Taste the Baron's highly regarded wines at the wine shop (*open daily*).

Above The beautiful rolling hills of Chianti, dotted with vineyards

🚗 *Return north on SP484, turn right at SP408 towards Gaiole. Fork left at SP2, then take SR429 into Radda in Chianti. Turn right at Piazza 4 Novembre to park.*

❽ Radda in Chianti
Siena, Toscana; 53017
The capital of Chianti in the 14th century, tiny Radda still retains its sense of import as one of the main towns in the Chianti League. Pride in its history is revealed by the family heraldic shields that adorn the front of the **Palazzo di Podestà** (now the town hall) in Piazza Ferrucci. This was where the *podestà* or magistrate was based. Across the square is the **Chiesa di San Niccolò**, its original Romanesque design still evident despite the fact that it was heavily remodelled in the last century.
🚗 *Drive back down the hill, turn right at the roundabout onto Via La Strada*

del Chianti/SP2bis (under SR429) towards Volpaia. Turn right onto SR114C, then right onto SP112.

The famous Gallo Nero
Archduke Cosimo III chose the black cockerel – Gallo Nero – as the symbol for the area's winemakers in the 18th century as he was sick of arguments about which was the "true" wine of Chianti. Since then, if the bottle has an image of the Gallo Nero in a red circle on the label on its neck, then it is Chianti Classico. However, it was Baron Ricasoli who first defined classic Chianti wine in 1874. It has to include 75 per cent Sangiovese and 25 per cent Malvasia and Trebbiano grapes.

❾ Volpaia
Siena, Toscana; 53017
This village was repeatedly damaged, then rebuilt as a result of its strategic position between warring Sienese and Florentine forces. Volpaia improved its economy during a period of stability in the 16th century. A central point for viniculture in the area, the village is essentially a large winery owned by the Stianti family. The village cellars, such as those in the crypt of 15th-century **Commenda di Sant'Eufrosino** *(guided tours by appointment; volpaia. com)*, designed by Michelozzo, contain vast wooden barrels, a wine bar, bottling plant and olive mill. The *enoteca* (wine shop) also sells a booklet mapping out various countryside walks.

Above Bell tower or campanile in the little hamlet of Volpaia **Below left** The façade of the Palazzo di Podestà, Radda in Chianti

EAT AND DRINK

NEAR CHIANTI SCULPTURE PARK
La Taverna Di Vagliagli *expensive*
This restaurant, between Castellina and Pievasciata, offers an intimate, elegant atmosphere with excellent service, superb food and good wine.
Via del Sergente 4, 53010 Vagliagli; 0577 322 532; closed Tue

RADDA IN CHIANTI
Le Forchette del Chianti *expensive*
On the town wall overlooking the valley. Run by two sisters serving traditional Tuscan dishes alongside a good wine list.
Viale Matteotti 5, 53017; leforchettedelchianti.com; closed Thu

VOLPAIA
La Bottega *moderate*
Come here for hearty, unpretentious country cooking, great views from the outdoor terrace and homemade cakes.
Piazza della Torre 1, 53017; labottegadivolpaia.it; closed Tue

---

DAY TRIP OPTIONS
There's plenty to do in this area, from a bird-watching picnic to a food and wine tour, and a historical trip looking at ancient and modern life.

Walk on the wild side
Starting from Greve in Chianti ❹ drive over to the Val d'Arno, visiting the villages of the Via Sette Ponti ❸ and picking up some local produce along the way. Stop at Ponte Buriano ❶ and pick up a map from the visitor centre to follow a trail through the Regional Nature Reserve, stopping for a picnic along the way.

Follow the drive directions in reverse, then retrace the route at the end of the day.

Red, red wine
In Castellina in Chianti ❺, visit the Enoteca Poggio Amorelli for a quick brush-up on the local wines, then buy some snacks in the deli. Visit Radda in Chianti ❽, then it's off to Volpaia ❾ to explore its ancient wine cellars and see its wine-production methods. Finally, drive back to Castello di Brolio ❼, to visit the castle and vineyard owned by the famous Ricasoli family.

From Castellina, take SR22, then SR429 to Radda in Chianti, then through Radda turn left onto SP2bis, right onto SP114c, SP112 to Volpaia. Return to Radda, down SP2bis, SR429, SP114a, left up SP408 and right onto SP484 to Brolio.

Ancient history, modern art
From Greve in Chianti ❹, explore the medieval market town, then drive to Radda in Chianti ❽, to see the architecture of a once powerful city. Then drive across to Castellina in Chianti ❺ for a look at evidence of ancient Etruscans. Stay for lunch and a glass of wine, then head to the Chianti Sculpture Park ❻, for a walk around the outside modern art sculptures in a natural setting.

From Greve in Chianti, take SR222 south, then SP114c to Radda in Chianti. Take the Via Strada del Chianti to Castellina in Chianti, then SR222 and SP102 to the Chianti Sculpture Park. Retrace the journey to get home.

TRIP 18

SACRED PATHS

San Miniato to San Galgano

HIGHLIGHTS

The pilgrim way
Follow in the footsteps of the pilgrims who travelled the Via Francigena from northern Europe to Rome

Etruscan heritage
Visit Volterra, city of the ancient Etruscans, and discover the exquisite art and culture of this fascinating civilization

Ancient abbeys
Experience the solitude and majesty of the pilgrim monasteries – Monte Oliveto Maggiore and San Galgano

City of culture
Explore beautiful Siena and marvel at the medieval city's masterful pre-Renaissance art and architecture

Rural idyll
Relax in the unspoilt countryside of the Val di Merse, dotted with sleepy agricultural hamlets

Panoramic view of San Gimignano's medieval towers

SACRED PATHS

A thousand years ago pilgrims travelled across these lands on their way to the holy city of Rome, bringing wealth to the churches, abbeys and towns along the routes. This trip starts with the spires of San Miniato, then meanders down the Roman Via Cassia to the monastery of San Vivaldo and magnificent Volterra. The route leads to San Gimignano, famed for its soaring towers and Vernaccia wine, and on to Siena, with its spectacular cathedral and pilgrim hospital. Further south lie the abbey of Monte Oliveto Maggiore, the woods of the Val di Merse and the soaring buttresses of San Galgano.

Above Rennaisance-style bust in an alabaster workshop in Volterra, see p183

ACTIVITIES

Attend a summer concert at the monastery of San Vivaldo

Visit an alabaster workshop in Volterra – maybe even take a class

Climb to the top of San Gimignano's Torre Grosso for spectacular views

Experience the surreal atmosphere of the roofless Abbey of San Galgano, which hosts summer concerts

Listen to atmospheric Gregorian chant at Monte Oliveto Maggiore

Ride a steam train from Buonconvento through the local countryside

Cycle through the Val di Merse's pleasant woods and sleepy villages

TRIP 18: SACRED PATHS

Above View over the surrounding countryside from Torre Grosso, San Gimignano, see p184

PLAN YOUR DRIVE

Start/finish: San Miniato to San Galgano.

Number of days: 4–5, allowing for half-days in Volterra and Siena.

Distance: Approx. 254 km (158 miles).

Road conditions: Generally well-signposted and well-paved roads.

When to go: The area has good conditions all year round. In spring the landscape is lush; summer is more crowded and hot, but also has many festivals; autumn has truffle festivals.

Opening times: Most shops are open 9am–1pm, then 4–8pm and closed Sun and Mon mornings. In bigger cities, shops are often open over lunch. Most museums are closed Mon. Churches tend to open 7am–12:30pm and 4–7pm, but hours may vary.

Main market days: San Miniato: 3rd Sun; **Monteroni d'Arbia:** Tue; **Castelfiorentino and Chiusdino:** Thu; **Volterra and Buonconvento:** Sat; **Colle di Val d'Elsa:** Fri; **Siena:** Wed.

Shopping: Volterra has shops selling hand-carved alabaster. Colle di Val d'Elsa is famous for fine crystal. San Gimignano is a good spot to stock up on local Vernaccia DOP white wine.

Major festivals: San Miniato: White Truffle Fair, last 3 weekends of Nov; La Luna è Azzurra (children's puppet festival), Jun; Kite Festival, 1st Sun after Easter; **Monteriggioni:** Medieval Festival, 1st weekend of Jul; **Siena:** Palio (medieval horse race), 2nd Jul & 16th Aug; **Buonconvento:** Crete d'Autunno (food festival), late May & Oct; **Torri:** Medieval Festival, Jun.

DAY TRIP OPTIONS

Families will enjoy a day trip from Volterra, clambering up **towers** and over a **castle** and well preserved **city walls**. Culture buffs will love Siena and the **art** of its **Duomo** and **museums**, as well as Monte Oliveto Maggiore's **abbey** and Buonconvento's **religious art**. For a country trip, head to the Val di Merse from Siena for a **hike/cycle ride**, then see an **abbey** and end at a **hill town**. For full details, see p187.

Above Road winding through Volterra's countryside

VISITING SAN MINIATO

Parking
There is parking in Piazza del Popolo and Piazza della Repubblica. For long stays, park in Piazza Dante Alghieri.

Tourist Information
Piazza del Popolo 1, 56028; sanminiatopromozione.it

Buying and tasting truffles
The main street through San Miniato has several *alimentari* (delicatessens) that sell white truffles. The butcher **Macelleria Sergio Falaschi** (*Via Augusto Conti 18–20*) specializes in truffle salami.

WHERE TO STAY

SAN MINIATO

Miravalle *inexpensive*
An inviting hotel in the historic centre with a restaurant serving Tuscan cuisine.
Piazzetta del Castello 3, 56028; hotelmiravallesanminiato.it

AROUND CASTELFIORENTINO

Le Boscarecce Country Inn *inexpensive*
A pleasant restored farmhouse with rustic rooms, a garden with a pool and a terrace (3 km/2 miles on the SP4).
Via dei Renai 19, 50051 (3 km/2 miles north on SP4); leboscarecce.com

VOLTERRA

La Locanda *inexpensive*
This small hotel, handily located in the historic centre, has comfortable rooms.
Via Guarnacci 24/28, 56048; hotel-lalocanda.com

Borgo Pignano *expensive*
This elegant hotel is 100 per cent eco-friendly. The pool is carved out of a limestone quarry and there are yoga lessons and a newly expanded spa.
Loc. Pignano 6, 56048; borgopignano.com

Top left Porta all'Arco, an ancient entrance to Volterra **Top right** Fresco at Collegiata di Santa Verdiana, Castelfiorentino **Right** The tower of Frederick rising above San Miniato

❶ San Miniato
Pisa, Tuscany; 56027

Like a sentinel guarding the Via Francigena, San Miniato's 13th-century **Tower of Frederick** (*closed Mon: summer*) still dominates the Arno valley. The German Emperor Otto I built a castle in San Miniato in 962 CE, and the town became the seat of imperial viceroys with jurisdiction over all of Tuscany. The **Duomo** (*open daily*) is dedicated to the Virgin Mary and San Genesio. A mixture of Gothic and Romanesque architecture, it has majolica plates embedded in its façade. The town is also famous for its highly prized white truffles.

🚗 *From Piazza Buonaparte follow signs to Via Fiancigena, then left into Via Castelfiorentino. Fork right into Via Meleto to a large roundabout. Just before Castelfiorentino take first exit right, then left and over the bridge. Park in Piazza John Fitzgerald Kennedy.*

❷ Castelfiorentino
Florence, Tuscany; 50051

Named after the castle that was built here on the Via Francigena (*p213*), Castelfiorentino is laid out like a fan below the now crumbling **fortress** and the **Chiesa di Santi Ippolito e Biagio** (1195). The **Collegiata di Santa Verdiana** in the lower town has a small museum celebrating the 12th-century contemporary of St Francis who visited here. It's also worth exploring the modern art museum **BeGo** (*Via Testaferrata; museobenozzogozzoli.it*), which has frescoes by the 15th-century artist Benozzo Gozzoli.

🚗 *Head south on SR429, left towards Volterra, then right on the overpass (SP4). Go straight over the roundabout, and on through Gambassi Terme. At Spillocchi turn right for Montaione, then left at Via Pozzolo and left again at Via Tre Ponti and into San Vivaldo.*

❸ The Holy Mount of San Vivaldo
Montaione, Florence, Tuscany; 50050

This extremely beautiful and rarely visited monastery (*reservations required for guide tours of over 10 visitors; montaioneintuscany.it*) is where the 14th-century hermit monk Vivaldo lived in a chestnut tree in the forest. Fra'Tommaso da Firenze, on his return from the Holy Land, replicated the holy sites in Jerusalem in 25 stunning chapels (1500–16). The 18 that remain contain large polychrome terracotta sculptures from the workshops of Giovanni della Robbia and Benedetto Buglioni. Concerts are staged here in summer (*Sun*) – check monastery website.

🚗 *Head south on SP65, following signs to Volterra. Drive most of the way through town, then turn sharp left up Viale dei Ponti, then right for covered parking at Piazza Martiri della Libertà.*

④ VOLTERRA

Pisa, Tuscany; 56048

One of the 12 city-states of the Etruscan League, Volterra had well-built walls and portals, and later, a Roman theatre. During the medieval period the town built its Duomo and fine civic buildings, and in the Renaissance the ruling Medici built a fort. Volterra is famous for its tradition of alabaster carving – look for the artists' workshops.

A two-hour walking tour

From the car park, head southwest and through **Porta all'Arco** ①, an Etruscan gate from the 3rd or 2nd century BCE. Continue up Via Porta all'Arco and turn left at Via del Marchesi to **Piazza dei Priori** ②. To the left is the **Palazzo dei Priori** ③ (1254), the oldest town hall in Tuscany with terracotta shields of the Florentine rulers of the 15th century. Turn down Via Turazza to Piazza San Giovanni and the **Duomo** ④, dedicated to Santa Maria. Founded in the 9th century, and reconstructed after an earthquake in the 12th century, the church has a Romanesque façade by Nicola Pisano. Directly in front of the Duomo is the eight-sided **Baptistry** ⑤, built on the site of a pagan temple. Pass the loggia of the founding hospital and turn right into Via Roma and Via Buonparenti. In Via dei Sarti, the **Pinacoteca e Museo Civico** ⑥ (open daily) is worth a visit to see Fiorentino's Mannerist masterpiece, *The Deposition* (1521). Turn into Passo del Gralduccio in Piazza Minucci, then right for excellent views of the 1st-century **Teatro Romano** ⑦. Retrace steps to Via dei Sarti, proceed downhill, turning right into Via Matteotti, a shopping street, and left into Via Gramsci, which becomes Via Don Minzoni. The **Museo Etrusco Guarnacci** ⑧, one of Tuscany's most important museums, has fine examples of Etruscan alabaster work. Don't miss the *Funeral Urn of the Married Couple* and the modern-looking statuette *Evening Shadow*. At the street end is the 16th-century **Porta a Selci** ⑨. Retrace steps and turn left up Via di Castello. Immediately ahead is the **Fortezza Medicea** ⑩, in two parts. The later building was added by Medici ruler Lorenzo il Magnifico to house criminals, and it is still used as a prison. Continue to the **Parco Archeologico Enrico Fiumi** ⑪ (open summer: until 5:30pm, winter: 4–5:30pm), the site of the ancient acropolis. Descend the stairs to the northwest into Via dei Marchesi and head left, back to Piazza Martiri della Libertà.

🚗 **Leave on SR68 east. Turn left at SP47. At the roundabout, take the 3rd exit onto SP1, go around Piazzale Martiri Montemaggio and park in Via dei Foss.**

Rondel in the style of Luca della Robbia

VISITING VOLTERRA

Tourist Information
Piazza dei Priori 19/20, 56048; volterratur.it

Alabaster workshops
Visits to Volterra's workshops can be arranged at the tourist office. The **Artists' Cooperative** (5 Piazza dei Priori) has an excellent showroom, and the **Alabaster EcoMuseum** (Piazza Minucci 2) has interesting displays of tools, techniques and alabaster sculptures.

EAT AND DRINK

SAN MINIATO

Pepenero *expensive*
Chef Gilberto Rossi serves innovative cuisine amid casual-chic decor at his restaurant in the Piazza del Duomo.
Piazza del Duomo 4, 56028; pepenerocucina.it; closed Tue & Sat lunch

AROUND CASTELFIORENTINO

Il Cigliere Del Rustico *moderate*
This family-friendly restaurant serves good Tuscan home cooking – 6 km (4 miles) from town, just off the road.
Via Onofrio di Paolo 24, 50051; open Jul–Aug: Sat eve; Sep–Dec & Feb–Jun: open Sat dinner & Sun lunch; cigliaredelrustico.it

VOLTERRA

Del Duca *moderate*
A refined restaurant where guests are made to feel very welcome. Great food, excellent wines and superb ambience.
Via di Castello 2, 56048; 0588 81 510; closed Wed

Osteria La Pace *moderate*
This is a small but lively restaurant in the historic centre. Try the homemade tagliatelle with truffle, or grilled meats.
Via Don Minzoni 55, 56048; osteria-lapace.com

Right The Romanesque Church of Santa Maria Assunta, Monteriggioni **Middle right** Brightly coloured ceramic wares for sale in Siena **Far right** The multi-towered medieval town of San Gimignano **Below** The Chiostro Grande in the Monte Oliveto Maggiore Abbey

WHERE TO STAY

SAN GIMIGNANO

Hotel Leon Bianco *inexpensive*
Right in the centre of San Gimignano, this good-value three-star hotel has elegant rooms and a breakfast terrace.
Piazza Cisterna 13, 53037; leonbianco.com

Hotel Relais Santa Chiara *moderate*
This modern and comfortable hotel is within easy walking distance of the town, with parking, pool and gardens.
Via Matteotti 15, 53037; rsc.it

La Collegiata *expensive*
This stunning 17th-century converted monastery offers stylish luxury less than 2 km (1 mile) from the historic town.
Localitá Strada 27, 53037; lacollegiata.it

COLLE DI VAL D'ELSA

Relais Della Rovere *moderate*
Pope Julius II built this villa just outside the town next to the monastery. Well-restored, it has elegant rooms.
Via Piemonte 10, 53035; relaisdellarovere.it

MONTERIGGIONI

La Canonica di San Michele *moderate*
This restored 13th-century villa has retained many original features and is set in an area of pristine natural beauty.
Strada di Fungaia 11, 53035; lacanonicadisanmichele.com

SIENA AND AROUND

La Grotta di Montecchino *inexpensive*
These self-catering farmhouse apartments, 2 km (1 mile) west of Siena, offer simple, rustic comfort with a barbecue and pool – good for families.
Strada Grossetana 87, 53010 Sant'Andrea a Montecchio; montecchino.it

Albergo Chiusarelli *moderate*
A frescoed Neo-Classical villa in the heart of Siena. The rooms are clean and comfortable, and Piazza del Campo is just a few minutes away.
Via Curtatone 15; chiusarelli.com

Certosa di Maggiano *expensive*
The epitome of luxury, this 14th-century converted Carthusian monastery, on the southeast edge of town, has everything – including a helipad.
Strada di Certosa 82/86, 53100; lacertosadimaggiano

⑤ San Gimignano
Siena, Tuscany; 53037
From far away, San Gimignano's medieval towers – 14 of the original 72 remain – are a sign of the prosperity brought by the Via Francigena *(see box)*. Don't miss the **Collegiata di Santa Maria Assunta** *(open daily)*, consecrated in 1148, with an interior decorated in the 15th century by artists such as Benozzo Gozzoli. Climb the 218 steps to view the panorama from the **Torre Grossa** *(open daily)*. The **San Gimignano1300** *(Via Costarella 3; open daily)* is a museum whose main exhibit is a scale model of the town in the year 1300.

🚗 *Follow signs to Colle di Val d'Elsa on SP1, turning right for SP36. At the T-junction, turn left onto SR68. At the 2nd roundabout, turn left into Via Armando Diaz/SP541. Follow signs for "P-ascensore" in Via di Fontibona. Use the free parking and lift.*

⑥ Colle di Val d'Elsa
Siena, Tuscany; 53034
This historic town is split into two sections, with Colle "alta" overlooking Colle "bassa". The town's location on the River Elsa enabled a papermaking industry to flourish, but it was glass-making, particularly fine crystal, that gave it wider fame. From Colle "bassa", take the elevator up to the **castello**, the oldest part of the town, near the tower-house where 13th-century sculptor and architect Arnolfo di Cambio was born. From here, it's a pleasant walk to the west and the twin bulwarks of the **Porta Nova**.

🚗 *Exit the car park, turning right and continue until left turn at Via XXV Aprile. Continue onto SP5, over the autostrada, then right onto SR2 towards Siena; turn left into Monteriggioni and car park.*

⑦ Monteriggioni
Siena, Tuscany; 53035
A rare example of a garrison town with an intact circle of walls, Monteriggioni safeguarded the Via Francigena and Siena's gateway to the Val d'Elsa. Fourteen towers guard a mere 570 m (1,870 ft) of walls, crowning a gentle rise in the valley. Enter **Porta Franca o Romea** into Piazza Roma and visit the simple, 13th-century Romanesque **Church of Santa Maria Assunta**, first mentioned in the 7th century.

🚗 *Follow signs for Autostrada Firenze-Siena RA3 towards Siena. Take Siena Sud exit. Turn right onto SP6, then second left at Via di Tuli. Drive through Park dei Tuli and right into the Via Fontanella car park. Follow signs for Piazza il Campo on foot.*

⑧ Siena
Siena, Tuscany; 53100
Many branches of the Via Francigena converged on Siena and perhaps no other city owes so much of its heritage to the pilgrim way. It is said that in

1288, the city contained as many as 90 hotels. Travellers entered through Porta Camollia to the north and Porta Romana to the south – the latter being especially magnificent. **Il Campo**, the central square, is one of the most famous in Italy and the location of the *Palio* (horse race). The huge **Torre del Mangia** and the 14th-century **Palazzo Pubblico** (open daily) form the apex of the fan-shaped square.

The Duomo, **Santa Maria Assunta** (open daily), completed in 1215, is a masterpiece of Tuscan Gothic. The beautiful interior includes inlaid marble floors, black-and-white banded marble pillars and carvings and sculptures by major medieval and Renaissance artists, including some early works by Michelangelo. One highlight is the 15th-century Piccolomini Library, with paintings by Pinturicchio of episodes from the life of Pope Pius II, founder of Pienza.

Opposite, the Museum and Art complex of **Santa Maria della Scala**

The Palio of Siena

The Palio is Tuscany's most famous festival and occurs in the Campo each year on 2 July and 16 August at 7pm. This is a bareback horse race and was first recorded in 1283. The jockeys represent 10 of Siena's 17 *contrade* (districts); the horses are chosen by the drawing of lots. Preceded by days of pageantry, processions and heavy betting, the races themselves last only 90 seconds. Thousands watch the race, and rivalry is intense. Animal rights campaigners have long lobbied to put an end to the Palio, claiming the horses suffer unduly from the summer heat and uproarious crowds.

(closed Nov–Mar: Tue), dating from 1090, was the biggest pilgrim hospice and richly endowed by the city of Siena. Today, it is a cultural institute, gallery and underground archaeological museum. Its most important exhibit is the fresco cycle in the Sala del Pellegrinaio, which provides amazing detail of both hospital and pilgrim life in the 14th century.

🚗 Return to *Tangenziale Siena Ovest*. Head south onto the ramp, following signs to Arezzo and merge onto SS223, then right again to Arezzo. Merge onto E78/SS715. Take exit for Taverne D'Arbia, onto SP438 to Asciano, then turn right onto SP451 and follow signs to Monte Oliveto Maggiore and car park.

Above Fresco from the Piccolomini Library at Santa Maria Assunta, Siena

9 Monte Oliveto Maggiore
Siena, Tuscany 53041

Surrounded by a serried array of cypress trees and accessed by a small drawbridge, the Benedictine abbey Monte Oliveto Maggiore (open daily) is still an active monastery. The main church is noted for its intricately carved wooden choir stalls and inlays. The library is of immense historical importance, but access is limited. The Chiostro Grande is the main attraction, illuminated by frescoes about the life of St Benedict created by Luca Signorelli in 1497 and Antonio Bazzi (called "Sodoma") in 1505. Another highlight is the atmospheric Gregorian chant (6:15pm daily).

🚗 Exit the monastery, then turn left at SP451 to Buonconvento. There is ample parking by the walls.

SIENESE PANFORTE

First recorded in the 1300s, *panforte* (strong bread) is a rich, chewy mix of flour, almonds, egg white and honey, with dried fruit and candied oranges. It provided sustenance for pilgrims and has become the signature fare of Siena. It is available in many shops in the city.

EAT AND DRINK

SAN GIMIGNANO
Trattoria Chiribiri *moderate*
Serves traditional Tuscan food. Try the *coniglio ripieno* (rabbit stuffed with meat and vegetables).
Piazza della Madonna 1, 53037; 0577 941 948; closed Wed

MONTERIGGIONI
Osteria Antico Travaglio *moderate*
A family-run *osteria*, known for its great fiorentina steak and desserts.
Piazza Roma 6A, 53035; anticotravaglio-monteriggioni.com

SIENA
Zest *inexpensive*
A quick and tasty lunch-stop, this bar also offer a good choice of wines.
Costa di Sant'Antonio 13, 53100; 0577 47139

Antica Trattoria Papei *moderate*
Just behind the Torre del Mangia. Serves traditional Sienese fare such as *pici al cinghiale* (pasta with wild boar sauce).
Via del Mercato, 6, 53100; anticatrattoriapapei.com

MONTE OLIVETO MAGGIORE
Trattoria La Torre *moderate*
Located within the abbey complex, this *osteria* serves typical Tuscan cuisine. Try the *ribollita* soup and pecorino cheeses.
Loc. Chiusure, 53041; 0577 707 022; closed Tue

Below White-marble façade of Santa Maria Assunta, Siena's stunning cathedral

Right Chiusdino, a beautiful Tuscan hill town overlooking the Val di Merse **Below left** Clock on the medieval town hall, Buonconvento **Below right** Attractive street in Buonconvento

CYCLING IN VAL DI MERSE

Biking holiday
Offering woodland trails and relatively quiet roads, Val di Merse is ideal terrain for biking. The tourism website **Terra di Siena** (*terresiena.it*) has route maps for the area.

WHERE TO STAY

BUONCONVENTO

Podere Salicotto Country Hotel *expensive*
This farm stay puts the emphasis on luxurious comfort with "Bed and Brunch" (for a lie-in) and a swimming pool.
Strada Prov. le Pieve a Salti, Loc. Salicotti 73, 53022; 0577 809 087

AROUND GRANCIA DI CUNA

Agriturismo San Giorgio *inexpensive*
This farm stay has four apartments and also offers B&B. Set in a quiet location with comfy rooms and good breakfast.
Strada Provinciale 34/B di Murlo, Loc. Colle Malamerenda, 53014; san-giorgio.net

TORRI AND AROUND

Antico Borgo di Torri *inexpensive*
This small, family-run B&B in the centre of Torri offers comfortable rooms decorated in a rustic, country style.
Vicolo delle Cantine 1, Loc. Torri, Sovicille; borgoditorri.it

Villa Ferraia *moderate*
This superb environmental leisure centre offers simple but stylish rooms as well as an organic vegetable garden, farm and astronomical observatory.
Loc. Tocchi, 53015 Monticiano; villaferraia.it

AROUND CHIUSDINO

Agriturismo Colli di Travale *moderate*
A former medieval convent turned into a rustic farmhouse, with exposed stone walls and beamed ceilings. The rooms are charming and spacious, and breakfast is included.
Loc. Colli Travale, 58026 Montieri; colliditravale.it

⑩ Buonconvento
Siena, Tuscany; 53022

The village of Buonconvento was always vulnerable to attack. After the Sienese defeated Emperor Henry VII in 1313, they built imposing walls, securing this important stop on the Via Francigena. The pleasant *centro storico* is home to the **Museo d'Arte Sacra** (open Tue-Sun), which has a fine collection of religious art. Also worth a visit is the **Museo della Mezzadria Senese** (open timings same as Museo d'Arte Sacra), an evocative display of farming history in the region. Steam buffs will enjoy the **Nature Train** (*terresiena.it*) that puffs from town to town in the area on special days.

🚗 *Head north on SR2 towards Siena. Take exit Monteroni d'Arbia Nord, turn left at Strada Statale Cassia/SR2 (south), then right onto Via Comunale. Park in Piazza della Grancia.*

⑪ Grancia di Cuna
Siena, Tuscany; 53014

This huge structure close to Monteroni d'Arbia is a medieval *grancia*, or fortified farm. Once a hostel providing shelter for pilgrims, it was taken over in the 13th century by Siena's Santa Maria della Scala Hospital, who, over the years, redeveloped it substantially, turning it into an administrative centre for their estates. The 14th-century centre of the *grancia* is still intact, with a courtyard and winding internal ramps that enabled mules to carry their loads to the storage rooms above what are now private dwellings. To the left of the entrance is a 1314 church dedicated to James and Christopher, the patron saints of pilgrimage and travel.

🚗 *Return to Via Cassia and turn right. At the roundabout turn right to bypass the town and right at Via 4 Novembre/SP23 signposted Castello di Grotti, then turn left for Bagnaia. Then turn right and left onto SP99 for Torri. Park in Piazza Borgo.*

⑫ Torri
Sovicille, Siena, Tuscany; 53018

The Val di Merse, southwest of Siena, is dotted with intriguing medieval villages such as Orgia, Stigliano and Torri, whose old mills and huge granaries attest to the fertility of the land. Next to Torri's church is the impressive 11th-century **Benedictine Abbey** (closed Tue & Thu), now privately owned. The abbey's beautiful cloister is regarded as one of the finest in Tuscany. It was built around a brick parquet courtyard in three elegant tiers – marble, brick and wood – in the 12th, 14th and 15th centuries, respectively. Note

Pope Pius II's (1405–64) family coat of arms – Piccolomini – over the doors.

🚗 *Return to SP99, turn left and left again on SP73bis (Massa Marittima). A little way after passing Frosini turn right onto Strada Provinciale di Chiusdino/SP31. Park in Piazza Giacomo Matteotti.*

⓭ Chiusdino
Siena, Tuscany; 53012

The hill town of Chiusdino lies between the Colline Metallifere (Metalliferous Hills) and the gentle Val di Merse, both areas of great natural beauty. The historic centre is a medieval warren of steep, narrow lanes. San Galgano was born here into a noble family in 1148. Instead of following a knight's life, he plunged his sword into a rock and became a hermit. The Chapel of Compagnia has a bas-relief (1466) of the sword in the stone and **San Galgano's house** *(open daily)* is now a chapel with a banded brick façade and a 13th-century relief – a copy – by Giovanni di Agostino. The original is in the **Casa Parrocchiale** along with a *Madonna and Child* by Niccolò di Segna of 1336.

🚗 *Exit on Via Piave/SP31, then fork left on the Strada Comunale di Le Vene. Turn left on Strada Provinciale Massetana/SP441. Turn right into the abbey and follow signs to parking.*

⓮ San Galgano
Siena, Tuscany; 53012

One of the most striking and poignant monuments in Tuscany is the roofless, ruined **Abbey of San Galgano**. It was built by Cistercian monks in the 13th century in a fusion of French-Gothic and Romanesque architectural styles, with a vaulted chapter house. On the hill above is the 12th-century **Hermitage of Montesiepi**. Its simple style is offset by a superb banded brick and stone cupola, and by St Galgano's sword in the stone (thought by some to be the source of elements of Britain's Arthurian legend). Although the abbey flourished for several centuries, it was all but abandoned by 1600, and in 1786 its roof collapsed. In summer, it becomes a magical setting for occasional open-air operas.

Above Inside the peaceful and poignant ruins of the Abbey of San Galgano

Above left Chapel built at the birthplace of San Galgano, Chiusdino. **Above right** The sleepy hamlet of Stigliano in the Val di Merse

EAT AND DRINK

SAN GALGANO

Salendo *inexpensive*
This wine bar with a terrace is on the road up to the Hermitage of Montesiepi, and offers typical local produce.
La Cappella 172C, 53012; 0577 756 270

AROUND GRANCIA DI CUNA

La Galera *inexpensive*
This bar-restaurant specializes in grilled meats, seafood and pizza.
Via Roma 193, 53014; 0577 374 024; closed Sat dinner

AROUND TORRI

Dal Cateni a Orgia *moderate*
A fine restaurant in Orgia, this serves excellent food – try the pasta with wild boar and the pine kernel tart for dessert.
Via dei Pratini 19, Loc. Orgia, 53018; dalcateniaorgia.it; closed Tue dinner, Wed & Thu

CHIUSDINO

Gastronomia Pizzeria *inexpensive*
A popular pizzeria where you can dine pavementside or in the lovely garden behind the restaurant.
Piazza G. Matteotti 1, 53012; 371 159 3518

DAY TRIP OPTIONS

Volterra and Siena are great bases for day trips. Kids will love climbing over walls and towers. Adults will enjoy the art that bridged the gap between medieval and Renaissance Italy. Everyone will enjoy the scenery.

Towers, castles and walls
From Volterra ❹, drive to the towers of San Gimignano ❺ and climb up the Torre Grosso's 218 steps. Stop off at the castle at Colle di Val d'Elsa ❻ for lunch and head on to the garrison town of Monteriggioni ❼.

Follow the instructions in the drive and return the same way.

Pre-Renaissance art
In Siena ❽, spend the morning exploring the art and architecture of the great city. Pick up a picnic and head for the frescoes of Monte Oliveto Maggiore ❾, followed by the religious art of Buonconvento ❿. Return via Grancia di Cuna ⓫.

Follow the drive instructions to Grancia di Cuna, then head for the SR2 and Via Roma back to Siena.

The Val di Merse
Pick up a picnic in Siena ❽, then head to Torri ⓬ and the Val di Merse. Enjoy a hike or cycle ride, stopping for lunch. Afterwards, learn about the sword in the stone legend by driving on to San Galgano ⓮. Finish the day with a drink in Chiusdino ⓭, which looks out on the pristine countryside.

Take Via Roma to SR2, then head north on "tangenziale" to take SP73bis. Turn left for Torri at Rosia. Return to SP73bis, then SS441 for San Galgano and Chiusdino. Return the same way.

TRIP 19

IN THE SHADOW OF A VOLCANO

Castiglione d'Orcia to
San Casciano dei Bagni

HIGHLIGHTS

Natural beauty
Walk in the pristine chestnut forests that cloak Monte Amiata's hillsides and head up to the clean air at the summit for glorious countryside views

Mountain villages
Explore the pretty medieval villages that ring the mountain, whose forts and simple stone buildings reflect a tough ancient way of life

Mountain spa
Relax in a natural hot spring, gushing down a limestone waterfall in a forest glade, or soak in a sulphurous, smelly but good-for-you mud pack

IN THE SHADOW OF A VOLCANO

Italy's largest extinct volcano, Monte Amiata, dominates the horizon of much of southern Tuscany. It has been important in other ways, too. The mountain's woods provided lumber for Etruscan ships, its heights were a sanctuary for medieval monks and its depths give up minerals for the modern age. This drive takes in a ring of villages around the foot of the volcano, each with its own culture and appeal. Visitors can enjoy the relaxing properties of ancient thermal springs, hike up slopes cloaked with rich chestnut and oak forests – teeming with game and forest fare – enjoy the respite from the heat Amiata offers in summer, or even indulge in exciting winter sports when it snows.

Above The crumbling remains of the castello, Castiglione d'Orcia, see p192

ACTIVITIES

Get up the mountain under your own steam on a mountain bike, or let a horse do the work

Soothe those aching limbs with a mud massage or sulphuric sauna at a spa in San Casciano dei Bagni or Bagni San Filippo

Walk in the forest along gentle mountainside trails beneath chestnut, oak and beech trees

Ski down Monte Amiata at speed in winter on its snow-covered ski slopes

Enjoy a taste of medieval beer with Monte Amiata's local brews

Tour a mining museum on a narrow-gauge train at Abbadia San Salvatore

TRIP 19: IN THE SHADOW OF A VOLCANO

Above The main piazza in the medieval heart of Piancastagnaio, see p193 Below The hills and soft valleys of a classic Tuscan landscape

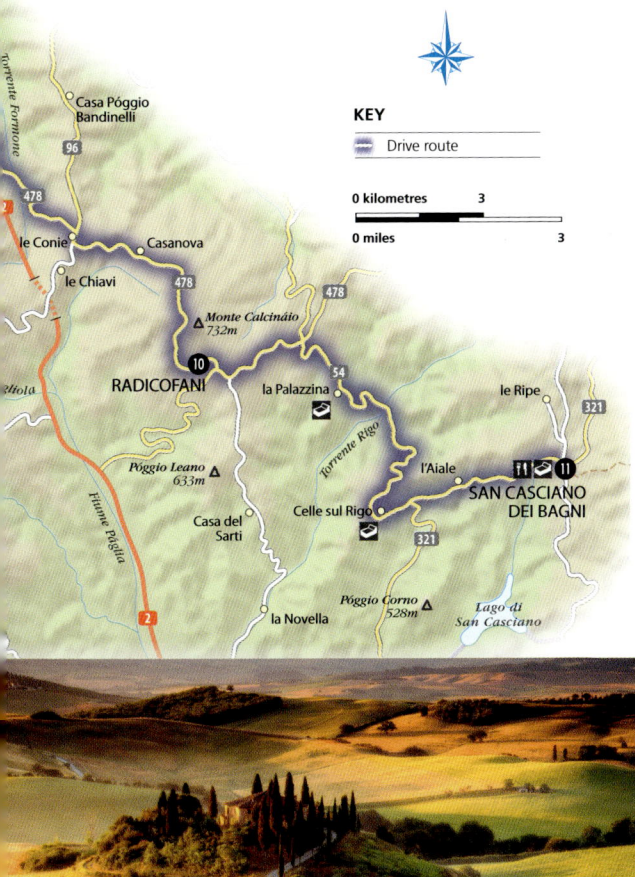

PLAN YOUR DRIVE

Start/finish: Castiglione d'Orcia to San Casciano dei Bagni.

Number of days: 2–3 days.

Distance: 117 km (73 miles).

Road conditions: Generally good road surfaces with good signposting. A little isolated in parts. During Dec–Mar, roads can be icy and snow chains are obligatory in mountain areas.

When to go: Mar–Nov is the best time. Aug is a peak season as holiday-makers escape the heat of the plain.

Opening times: Major museums are open 8:30am–7:30pm and closed Mon. Small museums often only open on weekends outside summer. Churches are generally open 7:30am–noon and 3–7:30pm. Shops open 10am–1pm and 4–8pm and close Sun & Mon mornings.

Main market days: Castiglione d'Orcia: Sat; Castel del Piano: Wed; Arcidosso: Tue; Santa Fiora: Thu; Piancastagnaio: 1st & 2nd Sat; Abbadia San Salvatore: Thu; Radicofani: 2nd & 4th Thu; San Casciano dei Bagni: 1st & 3rd Thu.

Shopping: Wooden handicrafts from Amiata's forests and organic preserves.

Major festivals: Castiglione d'Orcia: spring market, Easter Mon; Castel del Piano: Palio (medieval horse race), Sep; Montelaterone: La Festa della Pina (spring festival), Apr; Arcidosso: Sagra Della Patata Macchiaiola (potato festival), 3rd weekend in Aug; Santa Fiora & Piancastagnaio: chestnut festival, late Oct & Nov; Radicofani: Antichi Mestieri (old traditions), 1st weekend in Jun; San Casciano dei Bagni: Festa del Ciaffagnone (pancake festival), 2nd weekend in Jun.

DAY TRIP OPTIONS

Although the distances aren't great, mountain roads can be winding, so don't try to do too much on a day trip. Gourmets can enjoy the famous Amiata produce – **chestnuts**, **salami** and locally brewed **beer** – taking in the fine views on the way. Families with young children will find them intrigued by the history behind the area's many **castles**, **forts** and **walled medieval towns**. For full details, see p195.

Above The Peschiera, Santa Fiora, built to supply trout to the Aldobrandeschi court

VISITING MONTE AMIATA

Getting to Castiglione d'Orcia
From A1 Autostrada Rome-Florence, exit at Chiusi-Chianciano Terme towards Chianciano. Take SS146, then SP53. Turn left at SR2, then right at SS323. Continue to Castiglione d'Orcia, turning left at SS323, then left up Via Del Fosso.

Tourist Information
Castiglione d'Orcia: *Via San Giovanni 8, 53023; 0577 888 986.* **Arcidosso:** *Piazza Indipendenza, 58031; 0564 968 084.* **Santa Fiora:** *Piazza Giuseppe Garibaldi 37, 58037; 0564 977 142*

WHERE TO STAY

CASTIGLIONE D'ORCIA

Agriturismo Grossola *inexpensive*
A large stone 16th-century farmstead set in the country – good for walkers.
Via Grossola 4, 53023; agriturismo grossola.it

AROUND MONTELATERONE

Podere Legnotorto *moderate*
An old stone farmhouse turned into a stylish B&B. Ask for the room with the hot tub.
Loc. Pian di Ballo 29, 58033 Castel del Piano; poderelegnotorto.it

AROUND ARCIDOSSO

Thalassa Locanda *inexpensive*
This B&B has pretty rooms, some with nice views of the church, and a terrace where breakfast is served.
Via Talassese 94; thalassabeb.com

SANTA FIORA

Hotel Eden *inexpensive*
Experience old-world hospitality in this simple, rustic hotel.
Via Roma 1, 58037; hoteleden santafiora.it

① Castiglione d'Orcia
Siena, Toscana; 53023

Only a few ruins on a hill remain of the fortress that once controlled the nearby ancient byway, the Via Cassia. The heart of the town, built on the hillside below the fort, is Piazza il Vecchietta, a sloping cobbled square with a travertine fountain (1618) and the town hall, which contains a fresco removed from the original fortress.

From the town centre, take the steep Via della Rocca to the nextdoor village, **Rocca d'Orcia**, with a much better preserved bastion, **Rocca di Tentennano** *(open daily)*, and spectacular views of Mount Amiata and the Val d'Orcia.

🚗 *Drive south along SP323 past Poggia Rosa, then left at SP160. Continue past Seggiano to Castel del Piano. Park at Piazza Giuseppe Garibaldi.*

② Castel del Piano
Grosseto, Toscana; 58033

Sitting on the slopes of Mount Amiata, Castel del Piano has been inhabited since the Paleolithic era, but up until the 14th century, it was a stronghold of the Aldobrandeschi family. Spread across the slopes, the modern part of town dwarfs the historic centre, which is best explored from Piazza Giuseppe Garibaldi, an 18th-century attempt to emulate Siena's famous Campo. On Corso Nasini, named after the 17th-century family of painters born here, stands **Chiesa di Madonna delle Grazie** with a beautiful *Madonna col Bambino* by Sano di Pietro (1405–81).

🚗 *Head west on Via della Croce/SP64. Turn left onto SP26/Loc. Case Rosse and take a sharp right up Via Nouva to Montelaterone. Park in Via Nouva.*

③ Montelaterone
Grosseto, Toscana; 58031

Founded around 1000 CE, this is one of the oldest settlements in the area, with the inner of the two town walls dating from the 11th century. Later, from the early 1200s, the town came under the protection of mighty Siena. Winding streets and vaulted walkways offer an intriguing climb to the ruined 13th-century keep, **Cassero Senese**. The **Palazzo Pretorio** (town hall) from the same period is decorated with the coats of arms of Renaissance-era families. On the road to Arcidosso stands the 9th-century Romanesque church **La Pieve di Lamula**, largely reconstructed in the 12th century.

🚗 *Return to SP26 and head south to Arcidosso. On arrival, turn left up Via Roma to Piazza Indipendenza and park on Corso Toscana.*

Mountain chestnuts

Historically, mountain villagers relied upon the chestnut for survival during hard times. In autumn, they would collect the chestnuts, dry them, then grind them into flour used to make a type of bread. Once poor man's food, the flour is now used to make a rich cake – *castagnaccio* – with walnuts and pine nuts. The Amiata chestnut has a delicious sweet taste when roasted and even has Protected Geographical Indication (PGI).

④ Arcidosso
Grosseto, Toscana; 58031

Just outside Arcidosso, the **Santuario della Madonna delle Grazie** *(open daily)*, consecrated in 1348 and expanded in the 16th century, houses works of the 14th-century Sienese school. In 1121,

Above The twin hamlets of Castiglione d'Orcia and Rocca d'Orcia

Far left Pretty backstreets in the medieval heart of Montelaterone **Left** The distant Piancastagnaio seen beneath Monte Amiata **Below** Saxa Enoteca Contemporanea, Piancastagnaio, with its menu clearly displayed

BIRRA AMIATA

Beer drinkers must try the local brews from Birra Amiata in Montelaterone (birramiata.com). La Bastarda Rossa is made with Amiata chestnuts and has a rich red colour, while Aldobrandesca is a wheat beer made to a medieval recipe.

the town became a stronghold of the Aldobrandeschi family, who built the impressive **Rocca Aldobrandesca** *(open Sat & Sun)* – climb the tower for views. Little of the town's original walls remain, except for two original gates: Porta di Castello and Porta Talassese.

From Piazza Indipendenza follow signs to Santa Fiora. Take SP160, then turn left onto SP6 at Aiuole. Park in Via delle Fontane.

The Prophet of Amiata

In the late 19th century, a man from Arcidosso, David Lazzaretti, founded a church called Giurisdavidismo, which advocated a form of socialism and universal suffrage. Arrested twice by the alarmed authorities of the new Italian state and excommunicated by the pope, he was finally shot dead by the military police in 1878. A museum in Arcidosso's **Palazzo del Comune** *(Piazza Indipendenza; open Sat & Sun)* tells the fascinating story of his life.

⑤ Santa Fiora
Grosseto, Toscana; 58037

One of the prettiest Amiata towns, Santa Fiora's centre is entered through Porta al Palazzo into Piazza Garibaldi. Piazza di San Michele is dominated by a statue of the saint in *peperino*, a grey-brown volcanic tufa rock. In Piazza delle Arcipretura, **La Pieve delle Sante Flora e Lucilla** *(open daily)* has blue-and-white glazed terracotta reliefs by Andrea della Robbia from 1465–90. Via della Pescheria leads to a pond, constructed in the 12th century and filled with trout. Santa Fiora makes a good base for hiking through the forests on Mount Amiata's western and southwestern slopes. There's a pleasant signposted walk through the grove near the Peschiera and the Parco Comunale di San Rocco.

Return to SP6. The route is signposted "Roma". Then turn left onto SP18. At Piancastagnaio turn right into Viale Giuseppe Vespa, through the gate and park in Piazza Castello.

⑥ Piancastagnaio
Siena, Toscana; 53025

Its walls and town gates are mostly gone, but Piancastagnaio's medieval townscape endures. The hard stone streets of this mountain town reflect the harshness of life in the medieval era, when poverty was part of the infrastructure. Monumental **Rocca Aldobrandesca** *(open Jun–mid-Sep: daily)* looms over the town. After exploring the tower, head down Via Cavour to the main square, Piazza Matteotti, where the grand Baroque cathedral, **Santa Maria Assunta** *(open daily)*, first recorded in 1188, stands almost hidden behind a crowd of buildings.

Head northwest on Viale Giuseppe Vespa and follow SP18 to Abbadia San Salvatore. Fork right at roundabout, then left to park in Via Cavour.

EAT AND DRINK

CASTIGLIONE D'ORCIA

Il Cassero *moderate*
An unpretentious trattoria offering homemade pasta with Amiata mushroom and truffles. Dogs are welcome.
Piazza Cesare Battisti 1, 53023; 0577 888 950; closed Tue

La Cisterna nel Borgo *moderate*
Convivial hosts and traditional fare served with an innovative twist.
Via Borgo Maestro 37, 53023 Rocca d'Orcia; cisternanelborgo.com; closed Mon

CASTEL DEL PIANO

Antica Fattoria del Grottaione *moderate*
This rustic trattoria's specialties include *il peposo* (braised beef with black pepper). There's an outdoor terrace in the summer.
Via della Piazza, 58033; anticafattoriadelgrottaione.it

ARCIDOSSO

Il Bagatto *inexpensive*
This pleasant ice-cream place also serves quick lunches.
Viale Davide Lazzaretti, 1, 58031; 0564 966 207

Osteria Bastarda Rossa *moderate*
All the staples of Tuscan cuisine are served at this restaurant. Don't miss the tagliatelle with mushrooms and pig's cheek or the Tuscan tortelli with ragù.
Via Talassese 98, 58031; 328 123 1293; closed Wed

SANTA FIORA

Il Barilotto *moderate*
Generous portions of well-prepared meat and game, traditional but with an innovative twist. Good wine cellar.
Via Carolina 24, 58037; 0564 977 089

PIANCASTAGNAIO

Saxa Enoteca Contemporanea *moderate*
This place serves creative mountain food with gusto but the focus is on wine and artfully presented ravioli and desserts.
Piazza Giacomo Matteotti 11, 53025; saxaenotecacontemporanea.com; closed Mon, Tue & Wed

Above The typical dark volcanic stone of medieval Abbadia San Salvatore

WHERE TO STAY

ABBADIA SAN SALVATORE

Agriturismo Trefossata *moderate*
This simple farmhouse offers rooms all year round in a tranquil, no frills environment. Good for families.
Loc. Trefossata 196, 53021; agriturismotrefossata.it

SUMMIT OF AMIATA

Albergo Le Macinaie *inexpensive*
A family-run mountain hotel with lovely rooms. Amenities such as free bikes, quads and motorbikes available.
Loc. Prato delle Macinaie, 58033; lemacinaie.it.

BAGNI SAN FILIPPO

Agriturismo Selvella *inexpensive*
This Tuscan farmhouse features stylish rooms, some with marvellous views of the valley. Great pool for a cooling dip.
La Selvella SP478 km 29.5, 53040; selvella.com

AROUND RADICOFANI

Albergo La Torre *inexpensive*
Situated in the centre of town, this hotel features simple rooms with balconies. Breakfast-style buffet.
Via Matteotti 7, 53040; 0578 55 943

AROUND SAN CASCIANO DEI BAGNI

Locanda Quattro Vesta *inexpensive*
A beautiful farmhouse building, made of stone, with an outdoor swimming pool and a bar. Rooms are tastefully decorated in traditional Tuscan style.
Via della Crocetta, 53040; locandaquattrovesta.it

Fonteverde *expensive*
This glamorous spa resort offers pampering treatments, massages and highly attentive staff – good restaurant.
Loc. Terme 1, 53040; fonteverde spa.com

❼ Abbadia San Salvatore
Siena, Toscana; 53021

Lombard King Rachis established this abbey, one of the greatest in Tuscany, in 743 CE. For centuries it was the most important place in the region and held sway over the valley and the popular pilgrim route – Via Francigena. The magnificent **abbey church** *(open daily)*, in Via del Monastero, has a crypt that dates back to the original building. A town, built from the local volcanic rock, grew around the abbey and expanded due to the mercury mining industry. The mine is now the **Parco Museo Minerario** *(open summer: daily; museominerario.it)* with a narrow-gauge train to some of the sights.

🚗 To exit town, follow signs to the Vetta Amiata on Via Federico Hamman and then onto SP81. On arrival at the large turning circle, there is a car park to the left under the trees.

❽ SUMMIT OF AMIATA
Pianello Vetta, Grosseto, Toscana; 58033

Although usually snow covered from December until March, in summer the peak of Monte Amiata offers pleasant walks with spectacular views of the valley, from a large Crucifix and a statue of the Madonna.

A one-hour walking tour
Follow signs to Vetta Amiata (Amiata Summit) to the car park near the Albergo La Croce. Pass through a wood to a wide **grassy slope** ① – in winter this is the ski school slope. The walk up the paved path leads to the **Croce dell'Amiata** ②, a large iron cross. In 1900, for the new century, Pope Leo XIII decreed that the 20 highest peaks in Italy have a cross mounted on them. It took ten years and the four tons of iron were carried to the 1,730-m (5,676-ft) peak by the people of Abbadia San Salvatore. To the left of the cross is a **viewing platform** ③ looking down on the Val d'Orcia and the town of Abbadia San Salvatore. Due east, in the distance, is the Castello di Radicofani sitting atop a dark pine-clad hill. The path to the right goes past the bar-restaurant La Vetta, where walkers can stop for an aperitif of vin brulè (mulled wine). Further along the path to the left is a natural beech thicket **Macchia Faggeta** ④. The forest of Amiata has long been a useful source of lumber – the Etruscans used it to build their boats. In the 8th century, the Abbey took over the jurisdiction of the area, creating towns around the mountain. After the 18th-century suppression of the monasteries, the cooperative Società Macchia Faggeta was formed, and in 1944 it took over managing the woods, trails, ski runs and lifts.

The mountain path winds through the forest past huge granite boulders. On the largest outcrop is mounted the white **Madonna of the Scouts** ⑤. This second crowning of Mount Amiata was made by the Scouts of Grosseto. The statue was carried to the summit over ten days in 1961. Scouts from all over the world climb the rocks to tie their kerchiefs to the sanctuary. Retrace the route back to the car park.

🚗 From Abbadia San Salvatore, take SP18 towards Bagni San Filippo. Then fork right onto SP61, following directions for "Siena" and near the village is located Fosso Bianco.

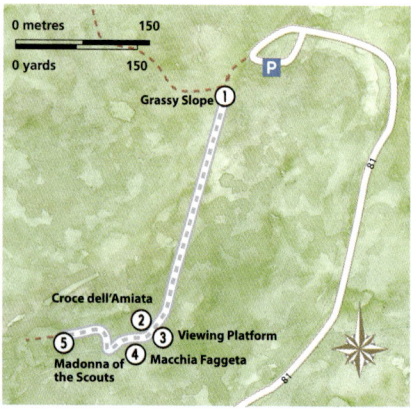

TRIP 19: IN THE SHADOW OF A VOLCANO

Left View of Radicofani, seen from high above on the Amiata Summit **Below** San Casciano dei Bagni, surrounded by pretty countryside

ACTIVITIES IN MONTE AMIATA

The ski season runs from around Dec to Mar and there are 60 km (37 miles) of ski runs and trails for cross-country skiers. For lessons, contact Scuola Sci Amiata West (*scuolasciamiataovest.it*).

To hire a bike and scale the mountain in summer, try Tondi Sport *(Via Matteotti 26, 53021 Abbadia San Salvatore; 0577 778 016).*

EAT AND DRINK

SUMMIT OF AMIATA
La Vetta *inexpensive*
This mountain-top bar/restaurant is useful for a quick hot chocolate, grappa or even a hearty mountain meal, such as polenta with *salsiccia* (sausage).
Loc. Vetta Monte Amiata 5, 53021; 0577 789 803

BAGNI SAN FILIPPO
Osteria Lo Spugnone *moderate*
A pleasant *osteria* with classic Tuscan dishes such as chunky salami and grilled vegetables drizzled with olive oil. Booking recommended.
Via delle Terme 4/6, 53023; lospugnone.it

SAN CASCIANO DEI BAGNI
Bar Centrale *inexpensive*
A local coffee bar that also sells sandwiches and cold dishes.
Piazza Matteotti, 53040; 0578 58 234

⑨ Bagni San Filippo
Siena, Toscana; 53023

The white limestone waterfall Fosso Bianco is an extraordinary natural phenomenon with hot mountain springs steaming with sulphurous vapours. In 1271, a Florentine monk and candidate for pontiff, Filippo Benizi, fled here to dwell in a nearby cave and discovered the spring. The Fosso Bianco and hot springs are accessed from a marked trail off Via del Bollore. The hot springs can be visited free of charge from Via del Fosso Bianco.
🚗 *Follow road down to SP61 and turn right. Take a right turn onto SR2, then left onto SP478. Park by the city walls.*

⑩ Radicofani
Siena, Toscana; 53040

Visible for miles around, hilltop Radicofani dominated the Roman Via Cassia and became a control point on the road between Rome and northern Europe. Etruscan in origin, the town came under the sway of the 8th-century Lombard king Desiderius. The tight cluster of houses are built of Amiata stone and the **Chiesa di San Pietro** has two works by the studio of Andrea della Robbia and an interesting 14th-century polychrome Madonna and Child. Walk up Via della Fortezza to the **fortress** *(open daily)* for spectacular views of the Val d'Orcia. The tower's history includes the time when it was occupied by a local gentleman bandit, Ghino di Tacco, in the 13th century.
🚗 *Head east on SP di Sarteano/SP478. Take a sharp right onto SP54 and turn left onto SP321, then turn right to Can Casciano and park by the city walls.*

⑪ San Casciano dei Bagni
Siena, Toscana; 53040

The Etruscans and Romans enjoyed the hot springs in this area – Emperor Augustus himself is said to have visited – and built baths here. In 2022, more than two dozen bronze statues were unearthed in the ruins of an ancient bathhouse. By the Middle Ages, a town and castle had been established in the tranquil landscape.

The turret of the **castello** (built in 1911, despite appearances) and the bell tower of the Collegiata Church dominate the town. Enter through **Porta di Sopra** (Upper Gate) and notice how the medieval structure of the town remains unchanged. Piazza Matteotti, just below the old town, forms a natural terrace with great views over southern Tuscany.

DAY TRIP OPTIONS
Eating local food, such as chestnuts, salami and beer, is a good way to get a feel for a place. Young kids may not like old buildings but they all love castles.

Gourmet day
Start the day at Santa Fiora ⑤ and buy freshly roasted chestnuts in season or the rich *castagnaccio* cake. At Piancastagnaio ⑥ buy homemade salami from a butcher *(macelleria)*. Drive up to the Summit of Amiata ⑧ for a walk and a picnic with a view. Then it's back down to Arcidosso ④ for a taste of local beer.

From Santa Fiora, follow the drive's instructions to Piancastagnaio, then go past Abbadia San Salvatore and up to Summit of Abbadia. From there, take SP81/SP35/SP58, then SP160 to Arcidosso.

Conquer a castle or two
Castiglione d'Orcia ① is a good place to start as it has two castles with great views. There's no fort at Castel del Piano ②, but it's a fine medieval town. Montelaterone ③ has everything – ancient walls, a historic centre and a ruined keep.

Follow the driving instructions to Montelarone and back.

TRIP 20

UMBRIAN HILLS, TUSCAN VALLEYS
Orvieto to Arezzo

HIGHLIGHTS

Renaissance masterpieces
Marvel at heaven and hell in Orvieto's Duomo by Luca Signorelli and Piero della Francesca's frescoes in Arezzo

Noble wine
Taste one of the great Italian red wines in the rustic wine cellars and restaurants of Montepulciano

Walled towns
Meander through the beautiful walled towns of Cetona, Lucignano and Cortona

Etruscan sites
Discover the ancient treasures of Orvieto, Sarteano and Cortona, showcased in magnificent museums

UMBRIAN HILLS, TUSCAN VALLEYS

This drive follows the Umbrian part of the important route between Rome and northern Europe, now the Strada Statale 71 (SS71), from Orvieto through the hilly hinterland to the north. This was once an Etruscan stronghold, where later, in the Middle Ages, villages passed from one feudal lord to another. The trip then crosses into Tuscany, passing through the pretty towns and vineyards of the Val di Chiana and Montepulciano, on to Val d'Orcia and Renaissance Pienza, through the rolling clay hills of the Crete Senesi. Finally, via the walls of Lucignano, the drive swings back to the SS71 at Cortona and Castiglion Fiorentino, before finishing at the provincial capital, Arezzo.

Above A hot-air balloon soaring above the clouds over Crete Senesi, Tuscany

ACTIVITIES

Explore the hills and nature reserves around Orvieto

Relive 1960s Italian style with a day's touring on a classic Vespa from Cetona

Learn traditional skills and **throw a terracotta pot** at a pottery near Ficulle

Enjoy a glass or two of celebrated DOC wine at Montepulciano

Sample the famous Pecorino di Pienza cheese in the heart of the Val d'Orcia

Photograph your own picture postcards of the rolling hills of the Crete Senesi

Sip prosecco in a hot-air balloon, soaring over the glorious Tuscan countryside

TRIP 20: UMBRIAN HILLS, TUSCAN VALLEYS

Above Cypresses in the Val d'Orcia near Pienza, see p202

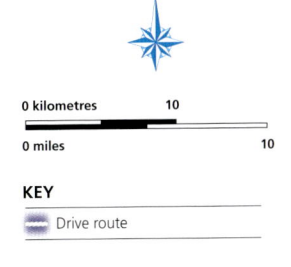

Above Arezzo's Piazza Grande, home to one of the largest antiques markets in Europe, see p205

PLAN YOUR DRIVE

Start/finish: Orvieto to Arezzo.

Number of days: 3–4 days.

Distance: 204 km (127 miles).

Road conditions: Generally good throughout and well signed.

When to go: This drive is good all year round. Festivals take place throughout the year, but the most important ones are in spring and summer.

Opening times: Major museums are open 8:30am–7:30pm, and closed Mon. Small museums are often only open at weekends outside the summer months. Churches are usually open 7:30am–noon and 3–7:30pm. Shops open 10am–1pm and 4–8pm and close Sun & Mon am.

Main market days: Orvieto: Thu & Sat; Montepulciano: Thu; **Ficulle:** Sat; Pienza & Castiglion Fiorentino: Fri; Città della Pieve: Fri; **Cetona:** Thu; Cortona: Sat; **Arezzo:** Piazza Sant'Agostino, Mon–Fri; Via Giotto, Sat; antiques, 1st weekend of month.

Shopping: Look for Pecorino cheese and Cinta Senese salami. Orvieto is known for its ceramics, while Arezzo is one of the gold jewellery capitals of Europe, and has some fine antiques.

Major festivals: Ficulle: bread and olive oil festival, Nov. **Città della Pieve:** Palio dei Terzieri (medieval pageant), Aug; **Sarteano:** green food festival, May. **Montepulciano:** Bravìo delle Botti (medieval spectacular), 3rd and 4th Sun in Aug; **Cortona:** Tuscan Sun Festival (international arts festival), late Sep; **Arezzo:** Giostra del Saraceno (medieval joust), 2nd last Sat in Jun, 1st Sun in Sep.

DAY TRIP OPTIONS

There are three tempting day trips. Families will love Orvieto's **Etruscan museum** and **tunnels**, Roman Ficulle's **castello** and Sarteano's **Etruscan treasures**. For art buffs, Cortona has **religious masterpieces**, Lucignano a **sacred reliquary**, while Arezzo has the finest **Renaissance fresco cycle** there is. Food and wine lovers can take things easy with a **wine tour** with tastings at Montepulciano and Pienza's **pecorino**. For full details, see p205.

Above Colourful flower-filled balcony in Sarteano **Above centre** View straight out of a Renaissance painting, near Città della Pieve **Above right** Perugino's *Adoration of the Magi*, Città della Pieve

GETTING TO ORVIETO
From A1 Autostrada Rome–Florence, take the Orvieto exit, keeping right to stay on SS205. At roundabout, take 2nd exit onto Via Angelo Costanzi. At the second roundabout, continue on SR71/Via delle Conce. Park (paid) at Parcheggio Campo delle Fieri.

WHERE TO STAY

ORVIETO
Hotel Corso Orvieto *inexpensive*
Value-for-money hotel in the historic centre with nice rooms and helpful staff.
Corso Cavour 339, 05018; hotelcorso.net

Palazzo Piccolomini *moderate*
This fine, centrally located 16th-century renovated palazzo was once the home of the papal Piccolomini family.
Piazza Ranieri 36, 05018; palazzopiccolomini.it

MONTELEONE D'ORVIETO
Agriturismo I Gergoni *moderate*
These self-catering houses have plenty for the sporting minded: bike hire and archery, canoeing and golf.
Vocabolo Gergone 3, 05017; igergoni.it

CITTÀ DELLA PIEVE
Locanda della Picca *inexpensive*
This hotel offers beautiful views of Val di Chiana. Rooms are spacious and elegant, each themed after a local wine.
SR142 Città della Pieve, 06062; locandadellapicca.it

CETONA
Il Caio *inexpensive*
The stone farmhouse has rooms or self-catering apartments ideal for families.
SS 321 Sud 12, 53040; ilcaio.it

① Orvieto
Terni, Umbria; 05018
Set on a huge slab of tufa, Orvieto was settled nine centuries before Christ and flourished in the Etruscan period as Velzna. After the Romans destroyed it in 264 BCE, the town didn't revive until the medieval period, when it became the residence of popes. Etruscan finds and medieval and Renaissance art and architecture make Orvieto a compelling place to visit. The travertine-and-basalt striped Duomo, **Cattedrale dell'Assunta**, has an Italian-Gothic façade with a large rose window, exquisite reliefs, gold tiles and bronzes. Begun in 1290 from plans by Arnolfo di Cambio, the building took 300 years to finish. Inside is Luca Signorelli's (c 1445–1523) *The Last Judgement* in the **Cappella di San Brizio** *(open daily)*, the finest fresco cycle of the Renaissance. The superb **Faina Archaeological and Civic Museum** *(closed Tue)*, opposite the Duomo, has a fine collection of Etruscan art. Nearby, explore Orvieto's **underground city** *(0763 344 891; open daily; orvietounderground.it)*, first excavated by the Etruscans.

🚗 *Descend from the rock (rupe) to Via Angelo Costanzi at Orvieto Scalo, taking third exit at roundabout onto SS71. At Ficulle, park to right of the main road.*

② Ficulle
Terni, Umbria; 05016
Strung along a ridge between two citadels, this tiny village dates back to when the Romans established the outpost Castrum Ficulensis (from the Latin *figulus*, or potter). Crafters still inhabit the village – near its southern entrance, Porta del Sole, is the family-run pottery of **Fabio Fattorini** *(Via Roma 40)*, started in 1834, and nearby **Vetro In** *(Corso della Rinascita 14)* is the stained-glass workshop of Michela Marilena. The medieval complex of **Castel Maggiore** is explored via a labyrinth of staircases and alleys.

🚗 *Head north on SS71 to Monteleone d'Orvieto. Take a slight left at Via Roma and park in Piazzale Marconi.*

③ Monteleone d'Orvieto
Terni, Umbria; 05017
Founded in 1052 as a feudal castle to defend the northern boundaries of Orvieto, this quiet castellated village has superb views from its medieval walls. Enter it through the medieval **Porta Nord**, rebuilt in 1848, and take Corso Vittorio Emanuele II to the village centre and Piazza Pietro Bilancini, home to the handsome 1888 Torre dell'Orologio (clock tower) and the medieval town well. Via della Ripa, above the western wall, gives views across the Val di Chiana and Monte Cetona.

🚗 *Head north on Via Crocifisso, then left at SS71/SR142 to Città della Pieve. Turn right at Via Beato Giacomo Villa, then right and park on the road.*

4 Città della Pieve
Perugia, Umbria; 06062

Almost completely built of brick, this Renaissance town is famous as the birthplace of the painter Pietro Vannucci, or Perugino (c 1450), who put the home landscape into many of his works. Enter town via **Fortezza** (open daily), built in 1326 and now home to the tourist office. It is a short walk to Piazza Plebiscito with **Perugino's house** (not open), on the left (No. 17), and the **Cattedrale di SS Gervasio e Protasio** – originally an 8th-century parish church. Heading north on Via Pietro Vannucci leads to the **Confraternita Santa Maris dei Bianchi**, housing a single painting – Perugino's glorious *Adoration of the Magi*, finished in a few weeks in 1504 using his trademark strong colours. On the left of the Well of the Casaline, is Via Baciadonne (Kiss the Women Street), one of the narrowest streets in Italy.

🚗 Turn into Viale Marconi and take SS71/SR142 towards Chiusi, left onto SP146. At the roundabout turn back and then right towards Chiusi and left at SP321, crossing over A1. Park on the way into town.

5 Cetona
Siena, Toscana; 53040

The first impression of Cetona is of the large square, **Piazza Garibaldi**, which seems too large and too modern for a medieval village. But it was the vision of one man, Gian Luigi Vitelli, who was made Marquis of Cetona in 1556 by Cosimo I de Medici, Grand Duke of Tuscany. The old town and

Below left View from the pretty terraces of Cetona **Below** Etruscan fresco in the Museo Civico Archeologico, Sarteano

its narrow streets straggle up the hill to the fortress, **La Rocca**, which Vitelli turned into a residence. Palazzo Vitelli, his family home, is on the main square.

🚗 Continue west on Via Martiri della Libertà/SP21. On arrival in Sarteano, at the roundabout, take the 3rd exit onto Viale Beato Alberto/SP478 and park in Piazza Domenico Barbagli.

6 Sarteano
Siena, Toscana; 53047

This charming village has an impressive **castle** (open summer: daily till late, restricted hours in winter) that provides a historical focal point as well as great countryside views. The streets and houses behind the main square still retain their medieval form and atmosphere, and parts of the village walls have been imaginatively incorporated into private housing.

Southern Tuscany was heavily populated by the Etruscans and the **Museo Civico Archeologico** (Via Roma 24; open summer: Tue–Sun, winter: weekends, Christmas holidays) has some extraordinary finds.

🚗 Head north on SP19 onto SS146 to Montepulciano. Turn right on Via della Circonvallazione and immediately left into Via di San Pietro and park in the dedicated parking areas.

Alternative travel
Drive around the hills of Umbria and Tuscany in true Italian style in a Fiat 500, or on a classic Vespa hired from **Slow Hills** (Piazza dell'amicizia 3 53045 Montepulciano; slowhills.com). Or leave the wheels behind and explore the countryside for truffles. **Truffle Hunting Tours** (truffle hunting.tours) organizes hunting expeditions in the forests around Orvieto, offering a chance to witness this century old tradition.

Above left The beautiful countryside surrounding Cetona **Above right** The magnificent façade of Orvieto's Duomo

POTTERY CLASSES
Take a pottery course in a lovely rustic setting on an old farm with potter **Paola Biancalana** (La Badia 8, 05016 Ficulle; paolabiancalana.it) who works with a range of ceramics, including terracotta, and likes to use a wood-fired kiln.

EAT AND DRINK

ORVIETO
Trattoria del Moro Aronne *moderate*
This central family-run trattoria offers home-style dishes. Try the *carbonara di fave e baffo*, an outstanding pasta dish with a sauce of puréed broad beans. Via S. Leonardo 7, 05018; trattoria delmoro.info/trattoria-del-moro-aronne; closed Tue

FICULLE
Osteria di Vitalonga *moderate*
Part of a vineyard serving local specialities. Try the pork with braised onions and the truffle soufflé. Strada Montiano 10, 05016 Tenuta Vitalonga; vitalonga.it; closed Mon & Tue

MONTELEONE D'ORVIETO
Seven Cafè *moderate*
White and black truffles, carpaccios and a variety of pasta dishes define this small modern restaurant. Via Sandro Pertini 28, 05017; seven-cafe.it; Closed Wed

CITTÀ DELLA PIEVE
Ristorante Zafferano *expensive*
Part of Hotel Vannucci, this elegant restaurant serves superb traditional cuisine with a contemporary twist. Via Vanni 1, 06062; hotel-vannucci.com; closed Tue, Wed & Oct–Apr

SARTEANO
Osteria da Gagliano *moderate*
A cosy tavern with a seasonal menu with local produce. Booking advised. Via Roma 5, 53047; 0578 268 022; closed Tue & Wed

Right (all) Montisi, a pretty town set among beautiful natural scenery that has attracted a thriving community of artists

VISITING MONTEPULCIANO

Tourist Information
Piazza Don Minzoni 1, 53045; prolocomontepulciano.it

WHERE TO STAY

MONTEPULCIANO

Osteria del Borgo B&B *inexpensive*
Marvellous city and valley views with comfortable rooms at this lovely B&B.
Via Ricci 7, 53045; osteriadelborgo.it

Locanda di San Francesco *moderate*
This central family-run hotel has large rooms and stunning country views.
Piazza San Francesco 5, 53045; locandasanfrancesco.it

PIENZA

Podere Spedalone *moderate*
Experience a tranquil stay at this farm with good rooms and a relaxing pool.
Podere Spedalone, 53026; poderespedalone.it

MONTISI

La Romita *inexpensive*
The Bindi family have run this relaxing hotel since 1633. It also has apartments.
Via Umberto I 144/150, 53020; laromita.net

LUCIGNANO

B&B Le Caselle "Il Baraccotto" *inexpensive*
Near the historic centre, this family-run B&B features Tuscan details and a garden with a pool. Good breakfast.
Via Mario Luzi 1, 52046; lecaselle.net

Below The early Renaissance façade of the Duomo in Piazza Pio II, Pienza

❼ Montepulciano
Siena, Toscana; 53045

Set at 600 m (1,970 ft), Montepulciano affords spectacular views of the surrounding landscape. Located on a major crossroads, it became an important conquest of Florence in 1511. The 1.5-km (1-mile) walk uphill into town, from Porta al Prato to Piazza Grande, the centre of the town, with the **Duomo** and the **Palazzo Communale**, is challenging, but worth it for the splendid views and charm of the old civic buildings.

Most visitors will know the name of the town from its high-quality red wine, the prestigious Vino Nobile di Montepulciano, the first in Italy to receive the Denominazione di Origine Controllata e Garantita (DOCG). It can, of course, be sampled in any of the cantinas around Piazza Grande.

Leave Montepulciano west along Via di San Biagio to see **Tempio di San Biagio** (open daily), the Renaissance masterpiece of a church designed by Antonio da Sangallo the Elder in 1529.

🚗 *Return downhill to crossroads with SS146. Turn right on Viale della Rimembranza to Tempio di San Biagio. Head south on Viale della Rimembranza, then turn right at SS146. At Pienza take the 3rd exit on the roundabout to Via San Gregorio, park here or on Via degli Archi.*

❽ Pienza
Siena, Toscana; 53026

This is one of the few places in the world where visitors can be in two UNESCO World Heritage Sites at once: Pienza and the Val d'Orcia, over which the town has a stunning view. The town was remodelled in 1458–62 by Pope Pius II, who left his symbol, a crescent moon, on every available surface. Pienza is an architectural marvel with an exquisite **Duomo** (1459) on Piazza Pio II – a landmark in Renaissance architecture. Zeffirelli's *Romeo and Juliet* (1968) and The *English Patient* (1996) were both filmed here. Visit **Palazzo Piccolomini** (closed Tue), the pope's former residence and now a museum of opulent interiors. Pienza is also famous for its Pecorino cheese – visit **Zazzeri** (Via Pian del Nocio 1/A) to taste and buy.

🚗 *Turn left at Via San Gregorio/SSP146 around to the right. Slight right at SP di Cosona/SP71, then carry on to Castelmuzio. Park in the lot on the right.*

9 Castelmuzio
Siena, Toscana; 53020

A living museum, this well-preserved medieval village, called "il Castello" by the locals, retains the typical structure of a fortified castle encircled by walls and bastions. There are a few shops inside the main gate and a single bar/pizzeria under the bell tower in the central piazza.

🚗 *Leave northwest onto SP71. At the stop, turn left onto SP14 and then right on Via Umberto I. Park on the right.*

10 Montisi
Siena, Toscana; 53020

This vibrant village dates back to the Etruscans, although much of what's visible was built during the height of the Sienese Republic (14th–16th century). Montisi has attracted a lively creative community over the years, and many artists offer drawing or painting classes. The 13th-century **Castello di Montisi**, at the top of the village, houses a small music academy which puts on summer concerts.

🚗 *Exit town and take SP38 left to Trequanda. Park in the lot on Via Caccinconti.*

The sheep's cheese of Pienza
The wild herbs of the Val d'Orcia are said to give the distinct flavour to the cheese made from Sardinian sheep's milk: **Pecorino di Pienza**. It's lovely with slices of crisp pear and can be aged in hazelnut leaves or straw and flavoured with truffle. *Fresco* (fresh) cheese is slightly soft; *semi stagionato* (part-aged) and *stagionato* (aged) are richer in colour and flavour.

11 Trequanda
Siena, Toscana; 53020

This sleepy village is even quieter when the central bar, **La Torre**, is closed *(Tue in winter)*, but it is a pleasant stop and home to the extraordinary **Chiesa SS Pietro e Andrea**. Founded in 1327, this single-naved Romanesque-Gothic church has a bizarre chequerboard façade of travertine marble and local tufa, and contains a fresco, *The Ascension*, said to be by Sodoma.

🚗 *Head east onto SP38, turn left and then turn right onto SP10 to Via Emoriccia. Turn left onto SS715/SP19, passing under SS715. Next, turn left on Via Licio Nencetti SP28 for Lucignano.*

12 Lucignano
Arezzo, Toscana; 52045

This pretty place is a fine example of medieval town planning, with walls and roads in concentric circles. Enter through **Porta di San Giusto** and the road to the north, now Via Roma, where the poor lived. Up against the walls stands the solid **Torre del Cassero**. At the heart of town, the **Collegiata di San Michele Arcangelo** (1582), the 13th-century **Chiesa di San Francisco** with its striped Gothic façade and the 12th-century **Palazzo Pretorio**, seat of the town council, formed a nucleus of religious and political power. The Palazzo Pretorio houses the **Museo Civico** *(open Jan–Mar & Nov, Dec: Fri–Mon, Jun–Aug: daily)* containing the 14th-century silver, gilded copper and enamel reliquary, the *Albero di Lucignano* (Tree of Life).

🚗 *Head east on Via Procacci/SP58 through Foiano and take a slight right at SP31 (over the motorway), following the signs to Cortona. On SP32, pass through Camucia centre, then go uphill on SP34. Park off Via Mura del Mercato.*

Above left Cycling in the countryside around Pienza **Above right** The chequerboard façade of the Chiesa SS Pietro e Andrea, Trequanda **Below left** Narrow street in the medieval centre of Montisi

ACTIVITIES IN MONTISI
It is hard to beat floating over the scenic fields and towns of the Crete Senesi in a hot-air balloon while sipping a glass of chilled prosecco. To have a go at this pleasurable activity, contact **Ballooning in Tuscany** (ballooningintuscany.com). Flights leave from Montisi.

EAT AND DRINK

MONTEPULCIANO
Osteria Acquacheta *expensive*
This *osteria* offers rustic food in a vaulted room and a traditional Tuscan dining experience. Book ahead.
Via del Teatro 22, 53045; acquacheta.eu

PIENZA
La Buca delle Fate *moderate*
A busy trattoria serving homemade pasta and ragù, wild boar, Tuscan steaks and delicious cakes.
Corso il Rossellino 38/A, 53026; labucadellefate.com; closed Mon

MONTISI
da Roberto *moderate*
This delightful, friendly restaurant with a garden serves food prepared with care in a relaxed atmosphere.
Via Umberto 3, 53020; tavernamontisi.com

TREQUANDA
Conte Matto *expensive*
Sit on the terrace and try great food from the gourmet tasting menu here.
Via Taverne 40, 53020; contematto.it; closed Tue; reservations required.

LUCIGNANO
Il Goccino *moderate*
Intimate, traditional restaurant with good wines and a terrace with a view.
Via Matteotti 90, 52046; ilgoccino.it; closed Mon

Above Restaurant in Piazza della Repubblica, in the heart of Cortona

WHERE TO STAY

CORTONA

Il Sole del Sodo *inexpensive*
This central B&B is a luxury Tuscan experience offering suites for 6 or 12.
Loc. Il Sodo 5, 52044;
ilsoledelsodo.com

Villa Marsili *moderate*
Set in the busy end of town, but this hotel's private villa garden and terrace allow for relaxation in peace.
Viale C. Battisti 13, 52044;
villamarsili.net

CASTIGLION FIORENTINO

Villa Schiatti *moderate*
This huge 19th-century villa, near the Castello di Montecchio, has pleasant rooms and a pool. Close to walking trails.
Loc. Montecchio 131, 52043;
villaschiatti.it

AREZZO

Graziella Patio Hotel *moderate*
A chic central boutique hotel inspired by the works of English travel writer Bruce Chatwin.
Via Cavour 23, 52100; hotelpatio.it

⑬ CORTONA
Arezzo, Toscana; 52044

One of the jewels of Tuscany, Cortona sits on a mountain spur facing south towards Lago Trasimeno and dominating the Val di Chiana, below. This walk takes in the major sights as well as visiting a few places off the beaten track to see a different side of this hill town.

A two-hour walking tour

Piazza Garibaldi ① at the eastern edge of town is the bus arrival point and a pleasant leafy terrace with wonderful views. Porta Garibaldi, the gateway to the town, leads to **Via Nazionale** ②, Cortona's main shopping street and home to the Tourist Information Office *(open daily)*. Via Nazionale opens out into beautiful Piazza della Repubblica. Dominated by the stone bulk of the **Palazzo del Comune** ③, the square is a mix of shops, wine bars and restaurants. Just off the piazza, at No. 4, is the **Palazzo Cristofanello-Laparelli** ④, now a bank. Built in 1533, the building is a striking architectural confection whose third floor of columns and pilasters looks like a Roman temple high above the square. Via Roma leads straight to the north-west gate, Porta Santa Maria. Around the right-hand side of the staircase, take a few steps into another square, Piazza Signorelli, named for Cortona's famous Renaissance painter, Luca Signorelli. It is dominated by the 16th-century façade of the **Palazzo Casali** ⑤ to the left, and the loggia of the 19th-century Teatro Signorelli to the right. The palazzo houses Museo dell'Accademia Etrusca e della Città di Cortona *(closed: Mon; cortonamaec. org)*, full of Etruscan finds. Between the Palazzo and the Theatre, Via Casali leads down to the **Piazza del Duomo** ⑥. The Chiesa di Santa Maria Assunta here has been rebuilt many times in its long history from its origins as a pagan temple. Little remains of interest except some Romanesque elements in the façade. Opposite the Duomo is the Museo Diocesano *(open summer: daily; winter: Fri, Sat & sun)*, which holds work by Signorelli, Fra Angelico (1395–1455) and Pietro Lorenzetti (1280–1348).

From the museum, return to Piazza Signorelli and the Teatro, often a venue for summer concerts in the Tuscan Sun Festival. Continue uphill to the piazzetta **Croce del Travaglio** ⑦. The road ahead, Via Dardano, leads to Porta Colonia and the car park beyond. Turn right into Via Maffei, a steep street lined with old residences and with only light pedestrian traffic. The road runs up to the Church of San Francesco *(open daily)*, built in 1245 by Brother Elias, St Francis' right-hand man.

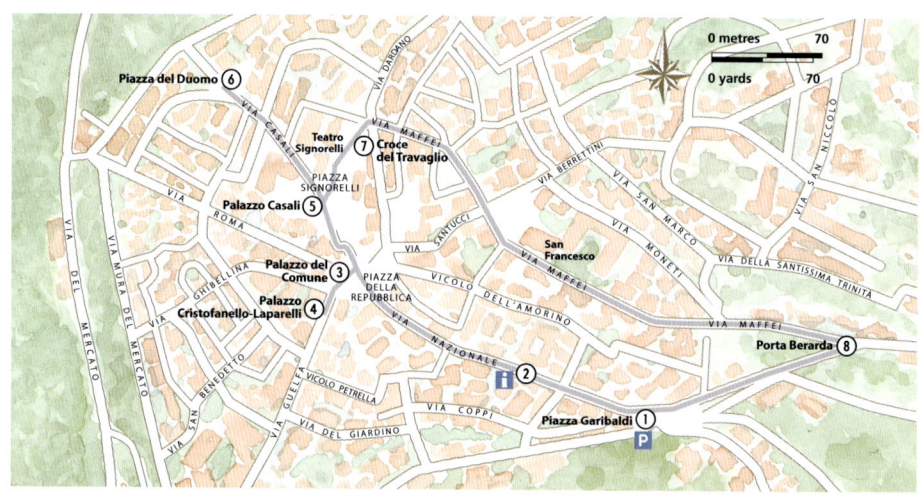

Far left The 12th-century Romanesque Santa Maria della Pieve, Arezzo **Left** View of Castiglion Fiorentino and the Val Chiana **Below** Beautiful frescoes inside the Basilica di San Francesco, Arezzo

EAT AND DRINK

CORTONA

La Bucaccia da Romano *moderate*
In ancient cellars in the heart of town, this restaurant serves traditional cuisine – chestnut ravioli, wild boar – with good wines, too.
Via Ghibellina 17, 52044; labucaccia.it; closed winter: Mon

Preludio *expensive*
Centrally located, elegant restaurant, set in a grand palazzo, serving innovative Tuscan dishes. Book ahead.
Via Guelfa 11, 52044; ilpreludio.net

AREZZO

Il Saraceno *moderate*
A cosy restaurant, famous for its rich and hearty food – thick Tuscan soups, steaks, roast meats and tiramisù.
Via Giuseppe Mazzini 6, 52100; ilsaraceno.com

Trattoria La Lancia d'Oro *expensive*
Owners Marzia and Maurizio host a happy restaurant with excellent mains and desserts. Outdoor tables are best on the day of the antique market.
Piazza Grande 18 (Logge Vasari), 52100; ristorantelanciadoro.it

The simple façade reflects the Franciscan rejection of wealth. Inside there is a painting by local master Pietro Berrettini (1596–1669).
Follow Via Maffei downhill to **Porta Berarda** ⑧. From here, turn right, and return down to Piazza Garibaldi.

🚗 Follow signs to Arezzo, on SR71, turn right to Castiglion Fiorentino. Follow signs to the centre and park in the big park at the end of the ascending street.

⑭ Castiglion Fiorentino
Arezzo, Toscana; 52043

Porta Fiorentina, well above the modern town and train station, leads to the historic centre and the **Piazza del Municipio** with its 16th-century nine-arched loggia designed by Vasari over a balcony with excellent views. Up past the Palazzo Comunale are the ruins of the fortress, **Il Cassero** (1347). The town's youth gather around Piazza Garibaldi on summer nights. To the south of town stands the romantic-looking 10th-century **Castello di Monticchio** *(open for concerts)*.

🚗 Head west on SP40, then right on SR71, then SS73 to the centre. At the next roundabout take the 3rd exit on Viale don Minzoni and carry on toward Bibbiena. On Via Amendola turn right at the roundabout on Via Sette Ponti and follow signs to Pietri parking lot. Take escalator to historic centre.

⑮ Arezzo
Arezzo, Toscana; 52100

A wealthy, bustling town, Arezzo has been an important commercial centre since Roman times. It has a beautiful medieval heart, whose highlight is Piero della Francesca's 15th-century frescoes, Legend of the True Cross, in the apse of the **Basilica di San Francesco** *(open daily; tickets: 0575 352727)*. The Gothic Duomo houses a lovely fresco of Mary Magdalene (left of the main altar) also by Piero. The main pedestrian street, **Corso Italia**, runs directly down the hill to the Romanesque **Santa Maria della Pieve** and **campanile** with double mullion windows. Behind this is the beautiful Piazza Grande, venue of the medieval pageant of the Giostra del Saraceno and a monthly antiques market.

DAY TRIP OPTIONS

Obvious themes here are Etruscans, which will appeal to families, Renaissance art and cheese and wine.

Etruscan treasures
Orvieto ❶ has a superb Etruscan museum and ancient tunnels. Pretty Ficulle ❷, a Roman village, has a good castle to explore. Enjoy pizza in walled Monteleone d'Orvieto ❸, then on to Sarteano ❻ for more Etruscan finds.

From Orvieto, take SS71 to Ficulle and Monteleone d'Orvieto. At Chiusi, take SS146, then SS476 to Sarteano. Return via A1 if in a hurry, or retrace route.

Renaissance genius
At Cortona ⑬, see Museo Diocesano's religious art and explore the town. Drive to Lucignano ⑫ for lunch and to see the *Tree of Life*. Then it's off to Arezzo for Piero della Francesca's sublime frescoes (book in advance).

From Cortona, take SP31 and SP28 to Lucignano, take SP25 to SP327, then SS73 to Arezzo. Return to start on SS71.

A rich palate
Using Montepulciano ❼ as a base, arrange a wine tour with the tourist office, then set off to Pienza ❽ to taste the best of its famous Pecorino cheese. Return for a Chianina steak, more fine wine and a semifreddo.

Take SS146 Montepulciano to Pienza.

TRIP 21

UMBRIA'S VERDANT VALLEYS

Perugia
to Arrone

HIGHLIGHTS

Fortified hill towns
Explore the medieval walled towns and fortifications of Trevi, Campello, Spoleto, Ferentillo and Arrone

Spiritual journey
See Assisi, the home of St Francis, and experience the same calm and solitude in his grotto at the hermitage

Roman era remains
Travel back in time to witness the power and glory of ancient Rome at Perugia, Spello, Campello and Spoleto.

Wild beauty
Enjoy the diverse natural features of the valleys, from woods and gentle rivers to steep gorges and rocky cliffs

UMBRIA'S VERDANT VALLEYS

Slicing through the green heart of Umbria are the Valle Umbra and the Valnerina valleys. The former was created by a river system from the Fonte di Clitunno, which eventually joins the River Tiber near Perugia. The latter was carved out by the River Nera, rising high in the Monti Sibillini to the east. This trip follows the Valle Umbra from ancient Perugia to the holy city of Assisi, home of St Francis, and passes Roman ruins and medieval villages on the way to the great Lombard city of Spoleto. From here, it joins the neighbouring valley and follows the River Nera, past ancient abbeys and once mighty fortresses.

Above The medieval heart of Spoleto, *see p214*

ACTIVITIES

Indulge in some of Perugia's famous chocolate

Walk in the footsteps of St Francis in the woods around the Eremo delle Carceri

Sample the fresh and fruity olive oil in Trevi

Try your hand at medieval crafts in a workshop in Bevagna's museum

Ride a bike along the mountain paths of the Valnerina

Head for the hills and try free-climbing at Ferentillo

Ride the rapids by white-water rafting on the River Nera

TRIP 21: UMBRIA'S VERDANT VALLEYS

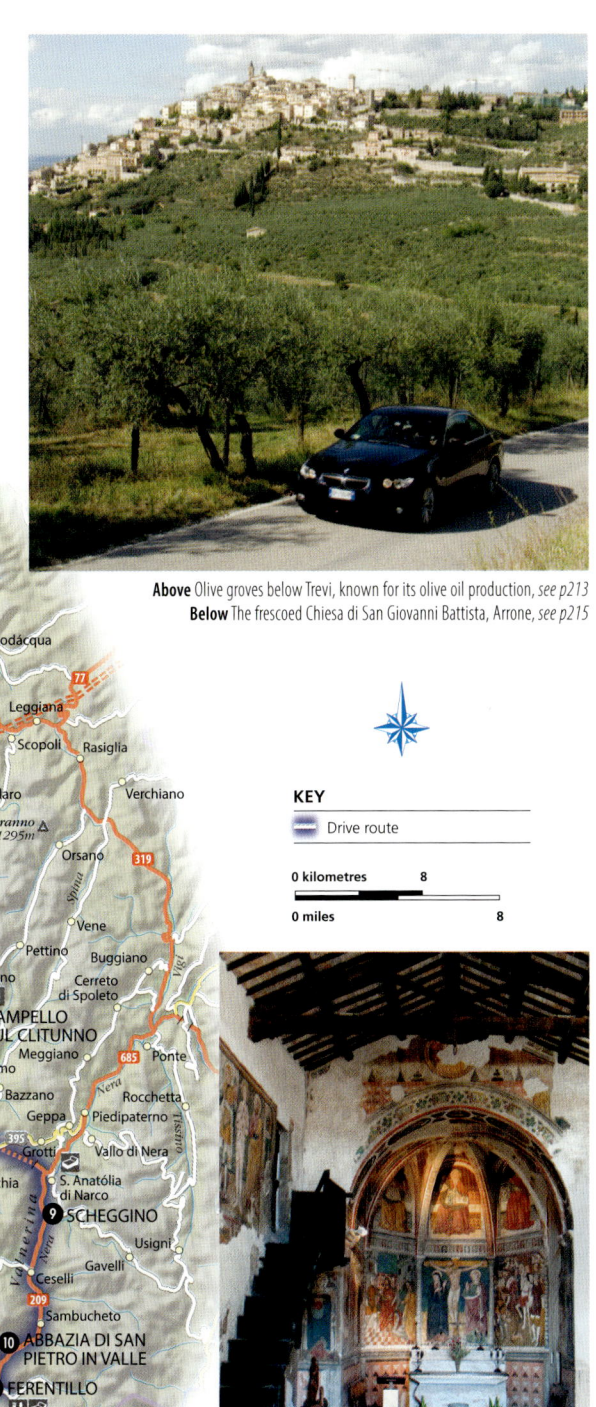

Above Olive groves below Trevi, known for its olive oil production, *see p213*
Below The frescoed Chiesa di San Giovanni Battista, Arrone, *see p215*

KEY

- Drive route

PLAN YOUR DRIVE

Start/finish: Perugia to Arrone.

Number of days: 3–4, allowing half a day to explore Perugia.

Distance: Approx. 150 km (93 miles).

Road conditions: Generally good but take the alternative route between Eremo delle Carceri and Spello in winter if the road over Mount Subasio is closed.

When to go: The valleys offer activities and interest all year round. Summer is best for sports and festivals. In autumn, the first pressing of olive oil is available.

Opening times: Major museums are open 8:30am–7:30pm and closed Mon. Small museums are often only open at weekends outside summer. Hours for churches vary but they are generally open 7:30am–noon and 3–7:30pm. Shops in Perugia and Assisi have extended trading hours, but others often open 10–1pm and 4–8pm and close Sun and Mon mornings.

Main market days: Perugia: Tue & Sat; Assisi: Sat; Spello: Wed; Trevi, Arrone: Thu; Campello sul Clitunno: 1st Sun of month; Spoleto: Fri. Ferentillo: Tue.

Major festivals: Perugia: Umbria Jazz, Jul; Euro Chocolate exhibition, Nov; Assisi: Calendimaggio (May Day festival) 1st Thu, Fri, Sat after 1 May; Bevagna: Mercato delle Gaite (medieval market), Jun; Spoleto: Festival dei Due Mondi (music and dance), Jun–Jul; Scheggiano: Trout Festival, Jul & Aug.

Shopping: Perugia has high fashion as well as chocolate. Assisi has all kinds of religious souvenirs. The area between Bevagna and Spoleto produces the excellent Sagrantino di Montefalco wine. Bevagna is also famous for medieval crafts: textiles, candles, parchment and handmade paper.

DAY TRIP OPTIONS

History buffs will enjoy the Roman sights – from **arches** and **theatres**, to **temples** and **villas**. Those interested in spiritual paths can follow in the steps of St Francis, from his **basilica** to the **grotto** where he prayed. Art lovers will enjoy the **frescoes** and **paintings** in the **churches** and **palazzos** of Perugia and beyond. For full details, *see p215*.

Above The Tempio di Sant'Angelo, Perugia, reputedly built over a pagan site

VISITING PERUGIA

Parking
Exit the motorway at Perugia Madonna Alta, taking the direction "stadio" to Porta Nova car park (3,000 spaces).

Transport
A shuttle train – *minimetrò* – runs from the car park at Porta Nova station to the historic centre at Pincetto.

WHERE TO STAY

PERUGIA

Chocohotel *inexpensive*
A fun chocolate-themed hotel with spacious rooms and a swimming pool.
Via Campo di Marte 134, 06124; chocohotel.it

Montecorneo Country House *inexpensive*
The grounds of this 18th-century villa feature apartments in three cottages.
Strada dei Loggi 136, 06121; montecorneo.com

Castello di Monterone Residenza d'Epoca *moderate*
A chance to stay in a real 13th-century castle – but in luxury – with frescoes and other original architectural details.
Strada Monteville 3, 06126; castellomonterone.it

ASSISI

Hotel Sorella Luna *inexpensive*
This charming hotel features bright rooms and a great terrace.
Via Frate Elia 3/5, 06081; hotelsorellaluna.it

Le Dimore di San Crispino *expensive*
A historic residence with elegant and refined apartments and good views.
Via Sant'Agnese 11, 06081; assisibenessere.it

❶ PERUGIA

Umbria; 06100

The capital of Umbria, this ancient Etruscan city grew into a mighty presence in the medieval period. From the 14th century it was ruled by a papal legate and, after violent feuding, went to war with the pope over the price of salt. This walk takes in the full history of Perugia.

A three-hour walking tour

From the Porta Nova car park, take the *minimetrò* shuttle to Pincetto station and emerge at Via Rupe. Turn into Via G Oberdan, then **Piazza Matteotti** ❶. Walk straight up Via Giuseppe Mazzini, then right into wide Corso Vannucci to **La Pasticceria Sandri** ❷, a historic café and pastry shop specializing in chocolate. Opposite is the **Collegio del Cambio** ❸ *(open daily, Sun am)*, two exquisite rooms of the Money Exchange Guild (built 1452–57) with frescoes completed in 1500 by Pietro Vannucci (Perugino). Further along is the **Galleria Nazionale dell'Umbria** ❹ *(open Tue–Sun)*, one of the finest museums in Central Italy with works by Perugino, Pinturicchio and Piero della Francesca. The museum is in the **Palazzo dei Priori** ❺, a civic building built in the 13th–15th centuries. The entrance in Piazza 4 Novembre, up a semi-circular staircase, leads into the Sala dei Notari *(open daily; closed for events and concerts)*. Its Gothic portal is surmounted by a griffin and a lion, the city's symbols, and the hall is supported by eight massive arches, fully painted in the late 1200s with biblical scenes. In the centre of the piazza is the **Fontana Maggiore** ❻, a majestic 25-sided fountain sculpted by father and son Nicola and Giovanni Pisano in 1278. The **Cattedrale di San Lorenzo** ❼ *(open daily)* flanks the piazza with the Loggia di Braccio (1423) and a statue of Pope Julius III (1555). Passing the façade of the cathedral, turn left, then right into Via Ulisse Rocchi, at the end of which is **Arco Etrusco** ❽ in Piazza Fortebraccio. This imposing structure, once the main gate into the city, was built in the 3rd century BCE. Proceed up Via Garibaldi, then turn right into Via Tempio to the round early Christian **Tempio di Sant'Angelo** ❾ *(open daily)*, with its 16 columns, built in the 5th–6th centuries. Return to Via Garibaldi, turn right into Via Rondine, left into Via Benedetta, then into Via Fagiano, which turns into **Via Acquedotto** ❿, an aqueduct (now a footway) built in 1254 to bring water into the city from Monte Paciano. At the end, turn right into Piazza Cavallotti, then up Via Maestà delle Volte and back into Piazza 4 Novembre. Stroll down Corso Vanucci to **Piazza Italia** ⓫ for views over the abbey of San Pietro to Assisi in the distance. In 1540, the ruling papacy sought to quell the rebellious populace by building a huge fortress over their houses. On the unification of Italy in 1860, Umbrians, free of papal rule, tore down the building and erected their provincial offices instead. On the west side of this building, an escalator descends into Via Baglioni, where

Below View of Rocca Maggiore, set on the hill above Assisi

shells of houses still remain in the foundations of the **Rocca Paolina** ⑫. Keeping to the left on the way down, exit the underground maze through Porta Marzia and turn left into Via Marzia to Via Guglielmo Oberdan and the entrance to the *minimetrò*.

For those with a sweet tooth, the Casa del Cioccolato Perugina *(Viale San Sisto 207/C, 06132 San Sisto; open Mon–Fri; perugina.it)*, just outside town, is a small museum that reveals the processes involved in making the city's delicious chocolates, including the famous Baci.

🚗 *Turn left on Autostradale Perugia-A1 towards Roma-Assisi, take Foligno exit onto SR75 to Assisi, exit Ospedalicchio. Follow signs to Assisi on SS147. Piazza Matteotti has an underground car park.*

> **St Francis of Assisi**
> Born around 1181 in Assisi, this high-spirited son of a wealthy cloth merchant had a vision that called him to a spiritual path and a life of poverty. He wandered far and wide, inspiring followers and founding the order of Friars Minor in 1210. His visions and profound faith changed the course of Christian history and he was canonized only two years after his death in 1226. St Francis (San Francesco) is the patron saint of Italy.

❷ Assisi
Perugia, Umbria; 06081

With an average of 5–6 million visitors every year, Assisi is one of the most important pilgrim sites in Italy. It is a small town that displays its artistic and religious patrimony well, but its back streets and alleyways still merit exploration. The central Piazza del Comune was the original Roman Forum and the splendid columns of the 1st-century BCE Temple of Minerva have been retained in the façade of the church **Santa Maria Sopra Minerva**. The German writer Goethe (1749–1832) thought it was the most beautiful building in Italy.

The town's most visited site, the **Basilica di San Francesco**, was commenced immediately after St Francis' canonization in 1228. In two parts, the lower and upper, the church contains frescoes by Cimabue, Giotto, Simone Martini and Pietro Lorenzetti that are the cornerstone of pre-Renaissance art. The **Basilica di Santa Chiara** – St Clare was a contemporary of St Francis – is a fascinating Gothic extravagance. Nearby, the 12th-century Romanesque **Cattedrale di San Rufino** is where both Francis and Clare were baptized.

🚗 *Turn right out of car park and take a slight right at Via Santuario delle Carceri/SP251, following brown signs for Eremo delle Carceri. Park after the left curve on the road.*

Above The Romanesque-Gothic Basilica di San Francesco, Assisi

EAT AND DRINK

PERUGIA

La Pasticceria Sandri *inexpensive*
A Perugian institution, this splendid café has been serving the finest chocolates and aperitifs since 1947.
Corso Vannucci 32, 06123; 075 572 4112

Da Cesarino *moderate*
By the Fontana Maggiore, enjoy typical Umbrian delights such as *penne alla norcina* (creamy sausage pasta).
Piazza IV Novembre 4, 06123; 075 572 8974; closed Wed

Trattoria del Borgo *moderate*
This antique trattoria in the centre of Perugia is one of the finest in Umbria. Try *cappellacci di capriolo* (venison pasta) or Chianina beef with porcini.
Via della Sposa 23/A, 06123; trattoriadelborgopg.it

ASSISI

Bibenda Assisi *moderate*
Fabulous wines are paired with gourmet cold cuts and cheese platters at this rustic *osteria*.
Vicolo dei Nepis 9, 06081; bibendaassisi.it

Pozzo della Mensa *moderate*
This traditional Umbrian restaurant is known for its lentil soups, baked wild boar with vegetables and desserts.
Via del Pozzo della Mensa 11; 075 815 209

Trattoria Pallotta *moderate*
Enjoy the rustic atmosphere and Umbrian cuisine – thick *strangozzi* pasta drizzled with olive oil and truffles.
Below l'arco della Volta Pinta; trattoriapallotta.it; closed Tue

Above View of Trevi, topped by the spire of the Duomo San Emiliano **Above right** Entrance to the secluded and peaceful Eremo delle Carceri **Below right** Simple choir stalls and wooden altar at Eremo delle Carceri

WHERE TO STAY

SPELLO

Antiche Dimore San Felice *inexpensive*
Immersed in lush greenery, this rustic country house features traditional rooms and a fabulous pool.
Via Ponte Custode 26, 06038; antichedimoresanfelice.it

Hotel Palazzo Bocci *moderate*
Lavish palazzo in the historic centre with frescoed ceilings and large rooms. Also features an outdoor terrace.
Via Cavour 17, 06038; palazzo bocci.com

BEVAGNA

Agriturismo Pian di Boccio *inexpensive*
Surrounded by open land, this ancient complex has three pools and a few tastefully furnished, rustic apartments.
Via Pian di Boccio 10, 06031; piandi boccio.com

Hotel Palazzo Brunamonti *inexpensive*
In the town centre, this lavish historic residence has spacious rooms and attentive staff. Secure parking.
Corso Matteotti 79, 06031; bruna monti.com

TREVI

Albergo Ristorante Il Terziere *inexpensive*
A short walk away from the city centre, this hotel has comfortable rooms and a pool. Bike and e-bike rental available.
Via Coste 1, 06039; ilterziere.com

③ Eremo delle Carceri
Perugia, Umbria; 06081

Clinging onto the steep slope of Monte Subasio, this is a 14th-century religious sanctuary where silence is required. Wander through medieval passageways and under low archways to reach, at the heart of the ancient hermitage, the **Grotto of St Francis** who prayed here in the 13th century. Outside, cross over a bridge into the forest to see the **Tree of the Birds**, a holm oak where the saint is said to have preached to the birds. Look for the sign of the cross scratched on boulders along the path by pilgrims. The tranquil hermitage is an ideal spot for a walk in the woods.

🚗 *Continue uphill on SP251 to go over Mt Subasio towards San Silvestro (faster route: SS75 towards Foligno and exit Spello). Turn sharp right at Via Subasio/ SP249 towards Spello centre. At the stop take SS75, then turn right at Via Martin Luther King for parking.*

④ Spello
Perugia, Umbria; 06038

Called Hispellum in the 1st century BCE, this delightful town, draped around a low ridge, still has some important Roman monuments. The entry gate Porta Consolare, the Piazza della Repubblica, originally the forum, and the magnificent Gate of Venus on the western side, date from the Augustan era. The highest part of the town is a knot of medieval lanes and houses. The cathedral, the 13th-century **Chiesa di Santa Maria Maggiore** *(open daily)*, has a Romanesque portal and frescoes by Perugino, but the highlight is the superb Cappella Bella, painted by Umbrian artist Pinturicchio in 1500.

🚗 *From car park, turn right, then left at Via Roma, then right at roundabout onto SS75 towards Foligno. Turn right into SR316 and exit Foligno Nord to Bevagna. Turn right to park off Via Alcide De Gasperi.*

⑤ Bevagna
Perugia, Umbria; 06031

Once the important Roman city of Mevania, Bevagna today has a more medieval air about it. The central Piazza Silvestri is flanked by the Gothic **Palazzo dei Consoli** and the 12th-century Romanesque **Church of San Michele Arcangelo** *(both open daily)*, notable for the bas-reliefs and mosaics on its portal. Mosaics of fabulous sea creatures, once the floor of the Roman baths, are visible from outside Via Porta Guelfa. The **Museo Comunale di Bevagna** *(closed Mon)* displays Roman funerary urns and tells the history of medieval guilds. It is also possible to book classes in paper, making, candle-making and weaving.

🚗 *Take SR316 south and after the bridge turn left to Montefalco. From there follow signs for Trevi, onto SP447 and over the motorway. Follow signs for Trevi "centro" and park in Piazza Garibaldi.*

❻ Trevi
Perugia, Umbria; 06039

Like a conical snail shell of medieval buildings, Trevi coils around a spur in the Valle Umbra. The town is enclosed by two circuits of walls and entered through Porta di Lago into Piazza Mazzini. At its centre, the highest point, stands the **Duomo San Emiliano** with its 11th-century façade. St Emiliano was thrown to the lions, but they licked his feet and face – look for the carvings. The **Museo Civiltà dell'Ulivo** (Largo Don Bosco; closed Mon), set in a former Franciscan convent, reveals the history of local olive cultivation.

🚗 Head south on SP425 and turn left after 5 km (3 miles) for Campello sul Clitunno. The Tempietto is on the right, not well marked and with little parking.

Above Clock tower and Palazzo Comunale, Piazza Mazzini, Trevi

❼ Campello sul Clitunno
Perugia, Umbria; 06042

A popular holiday destination in the Roman era, this area's later strategic importance is evident in the medieval castles and forts dotted over its hills.

Just outside Campello sul Clitunno, the **Tempietto del Clitunno**, decorated with Byzantine frescoes, is a gem of a late-Roman or early Christian church, whose perfect proportions and lavish Corinthian column screens inspired 16th-century architect Andrea Palladio.

At the **Fonti del Clitunno**, another 500 m (1,500 ft) further along the SS3, crystal-clear water gushes from the hillside into a series of lakes and ponds, creating an ambience of rare beauty that has inspired poets and painters from Virgil (70–19 BCE) to Lord Byron (1788–1804) and from Poussin (1594–1665) to Corot (1796–1875). The park, now privately owned, is ideal for children to explore and feed the ducks. The area is known for its olive oil and there are several *frantoio* (olive mills) around town worth visiting.

The SP458 leads southeast from the centre of Campello sul Clitunno. Turn left again and follow signs to the tiny fortified village of **Castello di Campello Alto**. Founded in the 10th century by the Baron of Burgundy, the village passed to Federico Barbarossa, Holy Roman Emperor, 200 years later. Set amid slopes cloaked in olive groves, it has well-preserved 13th-century walls.

🚗 Return down the hill and turn left into exSS3/Via Flaminia to Spoleto. Turn right at Viale Giacomo Matteotti (signed Spoleto), and left for car park.

The Via Francigena di San Francesco
This pilgrim trail follows the paths that wayfarers used on the journey from Austria to Umbria and on to Lazio, to visit the places where St Francis lived and worked. After the fall of Rome in the 5th century CE, roads were no longer maintained and were unsafe. Wheeled traffic was less viable, so travellers went on foot and mule, resting at pilgrim stops along the way. This drive roughly follows the trail from Assisi to Arrone, part of the Via Francigena di San Francesco. Religious and non-religious pilgrims still walk the Via Francigena, which is fairly well marked.

EAT AND DRINK

SPELLO
La Bastiglia *moderate*
A highly acclaimed restaurant offering Umbrian cuisine. It has an impressive wine cellar and rooms for stay.
Via Salnitraria 15, 06038; labastiglia.com

La Lanterna *moderate*
This charming restaurant serves good food such as asparagus, porcini and truffles with homemade pasta.
Via Torri di Properzio 37, 06038; ristoranteportavenere.it

BEVAGNA
Osteria Il Podesta *moderate*
Traditional central *osteria* with a cosy atmosphere and vaulted dining room.
Corso Matteotti 67, 06031; 0742 360 222; closed Wed

TREVI
Cantina Del Bartoccio *inexpensive*
This simple restaurant offers Umbrian dishes and a good house wine.
Piazza Giuseppe Mazzini 7, 06039; 349 399 7766

CAMPELLO SUL CLITUNNO
Ristorante Nuovo Parco del Clitunno *moderate*
Surrounded by the lake and trees, with a play area for kids – fish is the speciality.
Via Fonti del Clitunno 3, 06042; 0743 521 052; closed Mon

Ristorante Fonti del Clitunno *expensive*
Right by the springs, this traditional *osteria* provides good Umbrian food.
Via Flaminia 7, 06042; fontidelclitunno.it

Below left The fortified hamlet of Castello di Campello Alto **Below right** The Tempietto del Clitunno, an inspiration for Neo-Classical design

Above The Teatro Romano, Spoleto, still used for cultural events

WHERE TO STAY

SPOLETO

Gattapone *moderate*
Just below the Rocca, this hotel is especially popular with celebrities during festivals.
Via del Ponte 6, 06049; hotelgattapone.it

Palazzo Leti Residenza d'Epoca *moderate*
This former aristocratic residence has a magnificent Italian-style garden.
Via degli Eremiti 10, 06049; residenzadepoca.it

SCHEGGINO

Le Vaie *inexpensive*
Experience a traditional farm stay with four simple rooms in a rustic setting.
Loc. Vaglie, 06040 Sant'Anatolia di Narco; 0743 050 694

ABBAZIA DI SAN PIETRO IN VALLE

Abbazia San Pietro in Valle *expensive*
Stay in the 8th-century monastery in a superbly restored and tranquil hotel.
Via Case Sparse di Macenano 4, 05034; sanpietroinvalle.com

FERENTILLO

Il Borgo *inexpensive*
This country house B&B has a pleasant, rustic feel and comfortable rooms.
Vicolo S Anselmo 1, 05034; 329 228 7075

ARRONE

Fiocchi Residence *inexpensive*
Unfussy self-catering apartments near an adventure park, with access to pool.
Sta. Provinciale 17, Via Casale, 05031; residencefiocchi.com

Right top View of Spoleto, a strategically important city **Right bottom left** The River Nera, once Scheggino's first line of defence **Right bottom right** Fresco of San Sebastian in Arrone's Chiesa di San Giovanni Battista

8 Spoleto
Perugia, Umbria; 06049

Important since Etruscan times – and famous today for its summer arts festival – this delightful city has some interesting Roman ruins. The splendid **Teatro Romano e Museo Archeologico** *(open Thu–Sun)* is near Piazza della Libertà. Other Roman highlights to look out for are the **Arco di Drusus**, the triumphal arch into Roman Spoleto, and **Casa Romana** *(open daily)*, a villa with mosaics from the 1st century CE.

After the fall of Rome, Spoleto was the capital of the Lombard Duchy of Spoleto for over 600 years (570–1201), before falling to the papacy. At its heart is the **Duomo di Spoleto** (1175–1227) *(open daily)*. The Romanesque façade is outstanding, with rose windows, a huge bell tower and a Renaissance portico. Inside is just as impressive, with frescoes by Pinturicchio (1454–1513) and Fra Filippo Lippi (1406–69). The city is crowned by the **Rocca Albornoziana** *(open daily)*. Built by the militant Cardinal Albornoz to secure the papal dominions in the 14th century, this garrison fortress is divided into two large and elegant courtyards and was used as a prison until 1982. Highlights include the 15th-century frescoes in the *camera pinto* (painted room) and superb views. To the southwest is the spectacular **Ponte delle Torri**, a road and aqueduct with ten perfect arches.

🚗 *Exit car park right, then left, and left again onto SS3 north. Take Cassia/Norcia exit for SS685. After tunnel, take SR209 right, towards Roma. Turn left at Piazza del Mercato and park at Scheggino.*

9 Scheggino
Perugia, Umbria; 06040

This medieval hamlet built by the Duchy of Spoleto to defend a bridge over the River Nera is now easily accessed by a footbridge. The 12th-century walls form a classic triangle – with a watchtower at the apex – and managed to withstand a sustained siege in 1522. In the village centre is the 13th-century **Chiesa di San Nicolò**, with a Paleochristian chapel and fine frescoes attributed to Lo Spagna (died c 1529).

🚗 *Continue south on SR209. Turn right at Via dell'Abbazia following signs to the car park.*

⑩ Abbazia di San Pietro in Valle

Ferentillo, Terni, Umbria; 05034

This abbey (now a luxury hotel) was founded in the 8th century by the Lombard Duke of Spoleto. The duke had a vision of St Peter and built a church on the site of a 4th-century hermitage. He took monastic vows

and is buried in an exquisite tomb in the **church** (open Apr–Sep: 10am–1pm & 3–5pm Sat & Sun, 3–5pm Mon–Fri, Oct–Mar: by appointment; sanpietroinvalle.com). The church also has frescoes by the Umbrian School, which preceded Giotto by 150 years.
🚗 *Return to SR209 and head south. At Ferentillo Precetto, turn left onto SP74, then 2nd left onto Via della Circonvallazione. Park in Piazza Mazzini.*

⑪ Ferentillo

Terni, Umbria; 05034

Two castles, Matterella and Precetto, guard the Val di Nera at Ferentillo, where the valley narrows. They were constructed in the 12th century to protect the Abbazzia di San Pietro in Valle. The 16th-century **Church of** Santo Stefano, in Precetto, was built over an older crypt where bodies were naturally mummified. It makes a fascinating display: **Museo delle Mummie** (open daily). Ferentillo's cliffs make it a centre for the sport of *falesia* (free-climbing) – climbing without equipment; contact **Umbria Experience** (0744 198045; umbriaexperience.it).
🚗 *Return to SR209 and turn left. At Fontechiaruccia, turn left at the roundabout for Arrone on SP4. Park in Piazza Garibaldi.*

Mountain Adventures

The combination of mountains and rivers makes for exciting sports such as white-water rafting. Contact **Pangea Centro Outdoors** (348 771 1170; pangea-italia.com) or **Rafting Marmore** (330 753 420; raftingmarmore.com). Or try a thrilling, guided mountain-bike tour. Contact **Umbrian Mountain Bike** (0744 287 686; umbriainmountainbike.it).

⑫ Arrone

Terni, Umbria; 05031

This village defended the Valnerina Pass between Abruzzo and the Duchy of Spoleto. In the lower town is the **Chiesa di Santa Maria Assunta** (open daily) with fine frescoes. The walk up to the medieval upper town is tough but rewarding. Built as a 10th-century fortification, the houses nestle around the piazza with its **Torre degli Olivi** (Tower of Olives). The 12th-century Gothic **Chiesa di San Giovanni Battista** (the key holder lives next door) contains colourful frescoes depicting the martyr San Sebastian, the patron saint of plague victims, wounded by arrows.

Follow the drive's instructions, but don't stop at Trevi. Return the same way.

In St Francis' footsteps

Spend a day in the shoes of St Francis. Start at Assisi ②, to view the town where the young man grew up. Buy food supplies, then head for the Eremo delle Carceri ③, where he spent some time. Have a picnic on a walk through the beautiful forest.

Follow the drive's instructions from Assisi to the hermitage and back.

Above Narrow medieval street in the heart of Spoleto **Left** The fortified town of Ferentillo at the mouth of the Val di Nera

EAT AND DRINK

SPOLETO

La Lanterna *moderate*
A central trattoria; try *strangozzi* pasta with courgettes and saffron.
Via della Trattoria 6, 06049; 0743 49 815; closed Tue dinner & Wed

Pentagramma *expensive*
Celebrated restaurant serving top regional cooking with great wines. Booking essential.
Piazza della Libertà, 06049; 0743 223 141; closed Mon

FERENTILLO

Ristorante Piermarini *moderate*
This elegant restaurant specializes in farm-to-table truffles, spelt and lentils.
Via Fosso Ancaiano 23, 05034; sapori piermarini.it; closed Mon & Wed lunch

ARRONE

Trattoria Rossi *moderate*
Expect classic Umbrian cuisine at this popular family restaurant specializing in river crayfish, truffle and steak.
Voc. Isola 7, 705031; rossihotel ristorante.it

DAY TRIP OPTIONS

These valley towns were strongholds in Roman times, hence their many architectural sights and works of art.

Roman holiday

Enjoy the sights at the Roman town of Spello ④, then head for Bevagna ⑤ to see the artifacts in the town museum. Lunch at Campello ⑦, with its Classical church and lovely scenery, before stopping at Spoleto ⑧, with its collection of fascinating Roman architecture.

Medieval art

Start from Perugia ①, exploring its famous art gallery and palazzos. Next stop is Assisi ②, for its Gothic frescoes in the Basilica di San Francesco. Spello ④ also has some glorious 15th–16th-century frescoes by Perugino and Pinturicchio, as does Spoleto ⑧.

Follow the drive instructions from Perugia to Assisi. Take the SS147 and SS75 to Spello. Take the SS75 from Spello and then SS3 to Spoleto.

TRIP 22

LANDS OF MYTH AND LEGEND

Rieti to
Lago di Corbara

HIGHLIGHTS

Marvellous mountains
Head for the hills beyond Rome, once home to the Sabines, for good skiing in winter and enjoyable hikes in summer

Languor by the lake
Unwind by the calm waters of Lago di Piediluco, surrounded by painterly landscapes of hills and mountains

Roman town
Explore the atmospheric remnants of Carsulae, once a thriving Roman provincial settlement

Historic hill town
Visit splendid Todi, with its medieval squares, great cathedral and spectacular domed church

LANDS OF MYTH AND LEGEND

Northeast of Rome, the land of the Sabines stretches into the Apennine mountains, where, according to the Roman imagination, fortune-telling sibyls and all manner of mythical creatures dwelt. Nowadays, mountain areas such as Terminillo are holiday resorts for modern Romans, along with dreamy lakeside Piediluco and the waterfalls at Marmore – both on the Grand Tour itineraries of the Romantic poets and painters in the 18th and 19th centuries. This trip also follows the ancient Via Flaminia for a short way north through the well-preserved but little-known remains of Roman Carsulae.

ACTIVITIES

Go skiing or snowboarding at Terminillo or Leonessa

Follow in the footsteps of the ancient Romans along the time-worn stones of the Via Flaminia

Shoot the rapids on the River Nera near the Cascata da Marmore

Take to the water gently by going boating on Lago di Piediluco

Picnic by the Tiber near Todi, just like the ancient Umbrians

KEY

Drive route

TRIP 22: LANDS OF MYTH AND LEGEND

Above The pretty and peaceful lakeside resort of Piediluco, *see p221*

PLAN YOUR DRIVE

Start/finish: Rieti to Lago di Corbara.

Number of days: 3–4 days.

Distance: About 200 km (124 miles).

Road conditions: Generally good, except for Terminillo to Leonessa, which is often impassable in winter.

When to go: Apr–Oct, especially May and Sep. In winter, skiing is popular in Terminillo and Leonessa, but snow chains must be carried.

Opening times: Most museums open 10am–6pm, with small museums often only open at weekends outside the summer months. Churches are usually open 7:30am–noon and 3–7:30pm.

Main market days: Rieti: Mon, Fri and Sat; **Leonessa:** Fri; **Narni:** Fri; **San Gémini:** Tue; **Massa Martana:** Fri; **Todi:** Sat.

Shopping: Look out for truffles and truffle products, such as small jars of truffle butter, in Rieti and Leonessa. Todi has a linen and textile shop in Piazza del Popolo, and there are antique shops behind the Duomo.

Major festivals: Leonessa: Sagra della Patata (potato festival), 2nd weekend Oct; **Piediluco:** Festa delle Acque (water-based fun), last week Jun; **Narni:** Black Festival of Jazz, Dec; **Todi:** Festival of the Arts, last week Aug–Oct; **Massa Martana:** Gelato Festa (ice-cream festival), 2nd week Sep; **San Gémini:** Giostra delle Arme (medieval joust), 2nd Sun Oct.

DAY TRIP OPTIONS

Rieti in the land of the Sabines, on the slopes of the Apennines, is a good place from which to explore the **hills** and **mountains** of the region. **Watersports** in abundance are available on the **lake** at Piediluco and the **River Nera** at the base of Marmore **waterfalls**. Brush up your **history** by following the footsteps of the **Roman legions** from Narni to San Gémini and Carsulae. For full details, *see p225*.

Above Fountain in Rieti, once a prominent Sabine town **Right** Cascata da Marmore, a spectacular human-made waterfall

WATERSPORTS ADVENTURES

The **Centro Canoa e Rafting "Le Marmore"** (Via Carlo Neri 28, 05037, Papigno Terni; rafting marmore.com) organizes rafting and inner-tube river descents.

WHERE TO STAY

RIETI

Grande Albergo Quattro Stagioni *inexpensive*
This grand old-style hotel in the historic centre offers a wide range of facilities.
Piazza Cesare Battisti 14, 02100; hotel quattrostagionirieti.com

Hotel Miramonti *moderate*
Set in one of the oldest buildings in Rieti, this four-star hotel has moderately priced rooms and more expensive suites. Parking can be difficult.
Piazza Guglielmo Oberdan 5, 02100; hotelmiramonti.rieti.it

Park Hotel Villa Potenziani *moderate*
On a hill outside town, this villa enjoys all the benefits of a country location – silence, fresh air and top views. It's often used for weddings at weekends.
Via Colle San Mauro 6, 02100; villapotenziani.it

LEONESSA

Chalet Vacanze Il Daino *inexpensive*
Surrounded by nature, this wooden chalet is the perfect starting point for trekking and skiing tours.
Via delle Fonti, 02016; 392 211 0889

Right Fortified Labro, founded on a steep hill in the 10th or 11th century **Far right** Porta Spolentina, one of the main gates of Leonessa

1 Rieti
Rieti, Lazio; 02100

Before the Romans established their Empire, Central Italy was occupied by a number of warlike tribes. The Sabines lived on the slopes of the Apennines and fought often with their neighbour, Rome, before eventually being defeated in 295 BCE. Rieti was one of the Sabines' largest settlements and its medieval city walls are still standing around this bustling provincial capital, which is regarded as the geographical centre of Italy today, as marked in Piazza San Rufo. Unusually, the city centre has three linked piazzas, one of which (Piazza Vittorio Emanuele) was the old Roman Forum. The beautiful Romanesque arches of the crypt of the Papal Palace in Via Cintia are worth a visit. The **Basilica di Santa Maria Assunta** *(open daily)* has an impressive exterior and bell tower (1252), linked by a fine loggia.

🚗 There are many brown signs to Terminillo. Head for Via del Terminillo, SS4bis, uphill for 20 km (12 miles). Turn left into the car park at the village.

2 Terminillo
Rieti, Lazio; 02017

This accessible and modern ski resort is a winter playground for modern-day Romans. In warmer months the village and its surroundings provide welcome relief from the heat of the plains below. The area was first established as a resort in the 1930s and now has all the facilities of an alpine ski village. A pleasant 15-minute circular walk at Campoforogna provides spectacular views and a number of the original mountain huts (now abandoned) can be seen.

🚗 Follow SS4bis uphill, at the end of Piazzale Campoforogna, turn left for Leonessa, on SP10. The road circles the mountain down to Leonessa with amazing views. Turn left into SS471, and then left again at town gate to parking area. In winter, return to Rieti and take SS79 north to Leonessa.

3 Leonessa
Rieti, Lazio; 02016

Virtually hidden among the Monti Reatini, this lovely old town is a surprising find. Enter through the northern gate, the impressive Porta Spoletina, into the narrow Corso San Giuseppe, the main street by virtue of its shops, bars and 15th-century **Chiesa di Santa Maria del Popolo**. It suddenly opens out into the large Piazza VII Aprile, the scene of most of the town's social activity. The square is larger than in most towns this size as many of its public buildings were destroyed in an earthquake in 1703.

Left The pleasant lake resort of Piediluco, a good place for watersports **Below** Fountain in Piazza VII Aprile, Leonessa

EAT AND DRINK

RIETI
Bistrot *moderate*
Book ahead for this small and stylish, classic Slow Food restaurant.
Piazza San Rufo 25, 02100; 0746 498 798; closed Oct, Sun dinner & Mon

La Palazzina *moderate*
Since 1910, this trattoria has been serving delicious homemade pastas to hungry travellers.
Via Angelo Maria Ricci 107, 02100; lapalazzina.it; closed Sun & Tue dinner & Mon.

TERMINILLO
Sfizi di Iri *moderate*
Bright and busy little wine bar/trattoria on the main square of the village. Best to book during summer.
Piazzale Pian de Valli 39, 02100; 342 564 0336

LEONESSA
Trattoria Alesse *inexpensive*
Small, family-run trattoria on main street serving traditional local dishes.
Corso San Giuseppe 61, 02016; 0746 922 130

Leon d'Oro *expensive*
The centrally located Leon d'Oro serves classic dishes with a Roman influence.
Corso San Giuseppe 120, 02016; 0746 923 320; closed Mon & Sun dinner

PIEDILUCO
La Magia del Lago *moderate*
Beautiful lake views and friendly staff make for a lovely dining experience. Good selection of local specialities and pizzas, many of which are accompanied by truffle shavings.
Lungolago Armeno Armeni 5, 05100; lamagiadellago.jimdofree.com

Return to SS471 north, then turn left (west) at the large junction. Drive on SR521 to the crossroads with SS79 and follow signs on the right to Labro on SP5. Park near the town entrance.

④ Labro
Rieti, Lazio; 02010
This beautifully restored little town, clinging tightly to its steep conical hill, still keeps watch over the road below, which it was built to control. One of many fortified settlements in the area established in the 10th and 11th centuries, Labro was the seat of the Nobili family, who controlled much of the region and built the castle. The town's narrow alleys and stairways are paved with rough stone, and the castle is inhabited by the Nobili-Vitelleschi, descendants of its original occupants (*open for visits or tours: 0746 636 020*).

Head back to SP5, turn right onto SS79 towards Piediluco. Follow signs into town to the parking.

The Legend of the Falls
According to legend, the beautiful nymph Nera, from the valley, fell in love with the shepherd Velino, from the plains above. But the all-powerful goddess Juno disapproved and turned her into a river, now called the Nera. The distraught Velino threw himself off the cliffs and turned into a waterfall to join his love in an eternal watery union.

⑤ Piediluco
Terni, Umbria; 05100
Like a coastal resort, Piediluco is strung out along the shore of a lake with the same name. Even though it is only two streets the town has a large church, **St Francis** (*open daily*), built in the 13th century and decorated with 15th-century frescoes. There's no real piazza, but footpaths and small parks provide good vantage points. Excellent climatic conditions make the lake an ideal spot for water sports and it is home to the **National Rowing Centre** (*canottaggio.org*).

On the east side of town, there is a lido, where small boats and canoes can be hired. Or, opposite the Trattoria di Marilù, there is a kiosk where visitors can take a scenic lake tour or hire a boat (*collisulvelino.org*).

Return to SS79 and carry on to Marmore and Papigno, then turn right for Cascate Inferiore, then right again onto SS209. Stop by the road or enter the park a short distance further on.

⑥ Cascata delle Marmore
Terni, Umbria; 05100
The Roman consul Manlius Curius Dentatus created this astonishing human-made waterfall more than 2,000 years ago. As a way of draining the malarial plain of Rieti, in 271 BCE a channel was cut through the rock to allow the River Velino to flow down to the River Nera, in three distinct stages, creating the highest waterfall in Europe (165 m/541 ft). Its rampant energy is now harnessed to provide electricity, and the falls are turned on and off twice a day. Marmore is little more than a railway siding, but the steep path to the summit of the falls affords great views of the cascade (alternatively, drive to the top via Terni).

For Narni, return to Papigno and head towards Terni, skirting the edge of town to the south to get on the Via Flaminia Ternana SS3 (follow signs to Narni at the many roundabouts). The road runs straight into Narni. There is a large parking area to the right, and a lift into the town.

Above The Benedictine Abbazia di San Cassiano, Narni **Bottom left** Stretch of the Via Flaminia in Roman Carsulae **Bottom right** Piazza Garibaldi, the square at the heart of modern-day Narni

WHERE TO STAY

NARNI AND AROUND

Hotel dei Priori *inexpensive*
A convenient and pleasant little hotel in the oldest part of town with helpful staff. It's popular, so book early.
Vicolo del Comune 4, 05035; loggiadeipriori.it

Torre Palombara *moderate*
Sumptuous accommodation at a reasonable price only a ten-minute drive east from Narni. Expect a warm welcome in this tranquil, rural retreat.
Strada della Cantinetta 3, 05035; torrepalombara.com

SAN GÉMINI

Grand Hotel San Gemini *inexpensive*
Classy, modern rooms and a relaxing pool define this large hotel housed in a historic building.
Piazza Duomo 4, 05029; grandhotelsangemini.com

❼ Narni
Terni, Umbria; 05035

Despite being close to some of Umbria's most industrialized areas, Narni is a very beautiful town. The Romans conquered it in 299 BCE and established a settlement called Narnia, but its history goes back much further. Its simple main square, Piazza dei Priori, is graced by the elegant **Loggia dei Priori** by Gattapone (1300–83). There are some delightful medieval bas-reliefs and the tiny pulpit used by St Bernadino. In Via Mazzini, by the square, the beautifully proportioned **Chiesa di Santa Maria Impensole** *(open daily)* has hardly been altered since 1175.

On the wooded hillside west of town sits the 10th-century **Abbazia di San Cassiano** *(open for services only)*, built on the Via Flaminia to watch over the corridor between Rome and Ravenna – it's a lovely walk to the abbey.

Door carving from San Gémini

🚗 *Take Via Roma out of town and head for Narni Scalo. Take Strada dei Tre Ponti/SP1 downhill, turn right at SS3ter and cross the bridge. The Roman bridge is on the right. At San Gémini, park to the left of the entrance gate.*

❽ San Gémini
Terni, Umbria; 05029

This town sits on the Roman road, the Via Flaminia, which still forms its main street (called Via Roma). The main piazza is home to the **Chiesa di San Francesco**, which has some fine carvings on its portal. To one side of the Palazzo Municipio, the medieval **Porta Tuderte** leads to the oldest part of the town, where the **Palazzo Vecchio** is a fine example of early medieval architecture.

🚗 *Return to SS3 and head northeast. Turn right at the Fonte di San Gémini and on Via Carsulae follow signs to the car park at the archaeological site.*

❾ CARSULAE
Terni, Umbria; 05100

The Via Flaminia, which runs from Rome to Fano on the Adriatic *(see Drive 24)*, kept the ancient capital supplied with supplies from Northern Italy and abroad. The *municipium* of Carsulae grew up on this important road and its remains provide an insight into Roman life. It is thought that the city was abandoned after it was damaged by an earthquake.

A one-hour walking tour

On the road from San Gémini, the car park for the Carsulae Archaeological site is clearly marked. From the **car park** ①, steps lead to a subway beneath the road and along a path to the **ticket office** ②. There is also a small museum here, and although most of the larger items from the site have ended up elsewhere, there are still some good terracotta pieces from the 1st century CE. From the entry gate, the path winds downhill towards the main site. Cross a section

The Chronicles of Narnia

This hugely popular series of books (1949–54) by C S Lewis is based in part on the Classically educated author's detailed knowledge of ancient myths and legends. Some literary scholars believe that a map of early Rome in the author's possession is proof that he used the name of the Roman city for his series, as Narnia had been underlined. For the Romans, Narnia was an outpost on the edge of the known world, beyond which lurked all manner of mythical creatures, strange beasts and weird peoples.

of field to an unmistakable stretch of the **Via Flaminia** ③, made of large grey stones and rutted by the passage of countless carts and chariots. Standing in the middle of this historic road, it's easy to imagine the passing traffic through this once important provincial town.

Slightly ahead and on the right-hand side of the road stands the only intact building on the site, the **Church of Saints Cosma and Damian** ④. This dates from the 11th century, when a pre-existing building was converted to religious usage. The solid columns at the front come from the nearby Roman basilica and have been used to good effect to create a stylish loggia and entrance. Inside the church there are damaged frescoes of saints.

Opposite the church, the remains of a tight cluster of buildings and shops at road level show how the prime commercial space in a city centre was as much sought after in Roman times as it is today. Nearby, the **twin temples** ⑤, next to **the forum** ⑥ indicate the traditional layout of the settlement. Proceed along the Via Flaminia in a northerly direction to the **Arco di San Damiano** ⑦ – also known as Arco di Traiano. This is an archway from the Augustan era (1st century BCE), built as a symbolic northern entrance to the city. Just beyond the gate – and outside the walls – there are three large funerary monuments, similar to those found outside Rome along the Via Appia. These ruins give an indication of the importance of Carsulae.

Heading back along the well-worn Via Flaminia to the arch near the forum, turn left through scattered remnants of buildings. This is believed to be the site of the city basilica, which was not a church but an administrative centre and tribunal. Only bits of the foundations remain.

Beyond the basilica and a little further east are the **amphitheatre** and **theatre** ⑧, constructed in a natural valley in the terrain. These two buildings played an important part in the life of any Roman town and reflect sporting obsessions still current today. The elliptical-shaped amphitheatre was the scene of gladiatorial games and entertainments, ranging from athletic competitions to brutal fights to the death. The theatre, which predates the amphitheatre, was for more cultural events and both buildings reflect the Roman ability to build functional, safe and efficient buildings for large numbers of people.

From the theatre, head back to the car park.

🚗 From the car park, continue further on SP22 to SP113 and then turn right. Continue as SP113 becomes SP420. At the end of the street turn onto SR316, then turn right onto SP416 and continue into Colpetrazzo town.

Above The Arco di San Damiano, Carsulae, the northern entrance to the Roman city

EAT AND DRINK

NARNI

La Gallina Liberata *moderate*
A simple restaurant offering home cooking with no menu and no prices on display. Dishes vary daily.
Vicolo Belvedere 13, 05035; 351 888 5983; closed Mon

La Loggia *moderate*
This excellent little restaurant specializes in southern Umbrian dishes. Try the *manfricoli* pasta with broad beans, Pecorino cheese and pancetta. Booking advised.
Vicolo del Comune 4, 05035; loggiadeipriori.it

Il Gattamelata *moderate*
This old-fashioned restaurant overlooking the square and Duomo serves traditional food at reasonable prices. Worth it for a window seat.
Via Pozzo della Comunità 4, 05035; 0744 717 245; closed Mon

SAN GÉMINI

La Pecora Nera *moderate*
Bright and breezy *osteria* where the emphasis is on food and fun.
Piazza San Francesco 2, 05029; 334 882 4346; closed Mon & Tue

Below Via Garibaldi, a cobbled main street in the town of Narni

Above Network of passageways, part of Colpetrazzo's original structure as a castle

WHERE TO STAY IN TODI

Hotel Tuder *inexpensive*
Clean and comfortable mid-range hotel just outside the historic centre, a short walk into town.
Via Maestà dei Lombardi 13, 06059; hoteltuder.com

Hotel Fonte Cesia *moderate*
Situated in the heart of Todi, this old building has been nicely renovated but some rooms are quite small. There is a good restaurant and helpful staff. Free parking for guests.
Via Lorenzo Leoni 3, 06059; fontecesia.it

Relais Todini *moderate*
Umbrian luxury in picture-postcard countryside, ten minutes from Todi. Gorgeous views and well-appointed rooms and apartments.
Frazione Collevalenza, 06050; relais todini.com

⑩ Colpetrazzo
Perugia, Umbria; 06056
A former castle, this delightful little medieval town sits in an area of remote countryside. With one bar, one church and one small square, there is not a lot to see, but its simple layout, solid stone houses and arched alleyways give it a pleasant, close-knit atmosphere. A good place to stop and get a feel for the pace in an Umbrian farming community.

🚗 *From Colpetrazzo, continue north on SP416 to rejoin the main road/SR316. Turn right, and a little further on stands the Church of Santa Maria in Pantano. Park on either side of the road in front of the church. After seeing the church, carry on to Massa Martana.*

⑪ Massa Martana
Perugia, Umbria; 06056
The small religious complex of the **Church of Santa Maria in Pantano** *(open Sun)* has a slightly unorthodox appearance. Its large square façade, with a central rose window and doorway, leans out over the road and the chunky bell tower looks like it is part of a fortress. Dating back to the end of the Roman Empire, the church was built on the site of a temple next to the Via Flaminia. The structure contains building materials from the Roman era to the Renaissance. Note the pagan bas-relief under the window to the left of the door. Ask at the nearby bar for access to the church.

Ancient Massa Martana is not so much a walled town as a town within a fort – it has now been totally restored since it was damaged in the earthquake of 1997. There is an inscription that has been embedded in the medieval town gate, which records that Emperor Hadrian repaired the Via Flaminia in 124 CE.

🚗 *From Massa Martana, take SP414 to Todi – following signs. The road goes through Collevalenza, with its modern religious shrine, and across the plains to Todi on SP382. There are car parks around town and paid parking in the centre.*

⑫ Todi
Perugia, Umbria; 06059
One of the best known and most interesting hill towns in Umbria, Todi combines art, history and architecture in a thriving cultural scene. With Etruscan origins and later Roman reinforcement, the town enjoys a

Top right Elegant lakeside residences beside Lago di Corbara **Right** Piazza del Popolo, Todi, once the Roman Forum in the centre of town **Far right** Pretty cyclamens in the medieval town of Colpetrazzo

EAT AND DRINK

TODI

Cavour *moderate*
The alfresco dining area makes this a great venue on warm summer evenings – not to mention the excellent food and wine. Try pizza with black truffles and porcini or pasta with wild asparagus.
Corso Cavour 21, 06059; ristorante cavourtodi.com; closed Thu

La Mulinella *moderate*
Eat with the locals at this friendly trattoria near Todi. Homemade pasta, especially lasagne, is worth trying.
Loc. Pontenaia 29, 06050; 075 894 4779; closed Wed

Pane e Vino *moderate*
Cosy and interesting restaurant with an emphasis on local seasonal food and a good selection of local wines.
Via A Ciuffellii 33, 06059; panevino todi.com; closed Wed

Vineria San Fortunato *moderate*
Found right on the main piazza, this *enoteca* (wine bar) serves good local dishes. Excellent wine list.
Piazza Umberto 1, 506059; 0753 721 180; closed Mon

vantage point high above the Tiber, evolving to its present state in the late Middle Ages and Renaissance. The magnificent main square, **Piazza del Popolo**, was the Roman Forum and is now the site of splendid public buildings, including the 12th-century cathedral, the **Duomo di Santa Maria Annunziata** (open daily). The grand façade (the top half is unfinished) of **San Fortunato** (open daily) looms over an imposing set of marble steps. Its huge, airy Gothic interior contains an exquisitely carved walnut choir (1590) – engraved with the town symbol, an eagle – and high pulpits which enabled the Franciscans to preach to a large congregation. Beside the church, a pleasant park with panoramic views stretches across a space once occupied by a fortress.
Santa Maria della Consolazione (open daily), on the edge of town, echoes the style of the great churches of Rome and Florence. In the shape of a Greek cross, with a large dome and four apses, the church (built 1508–1607) is an impressive architectural confection.

🚗 *Follow signs out of town west towards Orvieto. The road runs downhill and joins the SS448, following the course of the Tiber to Lago di Corbara.*

The Eagle of Todi
Legend has it that an eagle revealed where Todi should be built. Long ago, a tribe of Umbri, led by Tudero, were feasting near the river when an eagle swooped down and seized the red cloth their meat was arrayed upon. It flew off and dropped the cloth high on top of a hill. This was interpreted as a sign from the gods to found a town there. The eagle clutching the cloth is still the symbol of Todi and can be found on the wall of the Palazzo dei Priori.

13 Lago di Corbara
Orvieto, Terni, Umbria; 05018

When the south-flowing Tiber reaches Todi, it turns sharply to the west towards Orvieto. It flows through verdant, undeveloped countryside and scenic valleys. The road runs beside the river, providing picnic spots and photo opportunities. The artificial Lago di Corbara and a huge area of the surrounding land are part of the regional **Parco Fluviale del Tevere** *(parks.it)*. The area is also famous for its wine.

Top left Todi (left) and the Church of Santa Maria della Consolazione (right) **Below** Vines growing beside human-made Lago Corbara

DAY TRIP OPTIONS
Easy day trips can be planned around activities such as skiing, walking or watersports. Evidence of the Romans abounds for history buffs.

Land of the Sabines
From a base in the Sabine town of Rieti ❶ it is an easy drive to either Terminillo ❷ or Leonessa ❸ for summer walks and, in winter, for snow sports. Access is good, as the roads are kept ploughed in winter.

Follow the drive instructions.

Lakes and waterfalls
Staying near Narni ❼ provides many choices for watersports enthusiasts. Pottering around in a motorboat on the lake at Piediluco ❺ is always a relaxing way to spend an afternoon. For more thrills, Cascata da Marmore ❻ and the Nera River offer exciting rafting, canyoning and kayaking.

Follow the drive instructions in reverse from Narni to Cascata da Marmore and on to Piediluco and back.

Following the Roman legions
From Narni ❼, follow the ancient Via Flaminia. From here the road is almost dead straight to San Gémini ❽, another Roman outpost. Next, drive on to the ruins of Carsulae ❾, where the paving stones carry the marks of ancient Roman chariots.

Follow the drive instructions and then back again to return to Narni.

TRIP 23

THE STONE OF THE APENNINES

Città di Castello to Jesi

HIGHLIGHTS

Ancient landscapes
Enjoy the countryside around Città di Castello, which is virtually unchanged since Roman times

Underground marvels
Explore the subterranean world at Frasassi, whose cathedral-size caves are filled with fabulous rock formations

Castelli di Jesi
The collection of ancient hilltop castles around Jesi are easy to visit and perfect for sampling the delicious local white wine

Secluded retreat
Breathe the pure air of the hills at the Eremo di Fonte Avellana, far from the everyday, industrial world

Romanesque abbey of San Vittore delle Chiuse

THE STONE OF THE APENNINES

Running the length of the Italian Peninsula, the Apennine mountains have long formed an important barrier, fiercely protected by forts and castles in the struggle for the fertile lands of Central Italy. In medieval times, the mountains also provided sanctuary for religious communities. Life here was harsh, and place names reflect the tough terrain – "Sassoferrato" (iron stone), "Frasassi" (between rocks) and "Pietralunga" (long stone). This trip starts in the Roman towns of Northern Umbria, passes over unspoilt terrain, and finally meanders through the gentle wine country of Le Marche.

Above The ancient town of Gubbio, built on a steep hill, *see p230*

KEY

Drive route

0 kilometres 7
0 miles 7

ACTIVITIES

Go truffle hunting and taste local delicacies in Città di Castello

Become a native of Gubbio by running around its fountain three times – keeping an elbow in the water

Learn how to watermark handmade paper at the paper museum in Fabriano

Go on an underground adventure at the caves in Frasassi – all equipment supplied

Sample some delicious Verdicchio wine from the hill towns around Jesi

TRIP 23: THE STONE OF THE APENNINES   229

Above Maiolati Spontini, one of the Castelli di Jesi near Cupramontana, see p234

PLAN YOUR DRIVE

Start/finish: Città di Castello to Jesi.

Number of days: 3 days.

Distance: 240 km (150 miles).

Road conditions: Good to excellent all year except in winter, when ice and snow are common and higher sections must be negotiated with care. Snow chains should be carried.

When to go: Spring and early summer bring clear days and wildflowers. Autumn is best for festivals and the grape harvest. Summer is pleasant in the hills but the beaches get busy.

Opening times: Most museums open 9am–7pm Tue–Sat (closed 1–3pm). Shorter hours in winter. Churches are usually open 8am–noon and 4–7pm.

Main market days: Città di Castello: Tue, Thu & Sat; **Gubbio:** Tue; **Cagli:** Wed; **Fabriano:** Sat (Piazza Garibaldi); **Cupramontana:** Mon; **Jesi:** Wed & Sat.

Major festivals: Città di Castello: Festival of Nations (music), last week in Aug, 1st week in Sep; Truffle and Mushroom Festival, 1st weekend in Nov; **Gubbio:** Festival of the Ceri (see p231), 15 May; **Cagli:** Distinti Salumi (charcuterie), last week in Apr–1st week in May; **Serra de Conti:** Festa della Cicerchia, (food festival) last weekend in Nov; **Cupramontana:** Wine Festival, 1st Sun in Oct; **Jesi:** Opera Season, mid-Oct–Dec (fondazionepergolesispontini.com).

Shopping: Truffle products (sauces, butters) are common in Città di Castello. In Gubbio, the ceramics and leather goods are of high quality. Fabriano is known for its handmade paper. The white Verdicchio wine of the Castelli di Jesi is crisp and clean on the palate and a good local buy.

DAY TRIP OPTIONS

From Città di Castello, explore the Roman townships – from Gubbio, with its **theatre** and **gate**, to Sassoferrato, site of a **historic victory**. Visit the **quiet hermitage** at Avellana for a **walk** and a **picnic**, then explore the **caves** of Frasassi. Tour the **wine castles** of Jesi, sampling the delicious **white wine**, **local foods** and Wine Label Museum. For full details, see p235.

Above The 17th-century façade of the Duomo di San Florido, Città di Castello, see p230

Above Roman amphitheatre in front of Gubbio's Palazzo dei Consoli **Below** Pretty Pietralunga seen from the road into town

WHERE TO STAY

CITTÀ DI CASTELLO

Residenza Antica Canonica *inexpensive*
Beautifully converted former presbytery in the town centre. All rooms and suites are former monks' cells. There are self-catering facilities and free parking.
Via San Florido 23, 06012; anticacanonica.it

Hotel Le Mura *moderate*
A small, comfy hotel built into the town walls, this place has good staff and a nice restaurant serving Umbrian cuisine. Conveniently located with parking.
Via Borgo Farinario 24, 06012; hotellemura.it

GUBBIO

Bosone Palace *inexpensive*
This is a lovely central 14th-century palazzo – Dante and Petrarch once stayed here. It also has a fine restaurant.
Via XX Settembre 22, 06024; hotelbosone.com

Hotel San Marco *inexpensive*
Historic hotel with spacious rooms combining antique furnishings with modern comfort.
Via Campo di Marte 2, 06024; hotelsanmarcogubbio.com

❶ Città di Castello
Perugia, Umbria; 06012

The Roman historian Pliny the Younger had a villa near Città di Castello and wrote in 96 CE of "this welcoming plain surrounded by mountains crowned with wild forests". Little has changed to this day. Ringed by medieval walls, this is a quiet country town with shops, good restaurants and some fine public architecture, such as the solid **Palazzo Comunale** (1322–38), built by Angelo da Orvieto.

Another local, Alberto Burri (1915–95), was renowned as a sculptor and abstract artist who pioneered the use of unusual materials such as burlap, pumice and tar. His work can be seen in the **Palazzo Albizzini** *(open Tue–Sun, reservation required)* and **ex-Seccatoio Tabacco** *(open Tue–Sun, reservations only; fondazioneburri.org)*. Autumn and spring are good times to hunt for truffles. Search for the elusive tubers with Saverio Bianconi *(075 851 1591; tartufibianconi.it)*, then eat your finds back at his farm.

🚗 *Take Viale V Veneto southwest, turn left under railway, then right onto SP106 to Pietralunga. Park near main square.*

❷ Pietralunga
Perugia, Umbria; 06026

Surrounded by the Apennines, this small mountain town has an old fortress that dates back to Roman times, but its most distinctive feature is the pentagonal 8th-century **Rocco Longobardo**, which dominates the central piazza. The **Santa Maria** church nearby was also built in the 8th century, and restored in the 18th century. The narrow medieval streets winding around behind the church offer occasional views down the Carpinella Valley.

🚗 *Descend from town and take SP201 south, then turn left onto SP204. At the roundabout, turn left onto SS219 for Gubbio. Follow signs for "Centro" and park in Viale del Teatro Romano.*

❸ GUBBIO
Perugia, Umbria; 06024

An unspoiled medieval citadel with an impressive Roman theatre, Gubbio's earlier heritage is revealed by its Eugubine Tablets. These spell out observances and rituals in Latin, Etruscan and Umbrian and are the only decipherable record of the original Umbrians.

A two-hour walking tour

The **Roman theatre** ① was built at the end of the 1st century BCE and is still used for summer concerts. From here, cross Viale del Teatro Romano and walk through a covered passage. Turn left into Via Cavour to **Piazza G Bruno** ②, lined with houses built from pale Gubbio stone. Turn right into Via dei Consoli, over a small bridge across the Carmignano – just a stream at this point. Then it's a short walk up to Lago del Vescovado and the simple 16th-century **Fontana dei Matti** ③ (Fountain of the Madmen). It is said that true citizens of Gubbio must run around the fountain three times – with an elbow in the water. Walk up the gentle slope of Via dei Consoli, past stylish leather goods and ceramic shops, to the splendid **Piazza Grande** ④. This beautiful square, at the heart of Gubbio, is flanked on three sides by historic architecture and has great views of the valley below.

The Romanesque-Gothic Palazzo dei Consoli is home to the Museo Civico *(open daily)* and the seven bronze Eugubine Tablets (3rd century BCE).

Just past the main square, the road becomes Via XX Settembre. On the left there is a sign for *"l'ascensore"* (lift), up to the **Museo Diocesano** ⑤ *(open Tue–Sun; winter Thu–Sun)*, with a

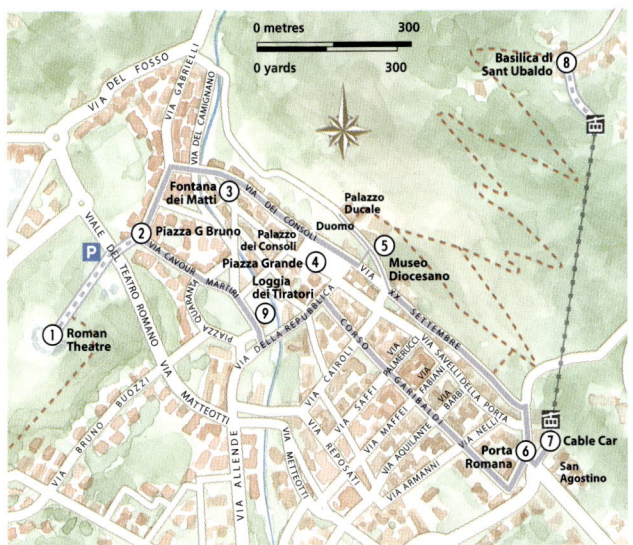

modest collection of religious art, and Gubbio's Duomo, perhaps the only one in Italy without a piazza. Next to the cathedral is the splendid Palazzo Ducale *(closed Mon mornings)*, built in 1480 by the Duke of Urbino, Federico da Montefeltro. Its elegant courtyard echoes the one in the Ducal Palace in Urbino *(see p243)* – enjoy the Giardini Pensili (Hanging Gardens), where a small bar provides drinks and snacks and stunning views.

Amble down the narrow lanes back to Via XX Settembre, and carry on to the towering **Porta Romana** ⑥. Outside the walls is the Chiesa di San Agostino (Saint Augustine), with 15th-century frescoes in its apse.

Just uphill from the church is the **cable car station** ⑦, which takes passengers to the top of the hill and the **Basilica di Sant Ubaldo** ⑧, where the 12th-century patron of Gubbio still lies in state above the altar. Return to the Porta Romana and take Corso Garibaldi to Via della Repubblica. Turn left towards Piazza Quaranta Martiri (Piazza of the 40 Martyrs), a grim reminder of a World War II atrocity in which the Nazis executed 40 people to avenge partisan actions. The piazza includes a public garden and the two-storey **Loggia dei Tiratori** ⑨, home of the Woollen Workers' Guild and a medieval hospital. These days, it often hosts an artisan market and displays of art. The piazza is the site for Gubbio's weekly market *(Tue)*.

From here it is a short walk back to Via Cavour and the car park.

🚗 *From Viale del Teatro Romano, follow signs to Scheggia. Exit town via a medieval gate with traffic lights onto SR298. At Scheggia, take Via Flaminia/SS3 left to Cagli. Park in main square.*

Festival of the Ceri

On May 15 each year, St Ubaldo's day, Gubbio erupts in celebration. *Ceri* is Italian for candles and the large wooden totems carried around town look like candles. (Some say they echo the phallic symbols used to worship Ceres, the Roman god of the harvest.) Each "candle" represents a saint and teams of enthusiastic men take it in turns to carry them up to the Basilica di Sant Ubaldo in a sort of race.

EAT AND DRINK

CITTÀ DI CASTELLO

Il Bianconiglio *moderate*
Enjoy classic Italian fare, including gnocchi with prawn tartare and lamb in raspberry sauce, accompanied by excellent house wines.
Corso Vittorio Emanuele, 42D, 06012; ristoranteilbianconiglio.it; closed Tu

Le Logge *moderate*
This offers sophisticated variations on well-known local specialities, including truffles. Try the *tagliatelle di castagne* (chestnut flour). Extensive wine list.
P Matteotti, Logge Bufalini, 06012; ristorantelelogge.com

Vineria del Vasaio *moderate*
Cosy underground restaurant in a restored pottery. The wine plays an important part in the menu and there is wine sampling by the glass with snacks.
Via della Cacioppa 4, 06012; 329 621 9056; closed Mon

GUBBIO

Alla Balestra *moderate*
Good-value, central restaurant serving Gubbian delicacies – try *Umbricelli alla norcina con tartufo* (truffle pasta).
Via della Repubblica 41, 06024; ristoranteallabalestra.it

All'Antico Frantoio *moderate*
Popular restaurant on the walkway to the Roman amphitheatre, specializing in delicious pasta and wood-fired pizza.
Via del Teatro Romano, 06012; 0759 221 780

Ristorante Picchio Verde *moderate*
This family-run restaurant has served typical Umbrian dishes for generations.
Via Savelli della Porta 65, 06024; ristorantepicchioverde.com; closed Tue

Below left The crenellated Palazzo dei Consoli, Gubbio **Below right** View of the thickly wooded hills around Gubbio

Above The summer landscape of Le Marche near Sassoferrato

WHERE TO STAY IN SASSOFERRATO

Country House Federico I *inexpensive*
An impressive hotel on the edge of town with country views. All the rooms are brightly painted.
Largo San Cristoforo 2, 60041; 0732 958 056

Vicolo Santa Chiara *inexpensive*
This B&B offers two bright, clean self-contained apartments overlooking the main square. The entrance in a charming medieval lane reflects the atmosphere in this part of town.
Vicolo Santa Chiara 1, 60041; 328 205 1370

Below left Stream in a limestone ravine near the Grotte di Frasassi Below centre The 13th-century Palazzo del Podestà, Fabriano Below right The Eremo di Fonte Avellana, in the hills of Le Marche

❹ Cagli
Pesaro, Le Marche; 61043

Cagli was one of the towns that sprang up along the Roman Via Flaminia. The impressive **Palazzo Pubblico** in the main square, Piazza Matteotti, indicates Cagli's importance in the late Middle Ages when it was a flourishing Comune. The square's fountain adds a touch of Renaissance style and there's a popular bar, too. The **Torrione**, or round tower, at the end of town is now a modern sculpture museum. Cagli's decline started as the Via Flaminia's importance diminished and was completed when the railway line was destroyed in World War II. The town is now a remote and relaxed place with a few Roman remains, some impressive Renaissance architecture, good restaurants and bars – and virtually no tourists.

🚗 Take SP424 towards Pergola, then after San Savino turn right onto SP53 to Frontone. Pass through Frontone on SP121; after the town centre, turn left onto SP106, following signs to Foce/Avellana. After 1 km (half a mile), turn left for the monastery.

❺ Eremo di Fonte Avellana
Pesaro, Le Marche; 61040

This beautiful monastery *(open 10am–noon & 3–5pm Mon–Sat; Sun & hols: to 5:30pm)* is home to a small group of Camoldesi monks and offers a perfect spot for contemplation. The grounds are open and there is a bar, a shop and picnic tables. There are hourly guided tours (in simple Italian) for a small donation. Of particular interest is the Scriptorum, which is beautifully illuminated with natural light. Below the monastery is a botanical garden devoted to plants of the region.

🚗 Return to SP52, at Serra Sant' Abbondio take a right to SP42 and again turn right to SP142/SP16. At the roundabout, turn back, take Via Cardinal Albornoz and park near the Rocca.

❻ Sassoferrato
Ancona, Le Marche; 60041

This attractive little town is famous as the place where Rome defeated the Samnites and the Gauls in 295 BCE. At the Battle of Sentinum – which took place just south of town – the Romans won control of the whole of Central Italy. There are a few Roman artifacts at the **Palazzo dei Priori** *(open daily)*.

Above the town, the square 14th-century **Rocca Albornoz** guards a small cluster of Renaissance buildings, squares and narrow streets. The park below the rocca has views of the countryside and mountains beyond.

🚗 Take SP360 southwest, then onto SP16. After about 4 km (2 miles) take the smaller left fork to Fabriano. Follow signs to "Centro", and park on the street.

Visiting the Grotte di Frasassi
To visit the caves, buy a ticket from the ticket office (frasassi.com) in the car park in La Cuna, as access to the caves is via a ravine that can only be reached by bus. The bus runs every 12 minutes and the fare is included in the cost of the entry ticket. Tours take just over one hour, and cover a walk of 1.5 km (1 mile). Enthusiasts can take the longer three-hour tour. It is pretty chilly inside the caves and a light jacket and sensible shoes are recommended for visitors.

Above Series of brick-built arched alleyways, Sassoferrato

7 Fabriano
Ancona, Le Marche; 60041

Its origins possibly go back to Roman times, but Fabriano only came to prominence in the Middle Ages. The magnificent **Palazzo del Podestà** (1255) and **Fontana Maggiore** (1285) in Piazza del Comune testify to its coming of age. Behind the altar in the Baroque **Cattedrale di San Venanzio** (open daily) are some wonderful 12th-century frescoes of the *Martyrdom of St Lawrence*. One of the most important painters of the early Renaissance, Gentile da Fabriano (1370–1427), was born here and his spectacular masterpiece, *Adoration of the Magi*, now in the Uffizi, Florence, is considered the high point of International Gothic.

Fabriano earned a reputation as one of the first places to make high-quality paper and the town is still known for its fine watermarked paper. The ancient processes of making paper by hand from rags are demonstrated in the fascinating **Museo della Carta** or the Paper Museum *(closed Mon)* in the San Domenico complex.

🚗 Take Via Dante, which joins SS76 towards Ancona. Exit for Sassoferrato Grotte Frasassi/Genga after 10 km (6 miles). Park in La Cuna's car park.

8 Grotte di Frasassi
Ancona, Le Marche; 60040

Speleologists regard the limestone caves at Frasassi as among the best in Europe. They are a vast complex of caverns, some the size of cathedrals, with amazing formations of stalagmites and stalactites, crystalline lakes and gleaming alabaster arabesques.

The caves were only discovered after World War II, when speleologists abseiled into the vast empty space of the Ancona Abyss. They were opened to the public in 1974 and the complex can now be entered from ground level. If caving does not appeal, then just along the road there is a Roman bridge with a small medieval tower and gate. This leads to the beautiful Romanesque abbey of **San Vittore delle Chiuse**. Built in the 10th century, this simple but supremely elegant building is an architectural delight.

The road to the caves runs through a ravine from where visitors can drive on to the town of **Genga**, which sits perfectly preserved, as though in a time capsule. Note how the houses have been built into the bedrock.

🚗 From Genga, follow directions to Arcevia on SP15. Turn right onto SP360. Near Arcevia, on Viale Martiri della Resistenza, take the left fork to "Centro" and park outside the walls in Via Mazzini.

Above View of the unspoilt verdant hills of Le Marche

EAT AND DRINK

SASSOFERRATO

La Rocca *moderate*
The garden terrace is a popular spot in summer, offering classical regional cooking and pizzas in the evening.
Via Cardinal Albornoz 1, 3 & 5, 60041; 0732 95 444; closed Wed

La Taverna di Bartolo *moderate*
Enjoy hearty rustic food such as *strozzapreti taleggio e radicchio* (home-made pasta with taleggio and red chicory) in the main square.
Piazza Matteotti 7, 60041; 0732 619 386; closed Mon

FABRIANO

Dal Brigante *moderate*
This simple restaurant serves good-quality local specialities. Good value and friendly service.
Via Cavour 92, 60044; 348 711 6220; closed Mon

Nonna Rina Ristorantino *moderate*
This restaurant has a quiet ambience and offers traditional local dishes served with a modern twist. Also features a vegetarian and vegan menu.
Piazza Garibaldi 25, 60044; nonnarina ristorantino.it; closed Sun & Mon dinner

Below Palazzo del Podestà and the Fontana Maggiore, Fabriano

Above Fields and vineyards on the hills around Cupramontana Above right The pretty central piazza, Cupramontana Below The Porta della Croce, the main entrance to Serra de' Conti

WHERE TO STAY IN JESI

Hotel dei Nani *inexpensive*
A modern hotel with plenty of facilities on the edge of the old town.
Viale del Lavoro 34, 60035; hoteldeinani.it

Hotel Federico II *inexpensive*
This modern hotel may lack character but it is on the edge of town and has plenty of facilities such as parking, pools, gym, sauna and a restaurant.
Via Ancona 100, 60035; hotelfederico2.it

Notti sulle Mura *inexpensive*
This tiny B&B offers colourful and smallish rooms in a characterful building close to the historic centre.
Via Spaldi 16, 60035; nottisullemura.it

⑨ Arcevia
Ancona, Le Marche; 60011

The old fortress, or rocca, of Arcevia at the top of the town was destroyed long ago. Only a few fragments remain in what is now a park. From here, the main street (Via Mazzini) leads through the town, past grand palazzos to the main square, Piazza Garibaldi. Further along, the **Collegiata di San Medardo** *(by reservation: 0731 9444)* has two fine paintings by Signorelli and a ceramic altarpiece by Giovanni della Robbia (1469–1529), whose fluency exceeded that achieved by previous artists.

🚗 *Descend from Arcevia toward Senigallia onto SP360. Follow signs to Serra de' Conti. Park below the city walls at Porta della Croce.*

⑩ Serra de' Conti
Ancona, Le Marche; 60030

One of the few brick-walled towns in the area, Serra de' Conti faces west across the Misa valley. Entry to the historic centre of medieval and Renaissance buildings is through the Porta della Croce. The **Chiesa di San Michele** is a fine Romanesque-Gothic building that is both simple and beautiful. The nearby church of **Santa Maria Maddalena** provides a stunning Baroque contrast inspired by the 15th-century architect Borromini.

🚗 *Leave on SP11 past Montecarrotto, and Moie. At Moie, take SS76 toward Ancona. Exit toward Castelbellino/ Monte Roberto and follow signs to Castelbellino on SP11. Head for "Centro" and park in Via Giacomo Leopardi, just under the town walls.*

Castelli di Jesi

In the hinterland west of Jesi, nearly every hilltop is fortified in some way. Known as Castelli di Jesi, these strongholds, which include Cupramontana, Staffolo, Monte Roberto, Castelbellino and Maiolati Spontini, are synonymous with the vineyards that produce Verdicchio, the famous white wine of the area. It is a light, dry wine, often served in fish-shaped bottles.

⑪ Cupramontana
Ancona, Le Marche; 60034

A town within a town, Cupramontana's old town is tightly clustered around its main piazza and church, while the rest of the town sits comfortably spaced around the old walls. The town has Roman origins (Cupra was a goddess of fertility), but its architecture is mostly Neo-Classical. The capital of the Castelli di Jesi area, Cupramontana is also the centre of the wine-producing area. It is surrounded by vineyards, and serious

wine buffs might like to visit the **Wine Label Museum** *(open hours vary).* *Head northeast on SP9, under the SS76, then cross the Esino on SP502. Join SP76 into Jesi. Park on the street.*

Local Musicians
Giovanni Battista Pergolesi (1710–36) was a celebrated musician who was born in Jesi. For someone who died at 26, he made an enormous contribution to music, virtually inventing *opera buffa* (comic opera). He also wrote serious secular and sacred music – his haunting hymn *Stabat Mater* is the best known. Gaspare Spontini (1774–1851), born in Maiolati Spontini, was successful during his lifetime, but his fame was relatively short-lived and his music is rarely performed today.

12 Jesi
Ancona, Le Marche; 60035

Jesi's main claim to fame is as the birthplace of Frederick II, Emperor of the Holy Roman Empire (1194), and

Above The River Esino, which runs from the hills of Le Marche into the Adriatic

the influential musician Pergolesi. The entrance to the town is through the Arch of Clementine (1734) to Corso Matteotti, the main shopping street. To the right is the **Pinoteca Comunale** in Palazzo Pianetti, a Rococo building featuring many works by Renaissance artists, including Lorenzo Lotto (1480–1557). A little further along is the Piazza della Repubblica and the grand Teatro Pergolesi. Continue straight on into the oldest part of town and the 15th-century **Palazzo della Signoria**, which now houses an important library of 115,000 books. The medieval reading room, the Sala Maggiore, still has its original wooden shelving. Further along still is Piazza Federico II, site of the Roman Forum and where, according to legend, Frederick II was born in a tent in 1194, much to the amazement of the locals. The **Cattedrale di San Settimio** *(open daily)* was rebuilt in Neo-Classical style in 1732 and retains only elements of its earlier form. The **Museo Diocesano** *(open Mon–Fri am & Sun late pm)* next door holds some interesting carved wood pieces from the old churches of Jesi.

Above Looking down Jesi's Corso Matteotti to the Arch of Clementine

EAT AND DRINK

CUPRAMONTANA
Trattoria Anita *moderate*
A traditional, family-run trattoria serving homemade food such as pasta, and lamb and rabbit dishes. Like everything else, the house wine is their own – and good.
Via F Filzi 5, 60034; 0731 780 311; closed Tue

JESI
Pasticceria Bardi *inexpensive*
A good stop for morning coffee and a well-made pastry.
Corso Matteotti 27, 60035; bardijesi.it

Rossintenso Enoteca Degusteria *moderate*
A contemporary *enoteca* (wine bar) that pairs food with wines. Try the carpaccios, the octopus soup and pasta.
Via Mura Occidentali 9a, 60035; rossointenso.it

Mare Mare *expensive*
This small diner with lovely decor features a highly curated menu of fish delicacies, including shrimp with sesame seeds and a special take on spaghetti with clams.
Corso Matteotti 88, 6003; mare-mare.it

DAY TRIP OPTIONS
The tour divides into three sections – for history buffs, for those looking for peace and quiet, and wine lovers.

Roman exploration
Start at Città di Castello 1, once Pliny the Younger's home town, then head to Pietralunga 2, with its Roman fortress. Travel on to Gubbio 3 with its Roman Theatre and Gate, then enjoy lunch. Finally, head to historic Sassoferrato 6, where the Romans won control over Central Italy.

Follow the drive's instructions from Città to Gubbio, then take SS298, SS360, SP360 to Sassoferrato, and back.

Woods and caves
Stock up on food in Cagli 4, then drive to Eremo di Fonte Avellana 5. Tour the monastery, then go for a walk and a picnic. Drive through Sassoferrato 6 to the Grotte di Frasassi 8 for a tour. Return home.

Follow drive's instructions from Cagli to Sassoferrato, then SP360 to Filipponi. Turn right to caves. Return the same way.

The wine castles of Jesi
Start at Serra de' Conti 10, with its fine churches. Then, head to Cupramontana 11, via the Castelli di Jesi of Monte Roberto, Maiolati Spontini and Castelbellino, sampling the wine along the way. At Cupramontana, visit the Wine Label Museum and lunch there, then head to Jesi 12, with its fine palazzos and churches.

Follow the drive's instructions and back.

TRIP 24

MONTEFELTRO MOUNTAINS
Rimini to Fano

HIGHLIGHTS

Coastal resorts for every taste
Splash about at glamorous lidos around Rimini, quieter beaches below the cliffs at Castel di Mezzo, and the family resort of Fano

Pristine wilderness
Get away from it all in the wild mountains above Pennabilli and the rock-filled Parco Naturale Sasso Simone e Simoncello

A Renaissance jewel
Enjoy the relaxed pace of Urbino, a beautiful town filled with some of the Italy's finest art and architecture

Impregnable fortresses
Discover the fortresses of San Leo, Sassocorvaro and Gradara, still in much the same condition as when they were built over 500 years ago

MONTEFELTRO MOUNTAINS

This trip starts on the Adriatic coast with its buzzing seaside towns, beaches and bars, then heads inland to the fairytale republic of San Marino, guarded by forbidding towers. Further inland lies Montefeltro, a region of unspoilt highlands, dotted with sleepy hill towns that are steeped in history. The atmosphere is quiet and peaceful and the air is pure – if it wasn't for the walls and forts guarding every town, it would be easy to forget that constant struggle shaped and defined the area. Even the beautiful Renaissance centre of culture and learning, Urbino, was paid for from the profits of war. Finally, head back to the coast and the spectacular cliffs at Gradara and Fano for more beach fun and the freshest seafood there is.

Above The impressive fortresss at San Leo, see p242

ACTIVITIES

Explore Roman Rimini – cross the Ponte di Tiberio, march through the Arco di Augusto and speak in the former Roman Forum

Clamber up the heights of San Marino and look hang-gliders and eagles in the eye

Hike among the rocks of the Parco Naturale Sasso Simone e Simoncello

Walk along the crenellated walls of the castle at Gradara

Go for a trek in the foothills around Carpegna

Swim in the Adriatic Sea from the beach at Fano

KEY

Drive route

TRIP 24: MONTEFELTRO MOUNTAINS

Above The twin rocky outcrops of Simone and Simoncello near Carpegna, *see p242*

PLAN YOUR DRIVE

Start/finish: Rimini to Fano.

Number of days: Approx. 3–4.

Distance: Approx. 230 km (143 miles).

Road conditions: Good, but often steep ascents/descents. Snow chains must be carried in winter months.

When to go: All year, though winter is not recommended. In spring and late autumn there may be some snow and ice on higher sections of road. In August, all the beach resorts are busy but the inland areas are not.

Opening times: Close to the coast, and in San Marino and Gradara, many attractions stay open late as visitors return from the beach. In summer, many bars and restaurants are open all week. Churches usually open 8am–12:30pm and 3:30–7:00pm.

Main market days: Rimini: Wed & Sat; **Santarcangelo:** Mon & Fri; **Urbino:** Sat; book fair, Wed; **Gradara:** 1st and 3rd Sun of month; **Fano:** Wed & Sat; antique market, 2nd Sun of month.

Major festivals: San Leo: medieval jesters festival, last weekend in Jul; **Pennabilli:** antiquarian festival, mid-Jul; **Carpegna:** Festa del Prosciutto, mid-Jul; **Urbino:** kite festival, 1st weekend in Sep; **Fano:** Jazz by the Sea, last week in Jul; Mardi Gras, 3 weekends in Jan–Feb.

Shopping: San Marino offers duty-free shopping on electronic goods, cameras and alcohol. In Urbino, try the soft and crumbly *casciotta d'Urbino* cheese. Fano is known for the local speciality *moretta di Fano* – coffee with a shot of liqueur and citrus peel.

DAY TRIP OPTIONS

There are distinct day trips to be enjoyed here. Visit **Roman ruins** and splendid **beaches**, then **towers** with **vertiginous views** and a **fort-cum-prison**. Tour a **palace**, rich in **art**, then visit a sturdy **castle** before going for a **hike** among huge rocks. From a **beach resort**, head to **clifftop villages** for **walks** and a **swim**, then round the day off with a drink in a **castle**. For full details, *see p245*.

Above Quaint street in the clifftop town of Fiorenzuola di Focara, *see p245*

Above Picturesque countryside en route to San Merino Below Torre dell'Orologio in Piazza Tre Martiri, Rimini

WHERE TO STAY

RIMINI

Savoia Hotel Rimini *moderate*
This contemporary hotel is right on the beach and has great views. Good for a swim and evening promenade.
Lungomare Murri 13, 47921; savoiahotelrimini.com

Grand Hotel Rimini *expensive*
Splendid "beau monde" hotel made famous by Italian film director Federico Fellini. Enjoy *la dolce vita* at the beach in luxury and elegance.
Parco Federico Fellini 1, 47921; grandhotelrimini.com

THE REPUBLIC OF SAN MARINO

Hotel Titano *inexpensive*
With great views from the top floors, this central hotel is a good base to explore town. Ask about parking when booking.
Contrada del Collegio 31, 47890; hoteltitano.com

Hotel Cesare *moderate*
Small modern hotel in a good central position with easy access to town.
Via Salita alla Rocca 7, 47890; hotelcesare.com

❶ Rimini
Emilia-Romagna; 47921

A busy seaside town, Rimini is the most popular resort on the Adriatic. But alongside the nightclubs, there is an interesting mix of Roman and Renaissance architecture. The **Piazza Tre Martiri** is the former RomanForum, where Julius Caesar addressed his troops before advancing on Rome in 49 BCE. Nearby, in Via IV Novembre, is the beautiful **Tempio Malatestiano** *(open daily)*, with its unfinished façade. This was commissioned in 1450 by the tyrant Sigismondo Malatesta, who had his and his wife Isotta's initials carved in the roundels.

The **Ponte di Tiberio** (14–21 CE) on the northern side of the town is built from Istrian stone and is a fine example of Roman engineering. On the southern side, the **Arco di Augusto** (27 CE) shows Rimini's importance in Roman times. (The battlements were added in the Middle Ages.) Piazza Cavour is the Renaissance hub of Rimini, with its palazzos, fountain and statue of Pope Paul V. The rough-hewn Castel Sismondo, started by Sigismondo in 1437, stands in Piazza Malatesta and provides a striking space for summer art exhibitions.

🚗 *Head inland on Via Marecchiese, turn right onto SS16 and left onto SS9 to Santarcangelo. In about 650 m (711 yards) turn left and park in the area on Via Federico Montevecchi.*

❷ Santarcangelo di Romagna
Rimini, Emilia-Romagna; 47822

Set on a small hill in the coastal plain, Santarcangelo offers a pleasant break from the beach culture of Rimini. Dominated by the **Rocca Malatestiana and Monastery**, this medieval town sits on a mass of catacombs dating back to early Christian times. Visit the Tourist Centre *(Via C Battisti 5; iatsantarcangelo.com)* for tickets to the catacombs. Wear something warm, as it is chilly underground. Many of the town's pleasant buildings are adorned by plaques bearing poems, a custom initiated by poet, screen-writer and local, Tonnino Guerra.

🚗 *Take SP14 west to Ponte Verucchio. Cross River Marecchia, then follow signs to Verucchio. There is plenty of parking.*

❸ Verucchio
Rimini, Emilia-Romagna; 47826

A key defensive post in pre-Roman times, Verucchio was the site of Iron-Age settlements in the 8th century BCE. **Museo Civico Archeologico** displays locally discovered artifacts. The town is topped by an imposing Rocca built by Malatesta in the 13th century.

🚗 *Take SP32 to San Marino "Centro". Use top car park P7, Cava degli Umbri.*

❹ THE REPUBLIC OF SAN MARINO
Repubblica di San Marino (RSM); 47890

The world's oldest republic is perched on top of the cliffs of Monte Titano and maintains its own army, mint and parliament. With a population of 32,000, it is effectively a part of Italy despite its independent status. The United Nations gave San Marino World Heritage Status in 2008.

A two-hour walking tour
From the car park, walk past tennis courts to Via della Fratta. On the right is a stone path (Salita alla Cesta) up to the **Second Tower** ① *(entry fee covers all towers)*. To the right is the pleasant Parco Naturals and the Third Tower (Montale), a former prison and lookout, is visible to the south. The Second Tower (Cesta) was built in the 13th century on the remains of a Roman fortress. It is at the highest point of Monte Titano and houses an armoury museum with exhilarating views – not recommended for vertigo sufferers. It's a testament to their skills that the medieval masons managed to create such elegant stonework on

this sheer precipice. Returning down Salita alla Cesta, there is a path to the right, Passo delle Streghe (Witches Way), through parkland to the **First Tower (Guaita)** ②. This slightly larger castle shares the views of its twin. It was used as a prison as recently as 1975 and still has prisoners' graffiti in some rooms. Continue down Salita della Rocca, past the trinket sellers. As the path sweeps around to the left, continue straight on into what looks like a restaurant, signed "Ingresso Giardino". This is a public right of way. Enter, then go down some steps into the Bishop's Garden. From here another stone staircase leads to narrow Contrada Magazzini, then into **Piazza Domus Plebis** ③. The Basilica di San Marino was built here at the beginning of the 19th century over a Roman church. It is grand but a bit empty. The sweet little church next door, the Chiesa di San Pietro, contains two beds carved into the rock. Believed to be those of St Marino and his companion St Leo, they are said by many to have healing powers.

Below the square to the right, **Contrada Omagnano** ④ leads to the northernmost point on the cliff, and the cable car (down to Borgo Maggiore, every 15 minutes). A sharp left into narrow Contrada di Pianello leads to **Piazza della Libertà** ⑤ and San Marino's Palazzo Pubblico – a mini palace for a mini republic. There is a Changing of the Guard *(May–Sep)* every hour on the half hour. Continue along Contrada del Collegio, but at the next junction take a slight left uphill along Contrada della Croce. At the city wall, turn right, down to Viale Donna Felicissima and **Piazza Garibaldi** ⑥. The porticoed loggia of San Francesco graces this busy little square. The church itself is now a small museum and picture gallery (included in the ticket for the towers). A few steps downhill is the Piazza del Titano and the state museum, the **Palazzo Pergami-Belluzzi** ⑦ *(open daily)*, which has some archaeological finds and minor artworks.

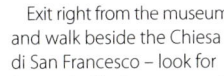

Statue of Liberty, Palazzo Pubblico

Exit right from the museum and walk beside the Chiesa di San Francesco – look for the Templar symbol in the stonework at the base of the church. Continue along to Piazza Sant'Agata, then follow the city wall left, up to Via della Fratta and the car park.

🚗 Zigzag down to Borgo Maggiore, turn left at the roundabout for San Leo and onto SP258 left to San Leo. Drive into town and park in the main square.

Left San Marino's elegant Palazzo Pubblico, built in 1884 **Below** Peaceful Santarcangelo di Romagna, a change of pace from Rimini

EAT AND DRINK

SANTARCANGELO DI ROMAGNA
Lazaroun *moderate*
Enjoy classic Romagnolo cooking, with well-presented dishes such as rabbit salad, pheasant with prunes and chestnuts, and amaretti semifreddo.
Via del Platano 21, 47822; lazaroun.it

VERUCCHIO
Ristorante La Rocca *moderate*
Stop in on the walk up to the Rocca – the quality of the food is almost as spectacular as the views.
Via della Rocca 46, 47826; 0541 679 850; closed Wed

THE REPUBLIC OF SAN MARINO
Cantina di Bacco *moderate*
Refreshingly old-fashioned place in the middle of town selling local specialities.
Contrada Santa Croce 35, 47890; cantinadibacco.net

Ristorante Bolognese *moderate*
Typically hearty Bolognese food. Try the *stringhetti al sugo di verdure* (pasta with vegetable sauce).
Via Basilicus 24, 47890; ristorantebolognese.com

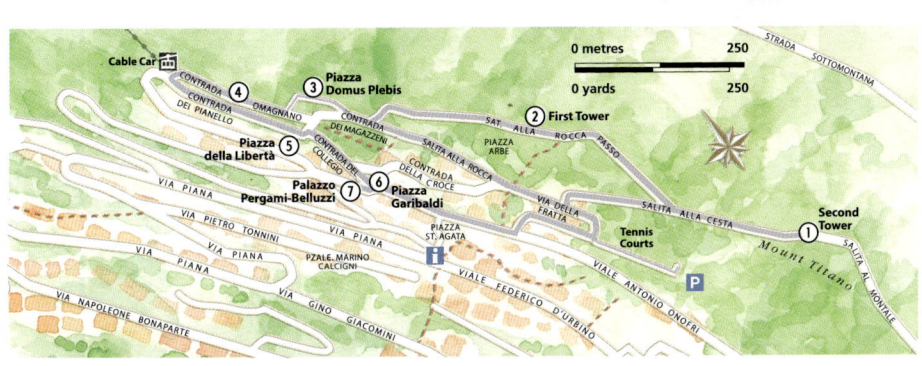

VISITING URBINO

Tourist Information
Located just inside the main city gate. *Via Puccinotti 35, 61029; vieniaurbino.it*

WHERE TO STAY IN URBINO

Albergo Italia *inexpensive*
With smart modern interiors and a central location close to the lift and car park in Piazza Mercatale, this hotel makes a convenient city stopover. *Corso Garibaldi 32, 61029; albergo-italia-urbino.it*

Hotel Raffaello *inexpensive*
In the very old part of town (ask for parking directions when booking), this old seminary has been transformed into a convenient, modern hotel. *Via Santa Margherita 40, 61029; albergoraffaello.com*

Albergo San Domenico *moderate*
Beautifully restored monastery opposite the Palazzo Ducale, complete with cloister and Roman cistern, but all modern conveniences as well. *Piazza Rinascimento 3, 61029; viphotels.it*

Top right Rocky outcrops of Simone and Simoncello **Below left** Fountain in Piazza Dante Alighieri, San Leo **Below right** Façade of the Chiesa di Sant'Antonio Abate, Pennabilli **Bottom** Countryside around Pietrarubbia, looking towards San Marino

⑤ San Leo
Rimini, Emilia-Romagna; 61018
This spectacular town enjoys the reputation of being the most impregnable fortress in Italy, built as it is on a near vertical cliff. Settlement began in the 8th century and its buildings are variously Longobard, Romanesque and from the Renaissance. For many years it was part of the Papal States, and its impressive **castle** became a prison for miscreants such as Count Cagliostro, an infamous charlatan and necromancer. It is now a lovely little place with two simple but beautiful Romanesque churches.

🚗 *From San Leo turn right towards Carpegna. Turn right onto SP6 towards Novafeltria/Maiolo – great views – do not take right turn to Novafeltria but head down to the Marecchia Valley and SP285. The turn left to Pennabilli is on a dangerous corner, so carry on to the roundabout and return. Park in town.*

⑥ Pennabilli
Rimini, Emilia-Romagna; 61016
The two fortresses of Penna and Billi were joined into one in the 14th century and the remains of the castles are visible above the still united town. The main square, Piazza Vittorio Emanuele II, with its redbrick Chiesa di Sant'Antonio Abate, sits between the two forts. It is a charming town of medieval streets and squares brightened up in summer by crimson geraniums in terracotta pots.

🚗 *Take SP1 to exit from town, then turn left onto SP84 towards Carpegna.*

⑦ Carpegna
Pésaro, Le Marche; 61021
A brief heyday in the late Middle Ages gave Carpegna just one impressive building. Planned, but not built until 1675, Palazzo dei Principi di Carpegna's main claim to fame is that it was used to hide much of Italy's art collection during World War II. Carpegna is also the headquarters of the **Parco Naturale Sasso Simone e Simoncello**. Sasso means "rock" or "stone" in Italian, and the two rocky outcrops or "sassi" are visible to the west on the road into Carpegna. For information on walking or trekking, pop into the Visitor Centre *(Via Rio Maggio, Carpegna; parcosimone.it).*

🚗 *Take SP1 east and follow signs to Pietrarubbia. On a hairpin bend on the right, a white road signed "Petrelle" leads to the rock. Either drive or walk.*

⑧ Pietrarubbia
Pésaro, Le Marche; 61023
A monumental outcrop suddenly emerges on the road from Carpegna to Pietrarubbia like a huge thumb raised to the heavens – locals call it the "Giant's Finger". Pietrarubbia itself is a good place to survey the Montefeltro region, from San Marino in the northeast and the Adriatic to the Apennines. The ruins of the medieval town and castle on the hill above town can be seen and visited from Pietrorubbia.

Far left Well-defended Sassocorvaro, set high on a hill **Left** The turrets and towers of Urbino, a centre of learning during the Renaissance **Below** The "Giant's Finger" rock formation on the road to Pietrarubbia

ACTIVITIES IN MONTEFELTRO

For horse riding, try the **Centro Ippico Montefeltro** *(Via Provinciale SP1, Carpegna; 349 526 3559)*. For details of organized treks, contact **Urbino and Montefeltro Consortium** *(Via Alessandro Manzoni 25, Urbino; eventi.turismo.marche.it/en-us)*.

From the "Giant's Finger" take SP1 towards Pietrarubbia. SP1 becomes the SP6 near Sassocorvaro, then SP3bis and SP37/SP67. There is plenty of parking.

Piadina

The *piada* or *piadina* is the perfect gastronomic symbol for the area and has been rather overlooked in favour of the pizza. Pellegrino Artusi (1820–1911) – the first writer to gather together recipes from all over Italy in one cookbook – didn't deem it worth an entry. But, properly made, the warm, round flatbread, filled with *prosciutto crudo* and *stracchino* cheese is paradise on a plate.

⑨ Sassocorvaro
Pésaro, Le Marche; 61028

The road to Sassocorvaro passes first through the pretty market district of Mercatale with views of the castle above and the lovely artificial lake. In the heart of Sassocorvaro, the fortress **La Rocca Ubaldinesca** *(open Wed–Sun)* is a fine piece of 15th-century defensive architecture. Its remote location and solid design meant it was never breached in earlier centuries, and during World War II it was used to hide many of Italy's artworks – it is now a museum. At the other end of the street there are pleasant views over the Fiume Fóglia lake, below.

Head out of town on Via Roma SP 67. Follow signs to Urbino on SS73bis. Follow the road around town to Piazza Mercatale, for underground parking.

⑩ Urbino
Le Marche; 61029

This enchanting city flourished under the patronage of Duke Federico da Montefeltro (1422–82). His university attracted painters, architects and mathematicians from far and wide.

The huge Palazzo Ducale, which houses the **Galleria Nazionale delle Marche** *(closed Mon)*, dominates the approach to Urbino from the south. The fairytale quality of the turrets that frame the duke's private quarters belies the strength of an undefeated military power. The courtyard is a masterpiece of the Greek and Roman humanist ideals that would become hallmarks of the Renaissance. In its day, the palace was the largest building in Europe.

The gallery's most famous works are Piero della Francesca's enigmatic *The Flagellation* (c 1460), often cited as the world's greatest small painting; *The Ideal City*, a perspective study attributed to Piero or his students; and the gorgeous *La Muta* (1507) by Raphael. The duke's private study is lined with finely worked wood panels and the servants' quarters and kitchens below stairs are worth seeing to understand how the other half lived.

Across the square from the palace is the **Cattedrale di Urbino**. Founded in 1062 but often rebuilt, it has an 18th-century Neo-Classical façade.

Near the Piazza della Repubblica, **Casa Natale di Raffaello** *(open daily)* has been preserved since the 19th century as a monument to the painter Raphael and retains its evocative atmosphere. Nearby the **Oratories of San Giovanni and San Giuseppe** *(open daily)* have frescoes by the Salimbeni brothers (c 1416). Blending International Gothic with a more natural approach, they are an exciting foretaste of the Renaissance.

Follow signs to Perugia/Pésaro on SP423; drive toward Pésaro to Montecchio, then turn left onto SP38 towards Gradara. Park in front of castle.

EAT AND DRINK

SAN LEO

Hotel Ristorante Castello *moderate*
With tables on the main square, this is the spot for a coffee, an aperitif, a light snack and a bit of people watching.
Piazza Dante 11/12, 47865; hotelristorantecastello.it

Osteria Belvedere *moderate*
This cosy restaurant offers fine alfresco dining – try *prosciutto di Carpegna* and local cheeses with *marmellata* (fruit jelly).
Via Tosselli 19, 47865; 0541 916 361

URBINO

Il Cortegiano *moderate*
Close to the Palazzo Ducale, this restaurant provides quick snacks or proper dining in the courtyard.
Via Puccinotti 13, 61029; 0722 320 307; closed Mon

La Trattoria del Leone *moderate*
This popular place in the historic centre is fairly small, so booking is recommended.
Via Cesare Battisti 5, 61029; latrattoriadelleone.it

Vecchia Urbino *moderate*
A restaurant serving delicacies such as truffles and porcini, as well as more adventurous dishes – *testina di agnello alla brace* (chargrilled lamb's head).
Via dei Vasari 5, 61029; vecchiaurbino.it

Above One of the many souvenir shops in the medieval town of Gradara

WHERE TO STAY

GRADARA

La Loggia di Gradara Relais *moderate*
Combining the ultra modern and the ancient, this tiny hotel is both unusual and interesting. As parking is outside the walls, guests are driven to the hotel in an electric car. Ask for a balcony room.
Via Dante Alighieri 2, 61012; laloggiagradara.it

FANO

Palazzo Rotati *moderate*
This boutique hotel in the historic town centre of Fano is a short walk to the sea. Rooms and suites are beautifully appointed. Guests enjoy a breakfast buffet or can opt for it to be served in their room.
Via Nolfi, 49 Fano 61032; palazzorotati.com

Siri Hotel *moderate*
On the main road into town, this ultra-chic modern hotel is well situated for both the beach and the historic centre. There's a shuttle to the private beach.
Viale Buozzi 69, 61032; sirihotelfano.it

Fano

Named after Fanum Fortunae, a temple dedicated to the goddess Fortuna, Fano became the terminus of the Via Flaminia (a consular road from Rome) and the largest Roman colony on the Adriatic coast. The Arco d'Augusto (2 CE), on Via Arco d'Augusto, is Fano's most significant ancient monument. In 1463, Federico da Montefeltro destroyed its upper section while besieging the town as a papal *condottiere* (leader of a band of mercenaries).

⑪ Gradara
Pésaro, Le Marche; 61012
This spectacular fortified town dates back to the 12th century and was gradually encased in a double line of medieval walls. The castle is now the **Museo Nazionale della Rocca** *(open daily)*. Superbly preserved, it is a fantasy fortress of crisp crenellations, towers and bastions (it is also said to be the location of the love story in Dante's *Divine Comedy*). Gradara buzzes with day-trippers and events in summer. In the early evening, once the coach parties have gone, taking a walk around the castellated walls is a great way to admire the sunset.

🚗 *Exit following signs to Cattolica/ Gabbicce Mare – under the A14 – take a dogleg, then follow signs for Gabbicce Mare/Centro. Follow Viale della Vittoria to the sea, then turn right into Via Panoramica uphill to Gabbicce Monte, then Castel di Mezzo and the Parco Naturale Monte San Bartolo.*

⑫ Castel di Mezzo
Pésaro, Le Marche; 61100
This is a tiny town in the centre of the 10-km (6-mile) strip of greenery, known as the **Parco Naturale Monte San Bartolo** *(parcosanbartolo.it)*. The green clifftops between Gabbicce Mare and Pésaro are a welcome relief from the long strips of organized lidos to the north, stretching as far as Trieste. The Parco Naturale Monte San Bartolo offers numerous walking trails and leisure activities. Castel di Mezzo itself is little more than a church, a restaurant and a few houses, but the town is certainly worth a quick stop for a short clifftop walk or a leisurely meal looking out to sea.

🚗 *Carry along the Strada Panoramica Adriatica to Fiorenzuola di Focara. Parking can be difficult but there are generally spaces along the road.*

Above Countryside around the fortified city of Gradara Bottom left Gradara's pretty town centre, popular with day-trippers Bottom right Bas-reliefs above the doorway of the Chiesa di San Michele, Fano

Love Story
Dante Alighieri (1265–1321) was the first great Italian poet to immortalize the tragic tale of Paolo and Francesca. Paolo was the handsome brother of the deformed Giovanni Malatesta. Francesca's father knew she would refuse Giovanni in marriage, so it was arranged for Paolo to perform the vows. Paolo and Francesca fell in love, but when Giovanni caught them embracing he murdered both of them in the family castle at Gradara.

13 Fiorenzuola di Focara
Pésaro, Le Marche; 61100
On a sunny day, this tiny fortress town can get crowded as it is a starting point for the trek to the stunning beach below. It still has the classic elements of a hill town and the old entrance gate and walls remain. Fiorenzuola was originally part of a defensive coastal network and a primitive lighthouse in medieval times.
Continue along Strada Panoramica Adriatica to Pésaro, then follow signs to Fano on SS16 along the seafront. At Fano, the road bends to the right and becomes Via Bruno Buozzi. Park here.

14 Fano
Pésaro, Le Marche; 61032
Although Fano has plenty to offer as a beach resort, it is also a working town with a history going back to the Roman era. That said, the impressive **Arco di Augusto** is virtually all that remains from ancient times. Close by the arch is the **Porta Maggiore**, built in 1227, but equally ravaged by time. Down the same street – once the Roman main road – is the **Cattedrale Santa Maria Assunta** (open daily). It has been restored many times, but retains its plain Romanesque exterior and contains medieval sculptures and other works of art by Renaissance artists. The small **Chiesa di San Michele** was built in 1494, and the bas-reliefs above the doorway date to 1511.

EAT AND DRINK

GRADARA

Il Bacio *moderate*
Dine under the shady mulberry tree in warm weather, and enjoy this restaurant's delicious specialities.
Via Roma 11, 61012; ristorante ilbaciogradara.it

Mastin Vecchio *expensive*
Just off the main street, Mastin Vecchio has a lovely courtyard for summer dining and offers cheaper (osteria) or more traditional (ristorante) options.
Via Alighieri 5, 61012; mastinvecchio.it

AROUND CASTEL DI MEZZO

Bar Panoramic *inexpensive*
On the road just beyond Gabicce Monte, this friendly bar has superb views and cheap drinks.
Via Panoramica 47, 61011; 0541 830 439

Taverna del Pescatore *moderate*
This excellent fish restaurant has a perfect clifftop position.
Borgata Casteldimezzo 23, 61121; tavernadelpescatore.it; closed Tue

FANO

Locanda dei Casta *inexpensive*
Local trattoria offering a menu of fish and meat dishes, including pappardelle with wild boar sauce.
Via Papiria 29B, 61032; locandadeicasta.it

Casa Orazi *expensive*
Inside the Hotel Augustus, this is one of Fano's best seafood restaurants. Casa Orazi specializes in brodetto Fanese, the excellent local fish soup.
Via Puccini 2, 61032; casaorazi.it; closed Mon & Sun dinner

Top left The unspoiled clifftop reserve of Parco Naturale Monte San Bartolo **Left** The medieval Porta Maggiore, Fano

---

DAY TRIP OPTIONS
There are some great days out to be enjoyed in Montefeltro, for families, art lovers, activity enthusiasts and those looking for a relaxing time.

A family day from Rimini
The resort of Rimini 1 – with its Roman remains – is a great starting point for a tour inland to San Marino 4. Take a walk up the tiny republic's steep streets with stunning views. Next stop is San Leo 5 and its formidable clifftop fortress. Return to Rimini for some relaxing beach time and a cooling dip in the sea.

Take SS72 from Rimini to San Marino to the top car park. Return the same way.

Renaissance and rocks
Spend the morning touring the Palazzo Ducale at Urbino 10, the city was the birthplace of Raphael and, in its heyday, it was a centre for the best minds of the time. Enjoy lunch before heading to Sassocorvaro 9 to see its sturdy castle, then drive to the "Giant's Finger" at Pietrarubbia 8 for a walk in the countryside.

Retrace the drive's instructions from Urbino to Pietrarubbia, and back.

Take a break from blue to green
From the lively beach resort of Fano 14, enjoy a change of pace by driving to the peaceful, green, clifftop oasis of the *Parco Naturale Monte San Bartolo*. Stop for strolls at pretty Fiorenzuola di Focara 13 and Castel di Mezzo 12, climbing down the cliff to the lovely beach for a swim. Visit romantic Gradara 11 and stay for a drink as the sun sets.

Follow the drive's instructions in reverse, from Fano to Gradara. If time is of the essence, return via the A14. If not, take SP47 back to the coastal road to Fano.

TRIP 25

THE HEART OF LE MARCHE

Loreto to Grottammare

HIGHLIGHTS

Pilgrimage destination
Visit the historic house from the Holy Land in Loreto's grand cathedral and see some exceptional art inspired by strong religious devotion

Majestic peaks
See the spectacular Monti Sibillini from viewpoints in quaint old towns along the way

Mostly marble
Enjoy a drink in one of Italy's most beautiful piazzas, the main square of delightful Ascoli Piceno – a town built almost entirely of travertine

Beachside fun
Wander along Grottammare's palm-lined promenade, relax on the hot sand or enjoy a meal of fresh seafood served with excellent local wine

Basilica della Santa Casa bathed in golden sunlight, Loreto

THE HEART OF LE MARCHE

Although not well-known to foreign visitors, the beach resorts of Le Marche buzz with activity all summer. But the region's inland treasures remain almost undiscovered. Starting at the holy city of Loreto, this trip sweeps over the Conero Peninsula and into the historic towns between the coast and the mountains. The famous opera town of Macerata, the serene abbey at Fiastra and the Roman ruins of Urbs Salvia are key stops. Next, the road climbs into the foothills of the Monti Sibillini, with spectacular views from the medieval towns of San Ginesio, Montefortino and Montemonaco.

Above The ancient fortress town of Grottammare, keeping watch over the modern coastline, *see p255*

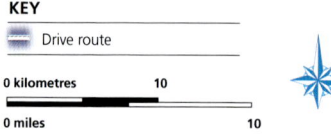

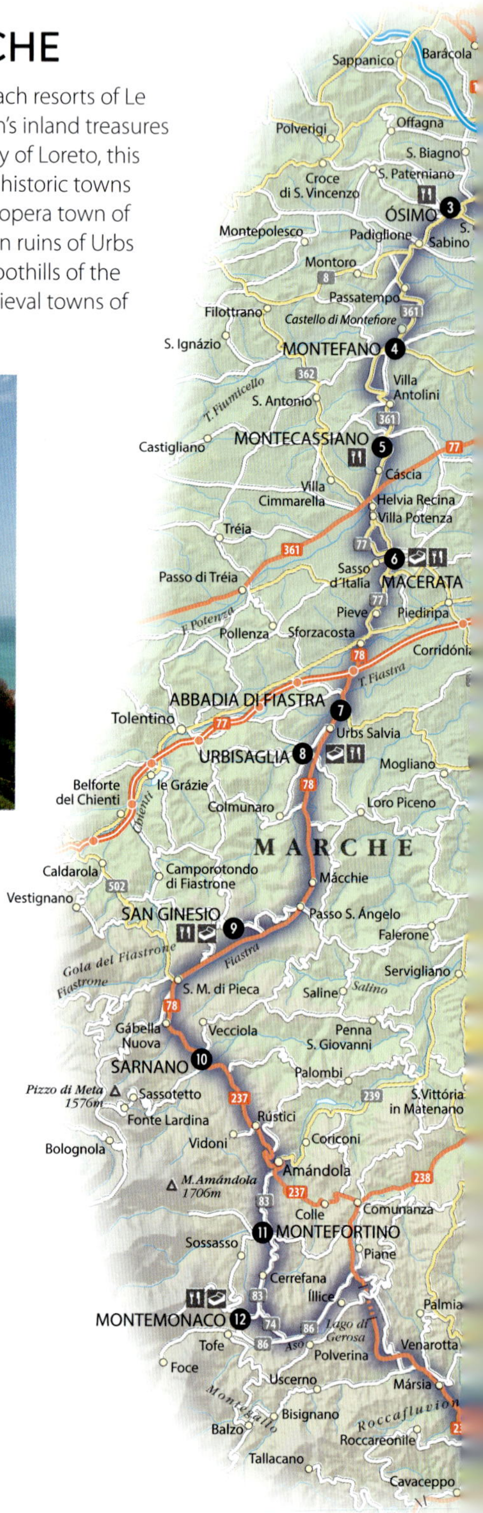

ACTIVITIES

Go for a swim at any of the beaches near Sirolo

Explore the underground cave system at Osimo, which dates back to BCE times

Enjoy an outdoor opera at the world-famous Sferisterio in Macerata

Choose climbing, walking or skiing on a visit to the Parco Nazionale dei Monti Sibillini

Taste some great wines in the province of Ascoli Piceno

Promenade at Grottammare, under palms imported from the Canary Islands

TRIP 25: THE HEART OF LE MARCHE

Above A narrow, cobblestoned street in pretty Ripatransone, see p255

PLAN YOUR DRIVE

Start/finish: Loreto to Grottammare.

Number of days: 3–4 days.

Distance: Approx. 240 km (149 miles).

Road conditions: Good-quality roads with one or two steep ascents.

When to go: All year round but best in spring and autumn. August is very crowded on the coast but quiet inland.

Opening times: Churches open 8am–12:30pm and 3:30–6:30pm. Shops in inland towns within driving distance of the coast stay open late in summer for those returning from the beach.

Main market days: Loreto: Tue, Wed & Fri; **Osimo:** Thu & Sat; **Macerata:** Tue; **San Ginesio:** Sun; **Sarnano:** Thu; **Ascoli Piceno:** Wed.

Specialized markets: Macerata: Il Barattolo flea market, 2nd Sunday of month; **Ascoli Piceno:** antiques market, 3rd weekend of month.

Major festivals: Macerata: Sferisterio (opera festival), Jul–Aug; **San Ginesio:** Palio (medieval festival), 13–15 Aug; **Ascoli Piceno:** Quintana (medieval festival), 1st Sun in Aug; Carnivale, late Feb–early Mar; **Offida:** Carnivale, Feb–Mar.

Shopping: In Macerata, look for Varnelli – an aniseed-flavour liqueur. Ascoli Province has great hand-made shoes. Offida is one of the best lace-making centres in Italy. In Grottammare, pick up handmade ceramics from shops such as Giancarlo Livori's atelier.

DAY TRIP OPTIONS

From the High Renaissance **architecture** of Loreto, it's a short drive to the **catacombs** in Osimo, where early Christians sheltered from persecution. The towns in the foothills of the Monti Sibillini provide ready access to the **national park**, where **churches** perch on clifftops, **castles** keep watch for invaders and **vineyards** stretch as far as the eye can see. The marble town of Ascoli Piceno is rich in **art**, **architecture** and **history**; beyond it lies perfect **picnic** country and Grottammare's **seaside** delights. For full details, *see p255*.

Above Secluded sandy beach on the Conero Peninsula near Sirolo

WHERE TO STAY

LORETO
Hotel Loreto *inexpensive*
Central, modern location with great countryside views from the terrace.
Corso Boccalini 60, 60025; loretohotel.it

MACERATA
Hotel Lauri *inexpensive*
Set right in the city centre, this hotel is housed in a charming 17th-century palazzo and features colourful rooms with modern amenities.
Via Lauri 6, 62100; hotellauri.it

Below Arco Gotico, the main shopping street in clifftop Sirolo Below right Typical Le Marche vineyard on the road to Macerata Bottom The tower of Castello di Montefiore, visible from a distance

❶ Loreto
Ancona, Le Marche; 60025
This small hill town is one of Italy's holiest sites and often throngs with pilgrims. It is also a place where Renaissance popes invested heavily in fine art and architecture. In the huge **Basilica della Santa Casa** *(open daily)* sits a small and very old building. Pilgrims come here to see where the Virgin Mary received the news that she was to become the Mother of God (The Annunciation). They believe that this is her actual house, carried by angels to Italy in 1294 from Nazareth in the Holy Land. Many famous 14th- and 15th-century architects, such as Bramante, Sangallo and Martini, worked on the basilica's decoration and the soldier pope, Julius II, gave it a military exterior. Of special interest is the large marble screen, designed by Bramante – one of many great works of art in the complex. The town's piazza, fountain and the quadrangle of buildings surrounding it all have a High Renaissance feel, which makes it like a mini Rome away from Rome.

From Loreto, take SP77 east. At the roundabout, head north towards Sirolo, then turn right onto SP23 to Sirolo and follow signs for "Centro". Park near Piazzale Marino.

❷ Sirolo
Ancona, Le Marche; 60020
Overlooking the Adriatic, Sirolo is a beachside town some distance from the beach. In a sense, this adds to its attraction – it gets a cooling sea breeze in summer and combines the ambience of a hilltown with ocean views. The main square, Piazzale Marino, offers the best views of the beaches of the Conero Peninsula, and the tiny medieval streets behind it buzz with activity in summer.

From Sirolo, drive west downhill onto SP2. Drive straight over roundabout, then turn left under the autostrada onto SP25. Then follow signs to Osimo. There are parking meters all around town.

The Santa Casa at Loreto
In 1291, Acre, the last bastion of the Christian crusaders, fell to the Turks, leaving the Holy Land under the control of Muslims. To protect their Christian heritage, a crusader family arranged to remove "Mary's house" to safety. That same year, the house arrived in Croatia, and in 1294 in Loreto. The stonework is similar to examples from Nazareth from around the time of the birth of Christ. Gradually the myth grew that angels had carried the *Santa Casa*, or Holy House, to Italy.

❸ Osimo
Ancona, Le Marche; 60027
The ancient Greeks, who colonized nearby Ancona in the 3rd century BCE, founded Osimo. In 174 BCE, the Romans took possession and some elements from this time still remain – great rectangular blocks in the town walls and a Roman fountain. The town's age shows in many of its public buildings, particularly the intricate Romanesque carvings around the doors of the **Cattedrale di San Leopardo** *(open daily)* and the official buildings in the main square, **Piazza del Comune**. Below the town is a labyrinth of catacombs, **Le Grotte** *(open daily)*, dating back to pre-Roman times. The tourist information office *(osimoturismo.it)* is in Via Fonte Magna, near the Roman walls.

Take Via C Colombo/SP361, following signs to Macerata. The Castello di Montefiore, with ample parking, is just before town.

Above Piazza Mazzini, Macerata, home of the weekly market

4 Montefano
Macerata, Le Marche; 62010

The imposing tower of the **Castello di Montefiore** is visible long before reaching Montefano. Little remains of the original polygonal castle built in the 14th century, except some of the walls and the keep. The tower withstood the artillery onslaught of six centuries of wars, but was damaged in World War II. Now restored, it is used as a summer concert venue and can be explored. Nearby Montefano is a pretty little town very typical of this part of Le Marche.

🚗 *Take SP361 to Montecassiano. Turn right onto ring road, Viale Giovanni XXIII. Park near one of the town gates.*

Rosso Conero
Red wines from the Monte Conero region have been highly regarded in Italy since ancient times; illustrious Roman authors Pliny the Elder (23–79 CE) and his nephew Pliny the Younger (61–112 CE) both praised the wines of this area to the south of Ancona. Today's "Rosso Conero" wines are strong, full-bodied reds. The main grape is Montepulciano, to which a small percentage of Sangiovese can be added. This inexpensive, readily available wine benefits from ageing.

5 Montecassiano
Macerata, Le Marche; 62010

With medieval walls and three robust gateways, Montecassiano is a set-piece historic village. The swallow-tail battlements of the **Palazzo dei Priori**, the loggia below, and the spire of the **Collegiata di Santa Maria Assunta** *(open daily)* behind the archway, make the main square, **Piazza Leopardi**, look like it should be the setting for an opera. During festivals held here in October, they make *sughitti*, a sweet polenta cake made from wine *mosto* (must), maize flour and local walnuts.

🚗 *Continue on SP361. At a major junction, there's a sharp left on to SP77, past Roman ruins at Helvia Recina. Stay onto SP77 to Villa Potenza, then SP37 to Macerata. Park in Piazza Mazzini (except Wed market day).*

6 Macerata
Macerata, Le Marche; 62100

When the Visigoths destroyed the Roman town of Helvia Recina in 408 CE, the people moved to the hill above. By the 12th century, Macerata had established itself and eventually became the provincial capital. Famous today for open-air opera at the **Sferisterio**, the town has a lively historic centre. Along Corso Matteotti, there are a number of Renaissance palazzos, the most striking being the **Palazzo dei Diamanti**. The street leads into the architecturally jumbled Piazza della Libertà. Its jewel is the small but perfectly formed **Loggia dei Mercanti** (1505), a fine example of Renaissance harmony. The tenor Beniamino Gigli (1890–1957) once serenaded the town from the loggia's balcony after a performance at the Sferisterio in 1930.

🚗 *From the parking on Piazza Mazzini, turn right on Sferisterio and take Corso Carioli south from roundabout. Then turn right around the city walls towards Via Roma/SP77 and continue on SP77. At Sforzacosta, follow brown signs to abbey on SP78; ample parking.*

EAT AND DRINK

LORETO
Ristorante Andreina *expensive*
At chef Errico Recanati's Michelin-starred restaurant, enjoy great pasta dishes such as *tagliolini al tartufo* (truffles) and *tagliatelle alla lepre* (hare). *Via Brodolini Industrial Area 2, 60025; ristoranteandreina.it; closed Tue & Wed lunch*

SIROLO
Trattoria Osteria Sara *moderate*
A small, characterful *osteria* in the centre of town, where the fish is fresh and cooked simply. Try *risotto di mare* or homemade tagliatelle with white fish. *Via Italia 9, 60020; osteriasara.com; closed Wed*

OSIMO
Mezzobaiocco *moderate*
An old farmhouse serving traditional and creative dishes, including gnocchi with herbs, tagliolini with fish ragù and some great seafood specialities. *Via Saragat 3, 60027 Campocavallo di Osimo; mezzobaiocco.it*

MONTECASSIANO
Nuovo Bar Centrale *inexpensive*
Underneath the loggia of the Palazzo dei Priori, this is a good place for a restorative drink or snack. *Piazza Unità d' Italia 16, 62010; 0733 290 479*

MACERATA
La Volpe e L'uva *moderate*
Enjoy good wine and top cuisine such as *quagliette con pancetta e salvia arrosto* (quails roasted with bacon and sage). *Via Berardi 39; volpeeuva.it; closed Sun*

Below left Passageway in the catacombs beneath Osimo *Below* Porta Amando Diaz on the west side of Montecassiano

Above The cloisters at the Cistercian Abbadia di Fiastra **Above centre** The wooded nature reserve of the abbey **Far right** Façade of the Collegiata della SS Annunziata, San Ginesio

WHERE TO STAY

URBISAGLIA

Locanda Le Logge *inexpensive*
Very chic, small B&B with three nice rooms and a restaurant – book ahead.
*Corso Gianelli 34, 62010;
locandalelogge.it*

AROUND SAN GINESIO

Il Casolare *inexpensive*
Views of the Monti Sibillini and food fresh from its own farm make this a traditional and enjoyable experience.
*Contrada Vallimestre 44, 62026
San Ginesio (on SP45 west of town);
0733 656 688*

MONTEMONACO

Hotel Monti Azzurri *inexpensive*
Set in the centre of town, this hotel makes a good base for touring and has comfortable rooms and home cooking.
*Via Roma 18, 63048;
hotelmontiazzurri.com*

7 Abbadia di Fiastra
Macerata, Le Marche; 62029

A Cistercian abbey, Fiastra has an extreme simplicity and a distinct lack of adornment that seems to add to its calming and spiritual atmosphere. The original population of monks came here from Milan in the 12th century and used the nearby Roman ruins for much of their building material. The beautiful and impressive Romanesque church, monastery and exquisite cloister now form a lively cultural centre in a large, thickly wooded **nature reserve** *(abbadiafiastra.net)*. This park is known as "La Selva" and is ideal for walking and activities such as bird-watching.

🚗 *Take SP78 south from the abbey, ignore a signed right turn to Urbisaglia. The ruins of Urbs Salvia appear on the left of the car park. To get to Urbisaglia, return to the signed turn off, turn left and follow the road uphill to the town.*

Below The small hill town of Montefortino, dating back to Roman times

8 Urbisaglia
Macerata, Le Marche; 62010

The scattered remains of **Urbs Salvia** *(open Jun–Sep: daily, Oct–May: weekends only)* indicate that this ancient town occupied a significant position in the Roman Empire. The road runs right past the Archaeological Park and its well-preserved town walls, amphitheatre, sanctuary complex and fresco-covered cryptoportico (underground passageway).

Urbisaglia, on the hillside above, emerged in the Middle Ages. The town has a typical medieval layout and its impressive, squat-bastioned 16th-century **Rocca** stands in architectural contrast with the more delicate Baroque **Chiesa di San Lorenzo** just next door.

🚗 *Return to SP78 south, turning right uphill to San Ginesio, as signed. There is plenty of parking available in town.*

9 San Ginesio
Macerata, Le Marche; 62026

At 700 m (2,300 ft) above sea level, San Ginesio nestles into the foothills of the Monti Sibillini. Entrance to the town is through the **Porta Picena**. To the right is the loggia of the **Ospedale dei Pellegrini**, established in 1295. To the left is a large church, **Santa Maria in Vepretis** *(closed)*, and the small park nearby has a sensational view towards the south. In the town's central square, Piazza A Gentili, the **Collegiata della SS Annunziata** *(open daily)* has a lovely ornate terracotta façade. The public gardens also have wonderful views to the mountains.

🚗 *Return to SP78 and carry on to Sarnano. Park near main square.*

Cistercian Architecture

The Cistercians were a monastic order that evolved in France in the 12th century. They believed that people of faith should live simple lives of hard work and prayer, and saw decoration as a diversion from spiritual matters. As a result, they built large, plain and elegant buildings. The Cistercians were great conservationists who built in remote locations, and after the drastic deforestation of the 10th and 11th centuries, developed systems of managed agronomy.

⑩ Sarnano
Macerata, Le Marche; 62028
Built almost entirely from brick, Sarnano still retains its medieval streetscape and ambience. From Piazza Alta, at the top of the town, the view of the terracotta roof tiles and the valley spread out below is enchanting. The square, eerily quiet for Italy, is sometimes called "the silent square" as there are no bars or restaurants. The town's main public buildings, the **Palazzo del Popolo**, the **Palazzo dei Priori**, the **Palazzo dei Podestà** and the **Chiesa di Santa Maria Assunta** *(open daily)*, all date from the late 13th century. The tiny ski resort of **Sassotetto** *(sarnanoneve.it)* is a 20-minute drive away, offering alpine and cross-country skiing.

🚗 *Continue south on SP78 through Amándola, turning right onto SP83 to Montefortino. Park just outside town.*

Below View from San Ginesio, in the foothills of the Monti Sibillini

⑪ Montefortino
Ascoli Piceno, Le Marche; 63044
Dating back to the Roman era, this town gave its name to a type of helmet worn by the Roman legions. **Porta Santa Lucia** is the main entrance to the narrow streets of the town. **Palazzo Leopardi** *(closed for renovation)* is a small museum known as the Little Louvre of the Sibillini. It contains a fine collection of Renaissance art, including works by Perugino, Carracci and others.

🚗 *Return to SP83, heading south to Montemonaco. Turn right at the sign for the town and park in Piazza Roma.*

⑫ Montemonaco
Ascoli Piceno, Le Marche; 63048
At 1,080 m (3,540 ft), Montemonaco has clear, sharp air, fantastic views and even a few medieval corners to explore. To the east, the view extends across a large swathe of Le Marche to the Adriatic. Walk uphill along Via Italia, and past the small 13th-century Palazzo Comunale. Continue to the **Chiesa di San Benedetto** *(open daily)*, which holds a relic of the right arm of San Bendetto encased in silver and a polychrome wooden crucifix from the late 15th century. Walk along the path to the **Parco Monteguarnieri** for breathtaking mountain views.

🚗 *Retrace route on SP83 and follow signs to Ascoli Piceno, turning right onto SP74, left onto SP86, then right onto SP237 to the Via Salaria SS4. Exit to Ascoli Piceno and follow signs to "Centro". Turn right at Via Adriatica and sharp left at Via Porta Torricella for car park.*

Above left Montefortino, set among towering peaks **Above** Brick-built Sarnano, a good base for exploring the Sibillini Mountains

EAT AND DRINK

URBISAGLIA
Locanda Le Logge *inexpensive*
This restaurant is highly regarded by the locals and offers a fixed-price gourmet menu of Marchegiana specialities. Booking advised.
Corso Gianelli 34, 62010; locandalelogge.it

SAN GINESIO
Terra Nostra *moderate*
Homemade pasta and desserts make this cosy central restaurant a good choice for local specialities such as wild boar and porcini. The menu also features Argentinian dishes.
Piazza Gentili 3, 62026; terranostrasanginesio.it

MONTEMONACO
Bottega della Cuccagna *inexpensive*
This place offers a mouthwatering selection of cheeses, salamis, wines and other local delicacies. Just buy a picnic lunch to eat outside. The adventurous might want to stay at their refuge on the mountainside.
Piazza Roma, 63088; bottega dellacuccagna.it; closed Wed

Above The medieval festival of Quintana, held in Ascoli Piceno's Piazza del Popolo in August

WHERE TO STAY

ASCOLI PICENO

Palazzo Guiderocchi *moderate*
This central, venerable building offers elegant rooms, Wi-Fi and a restaurant The annexe also has good-value rooms.
Via Cesare Battisti 3, 63100; hotelguiderocchi.it

RIPATRANSONE

Domus Petrae – Villa Tipaldi *inexpensive*
A modern villa turned into a B&B. Spacious rooms and a great breakfast.
Contrada Magazzini 11, 63065; domuspetrae.it

GROTTAMMARE

La Torretta sul Borgo *inexpensive*
This friendly B&B in the old part of town is a modern amenity with a historic feel.
Via Camilla Peretti 2, 63066; latorrettasulborgo.it

Above Ripatransone, viewed through a Gothic gateway into town

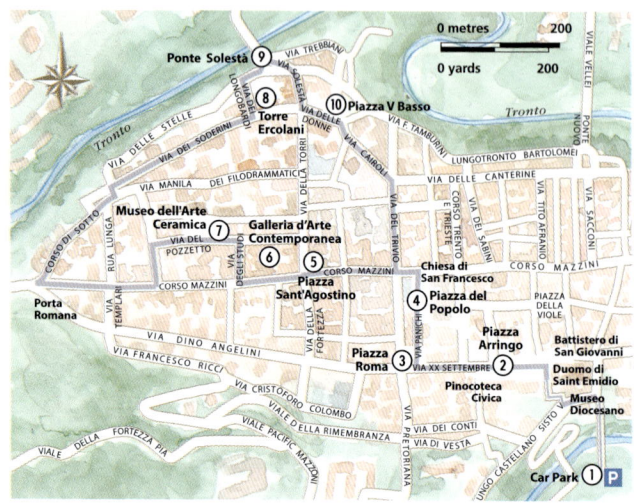

⑬ ASCOLI PICENO
Le Marche 63100

Originally a defensive site at the confluence of two rivers, Ascoli grew to prominence in the Middle Ages. Although it is often said to have the most beautiful piazza in Italy, what gives Ascoli its elegant charm is the fact that virtually every building is made of travertine marble.

A three-hour walking tour

From the **car park** ①, walk across the wooden bridge and take the lift to the city level. To the left there is a narrow lane into **Piazza Arringo** ②, the scene of many political speeches. At the eastern end is the Duomo di Saint Emidio *(open daily)*, home to a polyptych by the 15th-century artist Carlo Crivelli. Beside the Duomo stands the Battistero di San Giovanni *(open daily)*. Built in the 12th century, over a Roman temple, this beautiful building has a square base and an octagonal upper storey. The Palazzo Vescovile on the other side of the Duomo houses the Museo Diocesano *(open Tue–Sun)* with a fine collection of religious art. In the Palazzo Comunale is the Pinocoteca Civica with 15th- and 16th-century works by artists such as Crivelli, Titian, Reni, Guercino and other masters.

Exit the piazza by Via XX Settembre to **Piazza Roma** ③, a formal square with palms and an imposing bronze statue commemorating the city's war-dead. Turn right and cross the square to either Via Panichi or Via Macello. Both lead to **Piazza del Popolo** ④, hailed by many as the most beautiful piazza in Italy. One side is lined by Caffè Meletti, an elegant Liberty-style bar, and the other by a fine arcade topped by swallow-tailed battlements. Also on the square is the Gothic Chiesa di San Francesco, notable for its ribbed vaulting, a statue of Pope Julius II over the door and the Loggia dei Mercanti, a 15th-century addition. Also of interest is the 13th-century Palazzo dei Capitani, whose central clock tower and façade are decorated with reliefs and statues.

Head west along Corso Mazzini to **Piazza Sant'Agostino** ⑤ and its 13th-century Romanesque church. Across the square, Palazzo Merli's twin towers recall a time when Ascoli bristled with over 100 of them. Continue along Corso Mazzini. At the back of Sant'Agostino, the cloisters of the old convent house, the **Galleria D'Arte Contemporanea** ⑥, has a large collection of modern Italian art. Turn right from the gallery, then left into Corso Mazzini to Piazza San Tomaso and the **Museo dell'Arte Ceramica** ⑦. Cross the square to Via del Pozzetto, turn left (back to Corso Mazzini) and finish at the 1st-century Porta Romana. Turn right into Corso di Sotto, which leads into Via dei

Soderini. This part of town has a medieval feel. Continue to Via dei Lombardi and one of Ascoli's oldest towers, **Torre Ercolani** ⑧. The road leads to Via delle Stelle, along the city walls above the River Tronto. A bit further on is one of the ancient bridges into Ascoli, **Ponte Solestà** ⑨ built in the 1st century. The gateway and towers were built in the 13th century. Turning away from the river, walk up Via Solestà, then left into Via delle Donne, which opens into **Piazza V Basso** ⑩. Here, the Romanesque Chiesa dei SS Vincenzo e Anastasio has a façade divided into sections that once held frescoes of biblical scenes – it was called "La Bibbia dei Poveri" (the Bible of the Poor). Continue along Via Cairoli and turn right into Via del Trivio. On the right and behind San Francesco is the old cloister, now used for markets and performances. Turn right into Corso Mazzini and retrace steps back to the car park.

🚗 *Viale Indipendenza is the main road east, becoming SP235 to the coast. Turn left to Offida on SP43. Park in square.*

⑭ Offida
Ascoli Piceno, Le Marche; 63035
On the approach to Offida, the **Chiesa di Santa Maria della Rocca** appears as though floating on the cliff face. The church has an impressive Romanesque façade. The **crypt** *(open daily)* runs the full length of the church and contains 14th-century frescoes attributed to the Maestro di Offida. The centre of town is Piazza Vittorio Emmanuele II, given an elegant air by the arcades of 14th-century **Palazzo Comunale**, a handsome building with a clock tower.

🚗 *Head east on SP1, follow signs for Acquaviva Picena. Park near town walls.*

⑮ Acquaviva Picena
Ascoli Piceno, Le Marche; 63030
The medieval fortress that still forms the heart of this town dominates the hillside to the west. Known as La Rocca, it houses an ancient weapons museum – the **Museo delle Armi Antiche** *(open daily)*. The walk through its corridors and the views are worth the price of entry.

🚗 *Return along SP1 north, then turn right onto SP32. Park in town.*

⑯ Ripatransone
Ascoli Piceno, Le Marche; 63038
On the highest point between the sea and the mountains, Ripatransone had an advantage over its rivals. This generated the wealth that built the **Palazzo del Podestà** (1304) and the **Palazzo Comunale**, which holds documents in its archive dating back to 1216. Both buildings are in the main square, Piazza XX Settembre, known as the Belvedere del Piceno because of its excellent views in all directions.

🚗 *Take SP23 to Grottammare. At the fourth hairpin bend, turn left into Via Cagliata. Park on the edge of town.*

⑰ Grottammare
Ascoli Piceno, Le Marche; 63013
Originally built as a defensive bastion against raids from the sea, this tiny medieval fortress town now keeps watch over the beach below. The town has two churches, a ruined fort with curvy corbels and an excellent vantage point over the coast below. The **Chiesa di Santa Lucia** *(open daily)* is at the northernmost tip of the old town. The Chiesa di San Giovanni Battista now houses the **Museo Sistino di Grottammare** *(open summer: daily)*.

Above The tiled roof of the Chiesa di Santa Lucia, Grottammare, looking out to sea

EAT AND DRINK

ASCOLI PICENO

Migliori Olive Ascolane *inexpensive*
A lively venue on Piazza Arringo serving local delicacies, including *olive Ascolane* – olives stuffed with meat, coated in breadcrumbs and fried – as a takeaway snack.
Piazza Arringo 2, 63100; miglioriolive.it

Café Lorenz *moderate*
Right in the heart of the city, this café is known for its olive ascolane, artisanal beers and wood oven-baked pizzas.
Piazza del Popolo 5, 63100; lorenzcafe.it

GROTTAMMARE

Osteria dell'Arancio *moderate*
This well-regarded restaurant caters for discerning diners with good fish and meat dishes and excellent wines.
Piazza Peretti 4/5, 63066; 0735 632 214; open eves only; closed Wed

---

DAY TRIP OPTIONS
There are three distinct sections to this drive: the lowlands, the mountains and the coast.

The lowlands around Loreto
From Renaissance Loreto ①, it is a short drive for history buffs to Osimo ③ with its Roman fountain and walls and labyrinth of catacombs. A visit to the tower of Montefano ④ will intrigue budding military historians.

Take SP16 to Osimo, then SP361 to Montefano. SP82, then SP77 to Loreto.

Parco Nazionale dei Monti Sibillini
San Ginesio ⑨ is a good base from which to explore the national park. Drive to Sarnano ⑩ to visit the ski resort Sassotetto, either for skiing in winter or walking in summer. Head on to Montefortino ⑪ for Renaissance art, then on to Montemonaco ⑫ for a short climb and great views.

Follow the drive's instructions.

Ascoli Piceno to the sea
Spend the morning touring Ascoli Piceno ⑬, pick up some food and follow the drive to Ripatransone ⑯ – stopping for a scenic picnic along the way. Head on to Grottammare ⑰ for some time on the beach.

Follow the drive's instructions, missing out Acquaviva Picena. Return via A14 and RA11, if pressed for time.

INDEX

Page numbers in **bold** refer to main entries.

A
Abbeys
  Abbadia di Fiastra **252**
  Abbadia San Salvatore **194**
  Abbazia di Novacella (Neustift) **92**, 93
  Abbazia di Pomposa **136–7**
  Abbazia di Praglia **119**
  Abbazia di San Cassiano (Narni) 222
  Abbazia di San Fruttuoso 152
  Abbazia di San Pietro in Valle 214, **215**
  Abbazia di Sant'Andrea di Borzone 155
  Abbazia di Vallombrosa **164–5**
  Monte Oliveto Maggiore (Siena) **185**
  San Galgano Abbey **187**
Acceglio **46**
Accidents 19
Accommodation **22–3**
Acquaviva Picena **255**
Agriturismi 22, 23
Air travel 10
Alba **42**, 43
Alpe di Siusi (Seiser Alm) 102, **103**
Alto Adige **86–95**
Andersen, Hans Christian 155
Anghiari **169**
Aosta 34, **35**
Apennines **226–35**
  Ligurian 150, 153–5, 159
Aquileia **112**, 113
Arabba 102
Arcevia **234**
Arcidosso **192–3**
Arco 74, **75**
Arcumeggia **55**
Arezzo 204, **205**
Argenta **138**, 139
Arno, River 166, 172, 174
Arquà Petrarca 118, **119**
Arrone 214, **215**
Ascoli Piceno **254–5**
Asolo 128, **129**
Assisi 210, **211**

B
B&Bs 22, 23
Bacchelli, Riccardo 135
Bagni San Filippo 194, **195**
Bai de Dones 126
Ballooning 203
Banks 14
Barbaresco **42**, 43
Bardolino **83**
Barolo 42, **43**
Bars 25
Basilica *see* Churches and cathedrals
Bassano del Grappa **128–9**
Bellagio 60, **61**
Belluno **128**, 129
Berceto **145**
Bergamo **68–9**
Bevagna **212**, 213
Biella **34**, 35
Bolzano (Bozen) **100–101**
Bonassola **156**
Borro **174**, 175
Borromean Islands (Maggiore) **53**, 55
Borzonasca 154, **155**
Bra **43**
Breakdowns 19

Breaks, taking 19
Brenta Canal 120
Brescia 70, **71**
Bressanone (Brixen) **92–3**
Brunate **63**
Brunico (Bruneck) **95**
Buonconvento **186**
Burri, Alberto 230
Byron, Lord 147

C
Cafés 25
Cagli **232**
Camáldoli **167**
Camogli **152**, 153
Campello sul Clitunno **213**
Camping 23
Cannobio **54**, 55
Cantina Comunale di La Morra 43
Caprese Michelangelo 168, **169**
Caravans 21
Car hire 20
Carpegna **242**
Carsulae **222–3**
Casa Cavassa (Saluzzo) 45
Casa dei Nani (Orta San Giulio) 52
Casa del Fascio (Como) 60
Casa del Mantegna (Mantova) 85
Casa di Colombo (Genoa) 144
Casa di Petrarca (Arquà Petrarca) 119
Casa di Tiziano (Pieve di Cadore) 127
Casalzuigno **55**
Casa Natale di Raffaello (Urbino) 243
Casa Romei (Ferrara) 134
Cascate delle Marmore **221**
Casentino Forest **167**
Castel del Piano **192**, 193
Castel di Mezzo **244**, 245
Castelfiorentino **182**, 183
Castellina in Chianti 174, **175**
Castello di Brolio **176**
Castelmuzio **203**
Castiglione d'Orcia **192**, 193, 195
Castiglion Fiorentino 204, **205**
Castles and fortifications
  Castelli di Jesi **234**
  Castello di Duino 112
  Castello di Mesola **136**, 137
  Castello di Rivoli **37**
  Castello di Romena **166**
  Castello di Spessa 111
  Castello di Torrechiara **145**
  Castel Roncolo (Schloss Runkelstein) **101**
  Castel (Schloss) Prösels 103
  Castel Tirolo (Schloss Tirol) **91**
  Castiglia (Saluzzo) 45
  First and Second Towers (San Marino) 240–41
  Fortezza Medicea (Volterra) 183
  Monteleone d'Orvieto **200**, 201
  Rocca Albornoziana (Spoleto) 214
  Tower of Frederick (San Miniato) 182
  Trauttmansdorff castle (Merano) 90
  Tre Sassi Fort **102**
Cattedrale *see* Churches and cathedrals
Cavour, Count Camillo 42–3
Cetona 200, **201**
Chianti Hills **170–77**
Children, travelling with 17
Chiusdino **187**

Churches and cathedrals
  Basilica della Santa Casa (Loreto) 250
  Basilica di San Francesco (Arezzo) 205
  Basilica di San Francesco (Assisi) 211
  Basilica di Santa Chiara (Assisi) 211
  Basilica di San Vitale (Ravenna) 139
  Basilica di Superga (Turin) 33
  Capella degli Scrovegni (Padua) 119
  Cattedrale (Asolo) 129
  Cattedrale dell'Assunta (Orvieto) 200
  Cattedrale di San Leopardo (Osimo) 250
  Cattedrale di San Lorenzo (Alba) 42
  Cattedrale di San Lorenzo (Genoa) 144, 147
  Cattedrale di San Lorenzo (Perugia) 210
  Cattedrale di San Rufino (Assisi) 211
  Cattedrale di San Settimio (Jesi) 235
  Cattedrale di San Venanzio (Fabriano) 233
  Cattedrale di SS Gervasio e Protasio (Città della Pieve) 201
  Cattedrale di Urbino 243
  Cattedrale Maria Vergine Assunta (Saluzzo) 44
  Cattedrale San Giusto (Susa) 37
  Cattedrale San Giusto (Trieste) 113
  Cattedrale di Santa Maria Assunta (Fano) 245
  Chiesa del Gesù (Genoa) 144, 147
  Chiesa di San Lorenzo (Turin) 33
  Chiesa di Santo Spirito (Gorizia) 111
  Chiesa di Santo Stefano (Ferentillo) **215**
  Chiesa di SS Ippolito e Biagio (Castelfiorentino) 182
  Chiesa di SS Pietro e Andrea (Trequanda) 203
  Church of Saints Cosma and Damian (Carsulae) 223
  Church of San Francesco (Gargnano) 76
  Dom (Bressanone) 92
  Duomo (Belluno) 128
  Duomo (Bolzano) 100
  Duomo (Como) 60
  Duomo di San Moderanno (Berceto) 145
  Duomo di San Romulo di Fiesole 164
  Duomo di Santa Maria Annunziata (Todi) 225
  Duomo di Santa Maria Assunta (Cividale del Friuli) 110
  Duomo di Sant'Andrea Apostolo (Venzone) 109
  Duomo di Sant Emidio (Ascoli Piceno) 254
  Duomo di Spoleto 214
  Duomo (Mantova) 85
  Duomo (Montagnana) 118
  Duomo (Montepulciano) 202
  Duomo (Padova) 119
  Duomo (Parma) 146
  Duomo (Reggio Emilia) 146
  Duomo (Salò) 82
  Duomo San Emiliano (Trevi) 213
  Duomo (San Miniato) 182
  Duomo (Udine) 109
  Duomo (Volterra) 183
  La Pieve delle Sante Flora e Lucilla (Santa Fiora) 193
  La Pieve di Lamula 192
  Pieve di San Pietro di Romena 166
  Pieve di Santa Maria Assunta (Stia) 167
  Santi Antonio e Jacopo (Fontanigorda) 155

Churches and cathedrals *continued*
  Santi Pietro e Paolo (Sampeyre) 45
  Santuario della del Ghisallo (Bellagio) 63
  Santuario della Madonna delle Grazie (near Arcidosso) 192
  Santuario della Madonna di Montecastello (Tignale) **76**
  Santuario della Santissima Pietà (Cannobio) 54
  Santuario di Montallegro (Rapallo) 153
  Santuario di Montenero (Riomaggiore) 159
  Santuario Monte Lussari (Valbruna) 108
  Tempietto del Clitunno 213
  see also Monasteries and convents; Sacri Monti
Cima Grappa 128
Cinque Terre 147, **156–9**
Cinque Torri **126–7**
Cistercian architecture **253**
Città della Pieve 200, **201**
Città di Castello **230**, 231
Cividale del Friuli **110**, 111
Climate 9
Clusone 68, **69**
Cogne 34, **35**
Col du Mont Cenis **36**
Colle di Val d'Elsa **184**
Colli Orientali **110**, 111
Colma 63
Colpetrazzo **224**
Columbus, Christopher 144
Comacchio 136, **137**, 138
Como **60**, 61
Congestion charges 20
Corchia 147
Cormòns **110**, 111
Corniglia 156, **157**
Cortina d'Ampezzo **126**, 127
Cortona **204–5**
Corvara 102, **103**
Courmayeur **36**
COVID-19 13, 15
Cristo degli Abissi 152
Cuneo 46, **47**
Cupramontana **234–5**
Cycling
  Po Delta 135
  Val di Merse 186

D
D'Annunzio, Gabriele 82
Dante Alighieri 139, 166, 244, **245**
Della Robbia, Luca and Andrea **168**, 195
Dolomites 86–103, 122–9
Domodossola 53
Dronero **46**
Duino **112**, 113
Duomo *see* Churches and cathedrals

E
Eagle of Todi **225**
Electricity 15
Elva **45**
Emilia-Romagna 130–39, 145–6, 238–42
Erbusco 70, **71**
Este **118**
Etruscans 200, 201, 203, 204, 205, 210
Euganean Hills **118**, 119, 121
Exilles **36–7**

F
Fabriano **233**
Fano 244, **245**
Fegina 157
Feltre **128**, 129
Fénis **34–5**
Ferentillo 214, **215**
Ferrara **134–5**
Festivals 11
  Festival of the Ceri (Gubbio) **231**
  Palio (Siena) **185**
Ficulle **200**, 201
Fiesole **164**, 165
Fines 17
Fiorenzuola di Focara **245**
Fontanigorda 154, **155**
Food and drink
  Barolo wine 43
  Bergamo's polenta 69
  birra Amiata 193
  Collio: Strada del Vino **110–111**
  Franciacorta wine 71
  Gallo Nero wine **177**
  La Manifattura dei Marinati (Comacchio) 137
  mountain chestnuts **186**
  Pecorino di Pienza 203
  piadina 243
  Piedmontese 34
  Rosso Conero **251**
  Sienese panforte **185**
  Slow Food **42**
  Strada del Vino (Alto Adige) **101**
  Tuscan 175, 176, 177
  Tyrolean 93, 95
Franciacorta **71**
Francis of Assisi, St 168, **211**, 212, 213, 215
Friuli-Venezia Giulia 104–113

G
Gargnano **76–7**
Genga 233
Genoa (Genova) **144–5**, 147
Geoparc Bletterbach 100, **101**
Giotto 119
Gorizia **111**
Government advice 12
Gradara **244**, 245
Grancia di Cuna **186**, 187
Grand Canal (Venice) 120, 121
Greve in Chianti **174**, 175
Grinzane Cavour **42–3**
Grottammare 254, **255**
Grotte di Frasassi **233**
Grotto of St Francis (Eremo delle Carceri) 212
Gubbio **230–31**

H
Hannibal 36
Health 12–13
Hermitage of Montesiepi 187
Hofer, Andreas **91**
Holy Mount of San Vivaldo **182**

I
Il Bosco della Mesola **136**, 137
Il Campo (Siena) **185**
Il Vittoriale degli Italiani (Gardone) **82**
Insurance 12, 16
Iseo **70**, 71
Isola Bella (Maggiore) 53
Isola dei Pescatori (Maggiore) 53
Isola di San Giulio (Orta) 52
Isola Madre (Maggiore) 53
Issogne **34**

J
Jesi 234, **235**
Juliet's House (Verona) 118

K
Kreuzgang (Bressanone) 92

L
Labro **221**
Ladin language **103**
Lagazuoi (Lagació) **102**
Laghi di Fusine **108**
Lago della Rovina **47**
Lago di Brugneto **154**
Lago di Como **56–63**
Lago di Corbara **225**
Lago di Garda **72–83**
Lago d'Iseo **70–71**
Lago d'Orta **52–3**
Lago Maggiore **48–55**
Lago Maggiore Express **53**, 55
La Morra 42, **43**
Langhirano **145**
Language 15
La Spezia 146, **147**
La Thuile 36
La Verna **168**, 169
Lawrence, D H 77
Lazise **83**
Lazzaretti, David **193**
Le Marche 228–9, 232–5, 242–5, **246–55**
Leonardo da Vinci 172, 174
Leonessa **220**, 221
Levanto **156**, 157
Lewis, C S 223
Liguria 140–45, 147, 148–59
Lippi, Filippino 168
Lippi, Fra Filippo 214
Locarno 53
Lombardy 55, 56–71, 75–7, 82–5
Loreto **250**, 251
Loro Ciuffenna 174
Lucignano 202, **203**

M
Macerata 250, **251**
Malborghetto **108–9**
Manarola **158**, 159
Mantegna, Andrea 84–5
Mantua (Mantova) **84–5**
Maps 21
Massa Martana **224**
Menaggio 60, **61**
Merano (Meran) **90**, 91
Messner, Reinhold **95**
Michelangelo Buonarroti 162, 169, 185
Mobile phones 14
Mole Antonelliana (Turin) 32
Monasteries and convents
  Eremo delle Carceri (Assisi) **212**
  Eremo di Camáldoli 167
  Eremo di Fonte Avellana **232**
  Holy Mount of San Vivaldo **182**
  Monastery of Camáldoli 167
  Santuario della Verna **168**, 169

Money 14
Montagnana **118**, 119
Monte Amiata **188–95**
Monte Bianco 36
Montecassiano **251**
Montefano **251**
Montefeltro Mountains **236–45**
Montefortino **253**
Monte Grappa **128**, 129
Monte Isola (Iseo) **70**
Montelaterone **192**
Montemonaco 252, **253**
Monte Oliveto Maggiore (Siena) **185**
Montepulciano **202**, 203
Monteriggioni **184**, 185
Monterosso al Mare **156–7**
Montisi 202, **203**
Monti Sibillini 252–3, 255
Motorbikes and scooters 20–21
Motorhomes 21
Mountain roads 18–19
Museums and galleries
 Chianti Sculpture Park (Pievasciata) **176**, 177
 Civici Musei di Udine (Udine) 109
 Galleria d'Arte Contemporanea (Ascoli Piceno) 254
 Galleria dell'Accademia (Venice) 121
 Galleria Nazionale delle Marche (Urbino) 243
 Galleria Nazionale dell'Umbria (Perugia) 210
 MMM Ripa at Brunico **95**
 Musei Civici (Reggio Emilia) 146
 Musei Provinciali (Gorizia) 111
 Museo Alpino Duca degli Abruzzi (Courmayeur) 36
 Museo Amedeo Lia (La Spezia) 147
 Museo Archeologico (Bolzano) 100
 Museo Archeologico del Chianti (Castellina in Chianti) 175
 Museo Archeologico Nazionale (Aquileia) 112
 Museo Archeologico Nazionale (Cividale del Friuli) 110
 Museo Archeologico Nazionale (Parma) 146
 Museo Civico Archeologico (Sarteano) 201
 Museo Civico Archeologico (Verucchio) 240
 Museo Civico (Bassano del Grappa) 129
 Museo Civico (Belluno) 128
 Museo Civico (Cuneo) 47
 Museo Civico d'Arte Antica (Turin) 33
 Museo Civico e Gipsoteca (Savigliano) 44
 Museo Civico (Lucignano) 203
 Museo Civico Luigi Mallé (Dronero) 46
 Museo Civiltà dell'Ulivo (Trevi) 213
 Museo Comunale di Bevagna 212
 Museo d'Arte Contemporanea (Castello di Rivoli) 37
 Museo d'Arte Sacra (Buonconvento) 186
 Museo del Giocattolo (Bra) 43
 Museo della Carta (Fabriano) 233
 Museo della Farmacia (Bressanone) 93
 Museo della Mezzadria Senese (Buonconvento) 186
 Museo dell'Arte Ceramica (Ascoli Piceno) 254
 Museo delle Armi Antiche (Acquaviva Picena) 255
 Museo delle Mummie (Ferentillo) 215
 Museo delle Valli (Argenta) 138
 Museo del Merletto (Rapallo) 153
 Museo del Parco (Portofino) 153

Museums and galleries *continued*
 Museo del Prosciutto (Langhirano) 145
 Museo del Settecento Veneziano (Venice) 121
 Museo del Sigillo (La Spezia) 147
 Museo del Tesoro (Aosta) 35
 Museo del Vino (Bardolino) 83
 Museo Diocesano (Gubbio) 230–31
 Museo Diocesano (Jesi) 235
 Museo Diocesano (Udine) 109
 Museo di Santa Giulia (Brescia) 71
 Museo di Sant'Agostino (Genoa) 144
 Museo di Storia, Arte e Ammobiliamento (Turin) 32
 Museo Egizio (Turin) 33
 Museo Etnográfico (Malborghetto) 109
 Museo Etnográfico (Sampeyre) 45
 Museo Etrusco Guarnacci (Volterra) 183
 Museo Gaffoglio (Rapallo) 153
 Museo Glauco Lombardi (Parma) 146
 Museo Marinaro (Camogli) 152
 Museo Nazionale Atestino (Este) 118
 Museo Nazionale del Cinema (Turin) 32
 Museo Nazionale della Rocca (Gradara) 244
 Museo Nazionale di Ravenna 139
 Museo Sistino di Grottammare 255
 Museo Storia Naturale (Verona) 118
 Museo Tecnico Navale (La Spezia) 147
 MuseumPasseier (Val Passiria) **91**
 Parco Museo Minerario (Abbadia San Salvatore) 194
 Peggy Guggenheim Collection (Venice) 121
 Pinacoteca Comunale (Jesi) 235
 Pinacoteca and Museo Civico (Volterra) 183
 Ratti abbey and wine museum (Annunziata) 43
 Sciacchetrà Museum (Manarola) 158
 Torrione (Cagli) 232
 Victor Salvi Harp Museum (Piasco) 45
 WiMu (Barolo) **43**
 Wine Label Museum (Cupramontana) 235
Mussolini, Benito 77, 82, 83

N
Napoleon 36
Narni **222**, 223
National parks
 Parco Nazionale dei Monti Sibillini 255
 Parco Nazionale del Gran Paradiso 29, 35
 Parco Nazionale delle Cinque Terre 156
 Parco Nazionale delle Dolomiti Bellunesi 128
 Parco Nazionale delle Incisoni Rupestri 70
 Parco Nazionale dello Stelvio 90
Nature reserves
 Parco Naturale del Mont Avic 34
 Parco Naturale Fanes-Sennes-Braies 103
 Parco Naturale Monte San Bartolo 244
 Parco Naturale Sasso Simone e Simoncello 242
 Riserva Naturale Ciciu del Villar 46
Nesso 63
Nevegal **127**

O
Offida **255**
Opening hours 14–15
Orta San Giulio **52–3**

Orvieto **200**, 201
Osimo **250**, 251
Ötzi the Ice Man 91, 95, 100
Outdoor activities 215

P
Padua (Padova) 118, **119**
Palaces
 Palazzina di Caccia di Stupinigi (Turin) 32
 Palazzo dei Priori (Perugia) 210
 Palazzo del Bo (Padua) 119
 Palazzo Ducale (Urbino) 243
 Palazzo Feltrinelli (Gargnano) 76
 Palazzo Gemelli (Orta San Giulio) 52
 Palazzo Pergami-Belluzzi (San Marino) 241
 Palazzo Pubblico (Siena) 185
 Palazzo Reale (Turin) 32
 Palazzo Schifanoia (Ferrara) 134
 Palazzo Taffini d'Acceglio (Savigliano) 44
 Palazzo Te (Mantua) 85
 Palazzo Vescovile (Bressanone) 93
 Palzzo Municipale (Ferrara) 135
Palladio, Andrea 120
Paradisino (Vallombrosa) 165
Parking 20
Parks and gardens
 Chianti Sculpture Park (Pievasciata) **176**, 177
 Il Mulino del Po (Ro) **135**
 Parco Archeologico Enrico Fiumi (Volterra) 183
 Parco Arciducale Arboreto (Arco) 75
 Parco Botanico Alpino Valderia 47
 Parco dell'Antola 154
 Parco dell'Aveto **154**
 Parco delle Alpi Marittime 47
 Parco Fluviale del Tevere 225
 Parco Giardino Sigurtà (Valeggio sul Mincio) 84
 Parco Monteguarnieri (Montemonaco) 253
 Parco Museo Minerario (Abbadia San Salvatore) 194
 Villa Taranto (Verbania) 54–5
 see also National parks; Nature reserves
Parma **146**, 147
Passo dell'Erbe (Würzjoch) **94**, 95
Passo di Monte Giovo (Jaufenpass) **92**
Passo Gardena (Grödner Joch) **103**
Passo Pordoi **102**
Passports 12
Pedavena 128
Pennabilli **242**
Pentema **154**
Pergolesi, Giovanni Battista 235
Personal security 13
Perugia **210–211**
Perugino 201, 210
Petrol 18
Pfaundlerhaus (Bressanone) 93
Pharmacies 12
Piancastagnaio **193**
Pian del Tiviano **63**
Pian di Scò 174
Piantravigne 174
Piazza San Marco (Venice) 121
Piazza Vecchia (Bergamo) 68
Piazzetta dei Mondagli (Saluzzo) 45
Picnics 25
Piediluco **221**
Piedmont 32–4, 36–7, 38–47, 52–5
Pienza **202**, 203
Piero della Francesca 205, 243
Pietralunga **223**
Pietrarubbia **242–3**
Pieve di Cadore **127**

INDEX 259

Pieve di Tremosine **75**
Pieve to Tignale Road **76**
Pinturicchio 185, 214
Pius II, Pope 202
Po Delta **130–39**
Ponte Buriano **174**, 175
Ponte degli Alpini (Bassano del Grappa) 128
Ponte del Diavolo (Dronero) 46
Ponte delle Torri (Spoleto) 214
Ponte di Rialto (Venice) 120, 121
Ponte di Rualan 127, 129
Ponte Solestà (Ascoli Piceno) 255
Ponte Visconteo (Valeggio sul Mincio) 84
Poppi **168**, 169
Porta all'Arco (Volterra) 183
Portofino **152–3**
Porto Garibaldi 137
Porto to Pieve: SP38 (Garda) **75**
Portovenere 146, **147**
Postal services 14
Pottery classes 201
Pré-Saint-Didier **36**
Public holidays 9
Punta della Dogana (Venice) 121
Punto Bonfiglio 158
Pyramids of Zone **70**

Q
Quadrilatero (Turin) 33

R
Radda in Chianti 176, **177**
Radicofani 194, **195**
Rail travel 10–11
Rapallo 152, **153**
Raphael 243
Ravenna 138, **139**
Reggio Emilia **146**
Restaurants **24–5**
Rieti **220**, 221
Rimini **240**
Riomaggiore **158–9**
Ripatransone 254, **255**
Risorgimento 83
Riva del Garda **75**
Riva del Vin (Venice) 120
Riviera del Brenta **120**, 121
Road, arriving by 11
Road conditions 18
Road systems 16–17
Romano, Giulio 85
Romans
  Amphitheatre (Aosta) 135
  Carsulae **222–3**
  Casa Romana (Spoleto) 214
  Fano 244, 245
  Rimini 240
  Roman amphitheatre (Susa) 37
  Roman arena (Verona) 118, 121
  Roman theatre (Gubbio) 230
  Teatro Romano (Spoleto) 214
  Teatro Romano (Trieste) 113
  Urbs Salvia (Urbisaglia) 252
  Via Flaminia 223, 225
Rosengarten mountain range 102
Rules of the road 18
RVs 21

S
Sabines 218, 220, 225
Sacri Monti **53**
  Sacro Monte della SS Trinità di Ghiffa **54**
  Sacro Monte di Francesco (Orta) 53
  Sacro Monte di Ossuccio (Como) **60–61**
  Sacro Monte (Varese) 55

Salò **82**, 83
Saluzzo **44–5**
Sampeyre **45**
San Carlone (Arona) **52**
San Casciano dei Bagni 194, **195**
San Fruttuoso **152**
San Gémini **222**, 223
San Gimignano **184**, 185
San Ginesio **252**, 253
San Leo **242**, 243
San Marino, Republic of **240–41**
San Martino della Battaglia 82, **83**
San Miniato **182**, 183
Santa Casa (Loreto) **250**
Santa Fiora 192, **193**
Santarcangelo di Romagna **240**, 241
San Vigilio (Vigiljoch) **90**, 91
San Vito di Cadore **127**
Sarnano **253**
Sarteano **201**
Sassocorvaro **243**
Sassoferrato **232**, 233
Sassotetto 253
Sass Pordoi 102
Sat Nav devices 21
Savigliano **44**
Savonarola, Girolamo 135
Scheggino **214**
Seasons 9
Sea travel 11
Self-catering 23
Sentiero Azzuro (Cinque Terre) 156
Serra de' Conti **234**
Sestri Levante 154, **155**
Shopping
  in Biella 35
  in Torrechiara 145
  Tyrolean food 93
  in the Veneto 128
  in Venice 120
Siena **184–5**
Signorelli, Luca 204
Sirmione 82, **83**
Sirolo **250**, 251
Slow Food movement 40, **42**
Special requirements, travellers with 15
Speed limits 17
Spello **212**, 213
Spoleto **214**, 215
Spontini, Gaspare 235
Stia **166–7**
Stresa 52, **53**
Stroppo **46**, 47
Susa **37**
Synagogue (Ferrara) 134

T
Tarvisio **108**, 109
Teolo 119
Terme di Valdieri **47**
Terme Pré-Saint-Didier 36
Terminillo **220**, 221
Thun, Matteo **90**
Tiber, River 225
Tiepolo, Giambattista 109, 120
Tignale **76**
Time zone 15
Titian 127, 129
Todi **224–5**
Tomb of Dante (Ravenna) 139
Tor Cucherna (Trieste) 113
Törggelen **94**
Torre Apponale (Riva del Garda) 75
Torre Civico (Saluzzo) 45
Torri **186–7**
Torri del Benaco **82–3**
Torriglia 152, **153**

Toscana 160–99, 201–5
Tourist information 14
Traffic restrictions 20
Tree of the Birds (Eremo delle Carceri) 212
Trentino-Alto Adige 75, 86–103
Treponti Bridge (Comacchio) 137
Trequanda **203**
Trevi 212, **213**
Treviso 128, **129**
Trieste **112–13**
Turin 29, **32–3**

U
Udine 108, **109**
Umbria 197–201, 206–225, 228–31
Urbino 242, **243**
Urbisaglia **252**, 253

V
Valassina **63**
Valbruna **108**
Val Camonica **70**
Val Cannobina **54**
Val d'Arno **170–77**
Val di Fassa **102**
Val di Fiemme **101**
Val di Funes (Villnöss) **94**
Val di Merse 186, 187
Val d'Ultimo (Ultental) **90**
Valeggio sul Mincio **84**
Val Gardena (Grödnertal) **103**
Valle d'Aosta 34–6
Valli di Comacchio **138**
Vallombrosa, Abbazia di **164–5**
Val Passiria (Passeiertal) 91, 92
Val San Cassiano 102, **103**
Valsanzibio **119**
Val Senales (Schnalstal) 90, **91**
Varenna **62–3**
Varese 54, **55**
Vecchia Regina: the SP71 (Como) **60**
Veneto 82–4, 102, 114–29
Venice **120–21**
Venzone **109**
Verbania **54–5**
Vernazza **157**
Verona 118, 119
Verucchio **240**, 241
Via Francigena 184, 186, **213**
Via Sette Ponti **174**, 175
Villa Balbianello (Lenno) **61**
Villa Feltrinelli (Gargnano) 77
Villa Russiz (Friuli) 111
Visas 12
Vittorio Amedeo I, Duke of Savoy 44
Volpaia 176, **177**
Volterra 182, **183**

W
Walking, Cinque Terre 156
Wi-Fi 14

Z
Zone, Pyramids of **70**

ACKNOWLEDGMENTS

DK would like to thank the following for their contribution to the previous editions: Daniel Mosseri

The publishers would like to thank the following for their kind permission to reproduce their photographs:

(Key: a-above; b-below/bottom; c-centre; f-far; l-left; r-right; t-top)

Adobe Stock: Travelvolo 163tl.
Alamy Stock Photo: bozac 111bl; Ceri Breeze 15bc; Ian Dagnall 56; Faraway Photos 61tc; Garry Gay 13tl; Hackenberg-Photo-Cologne 110tl; imageBROKER com GmbH & Co. KG / . / . 10tr; Juergen Richter / Image Professionals GmbH 164br; LOOK Die Bildagentur der Fotografen GmbH 111br; Francesco Lorenzetti 10br; MARKA 14tr; Neil Setchfield 13br; robertharding / Gavin Hellier 150cl; robertharding / Karen Deakin 191bl; Ghigo Roli 142cl; shuckey51 / Stockimo 140; Stock Italia 17bl, 240bl; Universal Images Group North America LLC / DeAgostini / A. VERGANI 136br; Christine Webb 191tl.
Corbis: Alfredo Dagli Orti 119tr; Douglas Pearson 231br.
Depositphotos Inc: mitch.zul 104.
Dreamstime: Adogslifephoto 22tr; Leonid Andronov 135br; Olga Buiacova 13tc; Claudio Giovanni Colombo 232tl; Piero Cruciatti 5tl, 51tc; Ermess 137tc; Flaviano Fabrizi 222tl; Germanopoli 68br; Giuseppemasci 130; Janoka82 60tl; Petr Jilek 185br; Horst Lieber 7tr; Jenifoto406 148; Francesco Marzovillo 43tc; Elena Odareeva 147tl; Sean Pavone 146tl; Rinofelino 111bl; Saiko3p 48; Andrey Salam-chev 18tl; Massimo Santi 196; Solarisys13 152t; Stevanzz 188; Zoom-zoom 241crb. **Getty Images:** Atlantide Phototravel / Corbis Documentary 198cl; font83 244tl; Francesco Bergamaschi / Moment 38; Fani Kurti 46tl; Neil Maccormack / EyeEm 28; Andrea Pistolesi / Photodisc 160, 170; Maremagnum / Photodisc 195t; Michele Rossetti / Moment 64; Stefano Rupolo / EyeEm 122; Achim Thomae / Moment 96; Flavio Vallenari 212br; Vincenzo De Palo PHOTO / Moment 246. **Getty Images / iStock:** bluejayphoto 114; e55evu 226; euganeus69 86; franckreporter / E+ 178; Orbon Alija / E+ 236; starush 72. **Hotel Greif:** Annette Fischer 23tr. **Photolibrary:** Age fotostock/Alberto Paredes 13tr; Alamy/Hackenberg-Photo-Cologne 109tl, imagebroker 95tr; Giuglio Gil 27c; imagebroker 109bc, /Dr Wilfried Bahnmueller 95tc; Lonely Planet Images/Andrew Bain 95cl, /Mark Daffey 18bl; Mauritius/Torino Torino 112tr; PhotoEquipe153 10bl; Radius Images 94tl; Robert Harding Travel/ James Emmerson 91br, /Tony Gervis 90tr; The Travel Library/H G Schmidt 94b; Westend61 92tl. **Shutterstock. com:** Davide Calabresi 152ca; Danny Iacob 78; iacomino FRiMAGES 2-3; Jaro68 206; Mitzo 68tl; Redmason 216; Marco Scuderi 154tr; Robert Harding Video 71tr.

Dorling Kindersley would like to thank the many people whose help and assistance contributed to the preparation of this book.

Photographers
Anna Mockford and Nick Bonetti, James Tye, Christine Webb

Additional Photography
Dan Bannister, Demetrio Carrasco, Steve Gorton, John Heseltine, Paul Harris and Anne Heslope, Roger Moss, Kim Sayer, Helena Smith, Rough Guides: James McConnachie

Maps
Cartographic Production Lovell Johns Ltd, www.lovelljohns.com Source Data Base mapping supplied by Kartographie Huber, www. kartographie.de Elevation Data SRTM data courtesy of ESRI

Jacket
Front and Spine: **AWL Images:** Francesco Iacobelli. Back: **Alamy Stock Photo:** ronnybas crb. **AWL Images:** Marco Bottigelli cla; Francesco Iacobelli b. **Getty Images:** Filippo Maria Bianchi / Moment Open tl; Marco Bottigelli / Moment tr.

Pull-Out Map Cover
AWL Images: Francesco Iacobelli.

Illustrator
Arun Pottirayil

MIX
Paper | Supporting responsible forestry
FSC™ C018579

This book was made with Forest Stewardship Council™ certified paper – one small step in DK's commitment to a sustainable future. Learn more at www.dk.com/uk/information/sustainability

THIS EDITION UPDATED BY
CONTRIBUTOR Toni Di Bella
SENIOR EDITORS Dipika Dasgupta, Alison McGill
PROJECT EDITORS Charlie Baker, Anuroop Sanwalia
SENIOR ART EDITOR Vinita Venugopal
ART EDITOR Tanvi Sahu
PROOFREADER Caroline West
INDEXER Helen Peters
ASSISTANT PICTURE RESEARCH ADMINISTRATOR Manpreet Kaur
SENIOR PICTURE RESEARCHER Nishwan Rasool
DEPUTY MANAGER, PICTURE RESEARCH Virien Chopra
PUBLISHING ASSISTANT Simona Velikova
JACKET PICTURE RESEARCHER Claire Guest
SENIOR CARTOGRAPHER Subhashree Bharati
CARTOGRAPHY MANAGER Suresh Kumar
DTP DESIGNER Rohit Rojal
SENIOR PRODUCTION CONTROLLER Samantha Cross
DEPUTY MANAGING EDITOR Dharini Ganesh
MANAGING EDITOR Beverly Smart
MANAGING ART EDITOR Gemma Doyle
SENIOR MANAGING ART EDITOR Priyanka Thakur
EDITORIAL DIRECTOR Hollie Teague
ART DIRECTOR Maxine Pedliham
PUBLISHING DIRECTOR Georgina Dee

First edition 2012
Published in Great Britain by
Dorling Kindersley Limited, DK,
20 Vauxhall Bridge Road, London SW1V 2SA
The authorised representative in the EEA is
Dorling Kindersley Verlag GmbH. Arnulfstr.
124, 80636 Munich, Germany
Published in the United States by
DK Publishing, 1745 Broadway, 20th Floor,
New York, NY 10019, USA
Copyright © 2012, 2025
Dorling Kindersley Limited
A Penguin Random House Company
25 26 27 28 10 9 8 7 6 5 4 3 2 1
Reprinted with revisions 2015, 2018
All rights reserved.
No part of this publication may be reproduced, stored in or introduced into a retrieval system, or transmitted, in any form, or by any means (electronic, mechanical, photocopying, recording or otherwise), without the prior written permission of the copyright owner.
The publishers cannot accept responsibility for any consequences arising from the use of this book, nor for any material on third party websites, and cannot guarantee that any website address in this book will be a suitable source of travel information.
A CIP catalogue record for this book is available from the British Library.
A catalogue record for this book is available from the Library of Congress.
ISSN 1479-344X
ISBN 9780 2417 3589 3
Printed and bound in China

www.dk.com

PHRASE BOOK

In an Emergency

Help!	Aiuto!	eye-yoo-toh
Stop!	Ferma!	fair-mah
Call a doctor.	Chiama un medico	kee-ah-mah oon meh-dee-koh
Call an ambulance.	Chiama un' ambulanza	kee-ah-mah oon am-boo-lan-tsa
Call the police.	Chiama la polizia	kee-ah-mah lah pol-ee-tsee-ah
Call the fire brigade.	Chiama i pompieri	kee-ah-mah ee porn-pee-air-ee
Where is the telephone?	Dov'è il telefono?	dov-eh eel teh-leh-foh-noh?
The nearest hospital?	L'ospedale più vicino?	loss-peh-dah-leh-pee-oo vee-chee-noh?

Communication Essentials

Yes/No	Si/No	see/noh
Please	Per favore	pair fah-vor-eh
Thank you	Grazie	grah-tsee-eh
You're welcome	Prego	preh-goh
Excuse me	Mi scusi	mee skoo-zee
Hello	Buon giorno	bwon jor-noh
Goodbye	Arrivederci	ah-ree-veh-dair-chee
Good evening	Buona sera	bwon-ah sair-ah
morning	la mattina	lah mah-tee-nah
afternoon	il pomeriggio	eel poh-meh-ree-joh
evening	la sera	lah sair-ah
yesterday	ieri	ee-air-ee
today	oggi	oh-jee
tomorrow	domani	doh-mah-nee
here	qui	kwee
there	la	lah
What?	Cosa?	coh-sah?
When?	Quando?	kwan-doh?
Why?	Perchè?	pair-keh?
Where?	Dove?	doh-veh?

Useful Phrases

How are you?	Come sta?	koh-meh stah?
Very well, thank you.	Molto bene, grazie.	moll-toh beh-neh grah-tsee-eh
Pleased to meet you.	Piacere di conoscerla.	pee-ah-chair-eh dee coh-noh-shair-lah
See you later.	A più tardi.	ah pee-oo tar-dee
That's fine.	Va bene.	va beh-neh
Where is/are …?	Dov'è/Dove sono …?	dov-eh/doveh soh-noh?
How long does it take to get to …?	Quanto tempo ci vuole per andare a …?	kwan-toh tem-poh chee voo-oh-leh pair an-dar-eh ah …?
How do I get to …?	Come faccio per arrivare a …?	koh-meh fah-choh pair arri-var-eh ah…?
Do you speak English?	Parla inglese?	par-lah een-gleh -zeh?
I don't understand.	Non capisco.	non ka-pee-skoh
Could you speak more slowly, please?	Può parlare più lentamente, per favore?	pwoh par-lah-reh pee-oo len-ta-men-teh pair fah-vor-eh?
I'm sorry.	Mi dispiace.	mee dee-spee-ah-cheh

Useful Words

big	grande	gran-deh
small	piccolo	pee-koh-loh
hot	caldo	kal-doh
cold	freddo	fred-doh
good	buono	bwoh-noh
bad	cattivo	kat-tee-voh
enough	basta	bas-tah
well	bene	beh-neh
open	aperto	ah-pair-toh
closed	chiuso	kee-oo-zoh
left	a sinistra	ah see-nee-strah
right	a destra	ah dess-trah
straight on	sempre dritto	sem-preh dree-toh
near	vicino	vee-chee-noh
far	lontano	lon-tah-noh
up	su	soo
down	giù	joo
early	presto	press-toh
late	tardi	tar-dee
entrance	entrata	en-trah-tah
exit	uscita	oo-shee-ta
toilet	toilette/bagno	twah-let/ban-nyoh
free, unoccupied	libero	lee-bair-oh
free, no charge	gratuito	grah-too-ee-toh

Making a Telephone Call

I'll try again later.	Ritelefono più tardi.	ree-teh-leh-foh-noh pee-oo tar-dee
Can I leave a message?	Posso lasciare un messaggio?	poss-oh lash-ah-reh oon mess-sah-joh?
Hold on.	Un attimo, per favore	oon ah-tee-moh, pair fah-vor-eh
Could you speak up a little please?	Può parlare più forte, per favore?	pwoh par-lah-reh pee-oo for-teh, pair fah-vor-eh?
local call	telefonata locale	te-leh-fon-ah-tah loh-cah-leh

Shopping

How much does this cost?	Quanto costa?	kwan-toh cos-tah
I would like …	Vorrei …	vor-ray
Do you have …?	Avete …?	ah-veh-teh…?
I'm just looking.	Sto soltanto guardando.	stoh sol-tan-toh gwar-dan-doh
Do you take credit cards?	Accettate carte di credito?	ah-chet-tah-teh kar-teh dee creh-dee-toh?
What time do you open/close?	A che ora apre/ chiude?	ah keh or-ah ah-preh/kee-oo-deh?
this one	questo	kweh-stoh
that one	quello	kwell-oh
expensive	caro	kar-oh
cheap	a buon prezzo	ah bwon pret-soh
size, clothes	la taglia	lah tah-lee-ah
size, shoes	il numero	eel noo-mair-oh
white	bianco	bee-ang-koh
black	nero	neh-roh
red	rosso	ross-oh
yellow	giallo	jal-loh
green	verde	vair-deh
blue	blu	bloo

Types of Shop

antique dealer	l'antiquario	lan-tee-kwah-ree-oh
bakery	il forno /il panificio	eel forn-oh /eel pan-ee-fee-choh
bank	la banca	lah bang-kah
bookshop	la libreria	lah lee-breh-ree-ah
butcher	la macelleria	lah mah-chell-eh-ree-ah
cake shop	la pasticceria	lah pas-teei-chair-ee-ah
chemist	la farmacia	lah far-mah-chee-ah
delicatessen	la salumeria	lah sah-loo-meh-ree-ah
department store	il grande magazzino	eel gran-deh mag-gad-zee-noh
fishmonger	il pescivendolo	eel pesh-ee-ven-doh-loh
greengrocer	il fruttivendolo	eel froo-tee-ven-doh-loh
grocery	alimentari	ah-lee-men-tah-ree
hairdresser	il parrucchiere	eel par-oo-kee-air-eh
ice-cream parlour	la gelateria	lah jel-lah-tair-ree-ah
market	il mercato	eel mair-kah-toh
newsstand	l'edicola	leh-dee-koh-lah
post office	l'ufficio postale	loo-fee-choh pos-tah-leh
shoe shop	il negozio di scarpe	eel neh-goh-tsioh dee skar-peh
supermarket	il supermercato	eel su-pair-mair-kah-toh
tobacconist	il tabaccaio	eel tah-bak-eye-oh
travel agency	l'agenzia di viaggi	lah-jen-tsee-ah dee vee-ad-jee

Sightseeing

art gallery	la pinacoteca	lah peena-koh-teh-kah
bus stop	la fermata dell'autobus	lah fair-mah-tah dell ow-toh-booss
church	la chiesa la basilica	lah kee-eh-zah lah bah-seel-i-kah
closed for holidays	chiuso per le ferie	kee-oo-zoh pair leh fair-ee-eh
garden	il giardino	eel jar-dee-no
library	la biblioteca	lah beeb-lee-oh-teh-kah
museum	il museo	eel moo-zeh-oh
railway station	la stazione	lah stah-tsee-oh-neh
tourist information	l'ufficio di turismo	loo-fee-choh dee too-ree-smoh

Staying in a Hotel

Do you have any vacant rooms?	Avete camere libere?	ah-veh-teh kah-mair-eh lee-bair-eh?
double room	una camera doppia	oona kah-mair-ah doh-pee-ah
with double bed	con letto matrimoniale	kon let-toh mah-tree-moh-nee-ah-leh
twin room	una camera con due letti	oona kah-mair-ah kon doo-eh let-tee
single room	una camera singola	oona kah-mair-ah sing-goh-lah
room with a bath, shower	una camera con bagno, con doccia	oona kah-mair-ah kon ban-yoh, kon dot-chah
porter	il facchino	eel fah-kee-noh
key	la chiave	lah kee-ah-veh
I have a reservation.	Ho fatto una prenotazione.	oh fat-toh oona preh-noh-tah-tsee-oh-neh

Eating Out

Have you got a table for…?	Avete una tavola per … ?	ah-veh-teh oona tah-voh-lah pair …?
I'd like to reserve a table.	Vorrei riservare una tavola.	vor-ray ree-sair-vah-reh oona tah-voh-lah
breakfast	colazione	koh-lah-tsee-oh-neh
lunch	pranzo	pran-tsoh
dinner	cena	cheh-nah
The bill, please.	Il conto, per favore.	eel kon-toh pair fah-vor-eh
I am a vegetarian.	Sono vegetariano/a.	soh-noh veh-jeh-tar-ee-ah-noh/nah
waitress	cameriera	kah-mair-ee-air-ah
waiter	cameriere	kah-mair-ee-air-eh
fixed price menu	il menù a prezzo fisso	eel meh-noo ah pret-soh fee-soh
dish of the day	piatto del giorno	pee-ah-toh dell jor-no
starter	antipasto	an-tee-pass-toh
first course	il primo	eel pree-moh
main course	il secondo	eel seh-kon-doh
side dish	il contorno	eel kon-tor-noh
dessert	il dolce	eel doll-cheh
cover charge	il coperto	eel koh-pair-toh
wine list	la lista dei vini	lah lee-stah day vee-nee
rare	al sangue	al sang-gweh
medium	medio	meh-dee-oh
well done	ben cotto	ben kot-toh
glass	il bicchiere	eel bee-kee-air-eh
bottle	la bottiglia	lah bot-teel-yah
knife	il coltello	eel kol-tell-oh
fork	la forchetta	lah for-ket-tah
spoon	il cucchiaio	eel koo-kee-eye-oh

Menu Decoder

l'acqua minerale gassata/naturale	lah-kwah mee-nair-ah-leh gah-zah-tah/nah-too-rah-leh	mineral water fizzy/still
agnello	ah-niell-oh	lamb
aceto	ah-cheh-toh	vinegar
aglio	al-ee-oh	garlic
al forno	al for-noh	baked
alla griglia	ah-lah greel-yah	grilled
l'aragosta	lah-rah-goss-tah	lobster
arrosto	ar-ross-toh	roast
la birra	lah beer-rah	beer
la bistecca	lah bee-stek-kah	steak
il brodo	eel broh-doh	broth
il burro	eel boor-oh	butter
il caffè	eel kah-feh	coffee
i calamari	ee kah-lah-mah-ree	squid
i carciofi	ee kar-choff-ee	artichokes
la carne	la kar-neh	meat
carne di maiale	kar-neh dee mah-yah-leh	pork
la cipolla	la chip-oh-lah	onion
i contorni	ee kon-tor-nee	side dishes
i fagioli	ee fah-joh-lee	beans
il fegato	eel fay-gah-toh	liver
il finocchio	eel fee-nok-ee-oh	fennel
il formaggio	eel for-mad-joh	cheese
le fragole	leh frah-goh-leh	strawberries
il fritto misto	eel free-toh mees-toh	mixed fried dish
la frutta	la froot-tah	fruit
frutti di mare	froo-tee dee mah-reh	seafood
i funghi	ee foon-ghee	mushrooms
i gamberi	ee gam-bair-ee	prawns
il gelato	eel jel-lah-toh	ice cream
l'insalata	leen-sah-lah-tah	salad
il latte	eel laht-teh	milk
lesso	less-oh	boiled
il manzo	eel man-tsoh	beef
la melanzana	lah meh-lan-tsah-nah	aubergine
la minestra	lah mee-ness-trah	soup
l'olio	loh-lee-oh	oil
il pane	eel pah-neh	bread
le patate	leh pah-tah-teh	potatoes
le patatine fritte	leh pah-tah-teen-eh free-teh	chips
il pepe	eel peh-peh	pepper
la pesca	lah pess-kah	peach
il pesce	eel pesh-eh	fish
il pollo	eel poll-oh	chicken
il pomodoro	eel poh-moh-dor-oh	tomato
il prosciutto cotto/crudo	eel pro-shoo-toh kot-toh/kroo-doh	ham cooked/cured
il riso	eel ree-zoh	rice
il sale	eel sah-leh	salt
la salsiccia	lah sal-see-chah	sausage
le seppie	leh sep-pee-eh	cuttlefish
secco	sek-koh	dry
la sogliola	lah soll-yoh-lah	sole
gli spinaci	lyee spee-nah-chee	spinach
succo d'arancia/di limone	soo-koh dah-ran-chah/dee lee-moh-neh	orange/lemon juice
il tè	eel teh	tea
la tisana	lah tee-zah-nah	herbal tea
il tonno	eel ton-noh	tuna
la torta	lah tor-tah	cake/tart
l'uovo	loo-oh-voh	egg
vino bianco	vee-noh bee-ang-koh	white wine
vino rosso	vee-noh ross-oh	red wine
il vitello	eel vee-tell-oh	veal
le vongole	leh von-goh-leh	clams
lo zucchero	loh zoo-kair-oh	sugar
gli zucchini	lyee dzu-kee-nee	courgettes
la zuppa	lah dzu-pah	soup

Numbers

1	uno	oo-noh
2	due	doo-eh
3	tre	treh
4	quattro	kwat-roh
5	cinque	ching-kweh
6	sei	say-ee
7	sette	set-teh
8	otto	ot-toh
9	nove	noh-veh
10	dieci	dee-eh-chee
11	undici	oon-dee-chee
12	dodici	doh-dee-chee
13	tredici	tray-dee-chee
14	quattordici	kwat-tor-dee-chee
15	quindici	kwin-dee-chee
16	sedici	say-dee-chee
17	diciassette	dee-chah-set-teh
18	diciotto	dee-chot-toh
19	diciannove	dee-chah-noh-veh
20	venti	ven-tee
30	trenta	tren-tah
40	quaranta	kwah-ran-tah
50	cinquanta	ching-kwan-tah
60	sessanta	sess-an-tah
70	settanta	set-tan-tah
80	ottanta	ot-tan-tah
90	novanta	noh-van-tah
100	cento	chen-toh
1,000	mille	mee-leh
2,000	duemila	doo-eh mee-lah
5,000	cinquemila	ching-kweh mee-lah
1,000,000	un milione	oon meel-yoh-neh

Time

one minute	un minuto	oon mee-noo-toh
one hour	un'ora	oon or-ah
half an hour	mezz'ora	medz-or-ah
a day	un giorno	oon jor-noh
a week	una settimana	oona set-tee-mah-nah
Monday	lunedì	loo-neh-dee
Tuesday	martedì	mar-teh-dee
Wednesday	mercoledì	mair-koh-leh-dee
Thursday	giovedì	joh-veh-dee
Friday	venerdì	ven-air-dee
Saturday	sabato	sah-bah-toh
Sunday	domenica	doh-meh-nee-kah

DRIVER'S PHRASE BOOK

SOME COMMON ROAD SIGNS

accendere i fari	headlights on
attenzione	watch out, caution
autostrada	motorway (with toll)
banchina non transitabile	soft verge
caduta massi	falling rocks
centro	town centre
controllo automatico della velocità	automatic speed monitor
cunetta o dosso	bump
deviazione	diversion
traffico a due corsie	two-lane traffic
divieto di accesso	no access
divieto di fermata	no stopping
divieto di transito	no thoroughfare
dogana	customs
escluso residenti	residents only
fine del tratto autostradale	end of motorway
ghiaccio	ice
incrocio	junction
incrocio pericoloso	dangerous junction/crossroads
informazioni turistiche	tourist information
lavori in corso	roadworks
nebbia	fog
non oltrepassare	do not cross
pagare qui	pay here
parcheggio a giorni alterni	parking on alternate days
parcheggio a pagamento	paying car park
parcheggio custodito	car park with attendant
parcheggio incustodito	unattended car park
pedaggio	toll
pedoni	pedestrians
pericolo	danger
pista ciclabile	bicycle path
rallentare	slow down
scuola	school
senso unico	one way
sosta vietata	no parking
sottopassaggio	subway
strada a fondo cieco	dead end
strada camionabile	route for heavy vehicles
strada ghiacciata	ice on road
strada statale	highway
strada sdrucciolevole	slippery road
strada secondaria	secondary road
uscita camion	lorry exit
veicoli lenti	slow lane
zona a traffico limitato	restricted traffic area
zona pedonale	pedestrian zone

DIRECTIONS YOU MAY BE GIVEN

a destra	right
a sinistra	left
dritto	straight on
giri a destra	turn right
giri a sinistra	turn left
il primo/la prima a destra	first on the right
il secondo/la seconda a sinistra	second on the left
vada oltre …	go past the …

THINGS YOU'LL SEE

acqua	water
area di servizio	service area
aspirapolvere	vacuum cleaner
autolavaggio	car wash
autorimessa/autoofficina	garage (for repairs)
benzina	petrol
benzina senza piombo	unleaded petrol
benzina super	4-star petrol
casello autostradale	motorway toll booth
cera per auto	car wax
coda	traffic queue
deviazione	diversion
gasolio	diesel oil
gommista	tyre repairs
guidare a passo d'uomo	drive at walking pace
liquido tergicristallo	windscreen wiper fluid
olio motore	motor oil
raccordo autostradale	motorway junction
spegnere il motore	turn off engine
spingere	push
stazione di servizio	service station
tirare	pull
uscita	exit
vietato fumare	no smoking

THINGS YOU'LL HEAR

Vuole una macchina con il cambio automatico o manuale?
Do you want an automatic or a manual?

Esibisca la patente, per favore?
May I see your licence, please?

Mi fa vedere il passaporto, per favore?
May I see your passport, please?

USEFUL PHRASES

Could you check the oil/water level, please?
Potrebbe controllare il livello dell'olio/dell'acqua, per favore?
potreb-be kontrol-lare eel leevel-lo del ol-yo/del akwa pair fah-vor-eh

Fill it up, please!
Faccia il pieno, per favore!
facha eel p-yeno pair fah-vor-eh

I'd like 35 litres of 4-star petrol, please.
Mi dia trentacinque litri di super, per favore.
mee dee-a trentacheenkwe leetree dee soopair pair fah-vor-eh

Do you do repairs?
Effettua riparazioni?
ef-fet-too-a reeparatz-yonee

Can you repair the clutch?
Può ripararmi la frizione?
pwo reepararmee la freetz-yone

There is something wrong with the engine.
C'è qualcosa che non va nel motore.
cheh kwalkoza ke non va nel motore

The engine is overheating.
Il motore si surriscalda.
eel motore see soor-reeskalda

I need a new tyre.
Ho bisogno di una gomma nuova.
o beezon-yo dee oona gom-ma nwova

Can you replace this?
Può sostituirlo?
pwo sosteetoo-eerlo

The indicator is not working.
La freccia non funziona.
la frech-cha non foontz-yona

How long will it take?
Quanto tempo ci vorrà?
kwanto tempo chee vor-ra

Where can I park?
Dove posso parcheggiare?
dove pos-so parkej-jare

I'd like to hire a car.
Vorrei noleggiare una macchina.
vor-ray nolej-jare oona mak-keena

I'd like an automatic/a manual.
Vorrei una macchina con il cambio automatico/manuale.
vor-ray oona mak-keena kon eel kam-bee-o owtomateeko/ manwale

How much is it for one day?
Quanto costa per un giorno?
kwanto kosta pair oon jorno

Is there a mileage charge?
C'è un supplemento per il chilometraggio?
cheh oon soop-plemento pair eel keelometraj-jo

When do I have to return it?
Quando devo riportarla?
kwando devo reeportarla

Where is the nearest petrol station?
Dov'è la stazione di servizio più vicina?
doveh la statz-yone dee sairveetz-yo p-yoo veecheena

How do I get to …?
Come faccio per arrivare a …?
koh-meh fah-choh pair arri-var-eh ah

Is this the road to …?
È questa la strada per …?
eh kwesta la strada pair

Which is the quickest way to …?
Qual' è la strada più breve per …?
kwal eh la strada p-yoo breve pair

USEFUL WORDS

automatic	**con il cambio automatico**	*kon eel kam-bee-o owtomateeko*
bonnet	**il cofano**	*kofano*
boot	**il portabagagli**	*portabagal-yee*
brake	**il freno**	*freh-no*
breakdown	**il guasto**	*gwa-sto*
car	**l'automobile, la macchina**	*ow-toh-moh-beeleh, mak-keena*
car ferry	**il traghetto**	*traget-to*
car park	**il parcheggio**	*parkej-jo*
clutch	**la frizione**	*freetz-yone*
crossroads	**l'incrocio**	*een-kro-cho*
drive	**guidare**	*gwee-dar-eh*
engine	**il motore**	*mo-tor-eh*
exhaust	**lo scappamento**	*skap-pamento*
fanbelt	**la cinghia della ventola**	*cheeng-ya del-la ven-to-la*
garage (for repairs)	**l'autorimessa/ l'autofficina**	*ow-toh-ree-mes-sa/ ow-toh-fee-chee-na*
gear	**la marcia**	*mar-cha*
gearbox	**il cambio**	*kam-bee-o*
gears	**le marce**	*mar-cheh*
headlights	**i fari**	*far-ee*
indicator	**la freccia**	*frech-cha*
junction	**l'incrocio**	*een-kro-cho*
licence	**la patente**	*pa-ten-teh*
lorry	**il camion, l'autocarro**	*kam-yon, ow-toh-kar-ro*
manual	**con il cambio manuale**	*kon eel kam-bee-o man-wah-leh*
mirror	**lo specchietto**	*spekk-yet-to*
motorcycle	**la motocicletta**	*moto-chee-klet-ta*
motorway	**l'autostrada**	*ow-toh-strada*
motorway entry	**raccordo di entrata**	*rak-kor-do dee en-tra-ta*
motorway exit	**raccordo di uscita**	*rak-kor-do dee oo-shee-ta*
number plate	**la targa**	*tar-ga*
petrol	**la benzina**	*bendz-eena*
petrol station	**la stazione di servizio**	*statz-yone dee sair-veetz-yo*
rear lights	**i fari posteriori**	*far-ee post-airy-oree*
ring road	**raccordo anulare**	*rak-kordo anoolareh*
road	**la strada**	*stra-da*
spare parts	**i pezzi di ricambio**	*petzee dee ree-kam-bee-o*
spark plug	**la candela**	*kan-deh-la*
speed	**la velocità**	*ve-loh-chee-ta*
speed limit	**il limite di velocità**	*lee-mee-teh dee ve-loh-chee-ta*
speedometer	**il tachimetro**	*tak-ee-me-tro*
steering wheel	**il volante**	*vo-lan-teh*
traffic light	**il semaforo**	*seh-ma-foro*
trailer	**il rimorchio**	*ree-mork-yo*
caravan	**la roulotte**	*roo-lot*
transmission	**la scatola del cambio**	*ska-toh-la del kam-bee-o*
tyre	**la gomma**	*gom-ma*
van	**il furgone**	*foor-gon-eh*
warning triangle	**il triangolo**	*tree-angolo*
wheel	**la ruota**	*rw-oh-ta*
windscreen	**il parabrezza**	*para-bretza*
windscreen wiper	**il tergicristallo**	*tairjee-kreestal-lo*